Praise for F

ISLAND OF

"Other biographers have glossed over Roosevelt's two-year police stint, but Zacks shows it was a crucial period in the evolution of the 26th president. . . . The work propelled TR to national prominence, toughened his skin and, perhaps most important, established him as a reformer."
—*Smithsonian*

"Excellent. . . . A fish-out-of-water comedy, in that it tells the story of what happens when one of the virtuous clubmen—a square, incorruptible, 'law-and-order Republican'—is placed in charge of the New York Police Department." —*The Wall Street Journal*

"A cinematic saga about one of the reformer's early battles: trying to clean up the city that definitely never sleeps. Zacks . . . tells a clear-eyed immorality tale with cameos by Stephen Crane, Lincoln Steffens, exotic dancer Little Egypt, plus a cast of locals who'd have pleased Damon Runyon." —*Newsday*

"Jaunty and beautifully researched portrait of nineteenth-century New York. . . . Zacks, whose earlier books include *The Pirate Hunter* and *History Laid Bare*, seems to take a professional interest in scoundrels and sinners. He's right at home in fin-de-siècle New York, a time when the city had 30,000 prostitutes and 8,000 saloons." —*The Washington Post*

"Between risque anecdotes and vintage dirty jokes, [*Island of Vice*] provides a vigorous depiction of large-scale municipal politics in all its sticky, sweaty glory, and an ever-useful reminder that there are limits to even the most dynamic leader's ability to dictate personal morality. Sin-loving New Yorkers wouldn't have it any other way." —*Salon*

"Part of the pleasure of Richard Zacks's *Island of Vice: Theodore Roosevelt's Quest to Clean Up Sin-Loving New York* is in knowing how the story ends—that the stubborn, imperious young city official trying to reform Tammany-era New York would achieve greatness throughout his larger-than-life career." —*The Christian Science Monitor*

"The classic contest of cops vs. criminals. . . . One of the achievements of *Island of Vice* is that Zacks penetrates beneath the bluster into the psychology of this strange, restless man."
—NPR

"Competent, confident and extraordinarily energetic, the Republican Roosevelt had his work cut out for him. He had to get rid of corrupt cops, go toe-to-toe with Tammany Hall Democrats, enforce unpopular Sunday closing laws and quash dissent among his fellow board members. . . . *Island Of Vice* comes alive . . . when Zacks draws on trial transcripts to describe, in devilish detail, the complexities and contradictions of life in Victorian New York."
—*San Francisco Chronicle*

"From the opening pages of his rousing new book, *Island of Vice*, Richard Zacks plunges readers into the filth, debauchery and corruption of 1890s New York. When an ambitious young Theodore Roosevelt strides in to clean up the mess, the story, already brimming with incredible characters and jaw-dropping details, only gets better."
—Candice Millard, bestselling author of
The River of Doubt and *Destiny of the Republic*

"An irresistible force—young Theodore Roosevelt, the police commissioner, determined to wipe out vice—meets an immoveable object—the corrupt, pleasure-loving city of New York in the 1890s. And the result is: a whole lot of fun. What a marvelous time Richard Zacks must have had researching this story. The information is fascinating, the amazing tale moves with a headlong pace. I'm sure *Island of Vice* will be a bestseller, and it deserves to be."
—Edward Rutherfurd,
bestselling author of *New York: The Novel*

"It's been said that New York City politics were invented to scare young children. True, according to Richard Zacks whose riveting account lays bare the depravity and corruption of the Gilded Age—and the failed crusade of Police Commissioner Theodore Roosevelt to stop it. A must-read for any student of Gotham."
—Teresa Carpenter, author of *New York Diaries*
and winner of the Pulitzer Prize for feature writing

RICHARD ZACKS

ISLAND OF VICE

Richard Zacks got his book-writing start specializing in lewd and offbeat history. His *An Underground Education* and *History Laid Bare* are classics of their kind. He is the author of *The Pirate Hunter: The True Story of Captain Kidd*, chosen by *Time* in 2002 as one of the five best nonfiction books of the year, and *The Pirate Coast* (2005). His writing has appeared in *The New York Times*, *Atlantic Monthly*, *Time*, *Life*, *Harper's*, *Sports Illustrated*, *The Village Voice*, and other publications. He writes in a small office overlooking Union Square in New York City.

www.richardzacks.com

ISLAND

—— OF ——

VICE

THEODORE ROOSEVELT'S
QUEST TO CLEAN UP
SIN-LOVING NEW YORK

RICHARD ZACKS

ANCHOR BOOKS
A DIVISION OF RANDOM HOUSE, INC.
NEW YORK

FIRST ANCHOR BOOKS EDITION, SEPTEMBER 2012

Copyright © 2012 by Richard Zacks

All rights reserved. Published in the United States by Anchor Books,
a division of Random House, Inc., New York, and in Canada by Random House
of Canada Limited, Toronto. Originally published in hardcover in the United
States by Doubleday, a division of Random House, Inc., New York, in 2012.

Anchor Books and colophon are registered trademarks of Random House, Inc.

The Library of Congress has cataloged the Doubleday edition as follows:
Zacks, Richard.
Island of vice : Theodore Roosevelt's doomed quest to clean up
sin-loving New York / Richard Zacks. — 1st ed.
p. cm.
1. Vice control—New York (State)—New York—History—19th century.
2. Roosevelt, Theodore, 1858–1919. 3. Police administration—
New York (State)—New York—History—19th century.
4. New York (N.Y.)—Moral conditions— History—19th century.
5. New York (N.Y.)—Social life and customs—19th century. I. Title.
HV6795.N5Z33 2012
363.2'309747109034—dc23
2011028586

Anchor ISBN: 978-0-7679-2619-5

Author photograph © Kristine Y. Dahl

www.anchorbooks.com

Printed in the United States of America
3   5   7   9   10   8   6   4   2

For Georgia and Ziggy

CONTENTS

ISLAND OF VICE

PROLOGUE

A stunningly beautiful woman stood at the highest point of the Manhattan skyline. She was naked, perched on her tiptoes at the very top of the tower of Madison Square Garden at 26th Street, more than 300 feet off the ground. Fifty Edison lamps lit her up, revealing slim adolescent hips, pomegranate breasts, a hairless cleft. Late-night revelers staggering home from the taverns and clubs tipped their hats to her.

The woman's name was Diana. She was a thirteen-foot gilded copper statue of the Roman goddess of the hunt. Lovely Diana, virginal goddess, towered over the surrounding five-story buildings. Guidebooks touted her as drawing as many visitors as that *clothed* giantess of liberty in the harbor. Perfectly balanced on ball bearings, the statue could spin. For more than a decade, Diana's breasts and outstretched arm revealed the direction of the winds. New Yorkers knew that nipples pointing uptown meant breezes to the north.

Architect Stanford White had paid for her out of his own pocket and demanded a pubescent body that matched his desires. Famed sculptor Augustus Saint-Gaudens—better known for his equestrian heroes—had modeled this, his only nude female statue, after his young mistress, Julia Baird.

Under the respectable cloak of neoclassical art, Diana was the sly insider joke of these two famous men, a museum-worthy tribute to forbidden lust. And so she was the perfect symbol of New York in the 1890s, a city of silk top hats on Wall Street and sixteen-year-old prostitutes trawling Broadway in floor-length dresses, of platitudes uptown and bawdy lyrics on the Bowery, of Metropolitan Opera divas performing Wagner and of harem-pantsed hoochie-coochie dancers grinding their hips on concert saloon stages.

Manhattan, then growing in prestige by the minute, rated handfuls of superlatives: nation's financial capital (Wall Street), nation's leading commercial port (144 piers), dominant manufacturing center (12,000 factories and 500,000 workers), arts capital (museums and 100 theaters delivering a forty-week season), nation's premier residential address (Fifth Avenue), philanthropic center, cosmopolitan melting pot.

Almost two million people lived here, the wealthiest and the poorest crammed onto about a dozen square miles of one ideally situated island, with many neighborhoods joined by a mere five-cent cable car ride. The city housed more Irish than Dublin, more Germans than any city but Berlin, with pockets of Syrians, Turks, Chinese, Armenians, and with a new steady influx of Italians and Russians. The polyglot babble of the streets dizzied the minds of fifth-generation Americans. While the upper crust aimed at a stagey British enunciation, à la the characters of Henry James and Edith Wharton, the poor of New York garbled the language into a street slang that often required interpretation. When Billy McGlory, a notorious saloon keeper, testified about a prostitute stealing a man's wallet and refusing to give it back, he said under oath in a courtroom: "If the bloody bitch had turned up the leather, I wouldn't be in this trouble. It's the first time I ever called a copper in my house on a squeal and I get it in the neck for trying to do what's right."

New York was a thousand cities masquerading as one. Its noise, vitality, desperation, opulence, hunger all struck visitors. Department stores such as Stern's straddled city blocks; telephone companies linked 15,000 wealthy private customers. Convicted vagrants served time in workhouses on Blackwell's Island. Columbia College bought the land of the Bloomingdale Lunatic Asylum for a new uptown campus. The poorer districts smelled of sweat and horse manure. Many tenements had courtyard outhouses. The poorest slept in shifts. Uptown near Central Park, liveried servants helped veiled ladies into black enameled coaches, some bearing family coats of arms acquired by marrying European princes.

Not a single traffic light or even a stop sign regulated the mad flow of tens of thousands of horses, carriages, wagons, public horse and cable cars. Anarchy ruled the corners, and foreigners complained about the dangers of crossing busy streets. New York wagon drivers, paid for speed, cursed in many languages. Vehicles could ride in *any* direction on *any* street. The five-mile-per-hour speed limit was routinely ignored; the only faint attempt to aid pedestrians trying to dart across the streets was a squad of two dozen tall policemen stationed at major Broadway intersections.

Thieves stole more horses in New York City than in the entire state of California or Texas, and then raced to outlaw stables scattered around town—the equivalent of modern-day "chop shops"—to quick-dye horses' coats from dappled gray to black, clip tails, and repaint wagons. Four massive elevated train lines—on Second, Third, Sixth, and Ninth Avenues—striped the island north and south, casting shadows and coal ash, and allowing intimate glimpses into second-story apartments.

Above all, New York reigned as the vice capital of the United States, dangling more opportunities for prostitution, gambling, and all-night drinking than any other city in the United States.

A man with a letch, a thirst, or an urge to gamble could easily fill it night or day. Saloon owners, such as Mike Callahan, tossed their keys in the East River and never locked up. Richard Canfield ran his elegant casino—recommended guests only—at 22 West 26th Street, under the shadow of Diana. Swells in frock coats played faro and roulette for thousands, with no money exchanged, only elegant inlaid-ivory chips gliding across tables. A four-star chef waited in the basement for dinner orders. Other gamblers, wanting to bet on horse races as far away as New Orleans, could find "pool rooms" with telegraph tickers in the second floors of saloons and back rooms of hotels.

More than 30,000 prostitutes worked daily, from the expensive soubrettes of the Tenderloin brothels to the impoverished Russian Jewish girls charging fifty cents down on Eldridge Street. No man could walk far at night without being propositioned by a streetwalker. One do-gooder doing the math estimated that each prostitute averaged four clients a day and that on most days one out of every six adult men in New York City paid for sex with a prostitute. "The traffic in female virtue is as much a regular business, systematically carried on for gain, in the city of New York," conceded Thomas Byrnes, the city's leading police detective, "as is the trade in boots, and shoes, dry goods and groceries."

At a trial in 1895 of a police captain accused of sheltering brothels, a witness, a magazine illustrator named Charles Higby, recounted that his studio on 14th Street overlooked a seedy hotel used by streetwalkers. "What did you see? Tell us exactly," he was asked. "Fornication. Three windows at a time," he replied, adding that during the "intermission" a maid changed the sheets. Prosecutor: "Was it not offensive to you to see these different couples going in there and fornicating?" Higby: "Sometimes, [but] sometimes very amusing."

Around this time, French prostitutes in New York began offering oral sex, a taboo-in-America pleasure that cost twice the price of intercourse. Peddlers sold French postcards; gents went to audio parlors and paid a nickel to hear music or dirty jokes. ("She's a ballet dancer; first she dances on one leg, then on the other; between the two she makes a living.")

The Tenderloin, the most popular public vice district of the fin de siècle city, was a two-block-wide swath on either side of Broadway from 23rd Street to 42nd Street. Dance halls such as the Star & Garter and Haymarket, with orchestras playing waltzes, charged twenty-five cents admission for men; women entered free.

One song, with a cloying melody, ran:

Lobsters! rarebits! plenty of Pilsener beer!
Plenty of girls to help you drink the best of cheer;
Dark girls, blond girls, and never a one that's true;
You get them all in the Tenderloin when the clock strikes two.

Your heart is as light as a butterfly,
Tho' your wife may be waiting up for you;
But you never borrow trouble in the Tenderloin
In the morning when the clock strikes two.

New York City was the Island of Vice.

And then suddenly in 1894, after a series of particularly ugly police scandals involving brutality and shakedowns of even bootblacks and pushcart peddlers, Tammany lost the mayor's election.

And the new mayor, independent-minded William L. Strong, appointed Theodore Roosevelt as a police commissioner on May 6, 1895, with the understanding that Roosevelt, a law-and-order Republican, would be elected president of the four-man Police Board, the highest-ranking police official. It was a respectable return for the New York City native, whose career was petering out in a bureaucratic post in Washington, D.C., and whose books were never best-sellers.

———

Theodore Roosevelt was then a work-in-progress, years removed from San Juan Hill and the White House. He was energetic, stubborn, opinionated, with a fondness for manliness—boxing, hunting, military history—and a knack for head-on collisions with allies and enemies alike. "He was tremendously excitable, unusually endowed with emotional feeling and nervous energy," said William Muldoon, who lived not far from him on Long Island Sound, "and I believe his life was a continual effort to control himself."

Roosevelt ("Theodore" to his wife and friends, never "Teddy") was born into one of the city's wealthiest families. His Dutch ancestors had parlayed a hardware and plate-glass business into a real estate and banking empire; his namesake father had inherited the then staggering sum of $1 million in 1871.

After finishing his studies at Harvard, Roosevelt had dedicated himself to a career in writing and reform politics. He had served three years in the gritty New York State Assembly fighting Tammany Hall and boodle and kickbacks.

He lost his mother and first wife on the same day in 1884, salved his soul in the Dakotas, then was defeated for mayor in 1886. His reputation as an uncompromising reformer drew catcalls from the seedier elements of the city. Abe Hummel, a criminal lawyer, said Roosevelt's tombstone should read: "Here lies all the civic virtue there ever was."

Roosevelt had spent the last six years working in semi-obscurity on the Civil Service Commission in Washington. Clearly, that obscurity had chafed him.

"He went everywhere," wrote the *Washington Post* of those years, "pervaded the whole official atmosphere, turned up where he was least expected, bullied, remonstrated, criticized and denounced by turns. Never quiet, always in motion, perpetually bristling with plans, suggestions, interference, expostulation, he was the incarnation of bounce, the apotheosis of inquisition."

The thirty-six-year-old family man now had four young children—Ted Jr., Kermit, Ethel, Archie—to go with eleven-year-old Alice from his first marriage. He and his wife, Edith, had been maintaining a house in D.C. and one in Oyster Bay, and despite income from his inheritance and fees from his six books (such as the 541-page *Naval War of 1812*) and numerous magazine articles, he was having trouble paying his bills.

Roosevelt in 1895 was an outspoken crusader for a vast array of causes that would decades later be bannered under the umbrella of progressive reform, a term then unknown. He wore thick pince-nez glasses, stood five feet nine, often dressed nattily; he had a knight-errant quality about him, eager to call out the frivolous rich, the lazy poor, the sleazy politicians.

Reformers in New York City were ecstatic at his police appointment.

Everyone expected the fight to be tough and some thought it might be made even tougher by the man undertaking it. "There is very little ease where Theodore Roosevelt leads," conceded his longtime friend and future biographer, Jacob Riis.

Roosevelt had returned home to clean up the Island of Vice.

PARKHURST AND THE SIN TOUR

The battle started with a poorly researched sermon.

The Reverend Charles H. Parkhurst, adorned with an abundant goatee and steel-rimmed, thick-lensed glasses, just shy of his fiftieth birthday, stood on February 14, 1892, before about 800 well-dressed parishioners in Madison Square Presbyterian Church, at 24th Street off the park. The understated building—a long and narrow slab of drab brownstone with a classic steeple—evoked earnestness, in stark contrast to the exuberant yellow-and-white Madison Square Garden tower nearby, topped by nude spinning Diana. In the pews sat the city's elite; scrubbed boys and girls fidgeted but their parents certainly did not, not that morning.

Parkhurst sent no advance notice of the subject of his sermon nor did he distribute the text to the press during the prior week, but afterward almost every newspaper requested it.

Parkhurst didn't thunder from the pulpit. He spoke evenly and favored erudite words, befitting an Amherst graduate (class of 1866), one who had studied abroad at Leipzig and once penned an essay on similarities between Latin and Sanskrit verbs. He sometimes showed a sly dry wit.

On that Sunday winter morning, his calmly delivered words stunned his audience. He called the Tammany men ruling New York, especially the mayor, the district attorney, and the police captains, "a lying, perjured, rum-soaked and libidinous lot." He accused them of licensing crime, of polluting the city for profit. He said he would "not be surprised to know that every building in this town in which gambling or prostitution or the illicit sale of liquor is carried on has immunity secured to it by a scale of police taxation" as "systematized" as the local real estate taxes. He asserted "your average police captain is not going to disturb a criminal if the criminal has means."

Parkhurst was born on a farm outside Framingham, Massachusetts; he revered his rural roots. He had never seen vice until he moved to the big city.

He taught school till age thirty-three. For the past dozen years at Madison Square Presbyterian he had been praised for geniality and charitable works but was little known outside his congregation.

That would change overnight.

The minister, his quiet cadence building, wrapped his sermon in a biblical theme, charging that gambling places "flourish on all these streets almost as thick as roses in Sharon," that day or night, "our best and most promising young men" waste hours in those "nefarious dens." He said he had firsthand experience that the city government "shows no genius in ferreting out crime, prosecutes only when it has to, and has a mind so *keenly judicial* that almost no amount of evidence that can be heaped up is accepted as sufficient to warrant indictment."

He explained that, as the president of the Society for the Prevention of Crime, he had recently met with the district attorney and confronted him about McGlory's—a notorious den of prostitutes and thieves that thrived for years. The D.A. had replied that he had no idea that such "vile institutions" existed. "Innocence like that," added Dr. Parkhurst, "in so wicked a town ought not to be allowed to go abroad after dark."

Parkhurst promised his rapt congregation that he was not speaking as a Democrat or a Republican but as a Christian. He complained that the word *protest* was no longer driving "Protestants." He called for action.

"Every effort that is made to improve character in this city, every effort to make men respectable, honest, temperate and sexually clean is a direct blow between the eyes of the Mayor and his whole gang of drunken and lecherous subordinates."

———

Tammany Hall was a vast Democratic political club, a confederacy of strivers that had ruled the city since the late 1860s. The organization blessed lawbreaking mostly of a victimless nature in exchange for a payoff. Cops, many with Irish accents, closed their eyes, and police captains and Tammany grew rich with the blindness. The annual rakeoff totaled in the millions of dollars, back when the average annual wage topped out at $500 or less. The boodle was breathtaking. All the while, the great city, growing into a cosmopolitan masterpiece, prospered, with lip-service platitudes about morality by cynical Tammany Hall orators and everyday embrace of vice.

The Tammany machine prospered, despite the downfall of "Boss Tweed."

The machine engineered many landslide victories. The Democrats of Tammany, dominated by the Irish, harnessed the votes of new immigrants through gifts of coal and ice, and a job. "If a family is burned out," explained state senator George Washington Plunkitt, "I don't ask whether they are Republicans or Democrats, and I don't refer them to the Charity Organization Society, which would investigate their case in a month or two and decide they were worthy of help about the time they are dead from starvation . . . I just get [living] quarters for them, buy clothes for them."

Tammany harnessed the loyalty of fellow politicians and campaign donors through larger gifts than buckets of coal. A Tammany contractor, when confronted with delivering one-tenth of the agreed-upon amount of sponges to the sanitation department, replied under oath: "Hell, did you weigh them dry?" The current Tammany boss, Richard Croker, a hulking, inarticulate bruiser, discovered that "successful government in the American democracy was a vile exchange of favors, and his abiding offense is that he demonstrated the fact," wrote Thomas Beer, author of *The Mauve Decade*.

The cops often formed the front line in the corruption of the city, interacting with criminals and citizens alike. Employment records reveal that about two-thirds of the police force were undereducated Irishmen or first-generation Irish Americans, as were most of the top men in Tammany Hall. These tough fellows—whose ancestors had suffered through what they deeply perceived as centuries of British Protestant misrule and injustice—didn't give a fiddler's fart for the mostly Protestant, mostly wealthy reformers of New York.

Reformers boiled with indignation at this lawlessness, but Tammany—when it bothered to discuss the matter—privately defended its actions as giving the people what they wanted. The vast majority of New Yorkers wanted to drink beer in saloons on Sundays, their only day off from a fifty-hour workweek. *We take a cut to undo the killjoy misery the Republicans are trying to inflict.* Men who wanted to put a dollar on Lovely Lorna in the fifth race at Gravesend could find a Tammany-protected curbstone bookie. Poor girls who didn't want to earn a dollar a day standing for twelve hours in a Sixth Avenue department store could earn that amount in less than an hour in a brothel—if they so chose.

Parkhurst was in effect demanding a holy war on vice and government collusion. The next day, Tammany Hall officials, buttonholing any available reporter, voiced their utter outrage that a man of the cloth would dare pollute the pulpit with such *unsubstantiated* charges. Several fellow ministers and even some Republican politicians thought Parkhurst had gone too far. He expected a fight, but he was flabbergasted when Tammany district attorney DeLancey Nicholl called him before a grand jury on charges of libel.

The minister was in effect attacking the respectable wing of Tammany Hall—not the election-day thugs or street-corner bullies, but the elite corps of the organization: men in silk top hats, men who cut ribbons on new buildings, men who gave speeches about the paving of the avenues.

These men—many now wealthy and respectable in Democratic circles—didn't appreciate being called "a damnable pack of administrative bloodhounds . . . fattening themselves on the ethical flesh of and blood" of New York.

On March 1, that grand jury delivered a scathing presentment indicating that the minister had "no evidence" on which to base his statements; the Tammany judge, reading the report, sanctimoniously rued the day a clergyman would try to destroy lives based on "nothing but rumor, nothing but hearsay." Judge Martine added: "Well-meaning people who go off half-cocked are a terror and a stumbling block to every good cause."

Even Parkhurst himself would later concede of his February sermon: "I could not swear as *of my own knowledge* that the district attorney had lived an immoral life, that police officers were blackmailers, that police justices encouraged bunco-steering and abortion or that the entire Tammany organization was not a disguised wing of the Prohibition Party."

Reverend Parkhurst vowed that he would "never again be caught in the presence of the enemy without powder and shot in my gun-barrel."

He knew—and he knew that all those seemingly shocked Tammany officials also knew—that his charges of widespread vice and police complicity were absolutely true. Now he must go out and prove them. Parkhurst, the married middle-aged minister, hired a young private detective named Charlie Gardner to take him on the ultimate sin tour of New York City.

———

On the evening of Saturday, March 5, 1892, twenty-six-year-old Charlie Gardner, an independent detective trying to launch his own agency after five years at the Gerry Society for the Prevention of Cruelty to Children, showed up at Dr. Parkhurst's home at 133 East 35th Street. Gardner came recommended by a wealthy member of the congregation, though he was a rough-around-the-edges investigator—he'd had several run-ins with the police over the years. He dressed sharp, tried to act a bit jaded, and sprinkled his conversation with slang. Despite working for the Gerry Society, he liked to drink, especially beer and wine, and the police had accused a few of his partners of shaking down suspects. They also would later claim that his ex-wife had participated in a scheme to abduct girls for brothels. (Parkhurst knew none of this at the time.)

A strapping six footer, with blondish-red hair, pink cheeks, and a clipped mustache, he looked younger than his announced mid-twenties age. Gardner had a mischievous side and seemed very much to enjoy the prospect of corrupting the Madison Avenue minister. "I still flatter myself that I whirled him from the pinnacle of a church leader to the depths of criminal New York at a pace never taken by any other man," Gardner would later write in his memoir *The Doctor and the Devil*. Parkhurst, for his part, would very soon state from the pulpit: "I never dreamed that any force of circumstances would ever draw me into contacts so coarse, so bestial, so consummately filthy as those I have repeatedly found myself in the midst of these last few days. I feel as though I want to go out of town for a month to bleach the sense of it out of my mind, and the vision of it out of my eyes."

Gardner arrived at Parkhurst's townhouse; his fee had already been negotiated: the ample sum of $5 a night, plus expenses. A young devout parishioner had volunteered to go along with the reverend as another witness. Both the parishioner and Parkhurst had dressed for slumming.

Gardner took one look at the two of them and burst out laughing.

Parkhurst wore his oldest black broadcloth suit—frayed at the cuffs but still ministerial. Twenty-five-year-old John Langdon Erving—tall, thin, delicate, with large blue eyes and blond hair parted in the middle—wore clothes fished from the depths of his closet. The wealthy young man, with a Van Rensselaer in his family tree, looked like "a Fifth Avenue lounger . . . a fashion plate of a dead year," according to Gardner. Erving taught Sunday school, led polite high-society dances, and gave off a sheltered otherworldly air. His religious devotion sometimes worried his parents.

Gardner told Parkhurst and Erving that they would get barred from joints or perhaps beat up on principle dressed that way. He hailed a carriage and took them to his apartment at 207 West 18th Street for the slum tour makeover. The tall detective decked out Reverend Parkhurst in a pair of his own black-and-white-checked trousers "loud enough to make a noise in the next block," and Gardner cinched them up so high on Parkhurst's chest that "to get in his hip pocket, the Doctor would have had to run his hand down the neck of his shirt." He added a worn double-breasted sailor's jacket, but Gardner still found Parkhurst looking faintly churchly so he wrapped a ripped red sleeve around Parkhurst's neck as a scarf and soaped down the minister's wavy coiffed hair to a greasy, limp derelict look. The final touch was an old dirty brown slouch hat.

For Erving's makeover, Gardner slid the young man's delicate feet out of fine leather shoes and into big awkward rubber boots and gave him a pair of pants that didn't reach within five inches of the ground. He mussed his hair to remove that college-boy center part. A puffy red satin necktie provided the final found-in-the-ashcan touch.

The trio boarded the Third Avenue Elevated, traveling downtown from 18th Street to Franklin Square in the older part of the city. The disguises seemed to be working, as a pretty young woman irritatedly moved her skirts away from Dr. Parkhurst. Gardner had decided to start with the waterfront dives of Cherry and Water Streets that attracted alcoholics, prostitutes, and thieves, and go sleazier from there.

The Cherry Hill neighborhood was once fashionable enough to attract the likes of then president George Washington, but now gangs ruled the streets, including "Swamp Angels" who pulled heists, then disappeared into the city's sewers. Dilapidated buildings housed a mongrel mix of Irish and Italians and visiting sailors, with one block dubbed Penitentiary Row.

Gardner shepherded his wide-eyed twosome into 33 Cherry Street, a typical dive saloon in a ramshackle two-story building with a long bar and a moth-eaten green pool table in the back. The pool players peered over a five-foot partition and eyed the three newcomers as fresh prey.

Gardner introduced Parkhurst—who was about half a head shorter—as his "South Carolina uncle" to the bartender. To kick off the first night, Gardner ordered them each a ten-cent glass of whiskey from a bottle labeled "Manhattan Club Reserve." Dr. Parkhurst—maybe to settle his nerves or show his resolve—downed his in a gulp. (Gardner would find himself impressed by Parkhurst's "capacity for holding liquor," stating that the minister vomited only once in their several nights out.) Aristocratic Erving swallowed his but immediately poured himself a water chaser, "a breach of Cherry Street etiquette that brought a smile of contempt" from the bartender.

The young detective told the barkeep that his "South Carolina uncle" was looking to buy a "clock and slang" (i.e., a gold watch and chain). Tom Summers fanned out a stack of pawn tickets. (Summers's customers stole, say, a watch, pawned it for a pittance, maybe 10 percent of its value, bought drinks, then used the pawn ticket for a last round.) Barkeep Summers didn't ask many questions; neither did the pawnbrokers; neither did fellows buying pawn tickets from Summers.

Parkhurst's education was beginning.

He noticed several boys and girls, about ten years old, whose heads didn't reach the bar, motioning to the bartender and pointing to the pitchers and cans they were carrying. The children handed over coins, and the bartender filled the containers with beer, which the children tried not to spill as they hauled them outside. (Children "rushing the growler" for their parents, even at midnight, was a New York tradition.)

Parkhurst tried to hide his disgust. Gardner told Summers that none of the watches described on the pawn tickets suited his uncle. After drinking another whiskey, the trio exited, with only Erving staggering a bit. They meandered through the tumbledown, gas-lamp-lit neighborhood of low buildings until a handful of streetwalkers, including one "old enough to have been the mother of Columbus," linked arms and dragged them into 342 Water Street.

At a wooden table sat some down-on-their-luck women on the far side of forty. Several smiled missing-tooth smiles and tried to jolly the men into going upstairs. Two cheap chromos provided the only décor besides a ratty red carpet. After a glass of beer, with too many pleas echoing in their ears by ladies wanting to be "treated," the trio fled outside.

Down the next block, they heard music seeping out of 96 Cherry Street, a storefront with colored lights. Gardner led them into Jim Jensen's sailor dance hall, a large square room with a bar down one side. That block and others nearby featured saloon boardinghouses catering to the homesick sailors of various nations, such as this Swede joint. The bartenders and working women in each spoke the language of the home country. (The fleecing was swifter.)

In Jensen's, an old black man sat in the corner, playing a waltz on a "wheezy" accordion while a half dozen drunken couples danced and smoked at the same time. The tour guide Gardner identified the male clientele as mostly sailors, thieves, pimps, shoestring gamblers, and the women . . . if they were in that joint . . . as "abandoned."

Erving requested "ginger ale"; the scar-faced barkeep lined up three beers.

A "short, well developed girl" about nineteen years old came up to Parkhurst and said, "Hey, whiskers, going to ball me off?" which might have meant dance with her. Gardner intervened and convinced her to head out on the dance floor with Erving, whose tiny feet were ensconced in those giant rubber boots. Gardner later wrote in his memoir that the pretty young lady led the high-society man in an energetic, limbs-entwined waltz—never to be seen on Fifth Avenue—full of "vice and shame."

While Erving danced, a "200-pound" drunken woman elbowed her way over to Parkhurst and slurringly asked him to treat her. They drank together and she whispered to him that her name was "Baby" and added suggestively that she lived within a block of the place. Parkhurst declined the invitation as politely as he could and bought her another beer. She raised the glass and told Parkhurst to ask for "Baby" anytime he came down there.

The abrupt entrance by a Salvation Army band cast a pall on everyone's entertainment and ended their first night.

———

The next night when they met, Parkhurst told Gardner: "Show me something worse." That was his mantra, and for the next two nights Gardner tried to deliver in Little Italy, Chinatown, and elsewhere, all by way of preliminaries before their final night of maximum debauchery.

Gardner took Parkhurst to the back room at the East River Hotel. An economic slide that would turn into the Panic of 1893 caused as many as 50,000 men and women to seek temporary shelter on any given night. The hotel allowed anyone who bought a five-cent drink after midnight to sit, sprawl, cower, or sleep on benches or on the floor till morning. Hell's waiting room, some called it. The desperately poor preferred a night there to a park bench or a "penny hang," where seated people looped their arms over a rope till morning.

The long bar at the hotel was "stained yellow" by "innumerable quarts of tobacco" spit by customers; the bar's edge was "charred and burnt . . . by thousands of cheap cigars and cheaper cigarettes." Drunken women—"hair tangled and matted around rum-flushed faces"—tried to lure them to the stalls in the back. A fellow sawed "Bonnie Doon" on an out-of-tune violin while another tried to dance a jig.

They had sampled ten-cent-a-glass whiskey; now Gardner led them to try five-cent-a-glass whiskey. "If you [have never tasted it,] then you are a lucky man. It tastes like a combination of kerosene oil, soft soap, alcohol and the chemicals used in fire extinguishers, I fancy, although I have never touched a drink of that particular kind of brew."

In Chinatown, they saw Chinamen with single braided pigtails wearing bright-colored long silk robes running late errands from hand laundries. "Celestials" was the polite name for them; "chinks" or a sarcastic "John" was more common. Gardner introduced them to restaurant owner Lee Bing, who led them to an opium den in a rundown building on Doyers Street; the place was crowded with pipe smokers. Dozens of rugs covered the wood floor; white pillows abounded; cots lined the walls. The exotic scent of cooked opium pervaded the soft darkness. "But what struck Dr. Parkhurst most was the absolute silence," wrote Gardner, who called it a "silence that wraps itself around you until you want to shout, scream, yell, do anything to make a noise." (Young novelist Stephen Crane, visiting a similar opium den for the New York Sun, advised the first-time user not to expect hallucinations of "porcelain towers and skies of green silk" but rather a fine languor. "The universe is readjusted," he explained. "Wrong departs, injustice vanishes; there is nothing but a quiet harmony of all things—until the next morning.") Parkhurst asked Gardner to buy him an opium layout—long pipe, oil lamp, yen-hock needle—as a souvenir.

The next night, they wandered into Little Italy, a place notorious for crime and operatic violence. Italian men liked to play the "finger game" for money. "[They] would sit around a table in a dingy room and begin guessing at the number of fingers which each suddenly releases from his closed fist." A police officer called it "as fine a prelude to homicide as was ever invented."

Off the narrow streets of Mulberry Bend, sidestepping garbage, overhearing constant Italian, the trio gingerly walked down a few steps into a basement "stale beer" dive, which ranked as the lowest-type saloon in New York City. Dirt floor, a dark open underground rectangle with crude benches on the side, a plank for a bar. Unwashed tramps and derelict women clustered around kerosene lamps swilling ungodly brew from tomato cans. "If you ever went below decks on a slave ship, you smelled the same stench but nowhere else," later observed Gardner. He ordered them a round of two-cent beers and explained that the beer was commonly known as "dog's nose" or "swipes" because "it was the drippings left in barrels by Bowery saloon keepers, the leavings of glasses of Avenue A dive keepers, the floating scum of thousands of saloons, all over town." The two-cent whiskey there exhausted Gardner's stock of hyperbole; he called it "indescribably vile."

A fight broke out between two missing-toothed women competing to be treated by Parkhurst's party. Parkhurst, often the silent observer, commented: "Horrible, horrible, I had no idea such places could exist in a civilized town."

They later visited a big Bowery concert saloon, the Windsor; the female performers left the stage and sat on the laps of men. A woman in makeup applied "in liquid form by a fire engine" enticed them to buy twenty-five-cent brandies. One wore "a blue satin skirt that reached to her knees only."

At a "tight house" on Bayard Street, the women wore nothing but body-hugging toe-to-neck tights and danced with a party of soldiers on leave from Fort Hamilton in Brooklyn.

Within a block of police headquarters, at 300 Mulberry Street, the trio encountered at least *fifty* prostitutes walking the streets. "I suppose none of the police officers in yonder building know what is happening," commented Parkhurst dryly. Gardner was about to launch into a "wise up, Doc" speech when he realized the clergyman was kidding.

At the next joint, they witnessed a Bowery actress standing on her head while smoking a cigarette. She offered more private acrobatics for three dollars but they passed.

––––––

On Friday night March 11, 1892, Gardner delivered on his promise to show "something worse" . . . brothels and French circuses. Since several *hundred* brothels, mostly in nondescript walkup buildings, dotted the city, Gardner had plenty of options. He selected two of the city's main redlight districts: the Tenderloin (19th Precinct) and the area south of Washington Square.

Gardner had chosen a wonderful meeting place—the Hoffman House bar. The now-forgotten Hoffman House was then the most famous bar in New York City. Guests entered on 24th Street just west of Madison Square Park and found themselves in a high-ceilinged private art gallery primarily featuring nudes, with marble and bronze statues of "Eve" and "Bacchus" and paintings such as *Harem Princess*. Seventeen bartenders worked each shift, squeezing fresh fruit into elaborate cocktails, pouring rare French wines or fifty-year-old brandy.

But it wasn't the fine drinks, or even most of the artwork, that drew patrons, it was *one* painting, directly opposite the long mahogany bar, "unquestionably the biggest single advertisement any hotel in this country— probably in the world—ever had," according to William F. Mulhall, a former manager.

The massive canvas, painted with almost photo realism by W. A. Bouguereau in 1873, seemed to invite viewers to climb into a lush erotic landscape. In the eight-foot-tall *Nymphs and Satyr*, four voluptuous, naked young women are seen trying to wrestle a playfully reluctant male into the cold water and over toward another cluster of naked nymphs on the far side of a stream. Highlighted and of dazzling whiteness, one callipygian goddess dominates the tug-of-war, and perhaps never has a luminous backside been viewed so adoringly by so many men with cocktails in hand.

Parkhurst was late. While waiting, Gardner noticed two large men, seated at a table, staring at them. Since his guided vice tour had been going on for a few days, he suspected that these two fellows might be plainclothes cops out to catch Dr. Parkhurst in some compromising position.

Gardner tried an experiment. He took Erving and walked out onto 24th Street to see whether the men would follow; indeed they did. Gardner, no rookie at surveillance, boarded the Sixth Avenue El at 28th Street, as did their pursuers. Gardner waited till the train was moving, yanked open the gate between the cars, and jumped off and happily watched the detectives sail by.

Gardner sent a boy with a message to Dr. Parkhurst to meet them instead at the St. James Hotel at Broadway and 26th Street, a place that attracted "sporting men" and actors. ("Sporting men" might be defined as men who gamble, drink, do not work regular hours, and are rarely seen in the company of their wives.)

They met Dr. Parkhurst at the nearby hotel. From there, they walked to a Tenderloin brothel chosen for its proximity to Parkhurst's Madison Square Church. The threesome reached 33 East 27th Street around midnight, mounted the steps, and rang the bell. The building amid a row of attached buildings did not stand out. Hattie Adams, the madam, about forty-two years old, "a scraggly little thin woman" with curled "hay-colored" hair and wan green eyes, opened the door.

Gardner had slipped by earlier in the evening and said he would be returning with a friend, an "old man from the West" who had lost money gambling and needed cheering up. The three men—all well dressed enough to have been allowed in the Hoffman House—followed Mrs. Adams down a long dimly lit hallway to a comfortable back parlor, full of armchairs and sofas. Waiting there were seven young women—*not* garbed in the elaborate corseted, petticoated outfits of the era, but rather in "Mother Hubbards," light simple dresses, low cut and reaching well above the ankle.

"This is *rather* a bright company," said Dr. Parkhurst, with mock cheer. While the men waited for a servant to fetch beer—two large bottles—from a nearby saloon, Gardner bargained with Mrs. Adams for a "dance of nature," eventually knocking the price to three dollars per girl for five girls.

One of the prostitutes blindfolded the seven-dollar-a-week piano player because "the girls refused to dance [naked] before him." All was ready. Four of the five women then walked into the hallway and pulled a sliding curtain and undressed; the fifth just slipped behind an armchair. Removing a "Mother Hubbard" did not take long.

For the next fifteen minutes, to the piano plink of popular music, the nude women danced, sometimes alone, sometimes in pairs, wearing only stockings held up by garters. At one point, they linked arms for a brief nude *Folies Bergère*–style can-can. One of the naked girls, however, held aloof and refused to dance. "Hold up your hat!" she shouted to Gardner, who in turn yelled over to Parkhurst to toss him his black derby. Gardner stood up and held the derby about six feet off the ground. "The girl measured the distance with her eyes . . . and [she] then gave a single high kick, and amid applause sent the hat spinning away."

Various naked girls then took turns, scissoring a leg ceilingward and launching a hat. Flesh jiggled; girls giggled; the sightless "professor" played. The eyes of the bashful Columbia College graduate Erving darted from the floor to wobbling nipples and thickets of hair, and then back to the floor; the young man was judged a world-class blusher. The naked women kept inviting the men to dance. Gardner claimed he couldn't; Parkhurst refused, so once again Erving was drafted. Elegant in a "business suit," Erving danced a waltz with a naked prostitute for about two minutes. He held her left hand and perched his right hand on her naked hip.

The girl who had refused to dance suggested nude leapfrog. To boisterous piano music, each of the women put her hands on the squatting girl in front and launched herself upward and forward, legs splayed for clearance. A giggling heap of bodies was often the result.

After the performance, the girls put back on what Dr. Parkhurst described as their "summer outfits." A pair plunked themselves down on the laps of Gardner and Erving. They all kept whispering for the men to mount the stairs to the bedrooms. But the group drank one more round of beer, then left around 12:45 a.m., with Hattie Adams bidding them to come again.

They walked south about a mile through the cold night streets—some lit by gas, others by Edison arc lamps—discussing what they had seen; along the way, a friend of Gardner's, a smallish young tailor-turned-detective named William Howes, joined them, as an extra eyewitness. Gardner, promising "something worse," took them to the Golden Rule Pleasure Club on West 3rd Street. They opened the door to the basement of the four-story brick house and an electric buzzer alerted the hosts of their arrival. "Scotch Ann," a tall graceful woman, greeted them.

She guided them down a hallway that led to a cluster of small open-doored rooms, each with a table and couple of chairs. The men peered inside; they saw in each "a youth, whose face was painted, eyebrows blackened and whose airs were those of a young girl." They overheard the "youths" talking in a "high falsetto voice" and calling each other "by women's names."

Gardner whispered to Dr. Parkhurst that these "women" were men, that they were in a cross-dressing homosexual brothel. Parkhurst rushed through the hall, up the steps, and back out to the street. "I wouldn't stay in that house for all the money in the world," he told Gardner.

The tour group then wandered around so-called Frenchtown, the French brothel district of Wooster, Greene, and West 3rd and 4th Streets, today's New York University campus. With Gardner in the lead, the four men climbed the stone steps of a two-story house on West 3rd Street and found six young scantily clad women ranged along the side of a hallway, "pretty, painted, powdered and dissipated looking." The *filles*, in sleeveless gauzy frocks despite the cold, were speaking French and Dr. Parkhurst surprised them by joining in. "Whatever the Doctor said seemed to please the women immensely," later recalled Gardner.

As soon as they entered the parlor and picked out armchairs, "one of the girls, the plumpest and best looking in the lot, sat down on the doctor's lap." Parkhurst implored Gardner with his eyes to help him. (To get some idea of the heft, Sylvia Starr, a vaudeville actress then playing American Venus, stood five feet five inches and weighed 151 pounds, with a thirty-two-inch waist.) Gardner, amused, hesitated a long minute or two, then eventually beckoned the girl over to him. They drank some beer and left to go to another brothel.

Now came the climax of Dr. Parkhurst's sin tour: the French Circus at Marie Andrea's.

The four men walked to 42 West 4th Street and a woman in an upper window of the three-story brick house whistled down to them. A nightstick-twirling policeman stood nearby and apparently heard and saw nothing. They rang. Marie Andrea, a plump older French woman with small dark eyes, who spoke broken English, opened the door and greeted them. She guided them into a parlor on the left. They asked for music; she replied that she had something better: a "French Circus." She demanded five dollars per man with a trip upstairs included in the price, but Gardner bargained her down to four dollars each, with an extra performer thrown in.

Madame Andrea gave her orders in French. "A bevy of young and decid-edly pretty French women trooped into the room," Gardner wrote. "All of them wore the Mother Hubbard costume, of silk and gay satin, with stock-ings and shoes."

Each of the men could select a girl; Parkhurst chose first and perhaps out of compassion chose a "thin scrawny consumptive looking girl" about sixteen years old. Since the girls spoke only French, there was little conversa-tion as the other three men made their selections.

All the women trooped out; Marie Andrea attempted to describe in Franglais the upcoming acts; five women returned naked except for stock-ings.

So what exactly did Reverend Parkhurst and his three colleagues see that night? Charlie Gardner refused to reveal it in his book; Parkhurst also declined in his *Our Fight with Tammany*. The newspapers later drew a veil over the incident, the *New York Sun* calling "most of the testimony . . . unprintable."

But the *New York World* gave a subtle hint. The paper stated that a defense lawyer for the prostitutes later considered charging Reverend Parkhurst with violating Sections 29 and 303 of the New York State Penal Code. Sec-tion 29 concerned "aiding and abetting" someone in the commission of a crime. And a glance at the New York State law code reveals that Section 303, "Sodomy," states: "A person who carnally knows in any manner any animal or bird, or carnally knows any male or female person by the anus or by or *with the mouth* or voluntarily submits to such carnal knowledge, or attempts intercourse with a dead body, is guilty of sodomy and is punishable with imprisonment for not more than twenty years." A French circus featured oral sex. In the 1890s, men went to French brothels for oral sex, which was generally not available elsewhere. In this case, two of those French prostitutes performed cunnilingus.

The five French women at Madame Marie Andrea's finished their performance around 1 a.m. that night and "bowed and smiled like a successful lot of ballet dancers," according to Gardner. Servants hauled away the yellow cloth. The naked women sat on the clothed laps of all but Parkhurst.

The men stayed for their fourth one-dollar round of beers but passed on their trip upstairs. Once outside the building Parkhurst called it "the most brutal, most horrible exhibition that I ever saw in my life."

———

Just thirty hours after leaving Marie Andrea's, Parkhurst mounted the pulpit on Sunday, March 13, 1892, and lashed back at Tammany for accusing him of ignorance and charging him with libel. His theme was "The Wicked Walk on Every Side, When the Vilest Men are Exalted."

"Don't tell me I don't know what I am talking about," he told his congregation. He announced that he had the addresses of thirty houses of prostitution within blocks of the church. "Many a long dismal heart-sickening night, in company with two trusty friends, have I spent . . . going down into the disgusting depths of this Tammany-debauched town and it is rotten with a rottenness that is unspeakable and indescribable."

He explained: "To say that the police do not know what is going on and where it is going on . . . is rot . . . Anyone who with all the easily discernible facts in view, denies that drunkenness, gambling and licentiousness in this town are municipally protected, is either a knave or an idiot." He apologized for his frank language.

Reverend Parkhurst said he had been wincing under Tammany's criticisms and the criticisms of some fellow ministers. Now he was delivering to the district attorney 284 addresses of gambling joints, brothels, and after-hours saloons. His last line: "Now what are you going to do with them?"

———

After some hesitation, the district attorney, engulfed by so much publicity, brought disorderly house charges against four brothel madams visited by Parkhurst, including Hattie Adams and Marie Andrea.

The official's *unexpressed* goal seemed to be to inflict as much embarrassment as possible on Parkhurst in the process so the minister would not go snooping again. The press happily helped. Headlines ran: PARKHURST'S CAN CAN and PARKHURST'S SIGHT-SEEING.

Hattie Adams hired the leading team of criminal lawyers in the city: gargantuan William Howe "wearing a constellation of diamonds" and small shiny-domed Abe Hummel. "I do not know that I ever felt so much my inability to express my loathing and disgust for any man as I do for Parkhurst," said Howe. "In the words of M. Thiers, 'I cannot elevate him to the level of my contempt.'"

Hattie Adams claimed to run a boardinghouse that because of the neighborhood attracted mostly "actors and bicycle men and women" (i.e., traveling people). She was asked: "Are your guests single women?" She replied: "Not particularly single." But Adams was adamant that the Parkhurst party had arrived and asked for one of her boarders, a Miss Devoe, who had provided *all* the entertainment.

The defense trotted out another of those boarders, Charlotte Vanderveer, a "hatchet-faced" curly-haired brunette, who claimed to be Adams's seamstress. She testified that Dr. Parkhurst grabbed her "here" (indicating her bosom) and ripped her dress. "Now you undress and I'll pay you well for it," she quoted the minister as saying.

Parkhurst kept a steely calm both inside the courtroom and out.

Heir John L. Erving had a harder time. (Dr. Parkhurst had once dubbed him a "human sunbeam" because vice did not contaminate him. The nickname stuck when the newspaper boys shortened it to "Sunbeam.")

Q: Did [the naked dancer] put her arm around your neck?
A: No.
Q: Did she kiss you?
A: No, not then.
Q: When did she kiss you?
A: As I got up to go, she put her arms around my neck and kissed me.

The *New York World* reported that the blond Erving blushed so intensely it almost seemed as though he were bleeding. After testifying he collapsed and began muttering: "Where am I? What day is it?" He was quickly hauled away in a carriage.

A doctor at his parents' home in Rye, New York, diagnosed "extreme nervous prostration" and he was not allowed to return to the court, damaging the case against two other brothels. "What a sad picture we have here," said one of the defense lawyers. "This minister of the gospel taking the spotless youth from brothel to brothel, from orgy to orgy, merely to illustrate the existence of vice."

Despite expensive legal counsel, the two madams were convicted in May 1892; the judge sentenced Hattie Adams to nine months on Blackwell's Island, Marie Andrea to a year and a $1,000 fine. (Apparently, even a whiff of oral sex/French vice boosted the punishment.)

Parkhurst's Society for the Prevention of Crime was now riding high. Its detectives, including Gardner, then submitted affidavits to the district attorney against hundreds of brothels, gambling joints, and law-breaking saloons. Two Parkhurst detectives visited twenty-five brothels in the Tenderloin in twenty-four hours.

The Society also gathered evidence about saloons open on Sunday, hiring four detectives and giving them $50 in dimes to buy drinks. The men sipped beers in 254 saloons open after hours and on the Lord's day. "[Dr. Parkhurst] made the point that we four men had certainly sharper eyes than the 3,000 policemen or so in the city," Gardner later wrote.

That summer and in the months following, Tammany sweated; with so much scrutiny, the district attorney was forced to bring cases to trial, and police captains found it hard to ignore vice. The great corrupt money machine was clogged; the great lewd swaggering town was forced to be discreet, like a Philadelphia or even shut down like a Boston. Parkhurst, though criticized for slumming it a bit too enthusiastically, was looking triumphant.

––––––

Enter "Big Bill" Devery.

The Tammany police captain found out that Charlie Gardner, the lead detective for Parkhurst's Society, was investigating a prostitute in his 47th Street precinct. What if "Big Bill"—who stood five feet ten and weighed 225 pounds, with a fifty-inch waist and size seventeen shoes—discovered that the reform detective was trying to shake her down for a bribe? Demanding dollars to drop the whole thing? "All these amateur societies fall into the hands of blackmailers," Devery once complained, without a trace of irony. Then Devery could disgrace high-flying Parkhurst of Madison Square and could free Tammany from the endless meddling of these oh-so-pure reformers. And if Captain Devery couldn't catch Detective Gardner in the act, he could always frame the man.

"I seen my opportunities and I took 'em," as Tammany's George Washington Plunkitt once said.

Julius Caesar had his Rubicon; Big Bill Devery had a hooker and a sloppy private eye.

THE STING

William "Big Bill" Devery and Theodore Roosevelt were born within two years of each other in the Eighteenth Ward of New York City in private homes that were located eight blocks—and a world—apart.

Theodore Roosevelt Jr. was born on October 27, 1858, at 28 East 20th Street, a townhouse off fashionable Broadway and not far from Fifth Avenue; the baby boy joined one of the city's leading Knickerbocker families. Downtown, Roosevelt Street intersected Park Row. Respected Roosevelts dominated the hierarchy of elite clubs, such as the Union Club, and philanthropic organizations, such as Orthopedic Hospital.

William Devery was born on January 9, 1857, in a room over his uncle's saloon at 177 East 24th Street, a house address then off First Avenue, amid rough blocks of low buildings. Cripples dragged themselves along those streets to reach the charity wing of nearby Bellevue Hospital at 26th Street. Irish gangs ruled the corners. A married neighbor, Eliza Shaw, had her throat slit from ear to ear around this time.

Theodore's mother, Martha Bulloch, grew up on an azalea-filled plantation in Roswell, Georgia, attended by slaves; Theodore Roosevelt Sr. inherited a huge fortune.

Devery's parents escaped starvation poverty in Ireland; his father was a bricklayer who served in the Union Army, his mother a laundress.

Roosevelt was born into wealth with words of Christian good deeds and hard work echoing in his ears; his future nemesis was born into an angry clannish Catholic poverty, with centuries of hard usage by wealthy English Protestants coloring his every breath, tale, joke, gesture, accomplishment, failure.

Devery's mother, Mary Geoghegan, at age thirteen, sailed from Ireland to New York City, apparently with her older brothers, Stephen, twenty-two, and Andrew, seventeen, in 1852 in the wake of the catastrophic Potato Famine. Much of the family's early history in America must be pieced together from snippets of conflicting official records, but some Geoghegans do eventually make the newspapers . . . as criminals.

Mary's voyage over was miserably unpleasant. The escaping Irish were crammed together in the steerage deck, an unlit, stagnant-aired, low-ceilinged wooden prison, with each adult allotted a berth of eighteen-inch-wide pine plank for the six-to-eight-week voyage. Trunks, sacks, tools, all their worldly possessions cluttered the floor, making it near impassable. No privacy; no washing water; hundreds of perspiring emigrants flopped in bored, seasick writhing masses.

When storms hit, the steerage passengers were locked belowdecks for safety, all hatches closed, with nowhere to urinate or defecate except in a bucket or a corner or six feet below on the vile, unventilated, undrainable orlop deck amid cargo bundles and scurrying rats. The ever-aggregating stink would waft upward. After days or weeks at sea, the smell of vomit, urine, and shit choked the steerage deck.

Mortality rates veered toward 40 percent, much higher than slave ships. (Healthy slaves represented a profit to the ship's owners; living Irish peasants did not.)

Between 1845 and 1855 during the Potato Famine and its aftermath, about 1 million of the 8 million Irish died of hunger and disease in Ireland and as many as 2.5 million left the country, with the largest portion landing at New York.

The British government was Protestant; the vast majority of the population of Ireland was Catholic. Over the centuries, the wealth of this verdant land of Limerick and Tipperary tipped to the arriving Protestants, who by 1778 controlled 14 million of the 15 million cultivatable acres. Generations of Irish Catholics perceived the law as a one-sided arbitrary tool of the conqueror to separate Catholics from land, money, and power.

At varying times, Catholics could not hold office, serve as judges, print books, vote, purchase land, carry firearms, own houses beyond hovels. Catholic schools and churches were suppressed; Catholic orphans were raised as Protestants.

Embittered and impoverished, they reluctantly fled their homeland in the 1840s and 1850s. Uneducated rural peasants who had lived in huts, fiercely loyal to the Catholic Church, they arrived by the tens of thousands in New York City.

And here too they found a Protestant elite ready to *not* welcome them. "No Irish Need Apply" would appear in the classifieds, as would stereotyped cartoons showing "Paddy," the apelike laborer in a crumpled top hat, with a shillelagh in one hand and a beer mug in the other.

———

Big Bill Devery grew up neck deep in New York City vice, at least an Irish version of it. His family—mother, father, brothers, and sisters—worked for his uncle Stephen Geoghegan, who over time opened up a string of rough-house saloons on the tough Irish east side in the Civil War era. Guidebooks described the area as filled with squatters and "swine styes, bone-boiling establishments, masses of filth and putrid pools."

At Devery's birth in 1857, the city's East Side stage line stopped at 27th Street, but his uncle shrewdly opened oyster saloons along the future route of the line farther uptown.

Young Bill ran errands in his uncle's bars, mixing with Irish thugs and criminals. Geoghegan's "dram-shops" attracted so many armed burglars and other rowdies that the police threatened to pull the liquor license. In the 1850s and 1860s New York was a violent port town, with backroom bar brawls, roving street thieves, cockfights, dog pits. "In those days, you could do almost what you liked," Tammany boss Croker once wistfully mused to the *New York Sun*.

———

On the night of October 5, 1892, Tammany Hall loyalist William "Big Bill" Devery was smoking his eleventh or twelfth cigar of the day in his office at the 22nd Precinct on West 47th Street when the desk sergeant announced that he had a visitor. Charlie Gardner—recently promoted to lead detective for the Parkhurst Society—wanted to see him about executing a search warrant. History has failed to record Devery's exact curse.

"Big Bill," after a fourteen-year police career, was captain of this precinct, just north of the Tenderloin, stretching from 42nd to 59th Street, from Sixth Avenue to the North River (i.e., the Hudson), a precinct ripe with graft possibilities, since premier brothels and gambling palaces were moving uptown. A scant ten months into his first command, he was fast approaching the clover.

Police graft trickled to beat cops; it flowed to captains, delivered from prospective lawbreakers by plainclothes police detectives, called ward men.

Devery's bag man was his brother-in-law's brother, Edward Glennon, nicknamed the "Sphinx" for his taciturnity.

Big Bill Devery was a true Hell's Kitchen New Yorker, mixing charm and menace, and speaking New Yorkese. When he ordered his men not to drink in saloons in uniform, he told them: "Standin' up to a bar with the buttons on don't look nice." By all accounts, his men liked him; he could be brave in a dangerous situation, such as a riot, and could always be funny. He had a huge temper, but even his rants often veered into crazy humor, like when he talked about the "degenderates" coming out of the cross-dressing bars and going into the Fifth Avenue Hotel. He bet on the ponies. He was loyally married, with two daughters. He had quit drinking soon after becoming a cop. "I couldn't risk a load," he explained.

Above all, he was completely tolerant of vice—not violent crime, not murders, not beatings, not burglaries, but vice. *Take a payoff, let the people enjoy themselves.* He resented "silk stocking high hats" and ministers telling other people how to live. A reporter for a reform newspaper said Devery once came up to him on the street, grabbed him hard by the shoulders, and said: "Have you noticed any stray graft running around loose that I have overlooked?" Before the stunned reporter could answer, Devery laughed, let go of him, and walked away.

At age thirty-five, he was one of the youngest captains on the force, a clear Tammany favorite.

Charlie Gardner, always cheeky, walked into Devery's office, carrying the warrant for a brothel in Devery's precinct.

The latest strategy of the Parkhurst Society called for sending undercover investigators into three lush precincts: the 15th, south of Washington Square, full of French brothels and Thompson Street "Negro" streetwalkers; the 19th (the Tenderloin); and the 22nd, a growing hotbed of vice, as madams relocated uptown to be closer to the homes of wealthier clients. Parkhurst agents gathered enough eyewitness evidence to obtain a warrant from a reform-minded judge and then executed that warrant with the police, alerted the press, and hopefully shamed the Tammany district attorney into pressing charges.

Charlie Gardner infuriated Captain Devery that night by refusing to tell him the exact location for the brothel warrant. He claimed—correctly—that the police had tipped off this place and others in the past so that when the agents arrived it was empty, or a puzzled maid greeted them asking why anyone would want to search a nice respectable boardinghouse. Devery demanded to know the house number; Gardner refused.

The thirty-five-year-old born-and-bred New York Irish police captain and the cocky twenty-six-year-old New England private detective started shouting at each other. Gardner told Devery to his face that he hated bringing warrants to this precinct because of the way Devery was doing "business" with the prostitutes. "You know what happens to people who monkey with the police, don't you?" Devery yelled back at him, according to Gardner.

Devery gathered several plainclothes officers to accompany him and Gardner to execute the warrant; Gardner walked them north a few blocks, then motioned for the group to stop in front of 106 and 108 West 50th Street, the notorious French brothel of Lena de Meurville. "French Lena" was almost certainly the largest bribe payer in Devery's first command.

Gardner rang the buzzer; a "colored maid" opened the door and the group barged into the elegant foyer. Upstairs, Devery and Gardner found Louis Allen, a young lawyer at the criminal defense firm of Howe & Hummel, "French Lena," a housekeeper, and, asleep in one of the rooms, a sickly boarder. But no out-of-town businessmen, no underdressed harlots. Gardner nonetheless demanded the police arrest them all. Louis Allen, a married man, protested that he was merely consulting with a client. "Even if he is a lawyer, he doesn't need to have his clothes off and be playing cards with a lot of prostitutes," complained Gardner.

Allen was furious and vowed: "I will get square with you."

He was joining a long list of New Yorkers quite irritated with Charlie Gardner.

———

Captain Devery knew that the Parkhurst Society was investigating other prostitutes in his precinct, including one named Lillie Clifton. He set about laying a trap for Gardner. Lou Allen was willing to help; so was a police sergeant whom Gardner had crossed; so were Lillie and other madams wanting to stay open; so were many victims of previous Gerry and Parkhurst Society closures.

The newspapers later described Lillie Clifton as a "tall, well-developed woman" of hard-to-determine age, perhaps in her mid- to late thirties. She had opened her first brothel in the Tenderloin almost a decade earlier; she now had shares in three, including two in Devery's 22nd Precinct, just north of the Tenderloin. She had first met lawyer Louis Allen when Howe & Hummel had handled a lawsuit by her former longtime lover William F. Kidder, a patent medicine mogul. When the married Mr. Kidder had lost his fortune in 1890, he sued Clifton to recoup $6,000 in presents given to her from 1883 to 1890; the two sides settled on $2,700.

Lillie was born Catherine "Kate" Amos; she had passed occasionally as "Mrs. William F. Kidder." She was now registered at the Bryant Park Hotel as "Mrs. Stevenson." Shifty, playful Lillie shaped up as a fine adversary for Charlie Gardner.

Devery saw his chance when Lillie Clifton came to him to complain that a fellow named George Grant, a thirty-seven-year-old former agent for the Parkhurst Society, was trying to shake her down for protection money in the name of Charlie Gardner. Grant, a tall, muscular former Sing Sing guard with close-cropped graying hair, had shown up on a recent night and told her he wanted to arrange a meeting between her and Gardner to keep her place open.

Grant claimed Gardner agreed to this shakedown. Lillie Clifton's brothel had featured eighteen girls in its heyday but was now operating low key during the Parkhurst scare. Clifton would later admit that she was then doing "business very quietly," keeping only "three or four ladies" and that "every gentleman" must enter "through the basement."

Devery found out that Grant was having a hard time setting up a face-to-face meeting between Lillie and Charlie Gardner. So Devery stepped in. He sent a message to Gardner to come talk to him on Thursday, October 13, 1892; he sent the same message to Lillie Clifton and then he purposely didn't show up at his own precinct house. But he still had a problem, since those two didn't know each other. He needed someone to introduce them. So he had Louis Allen of Howe & Hummel just happen to be leaning against the railing outside the station house that night. When Lillie was leaving the building she ran into Allen, and then a bit later Gardner walked up. Allen, pretending to make nice with the private detective, suggested that all three go for some sherry at Boyle's saloon at 45th Street and Sixth Avenue.

According to Lillie's sworn testimony at a later trial, Gardner drank plenty that first night and confirmed to her that the Parkhurst Society was chasing after her; he was a smooth talker, she said, and he promised he'd wear a silk top hat when he raided her place. She sarcastically said she admired his "style." He hinted, though, that he might be able to help her and gave her his home address.

Lillie showed up at Gardner's rented rooms at 76 Lexington Avenue a few days later on Sunday night, October 16. He lived there with his nineteen-year-old pregnant wife, the former Florence Collins of Poughkeepsie. He had married her on May 14 in a hastily planned ceremony *inside* the Statue of Liberty; wags dubbed Gardner the answer to the riddle: What man ever married one woman while inside another?

Gardner introduced Lillie as "Mrs. Smith" and soon banished his wife to another room; he and Lillie then talked price and Lillie made her first monthly protection payment of $50 to Gardner. The pair sat together for a while and Gardner pulled out a long-necked bottle of red wine and then later a scrapbook with a "lot of disgusting pictures" including "photographs" of the type of circus act seen at Hattie Adams's house. They left his wife and went to a corner saloon for more wine.

A few days later, on October 19, Lillie met with Captain Devery, who advised her to keep making monthly payments while they figured out how best to snag Gardner with ironclad evidence.

On Wednesday, October 26, Devery sent Lillie and Charlie on a marathon night of carousing—an eight-hour binge while Gardner's pregnant wife stayed home alone—to amass incontrovertible proof of Gardner's character (or lack of it) for a future jury. Lillie and Charlie met that night at the corner at Sixth Avenue and 32nd Street around 8 p.m., downed a pint of champagne at Boyle's at 45th Street, then took a carriage (with a Devery spy driving) up past the grounds for the new St. John the Divine Cathedral, past the building site for the new campus for Columbia to a saloon at 132nd Street for a pint of wine, then enjoyed a leisurely dark ride through empty fields and scattered houses and on to the rural Beaconsfield Inn at 185th Street. Along the way, Lillie said Gardner confessed that he had done "everything on the calendar except keep a w-h-o-r-e." She said he even offered to distribute business cards for her brothel, if she'd give him a cut. They drank two quarts of champagne and ate some sandwiches with the proprietor/witness Mr. Boyer at the Beaconsfield, then on to dinner at Huber's near the bridge to the Bronx, then south to a MacDonald's saloon at 76th Street at 2 a.m. They then arrived at Lillie's brothel, which Gardner left at 4 a.m. when Lillie reminded him that he had a wife.

While Devery set his trap for Gardner, the Parkhurst Society struck again in Devery's precinct. On November 15, Parkhurst agents, led by Gardner, executed another warrant at French Lena's, only this time without contacting the police. A reform judge, Charles Taintor, had decided to allow the private society to execute warrants.

They hauled in the eight French prostitutes, none of whom spoke English. Judge Taintor, conducting the trial with a translator, convicted the women and sentenced them to six months in the penitentiary. He found them guilty under a statute that said: "An inmate of a house of prostitution with no other means of support is a vagrant." New York State did not have a law per se against prostitution (i.e., selling sexual favors).

Sentencing eight newly imported and lovely French *filles de joie* to prison clearly infuriated certain powerful people, including some at Tammany Hall, who set a plot in motion. Since the last afternoon Corrections Department ferry had departed for Blackwell's Island, and the 50th Street prison was undergoing renovations, Judge Taintor was advised that the eight women should be transferred to Jefferson Market Courthouse jail. The request appeared reasonable.

That night, though, a Tammany police judge there, Thomas F. Grady, signed an order requesting the women be released; the document required the signatures of at least two commissioners of the Department of Charities and Corrections to be valid. Commissioners Sheehey and Simmons (both Tammany men) signed the document. The French *filles* departed into the night, never to return to prison.

Clearly, the Parkhurst Society, now armed with its own warrants, was beginning to gum up the underworld. With word of the French Lena arrest spreading through the police department, Devery traveled to police headquarters at 300 Mulberry Street to consult with the new superintendent of police, Thomas Byrnes.

The tall, paunchy, and balding fifty-year-old Byrnes was then regarded as the nation's most famous detective; he had personally cracked some of the largest bank robberies, had made Wall Street safe by creating a "dead" zone for criminals south of Fulton, and had unraveled several high-profile cases involving the blackmailing of millionaires. Now, after a twenty-nine-year career spent largely in the parallel universe of the detective bureau, he was elevated to superintendent after his predecessor's sudden departure in the wake of the Parkhurst fiasco. Several newspapers hailed Byrnes—an independent Democrat not affiliated with Tammany Hall who often worked closely with the city's wealthiest Republicans—as the ideal man to reform the police.

Born in Ireland in 1842, Byrnes had arrived with the outbound wave of Potato Famine refugees, and his Irish accent reared only when he was flustered, which was rare. He had earned his fame by revolutionizing detective work in New York City, methodically cultivating and chronicling criminals. He and his forty detectives researched the habits and tendencies of thieves and murderers, building an extraordinary "Rogues' Gallery" of photos and biographical thumbnail sketches. "Joseph Lewis, alias 'Hungry Joe' is a very persistent and impudent bunco steerer [con man]. He is a terrible talker—too much so for his own good." "Sophie Levy, alias 'Lyons' is a notorious shoplifter, pickpocket and blackmailer . . . of late she has become addicted to the opium habit." "Col. Alexander C. Branscom, Forger and Swindler . . . 44 years old, good education, converses well. Right arm off at the elbow. His expertness with a pen is a marvel."

Ultimately, Byrnes paid Tom or pounded Dick to tell on Harry. Denying the old saw about "honor among thieves," he boasted that by cash or threat he could get any criminal to "peach on his confederates." He manipulated these criminal contacts into a vast network of stool pigeons.

One weekend, newspaperman Lincoln Steffens, dining out with his wife, reached to settle the tab and discovered his pay envelope missing. Recently assigned to the police beat for the prestigious *Evening Post*, he rushed to report the crime directly to top man Byrnes. The detective asked how much was in the envelope, what was written on it, and what route Steffens had taken home from work on Friday. "All right, I'll have it for you on Monday morning," Byrnes promised.

And indeed on Monday morning, Byrnes turned over the envelope with the cash intact and walked away without saying a word. Steffens, flabbergasted, sought out the other reporters, then playing poker in the basement of 301 Mulberry. For several minutes, the veterans ignored the rookie's question until finally one answered: "[Byrnes] knew what pickpockets were working the car lines you rode and he told the detectives who were watching them to tell them that they had robbed a friend of the chief's of so much money in such and such an envelope." Steffens must have still looked confused. The fellow added: "Byrnes passed the word that he wanted that dip back by Monday, and so of course, it came back Monday morning."

It was an open secret that Byrnes tolerated some petty thieving by certain crooks in exchange for their spying on bigger crooks. A popular saying in New York held that six hoodlums couldn't plot a heist without one of them being in Byrnes's pocket.

"He chased the thieves all the way to Europe," wrote Jacob Riis. He also gave wealthy out-of-town crooks permission to squander their loot at New York hotels and restaurants—provided they did absolutely no thieving in his city. Byrnes routinely ignored requests for extradition from other jurisdictions.

Byrnes had recently seemed hard-pressed to hide his irritation at the harsh criticisms of the Parkhurst Society, and its boundless unrequested help. Devery met with Byrnes, and the sluggish, somewhat amateurish effort to trap Gardner now rose to a new level of sophistication: exotic marked gifts such as handkerchiefs and cigars, covert signals, traceable cash.

On Sunday, November 20, 1892, Lillie showed up again at Gardner's rented rooms to make another $50 payment. She found Gardner's wife Florence there alone.

Madam Lillie—as part of the trap—gave Florence a beautiful necklace from Casperfield & Clavellans; she had commissioned the jeweler—almost certainly acting on Byrnes's advice—to inscribe four of the gold beads on the back with the numbers 2-2-0-5.

Waiting for Charlie, the two women talked for three hours; Lillie dazzled the sheltered upstate girl with tales of Manhattan high life.

Charlie finally returned home, admired the necklace, and allowed his wife to keep it. However, he soon asked her to leave the sitting room so he and Lillie could talk business; Lillie handed him another $50. "You're a nice girl," he said to the thirtysomething demimondaine, and told Lillie to meet him at the nearby saloon. Pregnant Florence would stay home.

Since it was Sunday, the saloon's front doors were locked. They each rounded the corner and entered by the side entrance; they drank two bottles of wine, in violation of the Sunday excise law. At some point, he warned her: "There is going to be a terrible rumpus in this town and you are on the list." He said dozens of houses in three precincts would be pulled during a mass crackdown. She claimed not to believe him; he offered to take her to the Society for the Prevention of Crime offices nearby.

When she and Gardner climbed the five flights late on that Sunday night, striking a match to light their way up, they encountered fellow agent George R. Clark. (Gardner would later claim he brought Lillie there to sign an affidavit against Grant for extortion.)

Gardner sent Clark out to fetch a fine bottle of red wine, yet another violation of the Sabbath law. Clark—who would later cynically describe his job by saying the Society paid for wine, champagne, girls, and "you stop short of co-habitating"—walked to the Hoffman House.

Both men bragged to Lillie that they would be reimbursed. Gardner showed Lillie a large ledger that revealed $100.50 in expenses for the past week, and $300 from an earlier investigation. "Lillie, you see these psalm-singing sons-of-bitches, they are all good for it, and I will get it all back."

Liquored up at this point, Gardner also opened the safe and showed her stacks of indictments against brothels, including hers: "22—Lillie Clifton" in red ink on the cover.

The two Parkhurst agents painted a picture of ruin for the prime madams of Manhattan. Lillie said she could not believe Gardner was going to treat her like the rest; he played it coy for a while, then offered her an escape . . . for the steep added sum of $150. Gardner took her number 22 folder and instead of returning it to the safe, he hid it in the bookcase.

On Friday, December 2, 1892, Lillie met again with Captain Devery to plan the endgame. Devery had taken a $100 bill to a grocery store and exchanged it for small bills, whose serial numbers he had the grocer copy down. He also prepared $50 and recorded the numbers. She left with $150 of marked identifiable police money.

Two nights later, she went to Gardner's rooming house.

The elderly landlady let her in and Gardner was lying on the sofa. "Where is our little wife?" Lillie asked. "Up to her mother's," he replied. "You are quite lonesome?" she asked. "Yes," he replied.

She paid him the marked money. Some of it wound up in the sewing basket and the rest in his pocket. "We will go and have a bottle of wine; you are a good girl," he said, and she replied: "And you are a good fellow if you come and treat." It was crucial that Gardner be in possession of the money.

They exited together. Lillie raised her handkerchief to dab her eyes. The waved hankie signal was apparently to alert Captain Devery and Sergeant Crowley, hiding in a nearby doorway. (The *New York Herald* later commented that "a detective story without a secret signal in it is not worth much.")

Lillie and Gardner climbed into a waiting cab; Crowley and Devery jogged after it, knowing the cab would be going only a few blocks to the nearby saloon. Crowley caught up to it just as the pair was stepping down, near some broken pavement. The police sergeant grabbed Gardner by the shoulder. Devery, jogging behind, yelled, "Search his left hand pocket." Crowley found nothing. Devery later said he saw Gardner throw something down with his right hand. A roll of bills lay in the gutter. Devery shouted at the cab driver: "Did you see him do that?" The man, William F. Smith, confirmed he did.

"If it was good enough for you to take," said Sergeant Crowley, "it is good enough for you to pick it up." Gardner snapped back: "Pick it up yourself." The cop retrieved the money. "You've got me now," said Gardner, "and I suppose you will pound me."

Gardner knew he was in trouble; he asked if he could stop for a drink on the way to the lockup. "It's Sunday night, old man," replied Crowley, suddenly a stickler for the Sabbath laws. (He did later allow Gardner to buy a cigar.)

At headquarters, Sergeant Crowley performed a thorough search—including instructing Gardner to drop his trousers—and found that the Parkhurst detective was carrying $1,556 in cash, an enormous sum, more than a year's salary for most, including a carefully folded-up $500 bill in a jacket pocket. The cash roll found on the street matched the serial numbers from Smith & Sills Grocery; none of the money found on Gardner did.

The next day Captain Devery, Inspector McLaughlin, and Sergeant Crowley arrived with Lillie Clifton to execute a search warrant at Gardner's rooming house. Mr. Merritt, the seventy-two-year-old landlord, a sometime Parkhurst man, tried to stall to keep them out since wife Florence was not home. "Don't give us any chin music," Crowley told him, "or we'll take you by the nape of the neck and fire you down the stoop."

The police found $50 in the sewing basket. The landlord wrote down the serial numbers—which, it turned out, matched Lillie's—and sealed them in an envelope. They also found eleven Parisian handkerchiefs, and a marked box of cigars. The landlord told them where to find the wife and they then went to Gardner's mother-in-law's house and found Florence wearing a gold necklace with numbered beads: 2-2-0-5.

———

On Monday, December 5, Superintendent Byrnes assembled the newspaper boys from across the street. He quoted Gardner as sarcastically telling Lillie that he had "100 school-teachers like you on my list." When reporters asked Byrnes to explain why Gardner was carrying $1,556 on him, the superintendent replied: "The payments of his other *school-teachers*, I suppose."

Byrnes was clearly enjoying himself. He said he opposed allowing private societies to execute arrest warrants. He accused Parkhurst agents of practicing "a regular system of blackmail." The Gardner arrest was splashed across the front pages of Monday-evening and Tuesday-morning papers.

Reverend Parkhurst defiantly defended "honest" Gardner. "If the police would only show as much interest and eagerness to suppress evil as they do to suppress the efforts of our Society there would be no cause for complaint."

———

On the morning of Gardner's showcase trial, on January 31, 1893, his very pregnant wife, weeping on the arm of her mother, entered the courtroom first. A triumvirate of reform lawyers—John Goff, William Travers Jerome, and Frank Moss—followed behind her, ready to defend her husband. Despite their spirited efforts, the jury would unanimously find him guilty.

Lillie Clifton made a fine star prosecution witness, with an extraordinary memory for dialogue that occurred while drinking immense quantities of alcohol. Elegantly dressed in a fur-trimmed dress, with a stylish two-plumed black hat, she testified for four hours behind a white beaded veil. She walked the jury through the entire sting, and was unshakable even during a brutal cross-examination that detailed how she lived off the sins of other women, how she had profited from adultery. "You are a BAD woman, are you not?" defense lawyer Jerome abruptly shouted at her at one point. She replied calmly, "No, not altogether." Throughout the trial, she seemed to be carrying on a flirtation with the jury foreman.

Gardner admitted the well-documented carousings, but he denied *ever* taking *any* bribes and claimed he was working undercover to make a blackmail case against former agent Grant. He also testified that Captain Devery knocked the roll of bills out of Lillie's hand and that Lillie planted the other roll in the sewing basket when he went to the bathroom. He contended her Sunday-night visit to Parkhurst headquarters was intended to get her to a desk with paper and pen but "she was too under the influence" to write an affidavit.

The prosecution, headed by the Tammany district attorney, made its case even stronger by parading a series of madams and saloon owners, who claimed under oath to have been shaken down earlier by Gardner.

Gardner also had to explain the extraordinary $1,556 he was carrying. He mentioned giving slum tours for $50 a pop and doing freelance detective work, but the D.A. had subpoenaed his bank records. In 1889, Gardner, while working six months at $80 a month for the Gerry Society ($480), had been able to deposit $1,400 in the 19th Ward Bank. At one point, he denied owning any real estate; at another, he claimed to have thirty-two lots in Westchester and new property in Rutherford, New Jersey. Gardner was tap-dancing, trying to hide that he was a wealthy young man.

The newspapers thought Gardner's best hope came from the daily presence of his adoring, often weeping, and very pregnant nineteen-year-old wife and from Reverend Parkhurst. The minister reported himself too ill to attend the trial but an odd deal was struck: he would testify at home and the district attorney would not cross-examine him. Parkhurst stated that in mid-October the Society had ordered Gardner to pursue Lillie Clifton for an affidavit about George Grant's bribery attempts, and also that the Society had decided, because of Grant's blackmail, not to pursue vice cases such as Lillie's in the 22nd Precinct.

———

All for naught. The guilty verdict was returned in six hours.

Even the pro-reform *New York Times* on its editorial page agreed with the decision, calling it "absolutely conclusive" and dubbing Gardner the "vilest" of men. "These creatures will work, as Gardner did, for their own profit, and will sell out their employers and their causes without scruple." The *Times* wondered if even Reverend Parkhurst could remain uncorrupted doing undercover vice work night after night.

———

The pendulum had swung back toward Tammany.

Gardner began his two-and-a-half-year sentence. And Devery received his reward. The Tammany police commissioners transferred William Stephen Devery on March 15, 1893, to the second most lucrative graft precinct in the city, the eleventh, on the overcrowded Lower East Side. Sphinx Glennon would collect and Devery would start making a bundle for the first time in his life.

Reverend Parkhurst—perhaps not overflowing with Christian love—would choose Devery's 11th Precinct for his next massive investigation, and send swarms of agents into the brothels there. "The police objected to Gardner's blackmailing anyone," Parkhurst would later write, "for the reason that they wanted the monopoly of the business themselves."

3

THE REWARD

Devery's 11th Precinct covered a scant nine-block square, one of the smallest precincts geographically, but it housed a quarter of a million people, mostly Russian and Polish Jews, crammed together in extreme poverty. Jacob Riis dubbed it "Jewtown" in his book. Reformer Frank Moss called it "New Israel" and judged it the most crowded slum in the world, topping Calcutta.

Signs in Hebrew advertised "Room to Let" but almost no one had an entire room to him- or herself. One reformer found a family of twelve living in two rooms, *and* taking in six boarders to pay the rent. People slept indoors in shifts, and on rooftops in the summer months.

Walking through the neighborhood, one heard the relentless whir of sewing machines; anyone taking the Second Avenue Elevated train—day or night—caught glimpses into second-floor tenement sweatshops, filled with men in shirtsleeves, and women and children, all making garments.

On Fridays, Jewish peddlers hosted the "Pig Market" on several blocks of Hester Street where they sold everything *but* pigs. Buyers bargained in a half dozen languages for peaches, cracked eggs, socks, suspenders, shoes, candlesticks, pickles.

And tens of thousands of New Yorkers ventured south all week long from uptown to these derelict streets seeking more than just bargain pants. "[Every] block in the Eleventh precinct . . . is . . . infested by a disorderly house connected with licensed saloons," wrote an investigator, "[also] cigar stores masquerading as such but really houses of ill fame, cider mills of the same character, gambling rooms, and 'crap' games, faro banks, coffee house dives and houses of assignation without number." He counted 242 saloons in the nine-block square and more than fifty brothels, including one at 81 Eldridge just eight doors from the police station house. (The back of this particular "disorderly house" lined up with the back of Synagogue Beth

Israel Anshe Poland on Forsythe Street, and congregants sometimes complained that their chanting was interrupted by rhythmic exuberant sounds of a very different character.)

Police statistics from 1896 reveal that the 11th Precinct sported the highest crime rate in the city—12,112 arrests for assault, disorderly conduct, robberies, and so forth—*almost double* the next precinct, the Tenderloin.

At night drunken men filled the crowded streets of Hester and Stanton and Allen. A snatch of song often echoed out of Steen's concert joint on Forsythe Street, where very young girls mangled popular tunes before offering themselves. A neighborhood fixture, five-foot-tall Rebecca Abramsohn tended bar on a ramp at her two-story beer saloon at 150 Allen Street; she rented beds upstairs by the half hour. Down the street, another saloon kept its "melodeon" playing deep into the night "while disorderly women and drunken men sang low songs." Respectable couples reported walking to synagogue and hearing half-dressed women yell at them: "I'm prettier than your wife" or "Hey, sweetie, you should come work here, you'll make more than your husband does." One witness cited brothels at 6, 8, 10, 12, 14, and 16 Delancey Street.

To Big Bill Devery, all this prurience represented a gold mine.

Within days of the captain's arrival, his "bagman" Glennon and Big Bill began visiting the brothels in plainclothes.

The pair showed up at 144 Chrystie Street, at the brothel of Katie Schubert, an especially pretty twenty-five-year-old German Jew who had broken into the business at age seventeen. She had owned her own brothel for two and a half years and kept five or six "girls" in her high-end parlor house, charging two dollars a customer.

Devery never mentioned money, he merely kidded around, smoked a cigar, and told her to obey Glennon. After the captain left, the Sphinx explained the fees: a hefty $500 "new captain" initiation fee and $50 a month, to be delivered to him at the precinct house in an envelope. "I would be protected to run along quiet and not make any disturbances, fighting or any noise," she later recalled being told. The captain didn't want any 2 a.m. piano music or loud singing to attract attention; he didn't want half-naked girls on the stoop or anyone calling down obscene offers from the windows.

The Sphinx knocked on the door of a brothel at 28 Bayard Street run by Charles Prien, a middle-aged Civil War veteran with short gray hair and a clipped mustache. Prien, who had been in business long enough to pay several "new" captains, was quite taken aback by the $500, especially since—to pay it—he had to sell a show dog that had won first prize at Madison Square Garden. Prien found Glennon aptly nicknamed. "We had very little conversation," he later explained, "it was only do the act." Prien slipped a tightly folded $50 bill to Glennon in a police handshake.

Rhoda Sanford, a stout fifty-five-year-old bottle-blond widow with four grown-up children, ran a brothel two doors down from Prien. She had gotten into the business late, when she had no other means and answered an ad to be a housekeeper; she discovered the place to be filled with women in short skirts. (When a prosecutor later asked her why she didn't leave, she answered: "I guess if you hadn't a dollar in your pocket, you would do anything, too.")

Sanford—clearly an intelligent woman—expressed shock to Glennon at having to pay a massive $500 initiation fee and $50 a month, especially since business was slow. (The stock market panic of 1893 was imminent.) Glennon, however, with little sympathy, told her the drill: he would appear like clockwork on the seventh of the month to collect. Sanford kept a tattered ledger of her fees, which revealed such entries as "$4 for shoes," "$2 for gin," and "$1.50 for Man Shark," which she explained meant any man, politician or beat cop, and finally the largest: "$500 for C," that is, Captain Devery.

Devery was looking at $500 from each of fifty houses, or $25,000. He was also charging the gambling games $50 a month and he raised the fee for numbers joints from $10 to $20 a month. Devery would have to share his newfound wealth, giving 10 to 20 percent to bagman Sphinx for taking the bigger risk of collecting the cash, and he was obligated to give a slice to his superior officer, Inspector Alexander "Clubber" Williams, for looking the other way.

On a hot early-summer night at Harry Hoffman's brothel at 180 Allen Street some of the eight women fanned themselves, waiting for dollar-a-roll customers, as the door stood invitingly ajar. Kate McCarthy, who'd worked in several brothels, leaned out of an upper window and called down to a portly man with a big brush mustache and a derby hat. She had downed a few beers and slurringly hollered, "Come up, darling, for a good time!" He turned for a second, looked at the building, and kept on walking.

At 9 a.m. the following morning, after Harry Hoffman had slept for three hours—his house always remained open till 6 a.m.—a policeman came to his door and ordered him to go down to the Eldridge Street precinct station house. They walked the five blocks together, past Rivington, Delancey, and Broome to Grand. A pair of green globes marked the entrance on Eldridge. Harry walked in and was escorted to the captain's office.

Harry Hoffman was a lanky thirty-four-year-old ex-con with a handlebar mustache who had served five years in Sing Sing on a burglary rap. He was renting from a former Tammany assemblyman, Phil Wissig, who owned the building and ran a rowdy lager beer saloon. Hoffman had agreed to pay Wissig $70 a month, and Wissig had written "Glennon" on the back of his business card. He told Hoffman to get right by the captain. Because he was the tenant of a Tammany big shot, he was being charged only $40 a month.

Bill Devery kidded around with Hoffman for a while—Devery was a funny man when he wanted to be. "So who exactly are you?" Devery eventually asked and Hoffman told him about his brothel over Wissig's saloon. "You son of a bitch, that is you, is it?" Devery said. "Well, if one of them women cows of yours calls me up again, I will take you by the neck and throw you out of the house."

Kate McCarthy had accidentally propositioned the captain the night before.

Devery didn't threaten to shut down the brothel; he merely informed him of a $10-a-month surcharge. Kate McCarthy had broken the cardinal rule of keeping it low key during the Parkhurst crusade. Devery said it was hard for him to look the other way when he was being shouted at.

———

As swiftly as Devery and Glennon started collecting dues, just as swiftly did Parkhurst start investigating. Gardner was locked in at Sing Sing but the Parkhurst Society sent other detectives, such as thirty-five-year-old John Lemmon and beardless Edgar Whitney. The pair found a struggling Jewish eyeglass peddler, who gave his name as "Franks" but was really Benjamin Ettenberger, to guide them to dozens of brothels.

The Parkhurst detectives posed as out-of-town rubes. Since they needed evidence but couldn't "co-habitate," they flirted, paid for illegal drinks, and ordered up a lot of striptease and high-kicking. One prostitute, who thought the agent was avoiding intercourse from fear of venereal disease, offered to go find a "condom" or to use a "syringe," a plunger-like device to give a thorough antiseptic douche. He pled a stomachache.

The agents—solo, in pairs, in groups of three—made repeated visits to Grace Walsh's brothel at 81 Eldridge Street and to Elizabeth Hartell's at 70 Eldridge Street about 150 feet or so from the police precinct house at 105 Eldridge. They wanted to build an ironclad case against these brothels that Devery passed every day.

Reverend Parkhurst sent a set of irate letters to Tammany mayor Gilroy, to Superintendent Byrnes, to the police commissioners, and to Devery complaining that the Tammany captain had failed to close fifty-three brothels and eleven gambling houses in the 11th Precinct despite offers of help—and precise street addresses—from the Society.

Parkhurst's missives were dismissed. Inspector Williams even issued a report confirming the absence of vice at those locations.

So on October 29, Parkhurst investigators, armed with stacks of eyewitness accounts, approached Judge Voorhis and received arrest warrants for four brothel owners.

After hauling in the defendants, longtime private eye John Lemmon testified to Judge Voorhis that on each of his three visits to 81 Eldridge Street he saw women in "sleeveless short dresses" and that "high-kicking" occurred. This provoked a gruff mocking cross-examination by the brothel madam's lawyer, Manny Friend:

FRIEND: *You* did some high kicking?
LEMMON: I cannot kick high.
FRIEND: How high can you kick?
LEMMON: I can kick high enough to reach you.
FRIEND: If any kicking is done, you will be the one to get it.

This vaudeville banter didn't amuse the judge, who threatened both men with contempt of court. Frank Moss, counsel for the Parkhurst Society, informed the judge that a man in the courtroom was attempting to intimidate the Parkhurst witnesses. Judge Voorhis requested the man be brought to the bench.

Slowly walking forward with a smirk was Max Hochstim, a notorious Tammany Hall saloon owner who along with a fellow owner, Silver Dollar Smith (aka Charles Solomon), and Democratic district leader Martin Engel ran the underworld of the Jewish ghetto. Hochstim helped recruit new Jewish girls for the brothels; he strong-armed residents to pay dues to his neighborhood association. He was feared throughout the 11th Precinct, almost as much as Devery.

Judge Voorhis questioned him; Hochstim denied all, especially tipping off the brothels about the raid. He said he was in Newark. The judge gave him a stern, demeaning lecture and ordered him removed from the courtroom. Hochstim, as he was passing lawyer Friend, stage-whispered, gesturing toward dandified bald Frank Moss: "Do you think it'd cost me a $100 [fine] to smash him in the face?"

The Parkhurst agents left the building and Hochstim's gang, reinforced by local bruisers, crowded in on them; the agents race-walked west along Broome Street. Members of the crowd jostled them and tried to punch them while—according to Frank Moss—police officers of the 11th Precinct stood by and watched and laughed. The Parkhurst agents at the Bowery jumped onto a passing Fourth Avenue streetcar but the mob—now 500 strong—grabbed the reins of the horses and surrounded the vehicle; a couple dozen men climbed aboard and began trampling the vice investigators. Police from the neighboring precinct, not having any order to ignore the action, eventually broke up the mob and freed the men.

That night Parkhurst rushed a typewritten complaint to newspapermen about the incident, singling out Devery and Hochstim.

Superintendent Byrnes read the minister's account of the thuggery in the morning papers; he told reporters he was "disgusted" and ordered an immediate investigation. Byrnes's doorman, Dan Strauss, seeing his boss arriving in such a sour mood, hid a lit cigar in his pocket to avoid detection and accidentally set himself on fire.

Devery quickly stitched together a report, citing twenty-seven shopkeepers who saw no mass harassment, merely a gaggle of boys trailing the Parkhurst men; Devery quoted a train conductor who said he had to restrain a Society agent from pulling his gun on the boys.

———

Parkhurst refused to allow the police to paper over Devery's profitable misdeeds. His agents testified before a grand jury, which on November 29, 1893, returned four indictments against Captain Devery for neglecting to close the brothels. (Judge Voorhis had found all four madams guilty.) The police commissioners, under pressure, shifted Devery from the juicy 11th Precinct to the graft-light 1st Precinct, Old Slip, near the southern tip of Manhattan. About the only shakedowns possible were excess construction site debris, maybe some sidewalk displays or overnight wagon parking. Straight-arrow Captain Moses Cortwright arrived in the 11th Precinct, and made 1,300 arrests in the next four weeks.

———

Devery's trial in April was front-page news. "For the first time in the history of the police department," the New York World announced, "one of its officials will be tried on a criminal charge of neglect of duty."

The stakes were high. As the small-circulation pro-reform paper the New York Times pointed out: If a police captain were actually convicted of neglect of duty, then all captains would be at risk, and then they'd have to shut down all the brothels and gambling joints. It was an astounding concept.

Dozens of blue-uniformed police officers packed the courtroom on April 3 to show support for this extremely popular captain. Devery had hired the fifty-two-year-old celebrity lawyer Colonel E. C. James, one of the nation's most heralded trial lawyers.

James rarely lost. Obviously, his services did not come cheap. Devery's legal fees would approach $5,000, an enormous sum when day laborers worked for a dime an hour.

Before the trial started, the defense caught (or created) a break: none of the four madams or any of the prostitutes working for them could be found. Many speculated the police had acted as fine travel agents, giving the women a choice of Europe or the East River.

James was a specialist in cross-examination, and his trial strategy for Devery grew quickly clear: discredit the Parkhurst agents.

Colonel James asked endless questions for the jury about the agents' experiences of "drinks," "merry-making," and "high-kicking" at 81 Eldridge Street. James asked twenty-eight-year-old Edgar Whitney very precise questions about garments worn. Hems above the knee? Plunging necklines? Had he not seen equally short, low-cut dresses at the opera? "Yes, but those women wore *tights* underneath," parried Whitney. Then James carefully explored the character of each investigator. He brought out that Whitney had been accused of stealing money as a traveling pants salesman in Vermont, skipping out on a hotel bill. He explored Whitney's stint in New York as an undercover investigator for the street railroads. Whitney would don a conductor's uniform and wander through the cars to make sure other conductors were ringing up every fare. Whitney was fired. "Was it not for appropriating nickels?" James asked.

The New York police detectives clearly did their homework for their captain. Whitney was forced to confirm that he had been arrested in an illegal gambling joint in Devery's former uptown precinct. Whitney denied vowing to get even.

All the Parkhurst agents admitted using numerous false names in their current and former detective jobs. Marcus Wishart, slack-jawed and laconic, stated he once worked for the Law and Order League of Pittsburgh collecting bounties for finding saloons open on Sunday, and that he was later arrested for attacking a constable in Pittsburgh.

Thirty-five-year-old John Lemmon, "most flippant" at first, had been using aliases for fourteen years as a detective in the West. He recounted how he had injured his hand during a recent investigation. "I had a fight somewhere on Fourth Street . . . in one of those coffee houses where they have the girl waiters. One of the girls came over and kissed me." Colonel James, shaking his bald head, interrupted: "Kissed you? Did you resist?" Lemmon: "I did not. Then a man came in and struck the girl. I hit him and we had a fight."

The lawyer made much of the agents kissing the prostitutes, then returning home to kiss their wives *with that same polluted mouth.*

Called to testify, Superintendent Byrnes explained that he had sent a pair of "fly" detectives from Central Headquarters to the 11th Precinct. Byrnes ordered the men not to inform Devery and to linger from 8 p.m. to 6 a.m. on several nights at the alleged brothel sites; the detectives returned with a report that 81 Eldridge was closed. Byrnes said he had known Captain Devery for a decade and his reputation on the force was "good."

The cross-examination of Dr. Parkhurst marked the trial's most dramatic moment. His "leonine" mane of now graying hair seemed to fascinate the press. He wore a black clerical frock coat buttoned up to his chin and kept on his gloves and overcoat while testfiying.

After the district attorney walked him through the Society's investigation and his many letters alerting the police to brothels, Colonel James asked during cross-examination: "Is the Parkhurst movement directed against the keepers of disorderly houses and gambling houses?"

Dr. Parkhurst replied: "It's primarily against the police department and the criminal collusion I believe to exist between it and the criminals."

Colonel James asked: "Do you include the District Attorneys' office?"

Dr. Parkhurst paused a moment. "Yes sir I do."

The spectators—en masse—emitted a sort of shocked simultaneous intake of breath. Then, after an awkward silence, Parkhurst looked directly at assistant district attorneys Bartow S. Weeks and John F. McIntyre sitting at the prosecution table and said with a weak smile: "Present company always excepted, sir." Unsmiling, A.D.A. Weeks rose and filed an official "exception" to Parkhurst's accusation.

The prosecution wrapped up its case late on Friday, April 7. Colonel James surprised the court by musing aloud that he might not call any witnesses. Dozens of officers, and possibly as many as 150 witnesses, stood ready to testify that 81 Eldridge Street was closed as tight as a jeweler's safe.

On Monday morning, fourteen police officers in full blue-and-brass uniforms sat rigidly near the front; another dozen or so came in plainclothes to back Devery. (He was extremely popular: he called reformers "little tin soldiers" and wondered if some of them had "angel's wings" under their coats; he advised beat cops who needed to go on a drinking bender to get a surgeon's note and take a few days off.)

Colonel James announced that he didn't need to call witnesses; the prosecution had failed to prove its case. James, in his summation, dismissed Parkhurst as an "enthusiastic ecclesiastic" who surrounded himself with "a set of vagabond detectives." He called the Society's true motive against Devery transparent: "They wanted to put up their job to trap this man who had laid by the heels the pet detective of the Society."

The A.D.A. devoted some of his closing argument to defending his own office from Parkhurst's accusations.

———

The case went to jury. The first vote came in 10–2 for acquittal. Eight long hours later, the jurors returned. The foreman of the jury stood and announced, "Not guilty." The *New York Sun* reported that the cheer by police officers could be heard blocks away; another newspaperman said he felt the "building tremble." Such was Devery's popularity; such was the unity of the men in blue. Devery reached into his breast pocket, extracted a cigar, and immediately lit up his victory stogie. Reporters noted his first good long drags created a big red glowing ash.

None of the policemen said it aloud for the press but the sentiment was clear: *If New Yorkers and tourists wanted brothels, why should the police stand in the way? And why shouldn't the police profit a bit for the favor?* The *New York Evening Post,* then a reform paper under E. L. Godkin, observed that the police force viewed the court decision as granting "the right of captains to discriminate among disorderly houses, which to break up and which to permit."

———

This verdict seemed to validate Tammany Hall's corrupt easygoing ways.

Reverend Parkhurst, looking back years later, called the Devery acquittal the turning point in the battle for reform. "No event has transpired during the history of our work that has operated more directly and powerfully to define and compact popular sentiment than the acquittal of Captain Devery." Parkhurst said intelligent citizens citywide saw transparently that Devery's guilt was proven but that corrupt forces—police, judge, district attorney, Tammany—had freed him. "Devery was about as thoroughly developed a product of the Tammany system as we ran against in all our encounters," assessed the reverend. "He was not lacking in a certain kind of genius but it all ran on depraved lines."

———

A New York State Senate committee was then halfheartedly probing the police force's role in election abuses in New York City.

Dr. Parkhurst—with the aid of some of the city's wealthiest citizens—decided to try to transform the sleepy investigation, generously fund it and replace the political hacks asking the questions with pit-bull reform lawyers, such as John Goff, Frank Moss, and William Travers Jerome. The reverend hoped to expose the corrupt inner workings of the police department, and do so more vividly and broadly than any prior inquiry in the history of American cities.

POLICE ON THE GRILL

The thirty-eight precinct captains ruled the 3,800 cops who ruled the streets; and Superintendent Byrnes *seemed* to rule the captains but insiders knew better. He wasn't exactly a figurehead—he oversaw day-to-day tactics, riots, training, ongoing investigations—but in many ways, he had his hands tied. In the byzantine command structure of the New York police, a four-member highly politicized Board of Police Commissioners controlled hiring, firing, transferring, and disciplining of the members of the police force.

Democratic and Republican politicians struggled mightily to gain a majority on the four-man board. Clearly, if policemen, especially captains, could rake in thousands of dollars in shakedowns, then Police Board commissioners (or the politicians who controlled them) could extract thousands from the policemen in exchange for promotions to sergeant and on to captain. Money flowed up—circuitously—from the brothel and dice game to the top politicians. And it wasn't just money; it was the power to do favors all over the city: to wink at violations or to flay enemies.

Since the mayor appointed the police commissioners, and since Tammany had won the mayoralty in seven of the last nine elections, the Republicans needed to find a way to get Republicans onto the city Police Board.

So the upstate Republicans, who controlled the legislature, had voted through an investigation of the New York City police, especially its role in monitoring elections. Political insiders viewed this probe as a kind of tribal war game. If Tammany Hall would agree to add a Republican police commissioner—the board had two Democrats, one Republican, and one vacancy—and would agree to legislation making the New York Police Board permanently bipartisan (two Republicans and two Democrats), then the Republicans would not investigate *too* hard and would certainly not expose graft that could profit both sides.

The governor, Roswell Flower, a *Democrat* and no timid poker player, vetoed the $25,000 appropriation for the investigation, and he vetoed the bipartisan police bill. He did so with some self-righteousness, pointing out how the Republican majority always found it necessary to investigate only *Democratic* cities such as New York and never Republican strongholds such as Syracuse or Rochester. He castigated Republicans for using public moneys to further their fight over the "division of political patronage."

Three days later, Tammany mayor Thomas Gilroy appointed James Murray, a stalwart Republican, to the last slot on the Police Board. The backroom deal seemed complete, creating an equilibrium in plunder on the board.

As Tammany's George Washington Plunkitt once pointed out: "Me and the Republicans are enemies just one day in the year—election day . . . the rest of the time it's live and let live with us."

The Republican investigation seemed dead. Then up popped Reverend Parkhurst. Hearing of the governor's vetoes, Parkhurst approached the Chamber of Commerce to pony up the missing $25,000 in appropriations. The Chamber quickly agreed. Parkhurst approached relentless anti-Tammany lawyer Goff to handle the investigation; Goff demanded absolute control.

Dr. Parkhurst and reform, in effect, had hijacked a show investigation, meant mainly to leverage the divvying of swag between the Republicans and Tammany Hall. Goff, who started on May 21, about six weeks after the Devery acquittal, actually intended to investigate, to probe everywhere in the New York City Police Department.

While political insiders knew about the widespread police corruption, it had never been publicly proven and splashed on newspaper front pages, and, moreover, no high-ranking police officer had ever broken the blue wall of silence.

———

The hearings were held, ironically enough, at the Tweed Courthouse, built at the obscene cost of $12 million, the work site of the so-called Prince of Plasterers, Andrew J. Garvey, a Tammany grand marshal, who received $133,187 for two days of plaster work. What better place to probe corruption than in the marble mansion of corruption?

The third-floor hearing room was packed on Monday, May 21. John

Goff, his face ruddy, his premature white beard and brows a mockery of kindly Father Christmas, interrogated the hale big-boned Republican police commissioner John McClave about his wealth. With more than a decade as a police commissioner, McClave—the owner of a city-block-sized lumberyard on West 21st near the North River—danced around most of Goff's questions. The fifty-four-year-old, who also served as Police Board treasurer, even seemed pleased to own up to an annual income of approximately $100,000 and to having recently bought a house on West 74th Street for $70,000.

But Goff relentlessly pushed for details of McClave's personal finances: Did he use the police pension fund to buy stocks for himself? Did he receive checks from men seeking to join the police force? McClave's indignation mounted. At one point, he shouted: "Anybody who told you that is a miserable contemptible liar."

Then Goff calmly requested permission to call another witness, Commissioner McClave's former son-in-law, Gideon Granger, who had just divorced McClave's daughter. Granger ambled to the witness box, chewing gum, "smiling as if he were going to the circus," as the New York World put it. Thirty years old, his thin waxed mustache curled up, his body posture exaggeratedly relaxed, Granger made it a point to declare that he bore his former father-in-law no ill will over the very recent divorce. Then he proceeded to describe his role during his six years of marriage as a go-between, funneling bribes to the police commissioner. Of one particular transaction to speed a hopeful cop into the ranks, he effortlessly recalled: "The money was in the form of a check on the Fifth Avenue Bank, dated May 17 and numbered 215." He told detailed anecdotes such as how a patrolman named "Ronk"—on the verge of dismissal for accidentally arresting the mayor's son—had handed him, in addition to a $100 gold certificate, a gorgeous live fox. Granger read bribe notations from his personal memorandum book: "Burns $280; Cohen $175; Cahill $250 Mehan $370; Farnsworth $300; Coleman $500; and Mead $250."

McClave, furious, turned shades approaching Goff's naturally florid Irish complexion, and, once back on the stand, denied all. He called his ex-son-in-law a "scoundrel" and a "forger," and he stage-whispered that he'd see him sent to prison.

Goff was off to a great start, so great that, it was later learned, around this time the Tammany Hall boss, Richard "Dick" Croker, secretly booked passage for himself and his son on the steamship Umbria to Europe.

Though praised for his grilling of McClave, Goff was having a hard time filling the witness box daily. The Lexow Commission—named after state senator Clarence Lexow, the Republican Party stalwart who had introduced the legislation—had the power to subpoena witnesses, to recommend arrest for those failing to appear, and, most importantly, to grant immunity from prosecution for anything testified. But the investigators soon discovered almost all potential witnesses were terrified of police retaliation, and feared being "railroaded to Sing Sing," or beaten with a "club" or a "sandbag," according to Goff.

Many fled, including approximately 100 Manhattan brothel madams who, it was later learned, formed an expatriate community in Chicago, not far from the Palmer House. But the police couldn't speed the exit of *everyone* involved. Parkhurst seeded the Lexow investigation with hundreds of leads from his Society probes, especially in Devery's precinct.

So began a daily parade of plume-hatted, silk-gloved madams, of comely and homely prostitutes, of mustachioed gambling impresarios, and of unrepentant counterfeiters who all soon mesmerized the city with tales of police shakedowns and of their days spent living the low life. Newspaper articles, syndicated around the country, reinforced New York's reputation for wickedness.

Lena Cohen, twenty-eight years old, testified that she ran a four-girl, fifty-cent-a-fling brothel at 378 East Houston Street and that the police had threatened to arrest her if she tried to leave the business. A detective named Farrell was not only collecting $50 a month, he was seeing—and not paying—one of her prostitutes nightly. When Lena balked, the detective arrested her husband, Morris, then her.

A gaunt blonde in a large hat, Louisa Miller testified that she had saved up from her years assisting a midwife and doing washing to open a respectable boardinghouse for single gentlemen and married couples. She paid $70 a month rent for 15 East 2nd Street. Detectives raided the house and, despite finding only elderly men sleeping there, pressed charges against her for running a disorderly house. Two detectives, Cohen and Schindler, demanded $10 each at first, then much more. She refused. Despite five witnesses telling the judge about the house's good character, she was convicted and fined $100. The detectives returned and told her, in effect: "You don't pay, you don't stay." She didn't, and the next time she was accused—and convicted—of personally soliciting an officer for sexual intercourse. The Lexow Committee had to retrieve her from the Tombs.

And so it went . . . an astounding array of shakedowns. Agents for the steamship lines arriving at the nation's busiest port testified to paying the police "from the time a ship sighted the Statue of Liberty until she had discharged her cargo." Czech beer saloons banded together into the Bohemian Liquor Dealers' Association and paid Detective Campbell $100 a month to stay open on Sundays. No shakedown was apparently too small. Italian bootblacks paid for select corners, and were forced to shine policemen's shoes for free. The owner of a seafood restaurant on Catherine Slip said he paid five dollars every two months to keep a glass case of clams and oysters on the pavement, in violation of the city's sidewalk encumbrance law.

Peddler Billy Mayston, a chatty fellow with a scanty mustache, sold whips and cutlery out of a satchel; he told how he paid his way. "I have given up more scissors to policemen than would supply all the people in this room." He told of another cop who judged Mayston's scissors too long and told him to leave a pair of nail scissors with the Italian greengrocer. "He is waiting for them yet."

Mayston, about thirty, a New Yorker of the streets, "full of natural humor and pawkiness," didn't seem eager to leave the stand. He described how he played the ponies and how the police allowed at least twenty "pool rooms" to remain open, even during the Lexow investigation. He advised the senators, if they planned on placing a bet at 23 Chambers Street, to carry a "pink sheet" to get in, that is, carry the *Sporting World* printed on pink paper. He looked in a little memo book, citing other locations such as the Merchants Hotel, second floor back, where plainclothes police detective Sheridan often spent afternoons and had recently helped the owner bum-rush a friend of Mayston's down the stairs. (The friend had wanted to place a bet below the hefty two-dollar minimum.)

Over the weeks, through other witnesses, it became clear that the police in many precincts not only charged for their blindness but helped settle turf wars among the criminals. They indeed regulated vice. A man named Pomeranz started a gambling game in the back of a saloon he bought at 82 Essex Street. Max Hochstim protested that it crimped his business. A neighborhood fixer named Santfman testified that police detective Schindler coerced two ex-cons to walk into Pomeranz's joint and start playing cards for money; the cops quickly entered, arrested everyone, and the only men that Tammany judge Hogan allowed to walk were the two ex-cons. Lawyer Frank Moss couldn't resist commenting: "You can see what power these men have when they have lots of men swearing to anything, and police officers to make arrests and judges holding them and discharging them at will."

Over and above the big shakedowns of brothels and gamblers and the little shakedowns of pushcart men, another side of some officers of the New York police emerged: rude, violent, and lazy.

The son of Tammany man Phil Wissig flirted with and insulted a man's wife near his father's East Side saloon. The husband testified that he confronted Wissig and the young man grabbed a policeman's nightstick and beat him; and two cops also pummeled him and threatened to arrest him.

A twenty-seven-year-old from Constantinople, George Alexander, owned a seafood restaurant at 103 James Street in a rough neighborhood off Cherry Street. The small fellow saw a man grab a lobster out of his glass case at 2 a.m. He threw off his apron, chased the man down yelling "thief," and grabbed him a few blocks away right near a beat cop. The thief smacked Alexander in the face with the lobster but as the crook tried to flee, he fell. The beat cop did nothing. Alexander, his face bleeding, yelled to the cop for help. "Go to hell," shouted back the cop. "What the hell do I care about your lobsters?" The thief ran away laughing.

After he filed a complaint at police headquarters, two detectives visited his place. The first threatened "prison"; the second merely said: "I will fix you."

Alexander feared that a plainclothes detective would pay him with a dollar and then claim he had shortchanged him, or that he had served him liquor after hours. "Who will protect me then?" the immigrant asked. "My word won't go there [in court], and as soon as they swear to that, I go to prison." Alexander closed his business.

————

On June 29, Goff announced a recess for July and August.

That same day, the Tammany-dominated Police Board informed the public it would commence departmental trials of corrupt officers.

An election loomed in November for a new mayor, sheriff, and other key posts, and Tammany could feel the heat of Lexow. In the most recent mayoral election, Tammany had won but a concerted effort by its political opponents, by Republicans, Reformers, anti-Tammany Democrats, and others—all riding the recent scandal—had a strong shot at victory. Tammany needed a speck of high moral ground to gain a handful of non-Tammany voters.

The Police Board brought charges that summer against four sergeants, four precinct detectives, and four captains, including Big Bill Devery, the heretofore bulletproof Tammany man. Bringing down a captain and dismissing him would mark a feat not accomplished for two decades. With Lexow testimony making the job easy, the board charged Devery with fifty-six counts of neglect of duty in not closing brothels.

Devery conveniently became quite ill. The family doctor diagnosed "active congestion of the brain" and described Devery's thirteen serious "symptoms" as including flushed face, buzzing noises, watery eyes, sleeplessness, rapid pulse, confusion, and inability to concentrate. His wife, Annie, refused to allow Inspector Peter Conlin to enter their house on West 28th. "My husband's life is more important to me than any rules of the police department," she said.

The Police Board carried on the trial without him. One of the first witnesses called was Louisa Scheuler, a cute fourteen-year-old in a white sailor suit, the daughter of the owner of the Atlas Hotel in Rockaway Beach. She testified that Captain Devery, vacationing a week earlier with his family, seemed "in the best of health" and had a "hearty" appetite.

A procession of brothel owners doomed him. Attractive Katie Schubert gave details about her monthly payments to the police. "Were you told after this thing is over, you can open again?" Katie: "I shall never open again." Why? "I got tired of earning money for other people to enjoy."

The board found Devery guilty, voting 3–1 to oust him. The lone dissenter, a Tammany man, pointed out that he thought Americans had a right to be present at their own trials.

The board also found eleven of twelve officers guilty and dismissed all of them, in an unprecedented housecleaning. Captain John Thomas Stephenson went down for, among other sins, accepting four crates of peaches to ignore sidewalk violations. The board wanted to show its toughness.

On September 6, the same day that Parkhurst returned on the White Star steamship *Germania* from mountain climbing in Switzerland, the police board voted to end the position of precinct detective, or "ward man"; from here on, if a plainclothes detective was needed, Superintendent Byrnes would send one from central headquarters.

Clearly, the current board members wanted to avoid the fate of Commissioner McClave, who had retired under doctor's orders.

Reformers were smelling victory in the upcoming election for mayor. The big question: on whom to bestow this plum. Early names included Dr. Parkhurst, John Goff, and Theodore Roosevelt. Former congressman Lemuel Quigg made a passionate pitch to Roosevelt down in Washington.

Theodore weighed the pros and cons. One major plus for this extremely competitive man would be erasing the sting of his 1886 defeat for mayor.

He discussed it with his wife, Edith, and she made it clear that she opposed running. She regarded the financial risks as too great. Edith always had financial fears since her father had squandered the family fortune and she had grown up in genteel poverty; she also knew her husband's strong suit was not managing the family budget.

She argued that he would need to quit his current job, spend money for the campaign, and he still might lose. Then he would be unemployed; the family would be pinched. Also, the five children were so settled in D.C.

Roosevelt listened to her arguments. He told Quigg not once but four times that he was flattered but refused to run.

Campaigns were much shorter then, and on October 5, a mass of mostly wealthy reformers, who dubbed themselves the "Committee of Seventy," anointed William L. Strong, a bearded avuncular sixty-seven-year-old businessman with no political experience.

Roosevelt later confided to his best friend, Senator Henry Cabot Lodge, his profound regrets over his decision. "I would literally have given my right arm to have made the race, win or lose," he wrote. "It was the golden chance which never returns."

Rounding out the ticket, John Goff accepted running for Recorder, the highest-ranking municipal judgeship, against Tammany's Frederick Smyth, who had presided over the Charlie Gardner case.

The Lexow Commission resumed in the fall; the witness chair was now dubbed "Goff's Griddle." The chief inquisitor's plan was clearly to array enough witnesses to build a corruption case against a high-ranking police officer, such as a captain or inspector, then use the threat of prosecution in criminal courts to force him to testify.

But so far, the police continued to stonewall. They answered Goff's subpoenas but denied or explained away the accusations.

In the meantime, Goff served up more horror stories.

On October 2, 1894, Goff delivered—in one single day's session—*ninety* police officers accused of brutality. The officers, a sea of blue coats, filled the gallery. The *New York Times* reporter observed that "some of the clubbers 'looked the part' but there were many mild-mannered appearing policemen among them." Goff said it took months of planning to synchronize this cattle call of malefactors. He complained that the Police Board rarely meted out harsh punishment to policemen guilty of brutality; he said that the board had dismissed only four officers in the past three years for brutality, and three of those cases involved violence against fellow policemen.

———

The Republican–Reform "Fusion" ticket defeated Tammany Hall, 154,000 to 109,000, in the mayor's race. William L. Strong was elected. Lexow lightning rod John Goff was elected to the post of Recorder by a slightly wider margin, defeating Tammany's Frederick Smyth, who had spent $3,500 of his own money on the campaign. Not since the Tweed scandal in 1872 had Tammany fared so miserably.

"The city is redeemed," proclaimed the *New York World*. "The wildest hopes of Republicans and Anti-Tammany men have been realized," announced the Republican paper, the *New York Tribune*. "It proved to be a landslide, a tidal wave, a cyclone, a political revolution of the most gigantic and far-reaching proportions."

———

John Goff and the reformers were not done with Lexow. The commission mandate allowed it nine more weeks, near perfect timing since Goff would begin his term as the city's highest-ranking judge in the New Year.

In the meantime, Goff was determined to crack the blue wall of silence, which was fortified by what he called the "cohesion of public plunder."

He still needed to build cases strong enough that the police captains would prefer to admit to the crimes in the hearing room and gain immunity rather than risk criminal prosecution. In most years, the captains had little to fear from a Tammany district attorney but this year was different. On the evening of December 12, Goff caught a break, as a jury convicted the dismissed captain John Stephenson of accepting four baskets of peaches and $38 in exchange for allowing a Duane Street fruit merchant to obstruct the sidewalk. Stephenson now resided in Cell No. 3 at the Tombs and was awaiting a sentence that could be as harsh as a $5,000 fine and ten years in prison.

Goff put Captain Timothy Creeden on the stand. Creeden, fifty-five, was a distinguished Civil War veteran, with classic Irish good looks, pale blue eyes, ruddy complexion, trimmed white mustache. Fellow officers deemed him a classy, fair commander; he had sworn off drinking and tobacco twenty-five years ago, soon after joining the force.

> GOFF: I am sorry, almost, that my duty compels me to ask you,
> Captain, knowing you to be an honorable man as a soldier and
> citizen, how much money did you pay to be made captain?
> CREEDEN: (*after a long pause*) I have not paid any money for my
> appointment.

Goff expressed his disappointment in Creeden, then began calling witnesses who painted a picture of how a sergeant bought a promotion to captain circa 1887. Creeden's friend Barney O'Rourke, a saloon keeper at 35 Forsythe, organized for him a collection of "loans" of $250 to $1,000 each from fellow saloon keepers and lodging-house men tallying $15,000; he had a middleman hand over the money to a hunchbacked, green-eyed petty politician named J. W. Reppenhegen, who would in turn hand money to another petty politician who could influence (or hand money to) Police Commissioner Voorhis, the anti-Tammany Democrat on the board. (Creeden, despite a captain's salary of $2,750, would be expected to reimburse his backers with money from shakedowns and favors.)

The following morning, Goff called Creeden back to the stand. The hearing room was so packed that onlookers camped on windowsills. Goff reiterated that none of Creeden's testimony could be used against him in a court or a Police Board trial. Goff began slowly by asking Creeden why he had denied paying for his captaincy. Creeden, in a deep voice, with a bit of a brogue, answered that he wanted to protect the men who had helped him. Goff brought out that Creeden had scored 97.82 on his captain's exam but was passed over repeatedly; Goff implied that Creeden was the victim of a shakedown.

> GOFF: And you are willing to take great risks even to your own
> danger in order to save your friends?

CREEDEN: Well, that was it.

GOFF: That is your nature, Captain?

CREEDEN: Yes, sir.

GOFF: And a distinguishing feature of your race?

CREEDEN: With my family, particularly so.

GOFF: For what reasons?

CREEDEN: Being revolutionists.

GOFF: Revolutionists in Ireland?

CREEDEN: Yes, sir.

GOFF: So that word "informer" carries with it a terrible significance there?

CREEDEN: It does, sir.

———

Goff had achieved a crack in the blue wall of silence with Creeden's admissions; he would now try to sledgehammer a major breach. Captain Max Schmittberger stood under indictment for extorting a $500 bribe for dock privileges from an agent of a French steamship line. Schmittberger's name was also mentioned in shakedown testimony by dozens of merchants, brothel keepers, and various criminals.

If he testified to these corrupt acts, he could make himself immune from prosecution. He started testifying late in the morning of December 21, then the committee broke for lunch recess. The *Tribune* would call his confessions "the Crowning Exposures." Word spread quickly. "Before the afternoon session was called to order, a battering ram could not have lodged another unshattered human being inside the room," stated the *New York Sun*.

Schmittberger—a tall, "handsome," imposing, forty-two-year-old officer, with black hair and large black mustache, sometimes called the "Big Captain"—sat stolidly in the witness box; he wrung his hands occasionally but he spoke in a loud clear voice.

He gave listeners a guided tour, precinct by precinct, through his two-decade career of vice and police corruption. His first assignment as a beat cop in 1874 was the Tenderloin. He recalled the disorderly dance palaces that flourished there: Haymarket, Tom Gould's, Star and Garter, Newport, Buckingham, Empire, Cremorne, Fashion, Arion, Lawrence Hall, Shang Draper's . . . places that stayed open all night with police permission. "These dives were resorts for the criminals of the whole country, who came there to meet women prostitutes."

> GOFF: And who was the captain to whom the money for protection
>   went directly?
> SCHMITTBERGER: Captain Williams.

Schmittberger was implicating one of the highest-profile officers in the city, Inspector Alexander "Clubber" Williams.

> GOFF: Was it a matter of common understanding among the
>   captains of the various precincts that they were to take
>   advantage of any opportunity that presented itself to make
>   money out of their respective precincts?
> SCHMITTBERGER: Certainly.

He later called it "a custom of the department."

The big German officer explained that the plainclothes detectives, called wardmen, would receive about 20 percent and the inspectors ranking above captain would receive 40 percent, leaving about 40 percent for the captain.

After sixteen years on the force, Schmittberger was promoted to captain. He said he didn't pay a penny but used the influence of a leading German newspaper publisher.

Schmittberger soon replaced a Captain Gunner in the 25th Precinct, and he asked him how much a month he should give to Inspector Williams. Gunner said he had been giving about $50 or $75. Schmittberger then went every month to central headquarters and slipped an unmarked envelope of cash to Williams. Goff asked why he needed to pay his superior officer. Schmittberger replied that the inspectors had the power to send central office detectives to raid gambling joints or Sunday saloons in any precinct and had to receive a cut not to do so.

The big German captain soon moved to the more lucrative 27th Precinct, which, thanks to three "pool rooms" (offtrack betting parlors) paying $200 a month each, delivered $900 a month before wardman and inspector shares.

At first Schmittberger didn't suppress or charge the saloons for Sunday liquor sales because word had spread through the department that Tammany had struck a citywide deal. But Thomas Byrnes, after he was named superintendent in the wake of the initial Parkhurst crusade in 1892, had gathered the captains and told them to crack down. He told them to stop making "show" arrests for Sunday liquor selling that rarely led to convictions and merely bulked up arrest statistics to impress the naive general public and press. Byrnes demanded legitimate arrests. Schmittberger followed orders and had two of his most trusted men arrest twenty-six saloon owners on the first weekend.

The arrested Bohemian bartenders cursed them in Czech and threatened the two officers and the captain. And soon after, one of the Tammany police commissioners, J. J. Martin, had all three transferred.

In order that Schmittberger not miss the point, he found himself newly installed in the Leonard Street precinct, which had almost no saloons. He complained to Superintendent Byrnes and next wound up in the 22nd Precinct, West 47th Street, where he lasted from May to December 1893. He collected about $500 a month from houses of prostitution and from "policy shops," mostly cigar stores that sold illegal lottery tickets. He in turn handed an envelope with about $150 a month to Inspector Thomas McAvoy, but he ran into a problem. "He did ask me one time if some of that came from disorderly houses . . . because he didn't want any money of that kind."

Goff asked Schmittberger why McAvoy didn't want it. "He is a very religious man."

Schmittberger could have collected more but he was told to lay off certain special brothels, though not for any reasons of faith. "I was given the tip, so to say, if I didn't want to burn my fingers not to have anything to do with [Georgiana Hastings], and I didn't. I never saw the woman, and I wouldn't know her now if she stood before me."

Georgiana Hastings ran a high-class establishment that attracted top politicians and judges. Goff couldn't resist informing the audience that the committee was having difficulty serving her with a subpoena, because last time a judge and another government official in the parlor had prevented the warrant from being executed. Goff announced that he knew the men's names. "Unless an absolute emergency arises where it is absolutely necessary," interjected chairman Lexow, "we should not smirch any private character."

Another protected house was Lillie Clifton's. Captain Devery "told me to take care of her . . . on account of the services she rendered in the [Gardner] case." Schmittberger complied even though Lillie was having her house on West 53rd Street run by a woman named Freeman.

Captain Schmittberger also recounted how one day he had sent a detective to the house of Mrs. Sadie West at 234 West 51st Street. She screamed at the detective "that Commissioner Martin was a friend of hers." When Schmittberger went to HQ to inquire, Tammany's Martin was furious. "Send that man back there and make him apologize, say he made a mistake." And he did.

Schmittberger again felt the cross-pulls of the superintendent battling a commissioner. A man with ties to Tammany commissioner Sheehy wanted to open a gambling palace off 42nd Street but Superintendent Byrnes threatened to "break" Schmittberger if he allowed it. He refused to let the gambler open up.

The commissioners transferred Schmittberger for the fifth time in three years. He was surprised to discover his destination: the Tenderloin. Then he was even more surprised to find that the Tenderloin yielded only about $200 a month. The Parkhurst crusade had inspired Byrnes to order captains to close down the brothels. "What is the world coming to: only $200 a month in the Tenderloin?" said Goff, sarcastically. "The golden days have passed."

Toward the close of the session, Goff asked why the captain had agreed to testify. Schmittberger replied: "I feel that the pillars of the church are falling and have fallen and I feel in justice to my wife and my children that I should do this."

When asked if he had any last comments, Schmittberger said that he thought Superintendent Byrnes was "an honest and fair man" who would do the right thing "if not hampered."

The *New York Tribune* summed it up: "Few well-posted citizens were really taken by surprise by Schmittberger's testimony" but the newspaper said there was "keenest gratification" that Goff "had gone up higher and bagged such large and heretofore elusive game."

———

Goff was seeking even higher game. On the very last day of testimony, Goff called Superintendent Byrnes. The papers had heretofore treated him with kid gloves. "Byrnes Alone in Favorable Light" ran a typical subhead.

Finally, the culmination: on December 29, around 5:30 p.m., Goff called out the name of Thomas Byrnes, and Byrnes, in a black cutaway coat, with gray pants, walked to the witness chair in the packed hearing room. Pinched for time, Goff racewalked Byrnes through the police promotions of his thirty-two-year career, then immediately asked about Byrnes's real estate holdings.

BYRNES: I own my residence at 58th Street.
GOFF: And it is worth?
BYRNES: $40,000.
GOFF: Free and clear?
BYRNES: Free and clear.

So began a near-surgical investigation of Byrnes's finances that revealed the policeman's net worth at "fully" $350,000, making him one of the wealthiest New Yorkers despite serving as a public employee earning $5,000 or less annually most of his career.

GOFF: Since you have been on the force, have you been in any other business?
BYRNES: No I have not.

The superintendent denied receiving a penny from vice payoffs or any police shakedowns but said that his position had brought him in contact with wealthy men, and "those gentlemen from time to time helped me to make money."

He explained that after he caught Colonel Howard Wells, the extortionist, in 1881 Jay Gould, the railroad financier, "wanted to make me a present of a large sum of money, which I declined . . . he was much astonished." Goff asked him what kind of reward he eventually received.

With the hearing room so crowded, with all those reporters present, Byrnes could not resist spending almost half an hour recounting how he had foiled Wells's blackmail plot, how he had supplied coded stock tips to the blackmailer, how he had assigned detectives to watch all mailboxes from 20th Street to 44th Street, Fifth Avenue to the North River, how he . . .

"This is all very interesting," interrupted Goff, "but please get to the point of your first investments with Mr. Gould."

Byrnes said that he finally agreed to let Gould invest $10,000 of Byrnes's own money for him. A decade later, when Gould died in 1892, the sum had ballooned to $185,000.

He also admitted that Gould's son, George, through shrewd trading had tacked on another $43,000 in the past two years.

What precisely did Byrnes do to warrant such stock tips from the lofty? The newspapers translated his vague answers to mean that for some families he encouraged unsavory suitors to return to Europe and leave wealthy American heiresses alone, and for others he did his usual job of protecting lives and property but did it more discreetly, keeping their names out of print.

On the Lexow stand, with the nation watching, Byrnes denied knowing that the captains were paying off the inspectors. The *New York World* commented: "If he did not know what was going on right under his nose, year in and year out, then he isn't detective enough to detect Limburger cheese without eating it."

But by and large, Byrnes owned up that the force was riddled with corruption at the highest ranks but he laid the blame squarely on corrupt politicians manipulating a corrupt Police Board. He said when he had tried to crack down on Sunday saloons by sending in undercover cops to make arrests, the board had passed a rule that only officers *in uniform* could enter saloons. He said the Police Board undermined him at every turn, promoting bad officers and transferring good ones to "Goatland" in the Bronx; it meted out punishments with a feather duster. Byrnes told the standing-room-only crowd that he advocated making promotions based on merit. Byrnes pointed out that he had taken the thick twenty-four-inch nightstick away from the men—except for riot duty—and replaced it with a slenderer fifteen-inch billy because he thought they were clubbing too many innocent people.

He singled out Tammany Hall, charging that Boss Croker was able to shut down the city's "pool rooms" last year during the Parkhurst crusade by simply giving an order to the police magistrates. "I have nothing but friendly feelings for Dr. Parkhurst and his Society although he has pounded me in every possible way," averred Byrnes, larding it on a bit thick. "He has created a public spirit in the city without which the reforms could not have been effected."

He defended the rank-and-file cops. "There is not anything on earth they would not do, if their commanding officers set them a good example."

Then, as time was running out by around 8:30 p.m., Byrnes dramatically handed to Chairman Lexow a copy of a letter dated December 13 that he had sent to mayor-elect Strong. Goff read it aloud. "I desire not to be an obstacle or an embarrassment to you in anything that you may propose to do with the police department . . . I, therefore, now place in your hands my request to be retired from the post of superintendent, to be used by you or not at any time after the 1st of January, as you see fit."

The crowded room seemed stunned. Byrnes was New York's most famous lawman. His comments immediately led the crowd to wonder whether Byrnes truly wanted his gracious face-saving offer accepted. He said that he and his detectives had put criminals away for almost 10,000 years of prison sentences—more than "Scotland Yard, Paris or New Jersey" combined—and stated that he was ready to offer "services, advice and information" to the new administration.

Goff dismissed him and Byrnes, a tad stooped, stepped down and took a seat.

———

The *New York Times* called the Lexow revelations heard over the last eight months "the sensation of the country." Thanks to telegraph and telephone, newspapers delivered sleaze from Manhattan to their readers. And editorial writers from Maine to California called for reform of the police in the nation's largest city.

The Lexow revelations had already led to thirteen criminal indictments of high-ranking officers; in addition, Lexow witnesses had leveled serious charges of corruption or incompetence against fifty-three men, including two current police commissioners, two former commissioners, three inspectors, fourteen current captains, two ex-captains, three sergeants, six detectives, eight former precinct detectives, and nine patrolmen.

The Lexow report would conclude: "It seemed as though every interest, every occupation, almost every citizen was dominated by an all-controlling and overshadowing dread of the police department."

New York's Finest—they already had the nickname—were accused of being New York's Filthiest. They ruled New York's street corners as an "established caste . . . with powers and privileges away above and beyond the people."

———

Mayor William L. Strong took office on January 1, with an overwhelming mandate to reform the city. He offered Theodore Roosevelt the job of . . . sanitation commissioner. Roosevelt agonized, declared himself eager to bust up the corrupt contractors, but ultimately found the post beneath his dignity.

Four months later, in April 1895, the mayor offered Roosevelt the post of police commissioner.

ENTER CRUSADER ROOSEVELT

The dawn of the reform era in the police department began on May 6, 1895, when sixty-eight-year-old mayor William L. Strong, a former bank president, in a brief 10 a.m. ceremony at City Hall, swore Theodore Roosevelt in as police commissioner. His salary would be $5,000 a year for five years. The mayor also gave the oath to Colonel Frederick D. Grant, forty-four-year-old son of the late Republican president, and Andrew D. Parker, a thirty-six-year-old Democratic lawyer. The three new men would be joining the sole remaining Democratic commissioner, thirty-one-year-old Avery D. Andrews.

Roosevelt—despite his reputation as headstrong and energetic—could not rule the show. By a recently passed law, the four-man board had to be bipartisan, that is, have two Democrats and two Republicans, but Mayor Strong implored them that morning not to be *bi*partisan, but to be *non*partisan, to banish politics and make decisions for the good of the city. In that era of bruising elections when Tammany Hall Democrats dominated New York City and upstate Republicans carried the rest of the state, Strong's request sounded quintessentially high-minded, and perhaps daft.

Three of these four men had never met before that day, and Roosevelt had but a passing acquaintance with Grant from various Republican dinners. Coming together on this "blind date" in governance were a reform Republican (Roosevelt), a loyal party Republican (Grant), an anti-Tammany Democrat (Parker), and a never-cared-for-politics Democrat (Andrews). Yet many key decisions of the board, such as promotions, would call for a unanimous vote; that meant one board member could scuttle the rest. By the middle of his tenure, Roosevelt would compare a bipartisan commission to a "Polish Parliament" where deadlocks are often ended "by killing the man who objected."

But that morning, they were all smiles and bonhomie and promises of cooperation to clean up the police department.

The four men, all well dressed for the occasion, strolled together uptown the mile from City Hall at Park Place to police headquarters at 300 Mulberry Street. They made a stately foursome: Andrews, the youngest, tall and lean, a devoted cyclist; Parker, also tall, with a precisely manicured beard; Roosevelt, mustachioed, strong but a bit stocky, just starting to add pounds to his thirty-six-inch waistline; Grant, the oldest, who, despite his comb-over, resembled his famous father. All four had blue eyes.

The walk was scenic in a classic New York sense. "The tenements stank," wrote a journalist of the blocks near police headquarters. "The alleys puffed forth the stenches of the night. Slatternly women hung out of windows to breathe or to gossip or quarrel across the courts; idle men hung half-dressed over the old iron fences or sat . . . on the stoops of the houses which had been the fine homes of the old families moved uptown." (The wealthy Roosevelt clan, for one, had moved from Maiden Lane to Union Square to 20th Street to 57th Street.)

As the four men approached 300 Mulberry Street, Roosevelt started to race-walk, more like a boy headed to the ball fields than a man in a suit heading to a job. The others struggled to catch up. Newspapermen, looking out from their basement digs across the street, abandoned their midmorning poker game to meet the new commissioners. Jacob Riis, veteran crime reporter for the *New York Evening Sun,* rushed outside; he had been there since 7 a.m., and he towed along his assistant Max Fischel, who had been there since 3 a.m. gathering the blotter report from the precincts. "Hello, Jake," Roosevelt called out to Riis, whom he had met briefly soon after the publication in 1890 of Riis's landmark book on poverty, *How the Other Half Lives.* With a wave of his hand, Roosevelt—who had never entered the building before—led the pack up the steps of police headquarters, past "Pat," the Irish doorman.

Roosevelt, all nervous energy, blurted out questions to Riis: "Where are our offices? Where is the boardroom? What do we do first?" He seemed to be moving fast enough to race right by the powerful ghosts of 300 Mulberry Street. He breezed past the office of the world-famous detective Thomas Byrnes; he didn't slow at the Rogues' Gallery of photos or the museum of crime paraphernalia.

This wide drab four-story building, with dirty awnings and a basement jail—located just north of Houston Street (pronounced "How-stin" by genuine New Yorkers)—represented the command center of the nation's largest police force, with almost 4,000 officers. A newly installed telephone service connected it to most of the thirty-eight precinct station houses and accepted calls from the rare private Manhattan caller wealthy enough to have a phone. The telegraph office still took the bulk of the incoming information, and hummed with complaints of dead dogs and loud saloons.

The four men gathered and chatted in Commissioner Andrews's office at 10:45 a.m. and waited for the departing commissioners to arrive to turn over their offices to the new men.

Roosevelt quickly grew restless waiting so Andrews took the men on a brief tour of the building. The new commissioners had no idea that they had inadvertently inspired a new dress code. "Every police attendant about Police Headquarters who possessed diamonds hid them carefully in his waistcoat pockets," observed the *New York Herald*. "It is not regarded as politic at the old building on Mulberry street to attract the attention of a reform Commissioner by the display of too much prosperity."

On their tour, Roosevelt greeted every workingman in the halls of the building, right down to the janitor in the sub-basement who spent his days shoveling coal into the steam boiler that ran the furnace. Roosevelt pointedly did not seek out Byrnes, the head of the police department for the past three years.

Each of the three men dropped his card off in the commissioner's office he would inherit, with Roosevelt and Grant on the third floor near the boardroom, and Parker and Andrews on the second floor.

The new board held its first meeting at 11:30 a.m. They sat around a large rectangular table with windows looking out on Mulberry Street. As prearranged, Andrews nominated Roosevelt for president and the three, with Roosevelt recusing himself, voted yea. He was now the highest-ranking police official in New York City—at least in title. His $5,000-a-year salary and single vote were equal to the others.

The board elected Major Avery Andrews treasurer to oversee the $5 million budget, and Andrew Parker would chair two committees: "Elections" and "Pensions." Grant was given "Repairs and Supplies" and "Rules and Discipline." Roosevelt, as president, was an ex-officio member of all the committees. The commissioners would hold three board meetings a week, and take turns presiding over once-a-week police misconduct trials.

Soon after, Roosevelt slipped away and met with his pal Riis, who had in tow twenty-nine-year-old Lincoln Steffens, a novice police reporter for the liberal *New York Evening Post* who would become famous for muckraking. "It was all breathless and sudden," wrote Steffens thirty years later in his autobiography, "but Riis and I were soon describing the situation to him, telling which higher officers to consult, which to ignore and punish; what forms were, the customs, rules, methods. It was just as if we three were the Police Board, T.R., Riis and I, and as we got T.R. calmed down we made him promise to go a bit slow, to consult with his colleagues also." (A careful reading of Roosevelt's letters shows that Steffens aggrandized his role a bit; Roosevelt referred to Riis as "my main prop and comfort," the "closest to me" during those years.)

Roosevelt readily admitted he "knew nothing of police management," but would try to frame that lack of preconceptions as a positive. He would describe the upcoming week as the hardest stretch he had ever worked in his life and report that he found the department completely "demoralized." That word, circa 1890, still packed more of the meaning of lacking any moral compass than depressed. Half the precincts lacked captains, because of suspensions and retirements.

The rest of the afternoon was spent in informal meetings; Andrews, whose office was connected to Roosevelt's by a wrought-iron spiral staircase, hovered close to TR. Before the mayor appointed him, this West Point graduate had described himself as a lawyer "with a minimum of clients and a maximum of free time." Even the most famous man in the building, Chief Byrnes, dropped in for a chat. To Roosevelt, Byrnes represented the old guard; to many others, he represented the greatest strengths of the department: modern crime-fighting skills.

Roosevelt in his sheltered life had had very few interactions with the New York police. On Wednesday, day three, Roosevelt and the other two new commissioners sat at the shoulder of Commissioner Andrews as he conducted the trials of nearly 100 policemen accused of misconduct by citizens or by supervisors called roundsmen. The four commissioners would rotate this once-a-week duty, and each could exonerate or levy small fines; heftier sentences such as dismissal required a majority vote.

Thus began Roosevelt's education in the day-to-day aspects of policing and of the rules: one patrolman was caught bringing a "can of coffee" to a fellow officer and claimed he went just "five feet off post"; others failed to report an unlit streetlamp, a dead dog, sunken street pavement. The more serious offenses involved letting a prisoner escape, assaulting a citizen, turning up in a saloon.

Andrews presided with curt righteous irritability. A patrolman named Dick Mullin claimed he went in uniform into a saloon to use the toilet and that he had told two young ladies on the street to alert the roundsman—if he should wander by—of that fact. Andrews: "Are there not hundreds . . . of people on Grand Street that hour of the evening?" The officer nodded and before Andrews could ask another question Roosevelt jumped in: "How is it that you should select two young ladies in whom to confide your business?" Andrews warned: "The officer who goes into a saloon takes his commission into his own hands." He promised to render a verdict later.

When street cops and court officers blamed each other for the escape of some prisoners from Jefferson Market Courthouse, Roosevelt and Parker asked a flurry of extremely pointed questions.

And so it went. The tone had changed. The old Tammany commissioners had joked with the men, and docked half a day's pay. Not these reformers.

That night Roosevelt attended the annual meeting of the New York Civil Service Reform Association at the City Club on Fifth Avenue and gave a rousing speech. A century-plus later it's hard to fathom the passion and contentiousness of something as bland sounding as civil service reform, but men such as Roosevelt considered it the bedrock for purifying politics and saving democracy. Until the 1880s, elected officials routinely handed out plum public-sector jobs to party faithful as rewards. Reformers envisioned a day when men would be hired based on merit alone (and not kickbacks or bribes).

Gradually Congress and presidents, governors and legislatures moved more and more jobs under civil service hiring rules. By 1895, about one-quarter of the 175,000 federal jobs were civil service, and about 13,600 of the 19,340 New York City public posts.

Roosevelt had fought for six years in D.C., irritating both Republican and Democrat alike, to locate and honor every single civil service job.

The party bosses, not surprisingly, detested civil service. "How are you goin' to interest our young men in their country if you have no offices to give them when they work for their party," asked George Washington Plunkitt, a New York state senator and member of Tammany Hall. "Isn't it enough to make a man sour on his country when he wants to serve it and won't be allowed unless he answers a lot of fool questions about the number of cubic inches of water in the Atlantic and the quality of sand in the Sahara."

The exam especially infuriated those who professed to have more common sense than book education. A Brooklyn cop—fresh from his exam—shared what he said were some of the questions with fellow officers. "What is the distance between Tokyo and Canarsie by ferry boat?" "Elucidate the forty-seventh problem of Euclid." "Is it better to have a clue without a case or a case without a clue?" "If a hen and a half lay an egg and a half in a day and a half, how long will it take three detective sergeants to catch three horse thieves?"

Carl Schurz, a longtime reformer and a leader in the German American community, introduced Theodore Roosevelt to the cheering audience. TR traced recent developments in Washington regarding postal, railroad, and customs workers, then he turned to his current job. He vowed "open competitive examinations for all positions" based on new physical, mental, and moral standards "without any regard to politics." He said that there would be only four exempt positions: a confidential secretary for each of the commissioners. And he noted that, as president, he was entitled to a stenographer too, but he would make sure his secretary could take dictation as well, thereby saving the department money and cutting one more potential patronage job. More polite applause from this audience full of some of the wealthiest, most influential reform men in the city, such as Richard Watson Gilder, *Century Magazine* editor, and E. L. Godkin, editor of the *Evening Post*.

On day four of his stint, Roosevelt hired a woman. Again, more than a century later, it is hard to appreciate the shock of that decision. Women were starting to make inroads as "typewriters" and stenographers in commercial offices but not at the New York City Police Department, which employed a few dozen matrons for the precinct jails and some housekeepers, usually police widows, to sweep the floors and make the beds. "Of Corset Will Be Necessary to Alter the Uniform" ran one mocking headline in 1887 at the hiring of the first matrons. "Their night stick will be of papier mache of a color to match their gloves and will contain a vial of smelling salts in the handle."

Headquarters was still a bastion of masculinity, full of beefy armed men dragging prisoners along. "[The hiring] took the breath out of the old stagers at Mulberry Street barracks," observed the *New York World*. Roosevelt added to the gender insult by hiring her at $1,700 a year to replace two men employed by the previous commissioner for $2,900 a year combined. Roosevelt was saving the department $1,200.

Minnie G. Kelly was "young, small and comely, with raven black hair." In her debut, she wore a wasp-waisted black dress and school-marmish spectacles and pulled her hair primly into a loose bun. Her job would not be easy: capturing the torrents of Roosevelt's words . . . he would write or dictate more than 150,000 letters in his lifetime.

(Years later, Roosevelt would declare himself pleased with her overall job performance but concede she made her share of mistakes. He recalled dictating a letter about an overly aggressive officer. "I was obliged to restrain the virtuous ardor of Sergeant Murphy, who, in his efforts to bring about a state of quiet on the street, would frequently commit some assaults himself."

That's what he said aloud; when Miss Kelly handed him the sheet, he read on the page: "I was obliged to restrain the virtuous ardor of Sergeant Murphy, who, in his efforts to bring about a state of quiet on the street, would frequently commit somersaults himself." TR later wrote his sister that he couldn't stop laughing long enough to reprimand her as he couldn't banish the mental image of the rotund sergeant rolling down the street.)

Even in the smallest ways in those first days, Roosevelt wanted to shake up the department and assert the reform agenda. Previous commissioners had voted themselves diamond-studded gold badges costing $400. Roosevelt and the new board voted to create a simple $15 round silver badge, with the city's coat of arms surrounded by blue enamel lettering: POLICE COMMISSIONER OF THE CITY OF NEW YORK. And even these inexpensive badges must be returned upon leaving office. "Personally, I should be content with a copper cent stamped P.C.," he told Riis. Frugality, incorruptibility.

After the board meeting on Friday, the commissioners shared a hack carriage to City Hall to lobby the mayor on a pending police reform bill. The police department then had no vehicles designated for the use of captains, chiefs, or commissioners; the officials either boarded a streetcar or elevated train or hailed a horse cab. The four men bounced along the cobblestone streets, then glided on the newly installed asphalt avenues.

While Roosevelt was pleased that hiring was now safely under the jurisdiction of the new Police Civil Service Board and promotions controlled by his board, he was appalled that the Republican-dominated legislature had recently passed a bill that would grant the chief of police full control over the weekly misconduct trials. Roosevelt had, of course, by now figured out that reorganizing the force centered on three basic management principles: hiring good new men, firing corrupt current officers, and disciplining to keep everyone in line.

Roosevelt rushed into the crowded, fadedly elegant room at 2 p.m., his colleagues trailing behind, and he approached the mayor, who suffered from gout and was sitting in a rocking chair. Roosevelt launched into a passionate diatribe, his hands sawing the air as he tried to convince the mayor to withhold his signature. "This bill is thoroughly bad and vicious," he said. "If it was drawn for the purpose of continuing the abuses in the department, it could not be better framed."

His arguments spilled out of him . . . Byrnes could undermine fair elections; he could cavalierly pardon bribe takers. "This bill has not one redeeming feature . . . nothing could be imagined more subversive of discipline." The mayor, whose receding hairline gave him something of an accidental Mohawk, sat, rocked, and listened.

What was amazing was that Roosevelt was rushing headlong on day five of his tenure to accuse the world-famous police chief of coddling crooked cops; TR was saying, in effect, that Byrnes could not be trusted. After fifteen minutes, Roosevelt abruptly stopped. (The *Washington Post* once uncharitably commented: "He slays a hippopotamus or cracks a flea with the same overwhelming ardor.")

Roosevelt had framed his argument in black and white, good and evil, and was painting the mayor into a corner.

Following Roosevelt's fire came Commissioner Parker, with his icy lawyerly manner. "No matter how grave the charge, no matter how monstrous the offense, the [chief] can sit in his office and say 'You shall not be tried.'" And Commissioner Grant wanted to help but felt somewhat inadequate. "If I were an eloquent man, I would pour out my eloquence in asking you not to sign the bill."

Mayor Strong, who said nothing, had that look of a man who had already made up his mind. He had never served in elected office prior to being anointed mayor by a coalition of reformers and Republicans, and Jacob Riis said he suffered from "the intermittent delusion that he was a shrewd politician." Commissioner Andrews called him "a lovable gentleman of the Old School" who had a "keen wit, a dry sense of humor, wore plain black clothes, [and] chewed tobacco."

The mayor immediately announced that he would veto the bill. Each commissioner went up and shook Strong's hand. As Roosevelt was leaving he could be overheard saying enthusiastically to Andrews, "The old man is a brick, isn't he?"

On Monday morning, May 13, Roosevelt made the three-mile commute from 689 Madison at 62nd Street down to Houston and Mulberry. (The Roosevelt family was temporarily staying for free at the elegant townhouse of his sister, Anna—better known as "Bamie"—who was then in London.) For a nickel, he could hop on the Third Avenue El at 63rd Street for eleven stops to Houston Street.

TR arrived early to the office and then to the boardroom and fidgeted waiting for Commissioner Parker, who, Roosevelt was discovering, often seemed to operate a bit on a parallel track all his own. When Parker showed up late at 11:23 a.m., TR immediately gaveled the meeting to order.

Roosevelt was feeling out his new colleagues. Parker, a former assistant district attorney, seemed an astute lawyer, with an eye for detail; Grant, a former minister to Austria, was congenial. By the end of the week, TR would confide to a close friend: "Parker is my mainstay; he is able and forceful but a little inclined to be tricky. Andrews is good but timid and 'sticks in the bark' [like an arrow that doesn't penetrate deeply into the tree]. Grant is a good fellow but dull and easily imposed on; he is our element of weakness."

Roosevelt, with his usual impatience, orchestrated a breakneck pace. The previous board in one of its last meetings had passed a resolution authorizing the annual police parade, a popular New York City civic event that ranked right up there with the Fourth of July and St. Patrick's Day. Roosevelt abruptly brought a motion to cancel the parade. Every year hundreds of thousands of people lined the streets as the men in blue marched by, not in a lockstep drill but rather as a kind of informal victory parade, with proud captains leading on horseback and police bands playing. Chief Byrnes was quietly making elaborate preparations. With no discussion, the board unanimously passed a motion to cancel; the only explanation given was that the board was too busy with other important matters.

Clearly this represented a symbolic quashing of Byrnes and the old guard. And Roosevelt privately told Jake Riis: "We will parade when we need not be ashamed to show ourselves."

Next item that morning: election reform. The police then oversaw elections, checking voter registration, monitoring polling places, and counting the votes. (That was Albany's stated reason for a bipartisan Police Board, not equal divvying of graft.) The board, to ensure fairness, passed a motion that all policemen must resign immediately from all political clubs and must stop giving donations. The Democratic Pequod Club was chockablock with Tammany Hall police officers, such as Big Bill Devery appealing his dismissal, and Inspector William McLaughlin, then on trial for bribery.

In a further effort to banish politics from policing, Roosevelt also suggested that all job applications no longer contain any reference to a man's party loyalties. He wanted the message out that ward heelers from both parties would find no jobs to hand out in the police department. "The ordinary politician is as keen to scent out places [jobs] as a pig is after truffles," Roosevelt told Steffens for an *Evening Post* article. So the board passed a measure mandating that even the janitors and laborers would become civil service appointees.

Next item that Monday: discipline. The board quickly agreed that it would double or triple the punishments, especially for drunkenness on duty. Andrews recited several cases, including the one of patrolman Peter MacDonald of King's Bridge precinct in the northern Bronx, who had been caught sleeping in a railway station *twice in the same night.* The old regime might have slapped him with a two-day fine. Checking the man's record, Commissioner Parker discovered that MacDonald had racked up thirty complaints, including many for being in saloons and bars. Parker recommended dismissal. Roosevelt suggested commuting the sentence to thirty days' fine but announcing to the force that this was special "leniency" by the new board and that all punishments hereafter would be much stiffer. (Two days later, they would fire repeat offender Joseph Flynn for being caught in a saloon. "It is time that an example was made of somebody," declared Roosevelt.)

The new board also voted to review the entire system of police discipline, which was then anchored in a poisonous relationship whereby roundsmen sneaked around the beats of patrolmen and spied on them. The more infractions the roundsmen found, the better their chances for promotion to sergeant. The board had the novel idea that roundsmen should be promoted when the patrolmen reduced crime on their beats and did their duty.

Next item: dismissal from the force. Roosevelt passionately wanted the right to fire any officer, without the fear of a court overturning the firing. "I want every decent man on the force to know that I am his best friend [but] every bad policeman we will get rid of as fast as we can," said Roosevelt. "We want neither loafers nor shirks, nor corrupt men of any kind." Under current rules, a dismissed officer could appeal to the criminal courts, which, in effect, meant that the board, to avoid being overturned, had to build rock-solid cases and use due process for witnesses and evidence. These standards were more rigorous and costly than a private employer firing someone. The board sent an urgent official message to Albany imploring the legislators to pass a bill denying dismissed policemen the right to appeal their terminations to the courts.

The board also discussed ways to deny pensions to corrupt cops, who might now rush to retire to avoid life under a reform board. Such a strategy might also help save the pension fund from an impending deficit. Parker would investigate. The board sent a memo to the chief that cushy "special assignments," such as guarding foreign dignitaries, should be based on seniority and valor instead of Tammany connections. To emphasize the positive, they discussed giving out more merit awards for bravery. The board immediately voted a medal of honor to patrolman Michael Nolan of the East 104th Street precinct, who had leaped into the fast-moving East River and saved a boy from drowning.

Those were just a few of the topics taken up at that Monday meeting. The *New York Recorder* commented that the new board accomplished more in this one meeting than former regimes did in four months; it certainly marked a strong collegial start for reform.

Around 2 p.m., a tall pale young man, with the build of a prizefighter, bounded up the steps of 300 Mulberry. Well dressed, in his mid-twenties, he sported a faint reddish mustache and matching side whiskers; he kept his identity a secret.

He sought out Commissioner Roosevelt and handed him an envelope, and then dropped off another with the clerk for Chief Byrnes. Roosevelt closed the door to his office and opened the envelope. He found copies of three letters—one to the mayor, one to the police chief, and one to a captain—all listing extensive charges against Captain Joseph Eakins.

Just as the Parkhurst Society had staked out a campaign in 1893 against Captain Devery for not closing brothels in the 11th Precinct on the East Side, so now it was orchestrating one against Eakins in the 15th. (This precinct covered a swath of Manhattan radiating outward from Washington Square, north to 14th Street, south to Bleecker Street; today, NYU occupies much of the area.)

The messenger would turn out to be Arthur "Angel" Dennett, lead investigator for the Parkhurst Society, who had kicked off the 15th Precinct probe by going on New Year's Eve with *New York World* reporter Nellie Bly to McAleer's Saloon on Thompson Street. They posed as a couple needing a bed, and paid twenty-five cents to mount the stairs. As they reached the landing, they heard loud lewd talk and also the sound of "the [metal-spring] beds in constant vibration." They saw an open door and entered a room with bare furnishings. Dennett asked the maid why there were no sheets or covers on the mattress and she explained that the customers "went to bed with [their shoes] on and would spoil the sheets if they used them."

So here TR was, a week into his new job, and he found Reverend Parkhurst eagerly trying to help him. Roosevelt would always publicly lavish praise on Parkhurst, but privately he said he sometimes found the reverend a bit *too* helpful.

Now Parkhurst was trying to oust an officer, Eakins, who just happened to be a well-respected Republican, a Civil War veteran, a high-ranking Freemason. Even the reform paper, the *New York Times*, had called Eakins a "man content to live on his salary," with an "excellent reputation."

Roosevelt summed up his first week in a letter to his sister. "I have never worked harder than in these last six days, and it is very worrying and harassing, for I have to deal with three colleagues, solve terribly difficult problems and do my work under hampering laws . . . I have rarely left the office until six in the evenings." (At times, one catches unintended glimpses of the privileged Knickerbocker Roosevelt.)

The next day a telegram from Albany reached police headquarters. The legislature planned to adjourn without passing any new police laws. TR and the board could not pencil in a list of officers to fire at will, and then achieve a sea change of personnel.

Roosevelt was disappointed—a key weapon for reform was being denied him. But hurdles or not, he still planned to go after the corrupt men.

Thursday morning Roosevelt presided over his first solo trial day. Close to 100 nervous bluecoats lined the halls of the second floor awaiting their turn. Roosevelt abruptly ordered a huge roundsman named Schauwacker to keep order. The room became unusually quiet—without the cops kidding each other in loud voices.

The *New York World* sent its star reporter, Arthur Brisbane—known for his "flippant audacity"—to cover the show.

"Sing, heavenly muse, the sad dejection of our poor policemen," wrote Brisbane for the front page of the city's (and the nation's) largest-circulation newspaper. "We have a real Police Commissioner. His name is Theodore Roosevelt. His teeth are big and white; his eyes are small and piercing; his voice is rasping . . . his heart is full of reform, and a policeman in full uniform, with helmet, revolver and night club, is no more to him than a plain every day human being. He is at work now teaching the force that it is paid to work, not to boss."

So began the front-page coverage in Joseph Pulitzer's *New York World*. Roosevelt and Pulitzer would have a rocky go of it over the next decade but for that first honeymoon month or so of TR's police job, the *World* and almost all the dailies treated the new commissioner admiringly.

> Think what must be the poor policeman's feelings when he comes up for trial before a man like Roosevelt!
>
> Roosevelt speaks English accurately. He does not say, "I done it" or "I seen it." He talks much more like a Boston man or an Englishman than like a New York Police Commissioner . . . When he asks a question, Mr. Roosevelt shoots it at the poor trembling policeman as he would shoot a bullet at a coyote. And when he asks a question, he shows a set of teeth calculated to unnerve the bravest of the finest. The teeth are very very white and almost as big as a colt's teeth . . . The lower teeth look like a row of dominoes . . . He has a knack of showing them all at once when he speaks quickly and when he does that he seems to say: "Tell the truth to your commissioner or he'll bite your head off . . .
>
> Under his right ear, he has a long scar. It is the opinion of all policemen who have talked with him that he got that scar fighting an Indian out West. It is also their opinion that the Indian is dead.
>
> But Roosevelt's voice is the policeman's hardest trial. It is an exasperating voice, a sharp voice, a rasping voice. It is a voice that comes from the tips of the teeth and seems to say in its tones, "What do you amount to, anyway?"
>
> In the good old days . . . the owner of such a voice as Roosevelt's would have been clubbed on general principles. Now the bravest policeman must listen to that voice, obey it and seem to like it.

Roosevelt was ready to clean the stables. He would hire fairly, fire as quickly as possible, and demand discipline. Jacob Riis, his staunchest ally, would say that TR brought a "moral purpose" to 300 Mulberry Street for the first time. "The ordinary attitude of Mulberry Street toward a new commissioner is one of good natured, half indulgent, half amused deference," wrote Riis. "The coming of Roosevelt has made a sudden and extraordinary change."

Lincoln Steffens, less hagiographic, interpreted TR's arrival a bit differently. "The police were excited . . . but . . . could not believe it all at once," wrote Steffens. "They laughed, they are cynics of the worst sort; 'the finest' are. They are confidently wicked; they have practiced corruption so long that they believe it is good; they know it is . . . for it pays."

Atop the chain of command stood the tarnished chief of police, Thomas Byrnes, whose offer of resignation had been ignored. (The mayor happened to like him.) "I think I shall move against Byrnes at once," Roosevelt wrote to longtime friend Massachusetts senator Henry Cabot Lodge. "I thoroughly distrust him and cannot do any thorough work while he remains. It will be a very hard fight, and I have no idea how it will come out."

SLAYING THE DRAGONS

By the time Roosevelt became a police commissioner, Thomas Byrnes was one of the most famous and recognizable New Yorkers, right up there with bulbous-nosed J. P. Morgan and hourglass-shaped Lillian Russell. (In that era, just a few years before newspapers could print photographs, being identifiable in public was rare.) "There is not, except among law breakers, a more popular man in New York City," wrote Shepp's *New York City Illustrated* in 1894, before Lexow. The guidebook advised readers bent on bird-dogging a celebrity that Byrnes, a tall heavyset man with a mustache, walked daily from his home at West 57th Street down to the Mulberry Street headquaters, smoking a large black cigar, and returned at 4 p.m.

Veteran police officers could leave their jobs in three ways: in a coffin, by resigning honorably on a half-salary pension, or by being dismissed in disgrace without retirement money. "To force Byrnes out publicly and to have every policeman on the force know that he has been forced out would do more good than anything else." That's what reporter Arthur Brisbane of the *World* claimed was Roosevelt's private opinion on the topic.

The dismissal drama at 300 Mulberry now turned into something of a game of chicken. Corrupt officers could risk keeping their jobs, hoping no charges would be brought against them, or they could try to retire immediately.

At the board meeting on Friday, May 17, Commissioner Parker slapped down a stack of more than two dozen pension applications. The board approved twenty-seven out of thirty applications, adding a hefty $20,375 to the department's pension burden. (The law clearly stated that all officers with no charges pending who had served twenty-five years—or twenty years for Civil War veterans—must be granted a pension.)

The reform commissioners found it especially galling to approve the honorable retirement of white-haired ward detective Edward Shalvey, thirty-four years on the force, who had admitted at Lexow being a bagman for six captains, including Eakins. His Lexow testimony had freed him from prosecution.

The board, with little choice, approved Shalvey's annual pension of $700. The lawyers, Parker and Andrews, had advised allowing this mass retirement as the quickest way to clean out the deadwood, but it was an open secret that Roosevelt was frustrated and vowed to prosecute wherever possible.

The Friday board meeting marked the new commissioners' continuing strides forward in tackling issues ranging from picayune to titanic to overhaul the department. Half the precincts—due to prosecution or retirement—lacked a captain and had sergeants filling in; the board would need to promote the right men. The current budget allowed for the hiring of 300 more patrolmen, but a new police civil service system needed to be created from scratch, with new physical standards—minimum height raised from five feet seven and a half inches to five feet eight inches over Roosevelt's objections—as well as new mental and moral standards.

The board wanted the police force to obey its order to quit political clubs but worried that captains might whitewash the effort. So the board voted that each of the 3,800 police officers must fill out and sign a form listing their club memberships. "I presume by the time the reports come in, the men will belong to very few clubs," Roosevelt observed.

The board also ordered that all future correspondence not include a man's politics or religion. Commissioner Grant joked that would free him from the temptation to help Republicans, while TR—echoing his credo to keep national politics out of police administration—said knowing a man was Republican "would have just the opposite effect upon me." (The baldness of the statement appalled the most powerful Republican in the state, boss Thomas Collier Platt, who called Roosevelt "a rich man with some force of character [but] more of a mugwump than a Republican.")

Roosevelt, point man for civil service reform, agreed to go in person to the Board of Estimate and request money to hire three clerks to administer written tests. While he was there, he would also ask for $2,500 to buy ten horses. Commissioner Grant modeled minimum equine standards for a patrolman's mount after the U.S. Cavalry, and for patrol wagon horses after requirements for hauling U.S. artillery.

"There is nothing of the purple in it," commented TR of the board's daily work. "It is as grimy as all work for municipal reform."

Roosevelt mentioned in passing at the meeting that he was disappointed to discover that many of the department's own rules of conduct for police officers, especially those governing walking a beat, were routinely ignored. The board voted to send out a directive that *all* the rules must be strictly enforced.

As Roosevelt had earlier requested, Chief Clerk Kipp now handed him a list of twenty-four officers with charges pending—including two captains and two sergeants. Roosevelt ordered that these cases be prepared and put on the calendar "at once." He wanted the corrupt officers out. The two unseen elephants in the room at that moment were Chief Byrnes and the charismatic Inspector Alexander "Clubber" Williams.

———

Byrnes's first move at the arrival of the new commissioners was quite shrewd. He announced himself to the newspapers as a grand crusader for reform, eager to root out police corruption. TR was outflanked.

The chief called a rare Saturday morning meeting of all the captains on May 18, 1895. These men in blue uniforms with two gold bars at the wrist and collar, some of the most powerful men in New York City, mounted the steps of 300 Mulberry Street and found themselves treated like schoolboys. Byrnes handed out pencils and sheets of paper and told the captains to take notes; he said he did not want to have to repeat himself.

McAvoy, Eakins, Schmittberger, and others squeezed into the school desks in the room where police civil service exams were usually held. The legendary detective—fifty-two years old, six feet tall, thinning hair, pale Irish complexion—said he expected immediate dramatic changes in the department. He ordered the captains to enforce every rule in the manual "no matter how long some of them may have practically been a dead letter."

One has to wonder what the captains were thinking. Was the chief mouthing pieties for the commissioners or did he really mean it? Rule 422 stated that begging was illegal and all beggars under sixteen must be brought to headquarters. Enforcing that rule alone could tie up half the force for months. Patrolmen were supposed to make a report in writing any time they left their post; no one, not even the grayest graybeards, could remember ever seeing one single written report. Another rule stated all policemen must refrain from "harsh, violent, coarse, profane or insolent language" (that would eliminate half their vocabulary, sniped a newspaperman), and they'd now apparently have to start "marching in military formation" when rushing to quell a riot. The manual comprised 100-plus pages of detailed regulations covering everything down to ticketing all sleighs driven without bells.

Byrnes, in addition, ordered that the captains enforce all laws, especially those against gambling and prostitution, and enforce the Sabbath laws preventing saloons from opening on Sundays. He warned that the department would check into any citizen's complaint and, if substantiated, the Board of Commissioners would put the captains on trial. Again, was the chief serious? Some saloons had been open Sundays since the Civil War. One expensive brothel on Bedford Street catered mainly to judges and legislators.

———

Byrnes went further to placate Roosevelt and Parkhurst and the reform movement. After he turned out the captains with their new orders, he called in Inspector Peter Conlin and told him to assign plainclothes detectives to investigate Captain Eakins's 15th Precinct. While roundsmen tracked lowly patrolmen daily, the New York police department at that time very rarely investigated at the exalted rank of captain.

Inspector Conlin—a by-the-book, low-key officer—assigned two men to see if any prostitutes were working the sidewalks in the area radiating out from Washington Square Park. Conlin told the men to accompany the young ladies-for-hire and to collect details about hotels and prices to see whether Eakins was ignoring disorderly houses. "Is that all Inspector Conlin told you to do?" twenty-eight-year-old officer Peter McCarty was later asked. "Well, the instructions was not to have any [sexual] intercourse with the females."

The dragnet was closing in on Eakins.

But that Saturday at noon, the tight-knit fraternity of police tried to help a fellow officer. Someone at HQ must have tipped Eakins to the police department's own investigation of him because he suddenly submitted to Chief Clerk Kipp an application to retire. In his retirement filing, Eakins stated that he had served twenty-nine years, which would by law guarantee him a half-salary pension *if no charges were pending.*

Did the Parkhurst Society accusations count as "charges"? No one knew.

———

Monday night Roosevelt had a secret dinner to attend; at it, he would have his first chance to talk at length with Dr. Parkhurst. (Not far away, that same night, another secret dinner of a very different sort would take place in a photographer's studio; Stanford White, Augustus Saint-Gaudens, "electrician" Nikola Tesla, and thirty others would drink 144 bottles of champagne until the dessert course, when a near-naked sixteen-year-old popped out of a massive pie.)

Few details have survived of Roosevelt's dinner. It's apparent the new police commissioner arrived leery of the unrealistic expectations of "reformers following the lead of Dr. Parkhurst," who hoped to quash "certain evils which I fear cannot possibly be suppressed in a city like New York in our present stage of existence." He also, like everyone else, had heard the vague stories of the minister playing leapfrog in a brothel. Lincoln Steffens wrote of his own meeting with Parkhurst, "[I expected] a wild man, ridiculous, sensational, unscrupulous, or plain crazy, [only] to call on him and find a tall slim smiling gentleman, quiet, determined, fearless, and humorous." Apparently, TR had a similar experience, soon dubbing him a "good fellow." Parkhurst evidently could be a charming dinner companion. Based on later events and opinions expressed, Roosevelt and Parkhurst discussed corruption in the police department and the efforts of the Society for the Prevention of Crime to help remove Big Bill Devery, Captain Eakins, and especially Chief Byrnes. Prostitution might have been too delicate a topic for either man.

———

By the start of their third week on the job, Theodore Roosevelt and the other commissioners were settling into a new routine: board meetings on Mondays, Wednesdays, Fridays at 10 a.m. (with Roosevelt arriving early and Parker arriving late), and marathon police misconduct trials on Thursdays.

Parker reviewed legal cases; Grant looked for waste in supplies, from harbor boats to horse feed. Andrews seconded Roosevelt. Roosevelt accepted all speaking engagements and interviews.

TR pronounced political "pull" and bribery dead. "If a man has President Cleveland, Gov. Morton and Mayor Strong behind him, it won't help him one particle."

Roosevelt was clearly developing a stump speech on police reform, a narrative he would deliver at least 100 times in the eight months remaining in 1895.

He stressed that civil service merit—passing physical, mental, and moral tests—would alone rule for new hiring and promotions. He stressed that the police would investigate the "moral character" of all applicants. (Roosevelt, for one, it would turn out, would not approve any man who had worked in a saloon.) He promised the civil service written test would be "simple, practical and common sense." (The first test would measure the applicants' talents in spelling, writing legibly, crafting a letter, simple arithmetic, and New York City geography.)

Roosevelt also unveiled a startling new directive. He wanted New York policemen to be polite. "We are bound to make all honest, brave and efficient members of the force who are bold in their dealings with the criminals and courteous in their dealings with the ordinary citizens, understand that we are their friends." He wanted them to regard "politeness as a sign of dignity not subservience."

Brisbane of the *World* was also present when Roosevelt reprimanded a patrolman for lounging against a wall and talking loudly at headquarters. "Officer, good manners are of importance," TR told the man, who, according to Brisbane, seemed quite baffled at what he was doing wrong. Brisbane added that he saw "a policeman in full uniform open a door for a man" without political pull.

It was as though the board was trying to end the era of tough undereducated men dominating the force.

————

Inspector Alexander "Clubber" Williams, also in Roosevelt's crosshairs, was just returning from a fifteen-day vacation and denied that he was quitting. "Why should I? I'm a young man yet and never felt better."

Williams, also known as "Fighting Aleck," was a former ship's carpenter, belligerent, blunt-spoken, still "full enough of brute strength and courage" that even at age fifty-five the *New York World* surmised he could survive in the ring with a Sullivan or a Corbett. Originally from Cape Breton, Canada, he was large, handsome, and cocky, with close-cropped hair and a beau D'Artagnan–style mustache. He intimidated people.

By one estimate, he had racked up a staggering 358 complaints, making him "the most venomously hated, frequently tried and most valuable of police officers," according to *Harper's* magazine. During his first days as a patrolman assigned to the corner of Broadway and Houston Street, he asked around to learn who were the toughest gang members in the neighborhood. He threw first one, then the other through a plate-glass window.

He was famed for breaking up riots and crowds. "In the days of the old walking matches at Madison Square Garden, when crowds were packed so dense about the doors that life was endangered," observed the *New York World*, " 'Fighting Aleck' and his club could always make a passageway."

Williams clubbed his way up the ranks. When he was promoted from a waterfront crime precinct to overseeing the city's up-and-coming vice district along Broadway from the 20s to the 40s, he said: "I've been living on rump steak since I been on the force; now I'm going to have a bit of Tenderloin." His nickname for the locale lasted half a century. He was said to receive a kickback for every shot of Hollywood Whiskey drunk in Tenderloin saloons. Miscellaneous complaints charged him with accepting, among other noncash items: a diamond ring, two cows, six pocket handkerchiefs, a gold-headed cane, a pistol, a pair of slippers, a velvet vest.

Like Devery, Williams was investigated numerous times. Roosevelt even took a crack at him back in 1884 when TR was a young crusading state assemblyman heading a committee probing corruption in New York City. Captain Williams—true to his reputation—was stunningly frank on all topics including prostitution. "I take a liberal view of the matter and don't believe that it can be suppressed," he told the committee. "There are 40,000 strangers in the city every day, and these all go to the places in my precinct, and not from curiosity I am sure."

Williams admitted that he allowed brothels to remain open if they stay "orderly." He said he opposed shutting them down because that would force the bawdy women into the streets and tenements. "It's like taking a small-pox patient into the street, it merely spreads the disease." Williams said he recommended creating a red-light district. At the end of his testimony, he asked if he could leave the hearing room immediately to go to a highly touted "walking match" at the Garden. "I suppose you find it even more interesting than the committee," said Roosevelt. "One is about as big a circus as the other," replied Clubber.

A decade later, committees were still probing Williams. The Lexow Committee asked why he allowed eighty-three brothels to stay open in the Tenderloin. Clubber hesitated, then replied: "Well, they were fashionable."

GOFF: Can't you give any other answer than that?
WILLIAMS: No, I can't say anything else about it. They were always there. When they were closed up, they would open again.

GOFF: Then you, the police officer charged with carrying out the laws and paid by the people for so doing, say that you left these houses open because it was fashionable?

WILLIAMS: Yes.

"Don't you know that's an extraordinary answer?" Senator Lexow interjected. "Well, I haven't any other," Williams replied.

The Lexow Committee had trouble pinpointing Williams's wealth but uncovered ownership of a building at 109 East 10th Street, a sprawling estate in Cos Cob, Connecticut, with a 100-foot stone seawall, a dock, and boathouse, and a $4,000 steam yacht named *Eleanor*.

Goff later asked Williams how he had amassed so much on a policeman's salary. The big inspector smugly answered: "Corner lots in Japan."

———

On the rainy, unseasonably warm morning of Friday, May 27, Republican commissioners Grant and Roosevelt traveled separately to work, although they lived a block apart. Soon after their arrival, genial Grant walked into Roosevelt's office carrying an envelope. The building was abuzz with whispers of dismissals, retirements, criminal charges. Roosevelt opened the envelope. Inside was Clubber Williams's application for retirement with pension. TR was furious. Roosevelt sent word for Parker and Andrews to come to his office. He wanted to figure out a way to reject it even though no charges were pending, but his three colleagues disagreed with him. Parker and Andrews, both lawyers, said the law was clear. Grant was generally sympathetic to veteran police officers, especially Republican ones. TR, still seething, dismissed the others and summoned Inspector Williams to a private meeting. The stocky president did not gladhand the towering officer. He apparently lectured him for a long time on kickbacks and community trust and honor. "Clubber" left, looking "annoyed and angry," according to a newspaperman lurking in the hallway.

This Williams brouhaha delayed the Friday Police Board meeting two hours till noon; the meeting, barely under way, was suddenly interrupted by a messenger delivering Jacob Riis's *Evening Sun*. The headline read: WILLIAMS GONE, BYRNES TO GO. TR was furious, since the board had not yet even voted on Williams's retirement. Roosevelt could be seen hunching over each of his seated colleagues and whispering pointed questions. He then barred the press and could be heard through the door yelling at Commissioner Grant, who, it was later learned, admitted he had leaked the story. (TR would later privately call Grant a "muttonhead.")

At 2 p.m. Williams approached the boardroom, knocked quietly, and entered. A few minutes later, Williams exited with a grim smile. Roosevelt followed soon after. "Inspector Williams has asked for retirement and the board has unanimously granted it; the law is mandatory and we were obliged to retire him." Roosevelt, very uncharacteristically, refused to comment further. The inspector would receive $1,750 a year for life.

"Clubber" went downstairs, took off his uniform, and lit up a big black cigar. His lifelong cop pals teasingly sang out to the *ex*-inspector: "Goodbye MISTER Williams" and he replied "Goodbye, boys." One newspaperman said these veterans "looked at him like the last rescue boat leaving a wreck."

Williams had one final profane statement to make. None of the newspapers could print it but that didn't stop him. The *New York Press* captured it best by inserting blanks instead of paraphrasing. "I leave this department without a stain on me. I ain't ashamed of anything I've done. That — — — that sat in the chair at the Lexow committee investigation and told those — — — lies about me, couldn't prove them. Then, after throwing — — all over me, he says he is going to take a mud bath in Carlsbad. He needs a mud bath, he does. I mean that big fat Schmittberger. The Extraordinary Grand Jury hunted through every bit of evidence against me. They went from hell to Beersheba for it. — — if they could find a — shred of proof against me."

A reporter shouted out a question: Would Williams go into business? "No, twenty-nine years of police service have unfitted me for that," he answered. And a surprised newspaperman added: "He said that last whole sentence without swearing. He did, really and truly."

Williams was gone but not in the manner TR had envisioned.

TR and the board spent the rest of that Friday afternoon in a very testy mood dealing with mundane matters such as civil service requirements and reinstatement applications. Several newly received citizen complaint letters were passed around for quick perusal including one by a Thomas McGregor that brutally criticized Byrnes. "Murderers and thugs continue to have their own way," it stated, "and bunco steerers and confidence men feel certain that they are safe in plying their business knowing that Byrnes . . . has got a great share in the swag." Commissioner Andrews absentmindedly handed a copy of it to a reporter who had asked to see it.

The building was humming with speculation that Byrnes would be forced out. The *Chicago Tribune* wondered . . . if bribery charges were brought, would George Gould explain "how he could give such good [stock] tips [to Byrnes] when he could not give them to himself?" It also quoted Byrnes as saying "I'm not thinking of getting out now. I am here to serve the public." He had repeatedly told his rich, powerful friends, such as the mayor, that he was staying.

On Saturday morning Chief Byrnes awoke to extensive column inches of negative comments about himself, rumors of his imminent departure, and big ugly helpings of that citizen's complaint letter. "[Byrnes] is worth $1.5 million and every dollar of it was wages of blackmail and corruption," McGregor had written. "As a police officer, [Byrnes] was never known to do any brave act but was always quick to take credit for that which was done by others."

Byrnes, the career detective, checked to find out about this McGregor and discovered that the New York City directory did not list a single Thomas McGregor. Byrnes grew more irritated; he mulled the indignities as he walked downtown from 57th Street on Saturday morning. He had been cooperating, ordering that impractical rules be followed, was investigating a respected captain, and yet the board allowed these anonymous charges to be published. By the time he arrived he was seething.

He marched straight to Commissioner Parker's office to complain. Parker, who knew Byrnes from years earlier, was acting as point man for the board; Roosevelt wanted nothing to do with Byrnes. After he left, Parker gathered the other board members for an informal meeting, and three out of four professed deep sympathy for Byrnes over the complaint letter and anonymous potshots. The board called Byrnes upstairs to apologize to him in person but Roosevelt left the room before Byrnes arrived. The board later issued a statement that it "deeply regrets" the publication of the letter and the members "unqualifiedly deny" making "derogatory" statements about Byrnes to the press.

The Byrnes circus was threatening to split the board. Lawyer Parker was trying to keep Roosevelt from bringing charges, which might take months and leave the department rudderless. Andrews sided with Roosevelt but Grant, malleable, liked Byrnes and was open to letting him stay. It fell to Parker to negotiate a compromise.

Parker met several times on Saturday with Byrnes. Neither man said a word to the press. Byrnes took the ferry to spend Sunday with his family near Red Bank, New Jersey. Monday morning, Byrnes arrived at 300 Mulberry before 8 a.m. looking glum. When Roosevelt arrived at 9 a.m., a reporter tossed an odd question at him: was it true that he would be the next police chief? "Just as much chance of it as I shall be made Admiral of the United States Navy."

Parker and Byrnes met again. "Never have I felt sadder at heart than during that talk with Chief Byrnes this morning," Parker commented later. At 11:45 a.m. the other three members of the board met on routine business. Almost an hour later, Parker still hadn't arrived in the boardroom. Roosevelt closed the session to the press; he could be overheard loudly talking to Commissioner Grant, who then went downstairs to find Parker and Byrnes. Parker returned alone at 1 p.m. to the boardroom carrying Byrnes's application for retirement.

Roosevelt clearly did not want to say anything pleasant about Byrnes so Parker, in this rare instance, spoke for the board. Parker once again denied that the board had issued negative comments about Byrnes and he noted that Byrnes had offered to assist in the future. However, probably per his agreement with Roosevelt, Parker conspicuously did not thank Byrnes for his long and illustrious career. In TR's eyes, Byrnes's profiteering negated all.

Chief Clerk Kipp called for a vote on Byrnes's application to retire with a $3,000-a-year pension. Roosevelt sang out the loudest of the four "Ayes."

A bit later, Byrnes, in a business suit, came upstairs and spoke to the board for ten minutes in private. Byrnes, usually the showman, then returned to his office through the quiet halls, and said very little, appearing subdued. The newspapermen found him looking somehow a tad more bald than the week before; Byrnes mumbled about the "fortunes of war." Then he made a brief dignified statement in which he said little more than "I have given thirty-two years of my life's work to the police force. I am proud of the service."

Sergeant Frank Mangin—Byrnes's right-hand man for decades—tried to control his emotions but started crying. "Why Frank this is nonsense. I have been here thirty-two years, and I'm glad to get out. Don't bother about this."

Grown men, who had wielded nightsticks and muscled thugs, had to wipe away tears. "Even the newspaper reporters at Headquarters showed more emotion than they usually do on hearing of a first-class murder or fire, and begged for a well-used club or some other little souvenir of his hard-working days." Several officers began muttering about "criminals coming back in shoals."

"Not one of us all who had known him long did not regret it," wrote Jacob Riis of Byrnes's departure, "though I for one had to own the necessity of it." Riis wrote that the chief represented the bad old days to too many people. "He was the very opposite of Roosevelt—quite without moral purpose or the comprehension of it, yet with a streak of kindness in him that sometimes put preaching to shame."

Roosevelt had wanted Byrnes run out of town on a rail but his small consolation prize came later that afternoon. The board voted unanimously to deny the retirement and pension of Captain Joseph Eakins. They also voted in as new acting chief fifty-four-year-old Peter Conlin, whom the *New York Times* called "a keen, handsome little man with a becoming gray mustache, polite and painstaking with just a trace of the soldier in his bearing." In one of his first deeds in office, Conlin cosigned with the Parkhurst Society lawyer, Frank Moss, a long list of charges against Eakins.

"I am getting the police department under control," TR wrote in his Sunday, June 2, letter to sister Bamie. "I forced Byrnes and Williams out, and now hold undisputed sway." Wife Edith also wrote Bamie that weekend. "I have never seen [Theodore] look better or more full of life energy."

MIDNIGHT RAMBLES

Long past midnight on Thursday, June 7, 1895, two oddly dressed men lingered on the steps of the Union League Club, a bastion of Republican wealth in the city. Despite the unseasonable eighty-degree heat, one wore a loose knee-length white duster over black formal attire, with a floppy hat pulled down; the other, despite the very late hour, wore green-tinted spectacles. The pair drew glances from the prestigious organization's night watchman.

They scanned the wide streets near the entrance at Fifth Avenue and 39th Street and saw little except for the occasional "Nighthawk" cab trawling for fares. Both men were of medium to short height, with cropped mustaches. One spoke with a Danish accent; the other had trouble whispering.

Theodore Roosevelt and his friend Jacob Riis, semi-incognito, were heading out on a stealth mission to hunt cops. Ever restless, TR wanted to find out more about the police department he thought he ruled "with undisputed sway." And Riis was thrilled to find a kindred spirit willing to stay up after midnight to explore. Were the policemen doing their duty? Were they professional? Efficient?

Roosevelt consulted the precinct map he had received from acting chief Conlin identifying the various posts of policemen. The 21st Precinct, a rectangle, stretched diagonally from the 42nd Street edge of Grand Central Depot, with its spectacular 200-yard-long arched glass-and-iron dome over the train platforms, down to Bellevue Charity Hospital at 26th and the East River, which housed the city morgue.

The pair headed east from Fifth Avenue to Third Avenue, then ducked into the shadows of the Elevated Railroad. Avoiding the geometric zigzags of light cast through the girders by the Edison arc lamps, they whispered excitedly.

Third Avenue—bisected by the spindly El—stretched out before them. A guidebook described it as "one of the longest and busiest streets in the city, lined with retail shops and tenement houses, with scarcely a single important building." Working-class people lived in the neighborhood. Almost daily, lunatics, criminals, and contagious patients shuffled through it to reach the new city pier at 26th Street to board the ferry to Blackwell's Island (now Roosevelt Island).

The two men meandered under the railroad girders and saw two uniformed policemen talking together at 41st Street, inside the first of ten posts on the precinct map. Roosevelt and Riis kept in the shadows and ambled south another block when TR decided that perhaps those officers might chat too long. (Cops at night were supposed to walk their beats alone, and converse with fellow officers only in times of emergency.) Roosevelt turned back and they retraced the deserted streets to check, but the officers were gone. He and Riis paced five times up and down that first beat along Third Avenue from 36th to 42nd Street—walking a mile and a half—but never saw the two bluecoats again.

They then trekked the half mile down to the precinct's southern boundary at 27th Street and didn't see a single police officer; they doubled back and decided to concentrate on finding the patrolman assigned to the smallest post, 27th to 30th Street on Third Avenue. They looked in doorways, alleyways, under illegally parked wagons (no overnight parking was allowed on public streets); they climbed the tall metal stairs to the El station at 28th Street and walked the platform. They descended.

All of a sudden, a pudgy man in an apron came rushing out of O'Neill's, an all-night coffee shop near 28th Street, and with a heavy club rapped three times on a lamppost. The sound echoed in the stillness of the night. "Where in thunder does that copper sleep?" shouted the man, as he banged three more times.

Riis yelled over to ask what the emergency was. The man, a night manager, said the Edison Electric Illuminating Company had recently hooked up O'Neill's and he was worried that the current wasn't working right and might spark a fire. "He orter'd tole me when he giv' up the barber shop, so's a fellow could find him." (Policemen on the late shift were notorious for finding a "coop" in which to spend part of the night.) TR and Riis retraced the beat four times before giving up.

Roosevelt was growing increasingly disgusted. The Tammany cops were fulfilling the reformer's worst expectations. In any case, pretty much every minute of his trek was an eye-opener for Roosevelt.

Although he had explored the wilds of Maine and the Dakotas, the castles of Europe and pyramids of Egypt, Roosevelt had rarely, if ever, walked the side streets of his native city after midnight. Wealthy men took carriages at that hour. In addition, TR had spent the last six years living in Washington, D.C. Ironically, he needed a guide to his own hometown, and he couldn't have found a better one than Jacob Riis.

The forty-six-year-old Dane had not only covered the police for almost twenty years for the *Tribune* and *Evening Sun* but in the late 1880s, he had taught himself flash photography and had produced *How the Other Half Lives*, which critics would judge a genuinely groundbreaking photo essay and exposé of the horrific tenement poverty in New York City. Riis's magnesium flash seemed to stun the poor out of their dimly lit oblivion: here was a family—from father to toddler—in a sweatshop sewing "knee pants" on Ludlow Street, over there dazed drinkers in a black-and-tan saloon on Thompson Street. Riis captured the bleakness, filth, overcrowding, disease, hunger, relentless poverty, but also the humanity.

When Roosevelt first read the book, he sought out the author at the *Evening Sun* offices. Missing him, TR left his card, with these words on the back: "I have read your book and I have come to help."

Now it was Roosevelt who needed Riis's help. Riis would one day call his years tramping with Roosevelt "the happiest by far" of his life and TR would write a deeply touching eulogy two decades later for "one of my truest and closest friends."

The pair walked over to Second Avenue and finally found a patrolman . . . asleep on a butter tub outside a grocer shop, his hat off, "snoring so that you could hear him across the street." Roosevelt woke the man up with an opening salvo of: "Is that the way you patrol your post?" The cop, instantly irritated, looked at the two short well-dressed strangers and snapped: "Come now, get a hustle on before I dump you." Roosevelt identified himself as a police commissioner, sternly lectured the man, and told him to come to headquarters the next morning. (That must have seemed like an extraordinarily bad dream for Officer Elbert Roberston.)

Roosevelt and Riis continued on Second Avenue and found another policeman . . . standing beside a woman, no doubt a streetwalker. The sleuths lurked in the shadows and watched the patrolman chat for a full ten minutes until Roosevelt could stand no more. He jumped into the conversation and confronted him: "Officer, is this the way you attend to your duty?"

Officer Thomas Connors, tall and handsome, was extremely peeved by the interruption. "What are you looking for, trouble? You see that street?" he said, pointing down Second Avenue. "Now run along, or I'll fan you and I'll fan you hard." Connors brandished his nightstick. Roosevelt didn't move. Connors turned to his companion. "Shall I fan him, Mame?" The doll's giggling retort: "Fan him hard."

Roosevelt abruptly ended the comedy. "Oh no, officer, you will neither fan me hard or easy. I am police commissioner Roooosevelt and instead of fanning anybody, you report at headquarters at 9:30 o'clock." TR clearly relished a sport that included hunting and defying bullies.

Around 4 a.m., Roosevelt and Riis visited the precinct house at 35th Street "to ascertain if the whole police force had dropped dead and the entire Coroner's office was in demand," as the *Evening World* glibly put it.

Sergeant James J. Fagan, surly at first, quickly straightened up when Roosevelt introduced himself and demanded that Fagan wake up the sergeant "on reserve" and send him out immediately to search for the missing roundsman and patrolmen.

Roosevelt and Riis left the station and resumed their tramp; they headed back north to 42nd Street and Third Avenue, where they found some of the precinct's missing officers: Roundsman White and patrolmen Magan and Mahoney. The burly blue-coated trio was standing outside a corner saloon amusing each other with stories.

Roosevelt interrupted: "Why don't you men patrol your posts?"

"What the %$#%$# is that your business?" demanded Roundsman White, and Patrolman Magan said, "Move on, now, or I'll pull you in."

Finally, Mahoney, reaching for TR's lapels, said: "Yeah, let's pull him in on general principles, he's suspicious looking, anyhow."

Roosevelt introduced himself. "The city pays you to do your duty. Report to my office at 9:30." TR and Riis returned to the station house and the commissioner informed Sergeant Fagan that all six officers (the butter tub sleeper, the chatty man, these last three, and the missing-in-action cop) must report to headquarters at 9:30 a.m.

Energized by their adventures, TR and Riis boarded a streetcar and rode down to the Hester Street stop in the city's most overcrowded slum, the notorious 11th Precinct, former haunt of Captain Devery. They saw sunrise amid the pushcarts as they entered the Eldridge Street station and later walked to 300 Mulberry at 6:45 a.m. "Is my room ready?" Roosevelt said to the white-haired sergeant on duty. "May I ask who you are and what room you occupy in this building?" A month into his new job, TR was still not well recognized in the city or even to some at police headquarters.

Roosevelt napped on a chaise longue. He was refreshed at 9:30 a.m. when the six officers arrived—"a line of huge frightened guardians of the peace" as he later gloated to his sister. Roosevelt severely reprimanded them for half an hour, a "raking down which they will not soon forget," especially critiquing them for the disrespect shown to him when they didn't know his identity. He expected roundsmen to maintain "military discipline." He extended a one-time clemency but vowed to fine them or any other officers in the future for such behavior.

Riis had promised Roosevelt that he wouldn't write up their mission, but apparently he was allowed to tell their adventures to the other press boys at 301 Mulberry. The newspapermen genuinely delighted in the street theater of someone, anyone defying police officers and they one-upped each other in supplying pithy dialogue. (The story of the cop offering "to fan" Roosevelt "hard" with his nightstick kept getting better.) The coverage, kicked off by Pulitzer's *Evening World* (HUNTS IN VAIN FOR POLICEMEN AFTER MIDNIGHT), was universally positive. TR was dubbed "Haroun el-Roosevelt" after the caliph in *Thousand and One Nights* who explored Baghdad at night in disguise. Editorialists and letter writers raved. "The passing policeman is afraid even to go to sleep on his beat lest the sleepless president of the Police Commission catches him in the act; he is afraid to club a night-walking citizen lest his locust [wood] may by accident collide with the head of the ubiquitous Theodore."

Privately, he was quite pleased as well. "These midnight rambles are great fun," he wrote his sister Bamie. "My whole work brings me in contact with every class of people in New York, as no other work possibly could, and I get a glimpse of the real life of the swarming millions."

———

TR's closest ally on the board, Avery Andrews, decided that he would imitate his reform mentor and also perform an unannounced inspection/ramble. At age thirty-one, Andrews was the youngest member of the Police Board and easily ranked as its most politically naive. He belonged to no political clubs, parlayed with no power brokers. He had landed the job in an almost otherworldly way that perhaps captured the best of the reform movement. He had written a detailed proposal on reorganizing the police and mailed it to Mayor Strong. The mayor had read it, liked it, and appointed him, hoping that an outsider such as Andrews would ignore politics and make decisions based on benefits to the city.

He chose for his mission to observe whether saloons were selling beer on Sundays, contrary to New York State's Sabbath and excise laws. The laws also forbade attending baseball games, horse races, and theater on Sunday or buying most anything except medicine.

Andrews lived with his wife in upper Manhattan, on West 130th Street, in a leafy oasis. Harlem then offered a greener, almost suburban feel compared to tenement-filled stretches downtown. Not too far from him, Riverside Drive, with its trees, mansions, and expansive Hudson River views, was touted by Shepp's guidebook as "probably . . . the finest avenue on the American continent."

At 9:30 p.m. on Sunday night, Andrews walked south to 125th Street, a wide esplanade flanked by an ever-increasing number of retail stores such as H. C. F. Koch's, and banks, theaters, and churches. Zeisloft's guide stated that the residents of Harlem—from the elite to the working class—enjoyed a nightly ritual of promenading along 125th Street, strolling to and fro from Third Avenue to Eighth Avenue, stopping occasionally at "the first class theaters," the "free concert halls" . . . or the "respectable restaurants."

Avery Delano Andrews—rail thin, tall, military bearing, long waxed mustache—followed the crowds on 125th Street and watched some men splinter off to the side entrances of various saloons. He entered with them and observed men with foam on their mustaches and steins of warm beer in their hands. He ordered a glass himself. "I drank it just to see whether it was really beer," he said later. "It was; it was not Weiss beer."

This glass of suds would occasion *Town Topics* sarcastically to call Andrews a "genius" for discovering what everyone knew. "The first thing we know some of those marvelous Commissioners will be finding out that bad women openly walk Broadway at night for business purposes."

Although this blue law against Sunday saloons had been on the books since 1857, it was honored more in the breach than the observance, at least in New York City. Sunday, the workingman's only day off, also marked the city barkeeps' most profitable day of the week. Police captains or Tammany Hall raked in a couple of dollars per saloon to look the other way. This pragmatism, though perhaps morally and legally murky, seemed to satisfy the vast majority of New York City residents.

Outside several of the saloons, Andrews saw policemen twirling their batons and oblivious to the dozens of thirsty men filing inside. After he had spent two hours unobtrusively wandering into joints in his uptown precinct, someone finally recognized the tall quiet chap as a police commissioner. Word spread surprisingly quickly, probably via policemen sending messages, and the joints bolted their side doors.

But Andrews, fit from his daily bicycling, decided to walk south from 125th Street to 42nd Street, along the poorer sections east of Madison Avenue. He passed the mostly Irish shantytown of makeshift cottages, with pigs and goats, up around 118th Street, heading farther south and farther east among the shoddy tenements that looked out toward Blackwell's Island, home to the almshouse, lunatic asylum, workhouse, and penitentiary.

All along the route, he found the side doors of saloons open and policemen staring the other way. "I did not see a patrolman putting forth a spirited effort to do his duty."

Andrews came to headquarters on Monday morning and recounted the Sunday beer sales to Roosevelt, who grew quite irritated. He immediately instructed acting chief Conlin to summon the police captains to headquarters. The telephone operator contacted the precincts; the blue-uniformed men traveled free on the various Els and streetcars to reach the Mulberry Street headquarters.

After more than two dozen captains arrived, Roosevelt lectured them on doing their duty and enforcing *all* laws. "I want you all to understand that your personal opinions or feelings on the Sunday opening question, or any other phase of the law, have nothing to do with enforcement of the law," he enunciated. "While the law is on the statute book it must be strictly enforced without question."

It is unclear whether Roosevelt realized how utterly utopian and otherworldly his orders sounded. Cops constantly used their judgment to *not* enforce all laws. Detective Cornelius Willemse wrote of beating up a drunk who was the sole breadwinner of a large family, rather than arresting him and putting the family on the brink of starvation and eviction. A standard guidebook—hardly a book of controversial political theory—Zeisloft's *New Metropolis* stated that New York cops were chosen not to act like soldiers but rather to make decisions on their own on the spot.

———

Rumors swirled around headquarters of an "earthquake" shake-up, with every single member of the force reassigned to uncomfortably new precincts. Roosevelt denied such a plan. He said the board would attack problems as they discovered them.

Roosevelt's turn to act as judge came up again on Thursday, June 13. He had sixty-three cases to race through and had no intention of adjourning without finishing. His staccato questioning kept the line of bluecoats moving. A Mrs. Bennett was testifying that a patrolman had tried to shake her down for a dollar to avoid a "drunk and disorderly" charge when shots suddenly rang out in the courtroom. Mrs. Bennett went scrambling to the corner. More rapid-fire shots rang out. Lawyer Levy, representing the accused policeman, whirled and ducked. Court clerk Peterson pressed himself against a wall between the windows. Meanwhile, Theodore Roosevelt calmly continued writing notes, then touched a blotter to the sheet of paper and moved it aside. "Mr. Peterson, I did not understand that this is Execution Day," he said, looking up for the first time. "Am I mistaken? If so, we will adjourn the trial."

The clerk nervously peered out the window and said that the sounds apparently came from a pack of firecrackers, now lying spent in the street. The New York World reported: "All felt ashamed, and took care not to meet the eye of President Roosevelt . . . but after a while they consoled themselves with the recollection that the President was a sportsman, and his experiences in the far West raised him above common mortals."

Roosevelt resumed his role as trial judge; he was sitting in snap judgment of officers mostly caught by roundsmen lounging or sleeping on the job. Burly men mumbled lame excuses about sitting down to tie a shoe or being compelled to use the saloon's urinal.

He found most of the patrolmen guilty of small derelictions but one case of accused brutality drew his sympathy and leniency. A bunch of Irish boys were shooting dice in the tough Irish tenements in the East Forties. An Irish plainclothes detective, John McMullin, decided to break up the game. When he grabbed a boy, a crowd gathered; a day laborer named Tom Hogan leaped off a beer barrel outside a saloon and tried to spring the boy. As the two men wrestled in the street, the kid escaped, to the bystanders' cheers. The officer drew his revolver—maybe he pulled the trigger or maybe Hogan kicked at the gun. In any case, a bullet wound up grazing Hogan's thigh. The mob tightened its circle around the officer, pummeling him, when another policeman, happening by, came to the rescue. The two officers yanked Hogan out of the crowd and then McMullin beat the already bleeding Hogan so badly with his club that Hogan spent the next four days in Bellevue Hospital. Now the brawler Hogan was bringing brutality charges against Officer McMullin. Roosevelt asked Hogan if he had been drinking. Had he ever been arrested? For what crimes? The surly answers in the affirmative led Roosevelt to decide that a brave police officer had used justified force to subdue and teach a lesson to a drunken thug.

———

At midnight that same night, TR once again exited the Union League Club, this time with a handsome young man at his side, thirty-one-year-old Richard Harding Davis. The pair, both elegantly dressed after eating supper at the club, strolled over to 42nd Street and Third Avenue, mounted the steps, and took the El train down to 14th Street. TR was taking a new partner on a midnight ramble.

Davis—born wealthy, educated at Johns Hopkins, managing editor of *Harper's Weekly*—already ranked, though young, among the literary lions of the city. He had kick-started his career by delivering accurate, empathetic coverage of the catastrophic Johnstown Flood; he had already written two successful books. His impeccable manners, elegant clothes, and the high fees he received from newspapers created a lot of envy among rivals.

Somewhere on 14th Street, TR and Davis met Commissioner Andrews and walked east toward the river and then downtown into one of the city's worst slum tenement districts. They tramped up and down Avenues A, B, and C, amid the bleak five-story buildings, every so often leaving the avenues and "venturing into narrow unlighted apologies for streets." The poor overcrowded 13th Precinct, east of Tompkins Square Park, used to be thriving "Kleindeutschland"—a thoroughly German neighborhood of Protestants and Catholics, of lager beer halls, oyster saloons, and Beethoven Hall, with signs everywhere in Gothic German script. Now the area, especially in the poorer districts toward the river, was being flooded with impoverished Jews from Eastern Europe.

For the next two hours, the three explorers were shocked to find policemen dutifully walking their beats, trying doors, peering into stores and alleyways.

"No bluecoat was lounging against a lamp-post receiving a complaint from a blonde young woman," wrote the *New York Press*. "Nor did a member of the force emerge from a saloon, wiping his lips and saying he was called in to quell a riot." The *New York Recorder* decided that these events, if true, "suggested a veritable departmental millennium."

TR and crew entered the precinct's Union Market station house at 1:55 a.m. and Roosevelt introduced himself to desk sergeant Joseph Saul. "Your precinct is in very good order, sergeant, and your men are doing their duty," he told the astonished officer. He added that hardworking policemen had a true friend in the new commissioners.

While wandering in the building, TR discovered a clue as to how this precinct had performed so well on his unannounced midnight inspection. On the wall of the men's washup room, someone had penciled an accurate drawing of TR; apparently, the first bluecoat who spotted him had warned the others. In this round of police cat-and-mouse, score one for the mouse.

———

Roosevelt was trying to pierce one of the odder, more secretive, closed societies on the planet, one with its own rituals, and loyalties. The 3,800-member police force was heavily dominated by Irish-born or first-generation Irish Americans, mostly Tammany Catholics.

New York policemen in the 1890s slept together. At night, the dozens of men "on reserve" bunked together in foul-smelling overcrowded barracks rooms in the precinct houses. They hung their dirty, often wet, uniforms on pegs along the walls, and plunked their overripe socks and shoes below. Small sinks provided the only washup. The beds often stood only eighteen inches apart, close enough to hear a "chorus of snores" and other nocturnal noises. The "shouting or singing of drunks" echoed up from the cells below. Every morning with military precision citywide, a doorkeeper came to wake the "reserve" men at 5:40 a.m. for the "dog watch" from 6 a.m. to 8 a.m. At one precinct, the fellow belted out daily: "Get up, you big bums! He who sits on a hot stove shall rise to shine again."

About 1,000 officers, or one-quarter of the police, remained "on reserve" sleeping at the station house every night, ready to quell any sudden riots or upheavals in this great "melting pot" city of foreigners, underpaid laborers, beggars, bomb-threatening anarchists, labor-rallying Socialists. That forced policemen to work 110 hours a week, to zigzag through a dizzying schedule of shifts—including midnight tour and six a.m. dog watch—with fifty hours on the streets and sixty hours spent on reserve. "It was a dog's life," said Max

Fischel, crime reporter for the *Evening Sun*. The starting salary of $1,000 a year put them just past the upper end of poverty.

A patrolman in Manhattan in the mid-1890s walked his beat alone, without a partner, for eight hours during daytime. Sore feet and bronchitis topped the complaint list. He knew every store owner from the butcher to the iceman; he often ate free. He had a "coop" where he sneaked to get warm in the winter; he was supposed to check all doors and coal chutes every evening; he looked for unlit streetlamps, for unemptied ash cans, for stray dogs, for thieves. He arbitrated marital disputes and saloon brawls. He nabbed truants, sham lunatics, reckless carriage drivers, abortionists, milk-waterers, fornicators, but mostly he collared "drunk" or "disorderly" persons, who accounted for more than half of 113,000 arrests made in New York City in 1895.

Whenever he needed backup, the cop blew hard on his small cylindrical metal whistle or he rapped his billy club three times on the pavement or a lamppost. If still unaided, he often drafted a bystander as messenger to run to the precinct house.

The policemen of a given precinct became especially close-knit, like an army platoon on a mission in a foreign country. They saw much more of their brother officers than they did of their wives—110 hours versus 58 hours per week less commute time.

They played pranks; they had hazing rituals. A veteran detective recalled his rookie hazing. At midnight a bunch of burly men in hooded black raincoats had stripped him naked, forced him to kneel on a stone, and painted him "shamrock green, their favorite color." Then they mummified him in adhesive tape. At Thanksgiving, he in turn had joined in when they grabbed a sleeping recruit, stripped him, and covered him in carrot tops and greens, then mercilessly pinched to see if the "turkey" was tender.

He also recalled that nobody could sit on the toilet and read a newspaper unless he folded it into a small square; otherwise someone would set it on fire.

All these hours sequestered together, filled with pranks and camaraderie, bonded the men together; the New York police evolved into a kind of paid, mostly Irish fraternity, with a deep streak of "us" versus "them," often not only "us" against the officers but "us" against the citizens as well.

The structure of police discipline reinforced this "us vs. them" attitude. Ambitious roundsmen—officers who literally made rounds—skulked around the beats of patrolmen looking for rules violations. Patrolmen might be caught chatting too long, drinking a "can of coffee," lingering in a warm shop, smoking a cigar, carrying an umbrella.

Cops perfected silent semaphore signals to alert each other—arms stretched out, for instance, meant roundsman approaching. With so many hours to kill "on reserve," they shared their prize escapes like epic lore.

Once, a patrolman on a frigid cold night was "cooped" up talking to a friend, an undertaker, when a small boy raced into the funeral home with a warning from a fellow cop that the roundsman was heading down the block.

The cop was trapped; the place had no back exits. He was broke and couldn't afford another fine or suspension. Five minutes later he was seen strolling along, and he casually tapped the shoulder of the roundsman still peering through the undertaker's glass. He wished his superior officer a pleasant evening and kept on walking down the block. But how had he done it? He had convinced the undertaker to load him in a coffin, wheel him out to a hearse, and trot the horses around the corner.

The New York police force back then had far more duties than today. They investigated housing violations such as out-of-repair "water closets" or the keeping of goats without a permit. They inspected boilers, did background checks for permits for liquor licenses, for carrying guns, for hosting masked balls (a great opportunity for lewdness), for all-night restaurants.

They shot "more or less mad dogs" and carried dead animals to Barren Island in the harbor; they chased smugglers near the piers; they reported fires and water leaks; they visited homes to view dead infants to check for abortion or infanticide.

The foreign-born nationality they arrested most in 1895 was Irish (21,628), followed by German (11,443), then Russian (7,172). "Black" Americans accounted for 2,843 arrests.

So, often Irish cops, avoiding Irish roundsmen, were arresting Irish citizens.

The vaudeville stage cop was portrayed as a portly Irishman with a faint brogue, leaning forward with his hand out behind him, palm upward. "Of course there are cops who have never taken a dollar, at least I've heard about them but I never saw one," wrote Detective Willemse. "However if they exist, I give them credit for being so good or for being on bum posts."

———

Roosevelt and his fellow investigators decided they had earned a break, and at 2:45 a.m. they headed over to Mike Lyons's all-night/all-day restaurant, a joint open *continuously* for almost a quarter century. (Management proudly announced they didn't own a front-door key.) Cops and criminals, pickpockets and politicians all enjoyed eating the corned beef at this Bowery joint. Located smack in the middle of dozens of sleazy concert saloons and variety theaters, the restaurant drew those who refused to call it a night.

"The Mayor of the Bowery, Johnny Matthews, used to swap yarns with Broken-Nose Burke," the owner once reminisced in a newspaper article, "while California George sat by and snorted and said he could tell a better [tale] with his feet." Inspector Byrnes rubbed elbows with out-of-town hoodlums there. "In those days to gamble was no sin," explained Mike Lyons, "and to take a fool's money was no crime, for the fool was buying the experience that made a man of him." Lyons had often locked up bankrolls of thousands of dollars for his clientele, no questions asked; he served 400 quarts of wine in one night; mornings, he gave out leftover food to the women of the Bowery.

The press—to this point—was having good-natured fun covering Roosevelt. "Three young men walked into 'Mike' Lyons restaurant on the Bowery just before 3 a.m. yesterday. One wore spectacles and had a short bristling brownish mustache. He looked like a trombone player in some east-side brass band, who after a hard night's work, had dropped in for a good-night chop and a bottle of beer," wrote an unidentified writer at Pulitzer's *New York World*.

"The second man had bright dark eyes and a pink boyish face. When he pushed back his coat, he disclosed a round silver badge on his waistcoat. Square-jawed, broad-shouldered, tanned featured and wide-mouthed was the third man and a leather belt held up his trousers. A farmer dressed up would have been a man-about-town's comment on him." (Gentlemen then wore suspenders.)

The three men ordered steaks and beer, and the Lyons cook was starstruck enough to come out of the kitchen to glimpse Roosevelt. Word of their tour now spread fast among the bluecoats but some officers were apparently too fast asleep to get the message.

After enjoying their meal and tipping a quarter, the trio wandered for a few hours till 6 a.m., heading west and then north, through dozens of posts. They found seven policemen either sitting down, missing, or too deep in conversation; three of the derelicts were caught in Captain Eakins's 15th Precinct near Washington Square Park.

Roosevelt and Andrews took the Broadway cable car back downtown and arrived at 300 Mulberry. TR wrote his sister that these rambles forced him to go forty hours without sleep. He announced that the first inspection tour's mercy would not be repeated and that he would stand as complainant against the seven delinquent officers.

Given the fierce rivalries among the dozen leading New York newspapers, it was astounding how near-unanimously positive remained the coverage of the new Police Board. "This [late night] work, Mr. Roosevelt is now performing . . . should win him the gratitude of every law-abiding citizen," stated the *New York Recorder*. "It means greater security for life and property . . . the meaning of this intense energy and vigilance on Mr. Roosevelt's part is that the police officer who desires to keep his place on the force must do his duty."

A cartoon ran of cowboy Roosevelt lassoing sleeping cops. "Mr. Roosevelt expects his dream of discipline to become a solid fact," stated the *New York Advertiser*. "There will be no politics, no pull, no anything that can make a subordinate expect favors from his superiors."

Pal Jake Riis wrote a worshipful piece for the magazine *The Outlook*. "It is a long time since a New York policeman has been brought into contact with a gentleman so intent upon doing his work and making others do theirs." Riis, along with the editors, praised Roosevelt for his zeal, his honesty, his efficiency, his writing, his character. "He is altogether a fine representative of the best type of the contemporary American."

Riding high in this honeymoon of favorable coverage, Roosevelt decided that the board should pursue the reform agenda "to the handle," as he liked to say, evoking the image of a knife thrust all the way in.

TR had plenty of political capital and newspaper backing; he could use it however he liked. His repeated words to the captains and to the press represented no mere political puffery. He meant them. He was opting for doctrinaire enforcement of *all* laws and, as a first crucial experiment, he chose to order the police to shut down *all* saloons on Sundays.

It seemed a Herculean order in a city that liked to drink.

THIRSTY CITY

Theodore Roosevelt rarely drank more than a glass of white wine at dinner parties; he would allow himself a flute of champagne at those formal public tributes at, say, Delmonico's. Already animated, he perhaps became a tad more so, according to friends, but no credible witness ever saw him drunk on the streets. He despised beer and red wine and never rushed to a saloon for a cocktail.

Embattled ex–police captain Big Bill Devery no longer drank alcohol at all. Neither did former police chief Thomas Byrnes. Nor did most of the top men of Tammany Hall despite their Irish surnames.

But by New York standards, Roosevelt and these Irishmen were the exceptions.

New York City in the 1890s was a hard-drinking town, a place where a man was never far from one of its 8,000 saloons and hundreds of hotels and restaurants.

An executive at a large local brewery estimated that he and fellow brewers delivered 460,000 quarter-kegs (nearly eight gallons each) of beer a week in Manhattan. That works out to about twenty pints or so per week per man and woman over the age of sixteen in the city.

Roosevelt was aiming to cut off that tap on Sundays.

New Yorkers also drank cheap California wines, which outsold imports five to one, according to Bonfort's *Wine and Spirit Circular*. They sipped Hungarian and German wines far more often than French or Italian.

They drank ten-cent shots of rye whiskey from Pennsylvania and Kentucky, shipped by barrel and blended, bottled, and watered down in New York. Among foreign imports, Holland Gin outsold the top Scotches such as Sanderson's Mountain Dew.

Roosevelt was corking all that on the Lord's Day.

He was ordering the mostly Irish and German police force to tell their kinsmen to skip the saloon on Sundays. He was sentencing workingmen to a sober Sunday with their families, on a day when the Sabbath law already forbade theater performances (except religious displays), all professional sports including baseball and football, circuses, minstrelsy, boxing, horse racing, "jugglers, acrobats . . . and rope-dancers."

Roosevelt intended to end the police blackmail and show the force that absolutely no bribes or blindness would be tolerated. Right from the start, he tried to frame it not as a crusade against liquor but rather against blackmail and selective enforcement of the law. Over the coming months, he would say loudly and repeatedly that he didn't make the laws, he enforced them. Enforcing all laws was right; and ignoring any law was wrong. Black and white. Good and evil.

Many parched New Yorkers, craving a beer, didn't care to parse the distinctions.

Another less publicized factor clearly played into Roosevelt's decision. His magazine articles reveal that he knew many saloons acted as unofficial political clubhouses for Tammany Hall; therefore he also knew it would mark a fringe benefit for the Republican and reform parties if hundreds of saloons went out of business due to lost Sunday sales.

"The saloons form on the whole the most potent factor in the political life of those Districts where the population is the most congested, where the people are poorest and most ignorant, and where the evils of machine domination are most acutely felt," wrote Roosevelt in his brief book *New York*, for the "Historic Towns" series.

"In consequence, the saloon-keeper is, nine times out of ten, a more or less influential politician. In Tammany Hall a very large proportion of the leaders are, or have been, saloon-keepers."

Roosevelt once again summoned police chief Conlin and told him—yet more forcefully—the police should now try very hard to close 8,000 saloons on Sundays across New York City, even though that would, in effect, deprive more than a million New Yorkers of beer on their only day off. "I do not deal with public sentiment," he wrote in a statement released to the *New York Evening Sun*. "I deal with the law." He promised: "If it proves impossible to enforce it, it will only be after the experiment of breaking many a captain . . . has first been tried."

This initiative may be seen as the official start of the civics experiment of dropping an incorruptible, by-the-book, no-compromises commissioner into the rough-and-tumble playground of bribe-happy New York. Commented one pro-reform magazine: "New York has never been so shocked and surprised in all its two hundred and fifty years of existence."

———

On Sunday, June 23, 1895, more than 2,000 policemen stood like slack sentries outside about half the saloons of New York. Another few hundred officers in plainclothes scattered to other watering holes.

The temperature hit a mid-afternoon high of eighty degrees; the sweltering humidity of 85 percent made the torpid air feel like the "inside of a cow's mouth," as the expression went. Parched men wandered the streets in search of a beer. They quietly knocked at side doors of their neighborhood bars but most received no answer. Many descended to the Bowery, figuring those Tammany types would never cave, but a flood of bluecoats had already shut the district.

An owners' sign of surrender on a Sunday was raising the shades so the police could peer inside. A disgusted reporter discovered more than half the Bowery bars had shades raised by noon and dirty floors exposed to unwonted sunlight.

Other drinkers tried the famed German brewery district, 74th to 94th Street on the East Side but found policemen at the doors of the biggest joints, such as Colonel Ruppert's. The more desperate fled to Coney Island, where bartenders eagerly served beer and whiskey, and the cops of Brooklyn—still a separate city until the 1898 Consolidation Act—ignored it all. "The Excise Law didn't bother us and we didn't bother the Excise Law," explained a sergeant on duty at the Surf Avenue police station. (The New York State excise law forbade the selling of liquor in saloons from 1 a.m. to 5 a.m. daily and all twenty-four hours of Sunday throughout the state.)

Many New York City voters deeply resented the Republican majority in the state legislature imposing its dour ways on the more convivial city. The respected *Brooklyn Eagle* estimated that 95 percent of New York City residents favored saloons being open at least part of the day on Sunday. "This city is ruled entirely by the hayseed legislators at Albany," groused George Washington Plunkitt of Tammany Hall. "The hayseeds think we are like the Indians to the National government—that is, wards of the State, who don't know how to look after ourselves and have to be taken care of by the Republicans of St. Lawrence, Ontario and other backwoods counties."

The original law dated back to 1857 but was revised many times over the years. Roosevelt himself, while an assemblyman in 1884, weighed in on the debate, opposing full Prohibition as "impractical"—being opposed by 19/20ths of the population—but he did favor a higher annual excise tax for bars selling liquor ($500) than for those offering only beer and wine ($100). He also drew a distinction between men having a beer while sitting down to a family meal in a restaurant or hotel as opposed to men standing at the bar tossing back shots of liquor.

That distinction—shared by other legislators—eventually made it into the revised law, and the city's hotels were now permitted to sell drinks to guests dining in the hotel restaurants or in their rooms on Sundays; also, the law didn't specifically address private clubs.

This pair of loopholes permitted the city's wealthiest, and the affluent out-of-towners staying at the Waldorf or the Fifth Avenue Hotel, to drink outside their homes on Sundays. For the poor, Sunday was a day of enforced rest.

Manhattan that Sunday, June 23, was dry, but not bone dry. Not all the pubs, wine rooms, and saloons submitted meekly to the crackdown. Many owners of the joints who were lucky enough not to have a bluecoat guarding the block tried to sneak loyal customers in at the side door. The "side entrance," "family entrance," or "ladies' entrance" was usually a simple, plain door up the block leading to a back room, with tables, chairs, maybe a piano. Wives entered there looking for wayward husbands; during rare police crackdowns, owners could wave recognizable regulars in and screen out temperance spies and undercover cops. Most hoped this Sabbath day marked a temporary display of virtue.

The commissioner himself spent the Sunday at his country estate, Sagamore Hill, at Oyster Bay, enjoying the breezes off Long Island Sound and playing with the "bunnies," as he called his youngest children. "Archie loves me better than anything in the world. Ted is so sweet; indeed they all are dear," Roosevelt wrote his sister. One Roosevelt niece, Corinne Robinson Alsop, recalled that the cousins adored "Uncle Theodore" and that one of his favorite games was to lead them, from toddler to teen, in traversing a dead straight line over *all* obstacles, no matter whether that meant climbing up a tree or over a barn. Dead straight. He also taught swimming by a swamp-the-canoe-and-rescue-the-sinkers method. His letters, even at his busiest, are filled with anecdotes about the children, whom he clearly loved.

In calendar year 1895, from June on, he would spend every Sunday there except for a handful.

———

All day Sunday, June 23, a steady stream of rough-looking workingmen headed to the side door of popular Callahan's at 12 Chatham Square, at the southern tip of the Bowery, touching Chinatown. The massive twelve-foot-tall front doors were shut under the black-and-gold marquee that touted "Lager Beer, Ales and Porter." Next door stood Callahan's Progress Hotel, "Rooms 25 cents."

Late that night, the bouncer opened the side door to a familiar face, when that familiar face came flying inward, followed by a stranger pushing him headlong forward.

Once inside, the stranger, a plainclothes rookie cop, found himself in the middle of the large square barroom, where he saw about forty men sitting around drinking. The clink of glasses and the laughter stopped abruptly. He heard the door slam behind him and the deadbolt slide into place.

Edward J. Bourke, a twenty-eight-year-old navy veteran, a by-the-book new officer recently sworn in by Roosevelt himself, had already raided Callahan's the previous Sunday, and while he was hauling the bartender under the shadows of the nearby Bowery El, the man had snarled: "Look here, you _____-_____, the next time, you come here, we'll bust your head open with an ax!"

Bourke took that as an invitation; he was back. He grabbed the bartender by the collar and started wrenching him along the bar. Just as Bourke was moving his prisoner toward the door, a squat, angry man blocked his way.

"Who the hell are you?" roared Mike Callahan, the owner. "King" Callahan had already been arrested several times for assaulting cops and detectives. The charges had always disappeared, since Callahan was an ex-assemblyman and a favored Tammany Hall stalwart whose cheap "Progress Hotel" next door could deliver 300 "floater population" votes to the Democrats.

Officer Bourke informed Callahan that if he interfered any further he would arrest him also. "You _____-_____. You arrest me!" Callahan punched Bourke hard in the face.

In that punch to the jaw, Tammany Hall Democrats began fighting back against Roosevelt's Sabbatarian crackdown.

Bourke reeled backwards and was disturbed to see Callahan's rough clientele picking up beer mugs and circling in, "getting ready," as he later recalled, "to play a prominent part in my funeral." Bourke wrestled Callahan to the sand-strewn floor. The officer purposely rolled over so that the bar owner was on top of him, "clinging so tightly to his burly frame, for the reason that while he was held thus, no beer glass, nor big feet, nor brawny fists could reach me."

While they scrapped, someone in the crowd yelled: "Axe the cop." Bourke managed to get a hand free and he pulled his revolver from his hip pocket and kicked Callahan away. "The first man who interferes, I'll shoot down like a dog," he shouted.

Officer Bourke dragged his cursing prisoners outside into the darkness. He blew his cylindrical whistle to call for help. The bar owner suddenly grabbed Bourke's necktie, and started yanking and twisting it. The bar crowd in the doorway was cheering. Bourke was losing air and couldn't pry Callahan's fingers loose so he smashed Callahan on the head with the butt of his pistol . . . twice. When the other officer showed up, he found the bar owner dazed and bleeding. The pair hauled Callahan and his bartender along the dark narrow streets to the jail at the Elizabeth Street precinct house.

Callahan slept down in the jail; Bourke slept up in the barracks and the next morning, Bourke hauled his two prisoners before a police court judge at the Tombs. "King" Callahan, bruised and with a "plaster" bandage on his forehead, expected an easy ride. Tammany Hall sent a couple of neighborhood heavyweights to speed Callahan's exit from justice: congressman-elect James Walsh and "Big Florrie" Sullivan, cousin of state senator Tim "Dry Dollar" Sullivan. They crowded around Clerk Solomon Rosenthal, also of Tammany Hall.

The trio helped Callahan skip the line of usual Monday morning drunks and brawlers, and Clerk Rosenthal's hearing seemed to give out when officer Bourke said he was adding a felony assault charge against Callahan on top of the excise misdemeanor. Rosenthal guided Bourke to speak to Judge Voorhis, who bounced him back to the clerk. The rookie cop Bourke was wavering, especially when he heard Callahan mutter he planned to charge the policeman with assault. Bourke was ready to skip the second charge, but then Lincoln Steffens, who happened to be covering arraignments, relayed to him that Police Commissioner Roosevelt had heard of his arrest and was hugely impressed.

Another officer, overhearing the exchange, told Bourke that with the president of the Police Board's backing, he should push the assault charge again. Rosenthal reluctantly did the paperwork, and Judge Voorhis approved assault charges and tripled the bail to $3,000 (which was paid by an uptown brewery).

Roosevelt, soon after arriving at Mulberry Street on Monday morning, announced that he was indeed delighted that a greenhorn cop had taken down a Bowery king and that political pull, especially Tammany pull, had failed. "All this talk about the impossibility of enforcing the [Sunday drinking] law is all nonsense," he told a reporter. "It can be done and it will be done."

This arrest sent the unmistakable message to the whole city that the board was not like other Police Boards. Editorialists started flinging the words *Sahara* and *New York* together. Roosevelt intended to press the excise board to revoke the licenses of places like Callahan's.

The president of the board once again called in the police chief, inspectors, and the entire press corps from across the street.

"I do not thank you nor anyone for doing his duty but I wish to express my gratification at what was done. It reflects credit on all of you. It is a great pleasure for me to say this. It seems almost ungracious to say more but I am convinced that you will understand me when I say that yesterday set a standard *below which* we must not go . . . Through you and your subordinates, I want to have it understood that the excise law, like any other law, 'goes' in New York."

Chief Conlin attempted to reply. "I can assure you that we will not fail—" Roosevelt cut him off. "I am sure of it. You have set the low water mark yesterday. It is good. We will do better by and by."

The next day, TR wanted to personally congratulate young officer Bourke, and was impatiently waiting for him at headquarters. But Roosevelt had to leave to catch the 11 a.m. train to Boston; he had agreed to attend his first Harvard reunion in fifteen years since graduation. He bounded down the stairs and bumped right into Bourke, his face still bruised and puffy. After hearing a breathless version of the fight story and "final arrest of the pugnacious proprietor of Never Close Up," Roosevelt praised the rookie— "You have done very well indeed!" And he promised: "This board is behind you, always remember that." That promise would come in handy later when Roosevelt sat as judge and swiftly dismissed the brutality charges brought by a friend of Callahan against Bourke.

The three other board members, though cast in the shade by Roosevelt, were working hard for reform as well. Commissioner Andrew, with help from Parker, presided all day on June 12, 14, 15, 18, 21, and 22 over the trial of Captain Eakins for not closing the Washington Square brothels. Roosevelt rarely lingered in the room, as the testimony often grew quite salacious.

> PARKHURST AGENT: We got into the bedroom and she says: "How do you want it, French or American?" With that she pushed me down on the bed and unbuttoned my pants quick. And I says "I am too full [i.e., drunk] now; I don't want any just now."
> LAWYER: When you did touch these women, what part of their person did you touch?
> PARKHURST AGENT: Their breast.
> LAWYER: If you didn't want to have intercourse with them, why did you touch their breast?
> PARKHURST AGENT: We have got to make a bluff sometimes.

The veteran police lawyer representing the disgraced captain aimed to drag out the case and force testimony lurid enough to make the board think twice before pressing charges against a captain wanting to retire.

The ushering out of Eakins was taking months. Meanwhile ex-captain Devery was fighting his way back in, with the help of his high-priced lawyer Colonel James. The city's corporation counsel, Francis Scott, advised on Tuesday, June 25, that it would be fruitless to appeal a recent Court of Common Pleas ruling reinstating Devery. He pointed out that the judges had called the two key witnesses, Rhoda Sanford and Katie Schubert, "notorious liars" and had stated that a defendant in America had a right to attend his own departmental trial. The board nonetheless voted to delay restoring Devery. (It would reinstate him on July 19, give him $2,237 for ten months' back pay, then promptly suspend him over a pending criminal charge of accepting a $100 construction site bribe.)

To offset the disciplinary trials, the board sought to reward heroism. It handed out an award and promoted lanky redheaded patrolman William H. Duggan, who had leaped into the Fourth Avenue railway tunnel to catch a burglar. It also honored harbor policeman Michael Gorman, who had saved his *twenty-fifth* drowning victim.

Roosevelt headed off to Boston, and the *New York World* prepared a little mischief. The newspaper staff knew that Roosevelt had Harvard meetings there at the Hotel Brunswick on Wednesday, so it seemed safe to assume that TR would not return in time for what was now his regular Thursday midnight ramble. (He had gone the previous week and caught Officer Bill Rath mid-slurp in an oyster house.)

Pulitzer's editors decided to fill that Thursday gap. They assigned cartoonist Walt McDougall, who resembled Roosevelt in age, height, mustache, spectacles, and most importantly, horse teeth. McDougall was the proper imp for the job.

He routinely inflated J. P. Morgan's nose to such gargantuan proportions that the plutocrat stooped to beg mercy from Pulitzer. (At the publisher's request, the cartoonist had agreed "to moderate" his "zeal.") His later caricature of the supreme court justices landed the newspaper in such trouble that McDougall not only had to apologize but had to "listen to a lecture by one of the justices on an off day that took the wave out of my hair and made a better man of me."

After midnight on Thursday, McDougall donned a floppy hat and set off with a reporter to walk down Sixth Avenue. He affixed a "wide toothsome grin" to his face and steered toward as many cops as possible. He found it "a very surprising sensation to be treated with such overpowering courtesy and respect" by large men who usually told him to "move on!" The cartoonist admitted misgivings about deceiving policemen but then he reasoned that he couldn't be blamed for being "handsome" like Roosevelt.

McDougall found his biggest problem in spooking cops was finding any cops actually walking their beats: "I had begun to think the police were on strike." He buoyed himself with the thought that Roosevelt outweighed him by fifteen pounds, so the commissioner's feet must have hurt even more than the cartoonist's.

McDougall, with his grin and small talk, succeeded in prying loose one cop from a bevy of adoring attractive streetwalkers. But when he walked up to two other officers, he was miffed when neither budged and both kept on chatting near a bicycle shop at Columbus Circle. They even gave him the polite brush-off, mentioning the late hour. The irritated *World* men decided to send the reporter accompanying McDougall circling back to try again.

"Say, old man, do you know who that was?" he asked one of the cops.

"Nah," the officer [badge No. 2206] replied. "What t' 'ell."

"Well, that's ol' Roosey out on another lark," said the *World* reporter.

"Holy smoke, is that right?" Officer No. 708 jumped as if a cannon cracker had gone off under him. "Now we are in for it."

"Aw, come off it," retorted No. 2206. "I know the cove. He's bigger than that." Then in a less confident tone. "Say is that straight goods? Been followin' him all the way up from the Ninth? Just my —— luck."

No. 708 jumped back with: "The duffer's coming back. The cabby's giving us the tip. Sneak, old man!" and officer No. 708 made a dash westward along Fifty-Eighth Street while No. 2206 with great dignity strolled down the avenue.

Cartoonist McDougall and the reporter wrote up their exploits for the Sunday *World*. McDougall was surprised that Roosevelt bore him a grudge for the impersonation lark for almost two years, since TR had "none of the false dignity of most great men," and "no man knew better the value of such advertising."

———

The real Roosevelt returned from Boston late Thursday quite pleased; he had been elected to Harvard's Board of Overseers, garnering 200 votes more than several prestigious candidates such as Charles Francis Adams. "Not only all my class, but all the alumni and undergraduates gave me a royal reception," he wrote to his sister. His New York exploits—saloon closings, midnight rambles, reform agenda—were vaulting him onto the national stage in a broader way than his gadfly years at civil service. That Friday night in Manhattan he found the energy for another midnight ramble, his fourth that month, wandering through the Tenderloin and other neighborhoods till three in the morning, catching seven cops shirking, including one walrus-sized patrolman belly up to the bar hoisting a frothy mug. The ginger ale excuse didn't wash.

The following morning, Saturday, at 11 a.m., several hundred angry Germans marched on City Hall. They paraded up the wide marble steps to complain directly to the mayor about the loss of their Sunday beer. Roosevelt, summoned from Mulberry Street headquarters, was rushing to City Hall to stand shoulder to shoulder with the sixty-eight-year-old mayor, but had not yet arrived there.

The meeting had been scheduled in advance, but the size of the delegation was unexpectedly large. The Germans trailed only the Irish in terms of population, and the massive German community in New York, spreading far beyond Kleindeutschland, prized its "Continental Sunday" at the biergarten with an almost religious fervor. "They quietly sip their beer as they listen to strains of an orchestra, and between steins munch pretzels, frankfurters and sauerkraut, Limburger sandwiches and other German delicacies," stated Zeisloft's guidebook. "On every side are family groups, father, mother and children, all merry, all sociable, all well-behaved," concurred another city guide. The Astors were originally German as were dozens of other leading mercantile families; the Metropolitan Opera favored performances of Wagner. There were still places in the city, such as Tompkins Square Park or the German Catholic Church on 3rd Street and Avenue A, where a passerby might overhear nothing but German.

Fifty representatives of the German American Reform Union reached City Hall first to confront the mayor. This was no fringe political club; this organization, a part of the anti–Tammany Hall movement, had supplied the key political puzzle piece that had helped elect Mayor Strong on the Fusion ticket of reform Republicans and Democrats.

The first speaker complained that in his campaign the mayor had promised a liberal approach to the Sunday law—such as allowing legal sales of beer and wine from 1 p.m. to 6 p.m.—but was now supporting Roosevelt's "harsh" and "tyrannical" enforcement.

Mayor Strong, trying to take a conciliatory tone, said he wished he could make an exception for the beer gardens but "it is impossible to discriminate" and, as consolation, he promised to lobby the legislature for a new excise law when it returned to session . . . six months later, on January 1.

Sheriff Edward Tamsen, a native of Hamburg and an influential book publisher headquartered at 52 Avenue A, asked what they should do until then. The mayor, known for his "dry sense of humor," said, "Honor the Sabbath." Tamsen, not amused, asked, "What's next? Shutting down the street cars on Sundays?"

Minutes later, at 11 a.m., Otto Kempner, a passionate former assemblyman with impressive thick swept-back black hair, arrived, marching in front of 200 perspiring followers of the United Societies for Liberal Sundays, a newly formed protest group of mostly German organizations. Roosevelt reached the white marble building just after them and jostled his way forward to the mayor's side.

"When the front door of the saloon is closed and the blinds are drawn, the law is enforced as much as it should be," stated Kempner, a native of Austria and a fierce opponent of Tammany. "This is the foremost city in America and it is up to date. You, nor no one else, Mr. Mayor, can put us in a spiritual strait jacket." He demanded the opportunity to read out loud candidate Strong's campaign promises for a liberal law.

The mayor, conspicuously looking at his watch, snapped, "I have something else to do but listen to you."

Kempner, his voice rising, accused the mayor of never having time for the needs of 125,000 voting German Americans in New York City. "You now attempt to enforce, by drastic means, antiquated and bigoted laws," he shouted. "Only bigots could enforce such laws. It is an asinine exercise of authority."

The mayor grew "flushed and Mr. Roosevelt glared through his eyeglasses in utter astonishment," according to the *New York Herald*. The raucous crowd was yelling encouragement in German and English.

Roosevelt could stand no more. He motioned for silence. "You people want me to enforce the law only a little bit, a little teeny bit. Well, your honor," said Roosevelt, turning to the mayor, "I do not know how to do such a thing and I shall not begin to learn now."

Then he turned back to Otto Kempner and the howling crowd. "You have threatened that it means political disaster to me to enforce this Excise Law. Now listen! If it meant a hundred political deaths for me to obey my duty, I would do it. I would not move an inch. It is true I may never be heard of again, but I will have kept my oath of office. You, Mr. Kempner and Mr. Grosse, stand here as the champions of a vicious and corrupt system of enforcement of the law."

Grosse, a fifty-year-old lawyer and popular German newspaper editor, shouted that the charge was not true. The crowd chanted, "*Nein, Nein*, he doesn't!" and someone yelled, "We are as good and law-abiding as you!"

Roosevelt tried to shout down the crowd. "You know the greatest source of corruption in the city is the partial enforcement of the laws. You are advocating a return to that system."

Grosse, also once an assistant district attorney and currently an Internal Revenue Service collector, shouted another denial.

Roosevelt, reddening, shook his finger at him and said, "You can deny it but it is true." Grosse replied that he wouldn't stand for such an accusation and began moving toward Roosevelt.

Mayor Strong slammed a gavel down on the podium and called for order. The rumblings of the German faction petered out. Roosevelt repeated his mantra that as long as the law was on the books, he would enforce it. He executed the laws; he did not legislate them. A huge groan filled the room. Later, as the angry crowd filed out, the mayor, with mock congeniality, smiled and said to the departing Germans: "Glad to have seen you, gentlemen."

––––––

Roosevelt kept his word and immediately met with Chief Conlin about increased enforcement. He pressed Conlin on Sunday vigilance and the chief conceded that probably about half the saloons had been closed the previous Sunday; he promised Roosevelt the police would shut down another third that weekend. He intended to assign 1,000 officers to work in plainclothes to supplement the 2,000 in uniforms. The two men also agreed on a very literal interpretation of the Sunday excise law, deciding that Sunday began precisely at 12:01 a.m.

Roosevelt, in effect, was trying to shut down Saturday night for the city at the stroke of midnight.

––––––

Sunday, June 30, was hot. A double shift of policemen on duty since 12:01 a.m. set out to close the saloons. Barkeeps were forced to seek out more clever ruses. An owner downtown let patrons enter through a private house next door, climb to the roof, then walk across a wooden plank three floors up over an alley and then down into the bar's back room. "Those who went to the trouble [decided] the risk of falling off the plank was greater than the satisfaction . . . from . . . one drink or even two."

By 10 a.m., some thirsty German Americans up in Harlem had convinced a bartender named Kirby to open up his side door at 125th and Third Avenue. A policeman locked the crowd inside until reinforcements came. All over town the blinds were raised, rooms remained empty. The poor had a much harder time this Sunday finding a beer, while the wealthy could go to a private club or a hotel for a meal and a drink.

The *Sun* reporter discovered that many hotels that rarely charged below twenty-five cents had created a low-price menu of ten-cent lobster salad and five-cent roast-beef sandwiches to satisfy the law. "A group of men sat around a table with a bottle of whiskey that supplied round after round of drinks, while three untouched sandwiches withered on plates pushed out of the drinkers' way."

On the poor East Side, even the "growler," or fill-it-up-and-tote-it-home, trade was quashed. New York had a long-standing tradition of families "rushing the growler," that is, fetching quarts of beer in various vessels to drink at home on Sundays. "Men, women and children with 'growlers' concealed in hat boxes, baskets and under aprons went from saloon to saloon until compelled to give up in despair."

The *World* tracked down a policeman who was willing—anonymously—to give an honest assessment. "The law is no good anyhow. These poor people like to have a glass or two of beer on Sunday, which without it is no Sunday at all to them. They can't afford to buy beer in bulk or in bottle to keep it on ice. I guess this crusade today is causing more suffering in poor families than anything else they have to bear."

That same day, Commissioner Andrews turned the crackdown into a family outing. He and his wife climbed into a carriage pulled by a pair of dapple grays and whirled around upper Manhattan to see whether the saloons were closed. (They were.) Elsewhere in town, some New Yorkers made a protest display on a fire escape on 1st Street, draping black crepe onto those pails that families used to fetch beer. Nearby a sign in a deserted saloon announced: WE VOTED FOR REFORM AND THIS IS WHAT WE GET.

The *Sun* summed it up: "So dry a Sunday and so dull a Sunday as yesterday has not been known in New York for years, if indeed such a day was ever known here."

For many New York newspapers, the honeymoon with Roosevelt was drawing to a very sudden close. Even that champion of reform the *New York Times* worried that the crackdown might sweep Tammany back into office. To most newspapermen, the idea of cutting off beer to the masses on Sunday was cruel and inhumane, especially with a hot New York summer approaching.

"If the Sunday laws were properly adjusted to the habits and reasonable wants of the people, they would be cheerfully obeyed," opined the editorial writer at the *New York World*. "There would then be no weekly repetition of the farce of pretending to enforce laws that cannot be enforced."

A cartoonist at the *New York Evening Telegram* portrayed Roosevelt happy at his Union League Club bar with a liquor menu on the wall behind him, listing "Champagnes, Claret, Burgundies, Sauternes, Sherry, Rhine, Ales, Porter, Brandies, Whiskies, Liqueurs, Cordials."

Town Topics, a tart weekly aimed at the upper class, wrote: "After making a tour of the beer saloons on Sunday last, disguised in pink whiskers and an Old Guard bearskin hat, Mr. Roosevelt repaired, I presume, to the Union League Club and bought a drink."

On that Sunday, June 30, the day of the most recent crackdown, Roosevelt found time at Oyster Bay to write a chatty letter to his sister in England, recounting his week. He mentioned his Tuesday trip to Harvard and his overnight stay with his pal Senator Lodge and joked about how one fellow alumnus, "Winty," drank too much at the Harvard dining club Porcellian. He also made a rare confession, one that he would never repeat to the general public of New York. "I have now run up against an ugly snag, the Sunday Excise Law. It is altogether too strict but I have no honorable alternative save to enforce it and I am enforcing it to the furious rage of the saloon keepers and of many good people too; for which I am sorry."

The citizens of New York would never hear the word "sorry" uttered by Roosevelt concerning Sunday liquor laws.

Neither would they ever hear about something else that was perhaps driving the commissioner to this crackdown: the recent tragic death of his brother Elliott, an alcoholic.

ELLIOTT

One year earlier, Theodore Roosevelt's younger brother, Elliott, was living under an assumed name on West 102nd Street with another man's wife, and drinking from wake-up to pass-out day after day. He teetered from charming to suicidal, one moment singing popular tunes, the next trying the window on the fourth floor.

And almost weekly, Elliott had to fend off requests for money from a former house servant named Katy Mann, who carried in her arms a baby—their child, so she said—whom she had named Elliott Roosevelt Mann. Though he had been married to a society belle, a woman so strikingly beautiful that poet Robert Browning had requested permission to gaze at her while she had her portrait painted in London, he now preferred to live in an alcoholic and opiate-filled haze with a woman identified as Mrs. Evans. To top it all, recently Elliott had drunkenly crashed his carriage into a lamppost and hurtled headfirst onto the pavement. "Elliott has sunk to the lowest depths," wrote Theodore's wife, Edith, in July 1894. "[He] consorts with the vilest woman, and Theodore, Bamie and Douglas receive horrid anonymous letters about his life."

———

Born sixteen months apart, the two brothers had often been exceptionally close growing up. For the first decade or so, Elliott had seemed the far more promising one: more outgoing, more charming, more confident, more athletic, more handsome.

"Teedie" and "Ellie," as they were called, shared the rarefied life of the Roosevelt clan on 20th Street. They had stood shoulder to shoulder at the second-story window and watched the Lincoln funeral procession in 1865; they shared private tutors (never attending public or private school) and performed scenes from Shakespeare under the direction of the family doctor; they endured dour family Sundays and took Grand Tours together to Europe and Egypt. They played in the gardens of Fontainebleau and floated down the Nile on a *dahabeah* for two months with thirteen servants. On that trip, twelve-year-old Elliott hadn't discovered hunting yet, but Theodore, with new spectacles, blasted birds with his new 12-gauge double-barreled French shotgun; then he gutted and stuffed them on the deck to preserve them as specimens. His blood-drenched clothes made him a family outcast, inspiring a limerick by Elliott.

There once was an old fellow named Teedie
Whose clothes at best looked so seedy
That his friends in dismay
Hollered out, "Oh, I say!"
At this dirty old fellow named Teedie.

As siblings often do, each carved out his niche. Elliott became the ball-room dancer, athlete, the charmer of women; Theodore was the bookish one who kept a diary and tried extremely hard at everything. TR would later reminisce about "dancing class" where Elliott far outshone him. "He was distinctly the polished man of the world from the outside, and all the girls from Helen White and Fanny Dana and May Wigham used to be so flattered by any attention from him."

They summered together, first in New Jersey, then at Oyster Bay; they rode horses bought for them by their father. Elliott excelled at sailing, while Theodore became the relentlessly determined rower.

Both suffered severe childhood illnesses that upended family outings, provoking immense worry by their parents and perhaps jangling relations between them. Theodore from age three endured frightening deep-gasping bouts of asthma, which he later combated with extraordinary gym workouts. Elliott seemed the golden child until suddenly at puberty he started having seizure-like attacks, diagnosed as "nerves/hysteria," with fainting, headaches, and night terrors.

Their philanthropist father, Theodore Roosevelt Sr., tried hard to prevent them from turning into the frivolous boys of Fifth Avenue. Father, known as "Great Heart," preached and also practiced an active Christianity that demanded good works. He founded the Newsboys' Lodging House to shelter hundreds of orphans sleeping in alleyways and gutters; during the

Civil War he had helped create the Allotment Commission, which encouraged soldiers to send their pay home to their families instead of squandering it on whores and saloons.

Theodore seemed challenged to live up to his father's lofty aspirations; Elliott often seemed chafed by them.

As part of a cure for Elliott's fits, the family sent him at age sixteen to a military outpost, Ft. McKavett in the wilds of Central Texas. Elliott wrote about bunking with a genuine cowboy in a tumbledown hut, sharing a blanket with the stranger, and deciding to use a dog as a pillow "partly for warmth and partly to drown the smell of my bedfellow." Theodore was very jealous.

Together, they weathered the sudden shock of their father's death in 1878. As they grew older, the lives of the two brothers intertwined less, with Theodore off at Harvard and Elliott still too troubled to study, but Elliott took his brother—just before Theodore's marriage to his first wife, Alice Lee—on a kind of extended bachelor party, a hunting trip out west as far as the Red River in Minnesota. Though they had no Indian adventures, the brothers shot more than 400 birds—geese, snipe, plovers, ducks—and nearly drowned, after upending a rowboat in Iowa. "I enjoy being with the old boy so much," Theodore wrote, and Elliott echoed the sentiment: "All the happier we are solely dependent on each other for companionship." Elliott appeared to be outgrowing the anxiety attacks, or perhaps he had discovered how to blot them out with cocktails.

Theodore described his twenty-year-old brother reaching Chicago during their trip: "As soon as we got here, he took some ale to get the dust out of his throat; then a milk punch because he was thirsty; a mint julep because it was hot; a brandy smash 'to keep the cold out of his stomach'; and then sherry and bitters to give him an appetite."

TR's flippant tone makes it unlikely he recognized his brother's incipient alcoholism, but clearly Elliott was downing more than a few. He obviously wasn't sloppy about it yet because Theodore asked Elliott to serve as best man at his Boston Brahmin wedding to Alice Lee on TR's twenty-second birthday. "She is so pure and holy, it seems almost profanation to touch her," Roosevelt wrote in his diary, but added that nonetheless he couldn't stop hugging her.

As a newly married man, Theodore embarked on his plans to be a writer and enter politics in New York. Meanwhile, best man Elliott sailed for India. Cavalier and footloose, Elliott hunted tigers south of Hyderabad, traveling by elephant, by horse, by servant-hoisted palanquin. Camp meals rivaled the catered baskets of Delmonico's as they dined on an assortment of curries, chicken, veal, salmon, duck, and tongue, washed down by a cool pitcher of beer.

Elliott proudly recorded that he had shot a nine-foot-long Bengal tiger as it was making its final lunge toward him. He wished his "brave, old Heart of Oak brother" could have been there. "It is the life, old man. *Our* kind. The glorious freedom, the greatest excitement." A London taxidermist deftly fashioned the tiger's skin into a rug that would cover the floor of the Roosevelt family parlor for years.

Elliott circled the globe, then returned to join the polo-playing, hard-carousing fellows of Long Island. On December 1, 1883, he married the regally beautiful debutante Anna Hall in "one of the most brilliant weddings of the season," attended by Astors and Vanderbilts. A crescent of diamonds held her veil in place. Anna, who almost a year later gave birth to daughter Eleanor and then five years after that to son Elliott, would remain beautiful enough to win accolades at society dinners. Elliott belonged to several prestigious Manhattan clubs and was working as a stockbroker.

Theirs seemed the perfect marriage, only it wasn't.

Elliott "drank like a fish and ran after the ladies," later commented a Roosevelt family member, "I mean ladies not in his own rank, which was much worse."

He also began having bizarre athletic accidents, probably from his recklessness and drinking. He fell attempting a double somersault during an "amateur circus exhibition" in Pelham, New York, in 1888 and cracked his ankle; a doctor's misdiagnosis of the injury as a sprain led to the ankle having to be rebroken to be set, all of which dragged out his recovery and probably accelerated his use of opium-based painkillers.

In late June of 1890, the twenty-nine-year-old German-born live-in house servant Catharina "Katy" Mann informed Elliott that she was pregnant with his child. Weeks later, Elliott and his wife Anna, their two children, and several servants (*not* including Katy) headed off to the elegant spas and hotels of Europe. The family's plan was for him to dry out. Count Bismarck entertained them in Berlin, as did Count Sierstorff, who intervened when Buffalo Bill, then touring there, offered Elliott a shot glass of whiskey.

Anna became pregnant again; Elliott remained sober for two months, feeding the pigeons in Piazza San Marco in Venice, sailing every morning with his two children near Naples. Then he cracked. Wife Anna wrote and asked if the most efficient member of the Roosevelt clan, unmarried older sister Bamie, would come over to Vienna to tend to her till she gave birth and try to convince her brother to dry out in a sanitarium.

Elliott had other ideas; he soon headed to Paris, inviting the family to tag along. Once there he would disappear for days, one time hunting boar with the Duc de Grammont. "The horns played a little, then we galloped in a single file up and down miles of beaten forest road," he wrote to one of his polo chums on Long Island. He complained that the only excitement possible in such a stage-managed hunt could occur if someone fell asleep and tumbled off his horse.

Back in New York, Katy Mann—pregnant, abandoned, and living at home in Brooklyn with her mother—approached the Roosevelt family, told her story, and demanded money. Older brother Theodore, then in D.C. serving on the Civil Service Commission, and brother-in-law Douglas Robinson (married to his younger sister, Corinne), in New York, handled the negotiations. TR at first did not believe the servant, until she said she had a locket and witnesses who had heard Elliott in her room. She claimed it was common knowledge that the other servants "chaffed" her about the master's attentions.

"It is like a brooding nightmare," wrote TR to his sister Bamie in Europe, painting the adultery in stark Victorian terms. "If it was mere death one could stand it; it is the shame that is so fearful."

TR wanted Bamie to convince Elliott to allow himself to be locked up in an asylum for a long cure. In any case, he expected his brother's living arrangements to change drastically. "Personally, I regard it as little short of criminal for Anna to continue to live with him and bear his children. She ought not to have any more children and those she has ought to be brought up away from him."

He advised his sister that as soon as Anna gave birth and recovered, she should bring the family home to the United States and leave Elliott in a foreign asylum, preferably a long-term, or possibly "permanent," arrangement. He added that if she couldn't persuade Elliott to go to one in Europe, he would have him locked up as soon as Elliott returned to America. "His curious callousness and selfishness, his disregard of your words and my letters and his light heartedness under them, make one feel hopeless about him." TR feared that "the Katy Mann affair is but the beginning."

Theodore regarded Elliott's drunken infidelity in black-and-white terms: Elliott was either "insane," that is, not responsible and deserving of treatment or . . . his brother was sane, responsible, and a "selfish, brutal and vicious criminal."

Katy Mann gave birth and demanded the large sum of $10,000. TR and his brother-in-law Douglas sent an investigator, carrying a picture of Elliott, to Brooklyn to examine the baby. He confirmed that it was probably a Roosevelt. "It is his business to be an expert in likenesses," wrote TR. They mulled a counteroffer of $3,000 or $4,000 in exchange for a quit-claim.

The Dutch Roosevelts, one of New York's oldest families, had never been touched by scandal. Most family members preferred to keep this quiet as long as possible, certainly not volunteer it to the press. Nonetheless, Theodore and Bamie—convinced they needed to protect Anna and the family fortune—applied to the New York courts for a writ of insanity against Elliott. With that filing, the scandal finally broke, with front-page headlines: DEMENTED BY EXCESS, WRECKED BY LIQUOR AND FOLLY, and PROCEEDINGS TO SAVE THE ESTATE. In his affidavit Roosevelt stated his brother had threatened suicide several times and had lost his power of self-control. Bamie stated that Elliott had been drinking to excess for the past three years but had turned irrational and violent in the past year.

However, Roosevelt's younger sister, Corinne, the flightiest and most emotional of the four siblings, refused to join in the court proceeding. Years earlier, she had written: "Dear Elliott has been such a loving tender brother to me . . . How different people are . . . there is Teddy, for instance, he is devoted to me too but if I were to do something that he thought very weak or wrong, he would never forgive me, whereas Elliott no matter how much he might despise the sin, would forgive the sinner."

The judge appointed a three-person commission of lunacy to evaluate the thirty-one-year-old bon vivant, currently in Paris. If he was ruled a lunatic, the court would appoint an executor to oversee his immense $175,000 estate. Throughout his letters, TR sounded a recurrent theme of wanting to preserve the estate for Elliott's wife and children, as Elliott was apparently blowing through about $1,500 a month skittering around Europe, which would exceed his annual investment income.

Each of the four Roosevelt siblings had received approximately $125,000 from their father and $62,500 from their mother.

Following his boyhood cowboy dream, TR had invested $85,000 to buy two ranches and herds of cattle in North Dakota; in one letter describing a sudden ice storm, he stated that he hoped to lose "less than half" the money. He had bought property and built a home for $45,000 in Oyster Bay. Thanks to his financial decisions, TR had seen his annual income drop from about $14,000 a year in the mid-1880s to $7,500 in 1894 prior to taking the police commissioner job. In one recent year, wife Edith's account books revealed an annual shortfall of more than $1,000. Roosevelt was eventually forced to sell off land in Oyster Bay. He even feared losing Sagamore Hill. He was famously impractical about money. Decades later, his daughter Alice noted that every morning her mother pinned a $20 bill in his pocket, and her father had no idea how he spent it.

On the other hand, the bulk of younger brother Elliott's inheritance—despite his high jinks and immorality—remained intact and was being invested through a stock brokerage managed by his uncle by marriage James Gracie.

Elliott had voluntarily parked himself at a retreat, Château Suresnes, outside Paris, where he somehow learned of the writ of lunacy. He issued a denial to the *Herald*: "I wish emphatically to state that my brother Theodore is taking no steps to have a commission pass on my sanity, either with or without my wife's approval. I am in Paris taking the cure at an *établisse-ment hydro-therapeutique*, which my nerves, shaken by several accidents in the hunting field, made necessary." His words sounded quite sane and his lawyers in America quickly found a jurisdictional flaw—an incorrect address—in Theodore's lunacy application.

Elliott seemed in the clear once again to pursue the life of a wealthy, hard-drinking, adulterous husband. In fact, he was already living with Mrs. Evans in Paris. His brother could not abide that.

Theodore said he feared for the well-being of Elliott's children and wife. His own wife, Edith, later admitted a further motive: "I live in constant dread of some scandal attaching itself to Theodore."

Boarding a steamer, Roosevelt headed for Europe in January of 1892 to confront his younger brother. They had a brutal meeting in which Elliott tried to laugh off TR's "stern" lectures, until he finally caved in, "utterly broken, submissive and repentant." He agreed to sign over two-thirds of his estate to his wife and to undergo two years' probation with no drinking before earning the right to rejoin his family. His rehabilitation would start with Dr. Keely's five-week Bi-Chloride of Gold cure in Dwight, Illinois.

"This morning, with his silk hat, his overcoat, gloves and cigar, E. came to my room to say goodbye," wrote Mrs. Evans. "It is all over ... Now even my loss was swallowed up in pity—for he looks so bruised, so beaten down by the past week with his brother. How could they treat so generous and noble a man as they have. He is more noble a figure in my eyes, with all his confessed faults, than either his wife or brother."

Although Elliott returned to the United States, stopped drinking, and was ruled sane later that same year, TR was adamant that his younger brother should not yet see his wife or children. His brother-in-law, real estate investor Douglas Robinson, gave Elliott a job managing properties and staff down in rural southwest Virginia, and Elliott thrived.

Still dazzling, wife Anna Hall Roosevelt attended a "beauty dinner" hosted by the Turkish minister in Bar Harbor in September 1892, and was regarded as the "belle of the occasion." Elliott kept writing letters, bragging of his sobriety to his mother-in-law. But a few months later at age twenty-nine, Anna Hall Roosevelt suddenly and shockingly fell ill and lay dying of diphtheria; Elliott wanted to see her one last time but her mother sent a terse telegram to him in Virginia: DO NOT COME.

Elliott, still exiled from his family by his brother and his mother-in-law, began drinking again; he tipped over an oil lamp while reading naked and severely burned himself. He moved back to New York City and wound up on West 102nd Street living with that same married woman, Mrs. Evans, as "Mr. and Mrs. Elliott."

"He is now laid up from a serious fall," Roosevelt wrote to his sister Bamie on July 29, 1894. "Poor fellow! if only he could have died instead of Anna!"

Two weeks later Elliott did die, with only a doctor and his uncle James K. Gracie at his bedside. He had started using "stimulants" again and while suffering from delirium tremens had tried to jump out of a fourth-floor window, but a policeman had restrained him. During his last hours he had called out for his daughter, Eleanor.

"The terrible bloated swelled look was gone," wrote sister Corinne to Bamie in London, "and the sweet expression round the forehead made me weep bitter tears ... Theodore was more overcome than I have ever seen him—cried like a little child for a long time."

In death, the raw emotions finally battered down Roosevelt's stout moral fortress and he wrote an extraordinary letter.

[Elliott] would have been in a strait jacket had he lived forty eight hours longer. His fall, aggravated by frightful drinking, that was the immediate cause. He had been drinking whole bottles of anisette and green mint—besides whole bottles of raw brandy and champagne, sometimes half a dozen a morning. But when dead the poor fellow looked very peaceful and so like his old generous, gallant self of fifteen years ago . . .

I suppose he has been doomed from the beginning. The absolute contradiction of all his actions and of all his moral—even more than his mental—qualities is utterly impossible to explain.

For the last few days he had dumbly felt the awful night closing in on him; he would not let us come to his house, nor part with the woman, nor cease drinking for a moment but he wandered ceaselessly everywhere, never still and he wrote again and again to us all sending me two telegrams and three notes. He was like some stricken hunted creature and indeed he was hunted by the most terrible demons that ever entered into man's body and soul.

His house was so neat and well kept with his bible and religious books and Anna's pictures everywhere, even in the room of himself and his mistress. Poor woman, she had taken the utmost care of him, and was broken down at his death. Her relations with him had been just as strange as everything else. Very foolishly, it had been arranged that he should be taken to be buried beside Anna but I promptly vetoed this hideous plan, Corinne who has acted better than I can possibly say throughout, cordially backing me up and he was buried in Greenwood [in the Roosevelt plot] beside those who are associated with only his sweet innocent youth, when no more loyal, generous, brave, disinterested fellow lived.

All his old friends came to the funeral; the church was filled; it was very very sad and behind it followed the usual touch of the grotesque and terrible, for in one of the four carriages that followed to the grave went the woman, Mrs. Evans and two of her and his friends, the host and hostess of the Woodbine Inn . . .

Katy Mann came in to Douglas' office with the child which she swears was his; I have no idea whether it was or not; she was a bad woman but her story may have been partly true. But we can not know.

Well, it is over now; it is fortunate it is over and we need only think of his bright youth . . . Poor Anna and poor Elliott!

For the rest of his life, TR almost never mentioned Elliott. But seeing all those empty liquor bottles beside the bed of his only brother must have made a profound impression.

Theodore Roosevelt had already suffered many tragedies in his life; he had seen his father die suddenly of stomach cancer at age forty-six and then his mother of typhoid fever at forty-eight and his first wife of Bright's disease at twenty-two, both on the same day, February 14, 1884. He couldn't blame those diseases but he could blame moral weakness and alcohol. He had witnessed close up how hard liquor had sped the ugly downfall of his brother Ellie.

LONG HOT THIRSTY SUMMER

During the sweltering summer of 1895, Commissioner Roosevelt intensified his efforts to shut down the saloons on Sunday. The more embattled he became, the louder and longer he talked about his commitment to absolute enforcement of law and order.

The small-circulation *New York Times* ran an editorial praising Roosevelt's "determined attitude" but most of the papers competed to show the people's outrage.

The *New York Herald* stationed reporters to tally figures from transit executives at the thirty-plus ferry boat and excursion lines heading to the likes of Coney Island, Staten Island, New Jersey, up-Hudson, and Connecticut, and estimated that one-quarter of the city's residents departed on Sunday. "Blue laws and blue skies conspired to attract the multitude to places where . . . the winds blow fresh and cool and where it is no sin to drink a glass of beer."

The *World* investigated whether the rest of New York State observed the Sunday law, and found that twenty-four of the twenty-nine largest cities ignored the law, either blatantly or at the side door. ALBANY'S MAYOR BLIND and NO THIRST AT NEWBURG ran typical headlines. As for the rest of the nation, the *World* found only six major cities bone dry on Sundays: Boston, Indianapolis, Kansas City, Philadelphia, Richmond, and Savannah.

In New York, thirsty citizens tried to outsmart the police, using ruses that would become popular thirty years later during Prohibition. Desperate people wandered to crowded restaurants and tried with a wink and a bit of code to finagle a drink.

For lager beer, they asked for "Weiss" beer; for whiskey, "cold tea"; for gin "plain soda"; and for Rhine wine "lemon soda." The *New York Advertiser* added: "If the drought continues, the proprietor will supply his patrons with a dictionary of the language of dry Sunday."

Desperate times called for desperate measures. A Tammany Hall politician, Colonel Tom Coakley, heard about a clever dodge: medicinal alcohol.

> Go into a drug store and tell the member of the Lucrezia Borgia
> family behind the soda water outfit that you want "Rainbow Syrup."
> Well, that licensed assassin will deal you out about three fingers of
> the rottenest whiskey this side of Flatbush. It'll keep you walking
> when you get it: you're afraid if you lay down, you'll die . . . I knew
> a man that drank some of it and he didn't do a thing but go over
> to Jersey City and stay all day. Thought he was having a good time,
> mind you, and hopped over there looking for fun. Well, when a man
> goes to New Jersey looking for fun, his mind is failing.

Beyond the jokes and clever anecdotes, the absolute proof of the crackdown's effectiveness could be measured in beer deliveries. By mid-July, a leading brewer reported that wholesale beer sales in New York City had fallen off by 92,000 quarter-kegs a week. That meant bartenders were selling about 3.6 million fewer five-cent beers every Sunday. He expected the industry to lose $4 million in revenue over the twenty-four weeks until the earliest time the legislature could reconvene in January and change the law. He estimated that 500 brewery workers would lose their jobs, and that 2,000 of the city's 8,000 saloons would fail, putting at least 4,000 bartenders out of work.

The heart of the Sunday crackdown fell along class lines. The poor couldn't afford bottled beer or liquor, couldn't chill it, and had nowhere pleasant to drink it. On the other hand, the "privileged few" could drink at their private clubs, with amenities such as bars, restaurants, reading rooms, pools, gyms, sleeping quarters. According to a tally in the *World*, 37,737 New Yorkers belonged to the city's premier clubs, including Roosevelt at the Union League, J. P. Morgan at the Century, and various other bluebloods at the Harvard Club or the Knickerbocker. Atop the white marble palace of the Metropolitan Club stood a magnificent roof garden "overlooking the Plaza and Central Park" where members and their guests enjoyed a "breeze that never reached the pedestrians on the avenue." The rich, "in easy chairs at low tables" could just ding the silver bell at the center of each table and waiters in white appeared to take their orders. Downstairs at the bar "a colored youth turned a crank to crush the ice and a mixologist concocted cocktails with dashes of cordials, liqueurs and imported bitters."

The *World* delighted in contrasting that oasis with conditions in the East Side tenements, where "the sun beat down" and turned any room into a "Russian bath"; the heat "made the water run lukewarm at the faucets," soured the milk, and "even sapped the moisture and coolness from the overnight watermelon."

Saloon owners such Mike "King" Callahan tried dodges to serve their customers. He hired carpenters to cut four new entrances to his joint: through Wing Lee's laundry on Doyers Street, through a doorway at No. 1 Doyers Street, through a paint shop, and through his "Progress" rooming-house. The plan was working well until a policeman thought he heard a cash register ring inside the saloon and noticed Wing Lee was doing a bustling "washee" business. On Sunday, July 7, at 7:30 p.m., patrolman Price barred the entrance to Wing Lee's. Callahan, who had once been a bouncer at Koster & Bials, came rushing out and cursed the officer: "I am not going to take any blank from any blankety-blank blank man." Callahan was arrested again. He sing-songed: "I suppose you want to shake Roosevelt's hand."

That same day, the owner of Quinlan's Saloon at 138 Park Row hauled all liquors, beers, and wines from his shelves and offered only soda water and sarsaparilla for sale. His sign proclaimed SOFT DRINKS ONLY; his place was packed. He was arrested twice that day and the precinct captain threatened to repeat the raid every Sunday.

Quinlan applied to Judge David McAdam for relief. The judge ruled on Friday, July 12, that selling fizzy water was not against the excise law, *but clearly violated the Sabbath law*. He quoted New York State statutes 266 and 267, which stated that food could be sold before 10 a.m. and prepared meals sold in restaurants all day Sunday but that it was forbidden to sell anything else with the exception of "prepared tobacco, fruit, confectionary, newspapers, drugs, medicines and surgical appliances." The penalty for the first offense: up to a $10 fine or imprisonment in a county jail, with escalating punishments for repeat violations.

"It is as much the duty of the police to arrest lemonade peddlers or druggists selling soda water on Sunday as it is to arrest saloon-keepers selling whiskey," explained the judge. McAdam was a Tammany Democrat with a sense of humor; he belonged to the "Thirteen Club," dedicated to defying triskaidekaphobia and to hosting dinners with coffin-lid menus, tombstone wine lists, and guests entering under stepladders.

The *Herald* explained it would now be illegal on Sunday to sell "soda water, mineral water, sarsaparilla, ginger ale, milk or buttermilk," and the paper feared the city would turn into "an arid desert" if the Roosevelt board fulfilled its promise to enforce all laws.

Newspapers now delighted in unearthing every dead-letter law imaginable to show the absurdity of Roosevelt's doctrinaire enforcement of *all* laws: no barber poles taller than five feet; no kite-flying south of 14th Street; no boarding a streetcar in motion (arrest half the men in the city); no placing of flower pots on windowsills (arrest half the women); no fishing off docks on Sunday (arrest the boys); no 5 p.m. opening of delicatessens to serve the "comfortable classes" who give their servants Sunday nights off; no ball playing within two miles of a church service on any day.

The *World* pointed out that it was illegal to bring oysters into New York City from May 1 to September 1 and wondered why Commissioner Roosevelt did not arrest Delmonico's for wanton violations. The fine was five dollars for the first hundred bi-valves and two dollars every hundred thereafter. Why weren't all beggars booked? Why could peddlers shout morning and night? What about Sunday organ grinders? The editors, perusing the 2,323-page New York State Revised Statutes, discovered that cursing was punishable by a dollar fine. ("Under this law, no doubt many millionaires have rendered themselves liable to the forfeiture of their entire fortunes.") They found it illegal to have a deck of playing cards in a college or on a ship. "The average citizen . . . has been leading a life of crime," the paper pointed out.

More ominously for the city's poorest workers, almost all sidewalk street vendors apparently lacked the proper licenses. Tens of thousands of New York's hardest-working citizens, those selling newspapers and flowers, suddenly feared the police would shut them down.

Roosevelt confided to Henry Cabot Lodge: "It is an awkward and ugly fight, yet I am sure I am right in my position and I think there is an even chance of our winning on it."

Around this time, he received the surprising news that his forty-year-old spinster sister, Bamie, would be marrying a U.S. navy man in London. Roosevelt regretted "dreadfully" that he could not attend her wedding in London, even though his sister Corinne and close friend Henry Cabot Lodge would be there. "I have plunged the [New York City] Administration into a series of fights," wrote Roosevelt. "To leave now would be to flinch; when you appreciate the situation here you will be the first to say that I could not honorably have left."

Roosevelt was growing used to attacks by newspapers, but almost no elected officials had dared to criticize him directly for enforcing the law. Then, one of the most prominent Democratic politicians in the state did just that in an open letter to the press. David B. Hill—a two-time former governor and current United States senator, and a Democrat not aligned with Tammany Hall—complained about the "narrow, harsh and unreasonable construction" of the law "now being enforced by the busy-body and notoriety-seeking Police Commissioners."

He argued that the Police Board's interpretation also made it illegal for people to hand a glass of wine to a friend in their homes on Sundays, or have a drink at a private club. He demanded that if the police commissioners were lenient enough to allow drinks at, say, a clubhouse, then they should be equally lenient regarding drinks with meals all over town. "A glass of beer with a few crackers in a humble restaurant is just as much of a poor man's lunch or meal on Sunday as is Mr. Roosevelt's elaborate champagne dinner at the Union League Club on the same day."

Hill advised against asking the Republican governor to call an immediate special session of the legislature because "the Puritans are 'in the saddle' now both in Albany and in New York City" and would not change the law. Not surprisingly, he advocated electing Democrats to fix the law.

The *World* on Monday gave Hill's attack favorable front-page coverage, and added sidebars about the reform police arresting boys for selling candy on Sunday. It dug up more forgotten laws and hammered on the issue of selling seltzer.

Hill's words and the *World*'s coverage lit Roosevelt's fuse. "It is a waste of time for the criminal classes and their allies to try to prevent us from enforcing the vital laws by raising a clamor that we are not enforcing other laws of less importance."

Pulitzer's newspaper was furious that Roosevelt lumped together all who opposed Sunday closings as villains, and the *World* called him "a little tin Czar" in an editorial and wondered what entitled him to judge one law more "vital" than another.

On the evening of Tuesday, July 16, Theodore Roosevelt stood in an obscure, overcrowded hall in Harlem, aiming to rebut the naysayers. He not only gave a rousing speech but took a surprisingly meaningful baby step onto the national stage of politics. His oratory captured his core values and hammered his law-and-order message—and it was picked up by many newspapers around the country.

The night began inauspiciously enough. Both Commissioners Roosevelt and Parker were running late. Six policemen tried to control an overflow crowd of at least 300 people packing the hall of a Good Government Club in East Harlem at 115th Street near Lexington Avenue. Hundreds of others milled outside; the ground-floor rooms "were as full as an L [train] at six o'clock and as hot as a bake shop." Perspiring well-dressed men sat elbow to elbow, whispering.

After almost an hour's delay, the club's leaders, Dr. Robert Kunitzer and Gustave H. Schwab, opened the meeting with speeches in German. The city coroner followed. Beloved but almost mascot-like at four feet ten with thick glasses and a thick German accent, sixty-two-year-old Dr. Emile Hoeber said he had great respect for "Rousss-ah-velt" but that no "policeman should spy around and entrap people to sell him a glass of beer." Loud applause filled the room. "What is right in the Union Club is not wrong in Terrace Garden; what is right in the Century Club is not wrong on the Bowery." More hearty applause. Around this time, Commissioners Roosevelt and Parker inched their way forward to the podium. Dr. Hoeber observed that a groundswell was building to repeal the Sunday law. "I know many Americans *who are as enlightened as any Germans* who are opposed to it." He uttered that final sentence "as solemn as an undertaker," according to the *World,* and received a huge unexpected laugh.

Dr. Kunitzer then introduced Commissioner Roosevelt, who received sustained clapping. (Except for the excise issue, the Good Government clubs were thrilled to have a reform administration in power.) Roosevelt turned to Dr. Hoeber. He said the doctor's remarks contrasting Germans and American-born citizens made him want to emphasize something before he began his prepared speech. "I come here to speak caring nothing for your creed or your birthplace," he said slowly. "I speak as one American to his fellow-Americans."

Then Roosevelt—with great enthusiasm, with his staccato hand gestures and broad smiles—painted a picture of the United States as an all-embracing land where the native-born and foreign-born citizens work together to elect officials in fair elections to pass laws that would be equally enforced on rich and poor, where fair play and hard work are rewarded.

Roosevelt excoriated Senator Hill for in any way advocating that city officials should ignore a clear-cut law closing saloons. "A more humiliating position was never taken by a public man," he said. "The question is merely: Are the laws to be enforced? The question to me is so simple, so easily answered, that I can hardly understand how any man who is both honest and intelligent, can fail to give us his support." Roosevelt stated any law selectively enforced "demoralizes" the community. "It is not possible to give the young a more dangerous impression than that the law has side-doors or back-doors."

He said this Sunday law was the single biggest corrupting influence on the police force; he promised that in future weeks, as manpower allowed, the police would tackle other ignored laws, such as Sunday soda water sales or street vendor licenses. He also vowed that enforcing Sunday excise laws would never deter the force from catching burglars or suppressing riots.

He struck again at his main theme: he and his fellow commissioners took seriously their oath to enforce the law "honestly and impartially." He said their opponents wanted to cherry-pick laws. Exercising his growing penchant for extreme rhetoric, he compared them to "lynchers and white-cappers" (i.e., white-hooded Klansmen) who claim that "popular sentiment" allows them to hang and mutilate Negroes accused of crimes. "For an official to permit violation of law whenever he thinks that the sentiment of a particular locality does not favor its enforcement inevitably leads to anarchy and violence."

Roosevelt hailed the movement that had swept reformers into office. He said it was a slur that some claimed this Sunday crackdown was motivated by race hatred or prejudice or class differences. "I am incapable of discriminating against any man . . . so long as he is honest and a good American citizen."

The hall erupted in cheers.

In those days, speech makers often supplied copies of their speeches in advance to newspapers. Roosevelt was certain that he had written a very fine speech, his cannon shot back at Senator Hill, at the *World*, at the "criminals and their allies." His words were reprinted around the country, especially in newspapers favoring reform. To many regions—far from "dry" New York— his vision of absolute unflinching law and order sounded desirable and plausible and very American.

He received a telegram from Senator George F. Hoar of Massachusetts. "Your speech is the best speech that has been made on this continent for thirty years. I am glad that I know that there is a man behind it worthy of the speech."

The implication was that it was the best oration since Abraham Lincoln. Roosevelt wrote that Sunday to his pal Lodge, the other senator from Massachusetts, "that was pretty good for the old man" and he was "greatly flattered." Letters of support began pouring in . . . even some from New York City.

The crackdown continued, with renewed zeal. Bushy-whiskered captain George S. Chapman, one of the rare reform zealots among the highest-ranking police officers, sneaked into a cellar under a saloon on Sunday, July 21, and poked open the trap door with his nightstick. Patrons stood on the door, until he threatened to shoot them off. Patrolman O'Malley grabbed one Cornelius McCarthy near a saloon carrying a pitcher of beer. "I'll sit in the electric chair before giving you a drop of this beer," shouted McCarthy. He was arrested.

"King" Callahan came up for a license hearing in front of the excise board in the wake of his two arrests. Roosevelt's favorite, young officer Bourke, testified against him. But Callahan had brought 200 neighborhood supporters and after the first few witnesses—including a female Christian missionary who called the bar more "orderly" than others nearby—the Tammany-friendly excise board cut off testimony and unanimously renewed Callahan's license. Callahan, in the flush of victory, told a reporter he was most proud that he had punched Bourke in the face. Excise commissioner Julius Harburger later commented that the reform movement should "raise its voice against this wholly un-American doctrine of subjecting the people to a system of espionage and restraint unprecedented in the history of our great city."

Roosevelt had promised to start cracking down on soda water sales, but calmer members of the board found a loophole so the shiny silver spigots could continue dispensing seltzer in drugstores. Parker noticed that the "syrups" that were often added made the drink "confectionary" and therefore legal under the Sunday sweets exemption. No one chose to ponder too deeply about plain seltzer.

Maybe it was the "lynchers" line, maybe it was thirst in humid July, but TR's speech and stance brought a renewed flurry of ridicule from his opponents.

The *Herald* described Sunday in Manhattan as "Roosevelt's Deserted Island." Tammany Hall veteran Colonel Tom Coakley used a circus metaphor for the *Washington Post*: "Roosevelt don't know how to lift the canvas and let his friends in and out." Cartoonists portrayed him as a buckle-shoed Puritan out with a lantern looking for sinners.

Town Topics complained: "New York is rapidly becoming a jay and hayseed village such as had the supreme felicity of giving birth to Dr. Parkhurst."

The turmoil energized Roosevelt, who sounded defiant in all his letters, but it also was beginning to wear him down. Edith wrote of her husband having a nagging chest cold and indigestion, and that the midnight strolls, with forty hours awake, had taken a toll. "For some time he has had such a worn and tired look as if he really needed rest that I hardly knew what to do about it," she wrote to sister-in-law Bamie in England. "Every night that he is at home he is in bed before 10 o'clock."

Roosevelt tried to move out to Oyster Bay for the summer but found the one- to two-hour commute each way by bike, train, ferry, train, and foot too grueling. Also, he would have to leave the office at 4:30 p.m. to catch the last train, so he was staying one or two weeknights at Bamie's empty house in the city. Edith, however, discovered drawbacks in that arrangement as well. "If he spends a night alone in town, he comes back to Sagamore so worried and fussed that it is some time before he calms down." She devised a fix.

"Edith, of course, persists in regarding me as a frail invalid needing constant attention," he wrote to Lodge, "and when I spend a night or two in town, she comes and spends it with me. In one way, however, I think this does her good because she gets away from the children and usually spends a quiet day in the Society Library."

———

The four-man Police Board until then had remained remarkably unified despite newspaper attempts to organize feuds. And it wasn't Sunday saloons that split them.

It was the Eakins trial, which was entering its third month, racking up large clerical expenses, and devouring swaths of the commissioners' time.

On Friday, August 2, Joseph Eakins, resplendent in gold-braided uniform, entered the witness box. Despite the open windows, the trial room was stiflingly hot; pitchers of water, infrequently replenished with ice, stood in one corner. Spectators cramming onto the benches made the room even stuffier.

The verdict, to be decided by the panel of four reform commissioners, looked like a foregone conclusion. Eakins wasn't even on trial for accepting bribes, but merely for failing to close brothels in the well-known brothel district, Frenchtown. Lincoln Steffens in the *Evening Post* called the case the "strongest and most hopeless" against a captain, with police insiders rating Eakins "as a goner," especially after the ample early testimony about "scores of houses of assignation." Also, Eakins's precinct had stayed bad after even the notorious 11th (Devery's Lower East Side) and the 19th (Tenderloin) had been significantly cleaned up.

But Joseph Eakins—a captain for two decades, one of the highest-ranking Freemasons in the city, a Civil War veteran—saw it differently. Indignant at the self-righteous questions hurled by Parkhurst's Frank Moss, the captain stated repeatedly that he had worked very hard to stop prostitution. He blamed certain judges for demanding that two different officers on two different days pay for and witness nudity before they would issue a warrant. He blamed Superintendent Byrnes for telling him not to list any suspected brothels. He asserted that his men had performed seventy raids during his eighteen months in the precinct. He displayed a thorough knowledge of the neighborhood, leading the listeners in the courtroom on a tour, building by building, mentioning names, nicknames, occupations, family histories. He confided that sometimes the most effective method of fighting vice was for him to go to the landlady and say to her: "You have got one of those daisies up here on the third floor, and you had better get rid of her or I will take you over to court."

He pointed out that one officer had made 468 arrests for street solicitation. He also said he worried about the accidental arrest of a respectable woman. "One mistake of that kind would do more damage than arresting a thousand of the others." He noted that very few men wanted the job of investigating prostitution because they were called "whorehouse detectives" and worse. In any case, his undercover men often became recognized, especially on Thompson Street. "Those colored wenches are just like a dog, they know a policeman just as far as they can see him whether he is in civilian's clothes or in uniform."

Prosecutor Moss wasn't buying any of it; he brought out the fact that most of those streetwalkers arrested had paid five dollars each to be bailed out by a 3rd Street saloon owner named Gus Blumenthal, and that most of the women were never convicted. He uncovered that Captain Eakins had never pursued a single landlord. Most damning of all, he maneuvered Eakins into admitting that he and his undercover officers knew the exact whereabouts of brothels. Moss continued to hammer the point block by block.

MOSS: You and Zimmerman knew the location of the tainted houses, didn't you?

EAKINS: Of course, we did.

MOSS: And talked them over?

EAKINS: I cannot say we had any particular conversations about them.

MOSS: He told you what he discovered?

EAKINS: I had something else to talk about except whorehouses. I had other police business to talk about and I did not spend all my time talking about whorehouses. Now that is all. I done the best I could.

The angry word *whorehouse* echoed in the hot courtroom but of course never made the newspapers.

When he calmed down, Eakins stressed that he did a fine job. "Law and order was my motto; I spent 18 hours out of 24 there." And he told Moss that he didn't know of any other organization besides Parkhurst's "that would do anything like what your Society has done."

MOSS: What do you mean by that?

EAKINS: Making charges of this kind against me.

MOSS (with sarcasm): You think this is a crime?

EAKINS: I think it is a crime and you cannot blame me for it.

Around 7:45 p.m., after a very long day, during a brief break as the testimony was winding down, Captain Eakins walked over to the pitchers and poured himself a glass of ice water and when he returned his eyes were red, almost brimming with tears. Commissioner Grant, who had stayed largely silent, noticed that and stepped in to ask Captain Eakins a few questions.

GRANT: How old are you?

EAKINS: Fifty-one.

GRANT: How long have you been on the force?

EAKINS: 29 years.

GRANT: And you have had only two charges preferred against you?

EAKINS: Both dismissed.

Grant, always sympathetic to military veterans, then asked what real estate Eakins owned and found out he had a 125th Street building, valued at $24,000, but a mortgage of $12,000 on it. He had rental tenants on the top floors of his home.

GRANT: That $12,000 represents the savings of 29 years?

EAKINS: That and about $2,000 more.

GRANT: How much has the trial cost you?

Lawyer Charles Hess said, "Tell the commissioner, I have no objection; in fact I am very glad he asked the question."

The tears brimmed again. The *New York Journal* claimed several spilled down Eakins's cheek.

EAKINS: I have paid $1,000 to the stenographer and $3,000 to Mr. Hess.

GRANT: That is a quarter of your life savings, is it not?

EAKINS: (*faintly*) Yes, sir.

GRANT: I think I heard you say that you thought this trial was a crime. Did you not say that?

EAKINS: I did.

Commissioner Grant rose from his seat, slowly buttoning his frock coat. "Well, I agree with you," he said, then walked out of the room. The phrase lingered in the air.

Commissioner Andrews and prosecutor Moss looked at each other in stunned silence. Hess came over and patted Eakins on the shoulder.

———

Grant's words split the board for the first time. Roosevelt was "astounded" when he read them in a newspaper the next morning. So was Parker.

Grant arrived first at 300 Mulberry on Saturday morning for the board's usual half day and was unrepentant. He answered the newspapermen's questions. He said not only was it a "crime" to bring charges against Captain Eakins, but that he thought Eakins deserved to be promoted to inspector. He blamed himself for not "sifting" through the charges more thoroughly. He apologized that he was "not a good talker" but he still stood by his words.

Grant regarded it as impossible for a police captain to clean up some districts and he found it absolutely intolerable to ask respectable plainclothes officers to go into brothels to witness immoral acts. "I would not do it if I were a policeman."

Grant spent most of the day holed up in his office working on a plan to merge the steamboat squad and the harbor patrol; he expected to free up sixty-one officers for other duties.

Parker, Andrews, and Roosevelt did not seek out Commissioner Grant; they met privately from 3 p.m. to 5 p.m., drafting a statement.

At 5 p.m. Commissioner Parker read their breathless, angry joint statement to the press.

"We deeply regret the necessity of making public the circumstances attending any difference of opinion among us as Commissioners but as Commissioner Grant, one of the judges of Captain Joseph B. Eakins, now on trial, has seen fit, while so sitting as judge, and during the pendency of the hearing, publicly to announce his opinion of the inquiry, and, without having heard the evidence, to declare beforehand his verdict and inferentially to designate his colleagues as criminals, we consider it our duty to make public the following facts."

They pointed out that Grant had personally signed the paperwork against Eakins on May 28, adding—a bit cattily—that Grant once said he would vote to dismiss without even reading the voluminous trial record (already 3,000 pages) and that he had seemed to grow *more,* not less, convinced of Eakins's guilt. The trio estimated that Colonel Grant had heard less than 10 percent of the testimony, a low water mark shared by only Roosevelt, but the statement stressed that Roosevelt "has not given an opinion." They also alluded to the fact that Grant had been approached by Eakins for sympathy as they were both Republicans, war veterans, and Methodists. The three commissioners said they were not to blame for Eakins's trial expenses, and they, for their part, all promised to read and carefully weigh all the evidence before rendering a decision. This statement was also clearly aimed at any appeals judges.

Roosevelt, who had nodded emphatically during the reading, dashed for his train to Oyster Bay; he invited Commissioner Andrews to join him.

Reporters raced from the boardroom to Commissioner Grant's office to read him the joint statement. He seemed dazed and disappointed, calling it "not a fair interpretation." Grant repeated that he meant no slight on his colleagues and considered them "gentlemen of the highest order." He said his earlier comment about voting Eakins guilty without reading several thousand pages had been a "joke."

That night a reporter for the *Herald* knocked on Grant's door on 62nd Street. "I spoke perhaps with more warmth than I should have," said the commissioner. "It seemed to me a piteous thing that a man of near 30 years service should be deprived of a third of the savings of his life through no fault of his." Grant also resented the prosecution's tone, and he repeated that he would vote for acquittal. "If my means permitted it, I would refund to the Captain all the costs of his trial for I realize he has been put to this great expense through my fault."

———

On Monday morning at 10:45 a.m. as the scheduled board meeting was about to begin, Commissioner Grant requested a private meeting with Board President Roosevelt. The two men remained in TR's office for almost three hours. When they left the room, Colonel Grant looked grim and Roosevelt was perspiring.

While announcing he had no intention of resigning, Grant did issue a partial apology. "I admit it was wrong to express my feelings in the Eakins matter at the time I did . . . It was injudicious for me to do so but I said what I felt and gave expression without thinking." But he said he still believed Eakins should not have gone to trial.

All four commissioners attended the long-delayed board meeting and put on a brave show of harmony. "I am sorry that all of you reporters have been disappointed," Roosevelt said as the meeting ended, "if you expected a sensation here today."

From then on, all four commissioners tried to downplay the incident. Roosevelt, however, was extremely candid about it in a later letter to Henry Cabot Lodge.

Grant is a good-natured, brave, generous fellow but he is certainly very dull and at times very obstinate, and his wife makes him very jealous of me. Moreover he is inflated to a very extraordinary degree with the idea of his own powers and his career in the future. He told me he thought it a "degradation" that he, who had been Minister to Austria, should accept this Police Commissionership; and only his good nature and genuine sterling honesty save him from being intolerable. All of his bad qualities combined with one good quality, his sympathy for an old soldier in distress, to make him go wrong in the Eakins business. I had treated him with extreme deference and gentleness up to that time. I thought it necessary then to give him a thorough dressing down. So all three of us joined, publicly first, and afterwards privately, to *give him the plainest talking to that I have ever taken part in; I told him the exact truth. For forty-eight hours he was furious; but it had a most healthy effect. He has been entirely tractable ever since. He will, undoubtedly from time to time, make very foolish breaks and will leave us on important issues, and especially when we come to make war on some corruptionist; but he has neither the wit nor the wickedness to go into a course of steady opposition to us. Indeed I think he rather likes me and wishes to work with me.*

But Roosevelt misread his man. He would learn that he had inflicted a deeper wound than he realized and that Grant—in very crucial moments— would be primed to split off from him.

———

The August heat made those thirsty on Sunday even testier. Roosevelt's righteous, unbending stance provoked many. A suspicious package arrived at the post office Monday addressed to "Mr. Theodore Roosevelt." A young female postal inspector performing her routine job of inspecting Fourth Class mail for illegally enclosed letters and contraband opened the five-inch by two-inch by two-inch box. As she slid off the wooden cover, three parlor matches hit a sandpaper strip and sent up a curl of smoke.

She screamed and called a supervisor. Inside he found a two-and-a-half-inch-long gun cartridge, with an Irish shamrock glued to it. Two police detectives carried the package to the inspector of combustibles, who observed that the cartridge shell was filled with an odd light-colored powder. "Inspector Murray pinched it, thumped it, smelled it and tasted it on suspicion that it might have nitroglycerin in it, and then solemnly said: 'Saw dust!'" The assembled officers laughed.

When Roosevelt was told of the "infernal machine," he flashed his piano-key grin and said, "I don't care a snap of my fingers for any bomb." The *World* ran a front-page cartoon showing TR holding an exploding cigar-shaped bomb in his teeth; he stands unharmed in a dapper outfit with a sash while two of his three colleagues lie near-dead on the floor and all that can be seen of Grant are the soles of his shoes, as he has been blown out the window.

The Eakins trial resumed at 2:45 p.m. that Monday afternoon for the final day of testimony. Avery Andrews presided and the other three commissioners stayed safely out of the room. The Parkhurst Society unveiled a secret witness they had been hiding for almost two weeks: streetwalker Gertie Long. Long had told the Society that she had been paying off cops in the 15th Precinct for more than twelve years.

Gertie Long was a "stout, gaudily dressed woman." She wore a pinch-waist striped dress with puffy sleeves, high collar, hem to the floor, and a flouncy hat with three cascading plumes; she had on gold and diamond ear-rings and rings and a glittering heart-shaped brooch. She also wore a veil until defense attorney Hess asked her to remove it. She admitted to hav-ing celebrated her fortieth birthday but grew irritated at repeated questions about her forty-first.

The more she testified, the clearer became her motives. She had been double-crossed by her police protectors and now she was furious . . . furious enough to risk her life and livelihood to testify. During the previous year's Lexow hearings, the police had begged her not to appear before the com-mittee—"Officer Schick is not sleeping nights," she was told; brothel keeper Jennie Moran pleaded with her not to disrupt business for them all—and the police had promised to go easy on her, but the day after the Lexow Com-mittee had adjourned, the shakedowns began anew and were harsher than before. Besides Officer Schick demanding his usual $2.50 a week for granting her the privilege of streetwalking in the Fifteenth, he sometimes surprised her in the sleet and snow of January and threatened her: "I'm going to pound you" or "The Old Man [i.e., the captain] is right around the corner." It was always about handing over more money.

Then just recently, in May, she fell ill (she called it "rheumatism") and couldn't work for two weeks. When she returned to the streets, the cops immediately wanted money and she said she didn't have it. She refused to pay them and they kept at her until they arrested her two weeks ago, on July 21. Plainclothes officer Schick hauled her to the precinct house and she said she was screaming that cops were shaking her down for one dollar a night; she said Captain Eakins stood in the doorway and heard all of it but did nothing. She threatened to go to the Parkhurst Society.

When she said "Parkhurst," Officer Schick and Officer Zimmerman got mad and told her if she didn't start paying again, they'd "throw her down with the niggers" and she'd get "railroaded" to Blackwell's Island. When released the next day, she nonetheless went to the Parkhurst offices. Agent Arthur "Angel" Dennett took her statement, carefully hid her, and now deliv-ered her to police headquarters for the Eakins trial.

Between Prosecutor Moss's gentle guiding and defense lawyer Hess's aggressive grilling, Gertie Long painted an extensive picture of the life of a streetwalker in the 1890s and of the crooked cops who profited from her. (Most of her testimony was too risqué for newspapers to publish.)

Gertie Long started working each night around 7:30 p.m. and continued till midnight. She charged two, three, or five dollars, whatever she could hustle, her highest being $17 once; she averaged three or four customers a night, but some Saturday nights went with six or seven different men. She generally took her clients to "Daly's Hotel," which was not a licensed establishment but rather a bunch of rooms over a carpenter's shop at 50 East 13th Street. The place charged one dollar for an hour and kicked back fifty cents to the prostitute. In that era before photo identification, the desk clerk required every man to sign a name into the ledger, and Gertie always made sure to whisper to him to add "and wife." Many nights four different Mr. Smiths signed her in.

She said she paid the "fly cops" (i.e., the plainclothes cops) varying amounts at various times: Zimmerman ("$2.50 a week"), O'Rourke ($5 a week), Durrigan, Gilmartin, Schick, and others.

PROSECUTOR MOSS: What were those payments made for?
GERTIE LONG: To let you alone on the street and to take the other
    girls that was in your way that didn't pay.

Gertie Long testified that not all of the fifty or so regular streetwalkers in the precinct had to pay to work. The "copper girls" such as Chicago Lil and Irish Lelia were exempt. What was a "copper girl"? Gertie Long at first answered a bit vaguely: "women that is in with officers." She mentioned that Officer Jimmie Durrigan had one for six years and kept her even after he got married; Officer Zimmerman had Sadie Green. Roundsman Foody even had one.

Gertie later clarified: "The [cops] have got their fling on these women." The expression "have a fling with" means "to have the pleasure of, to sow wild oats with." In case any confusion remained, lawyer Hess later asked whether "copper women" were "intimate with the policemen?" Yes, sir. "They have them girls that they can go to see."

Another perk for the women of these officers was that unlike the others they could leave the side streets and trawl prime Fifth Avenue for clients.

Also, when the officers needed to make some token arrests to raise precinct statistics, they never chose their own women. Gertie, no longer in her prime, seemed to resent these girls' privileges.

She also recounted that she had been arrested about a dozen times; each time the aftermath involved some kind of payoff to someone. One arresting officer said she could avoid sleeping in the jail if she paid five dollars for bail, and he rounded up a saloon keeper to take her money and sign the papers. She also paid five dollars to "Blumenthal" twice. Another time, $15 got her thirty-day sentence on the Island terminated on day one.

This past winter the cops had frequently hassled her. Officer Zimmerman cornered her one night and dragged her into the shadows by Denning's Dry Goods store. (He was a big strong "Hebrew" officer who sometimes forced his way into neighborhood brothels for "flings.") "I was always afraid of him," Gertie admitted. "How much coin ya got?" he snapped. And though she had $70, she told him $5 and he said, "Five dollars aint in it." So she took off her diamond ring and told him to hold it. She said she'd meet him the next night, give him another five dollars, and then he'd give the ring back. In the courtroom she showed off the ring, bought from a Mrs. Friedman, in 1887.

Gertie Long said the unwritten rule was that it was not okay to solicit customers if you saw the captain. She said Captain Eakins personally cleared out 13th Street about twice a month. The streetwalkers would scurry to another block until some scout reported him gone. She admitted she never knew anyone who paid money directly to Eakins. "I am not against the captain but against those men that took the money from me, those hounds."

Defense lawyer Hess tried to trip her up on details.

Gertie Long repeatedly held her own in exchanges with Hess.

She called testifying the "first dirty thing I have ever done" despite twenty years of streetwalking. She said she always wanted to quit the business but the cops kept taking her savings. She estimated she had shelled out about $8,000 to the police over the years. "How are you going to be respectable when you give those fellows the money you make?"

She vowed she would never take any hush money from the cops. "I meant to come down here, if they would hang me, [to speak] against those hounds." Lawyer Hess, a bit ominously, asked her if she would wait to confer with him after the session ended. She agreed. Was it to offer her money? Was it to give her a warning or to allow someone time to come to 300 Mulberry to follow her?

Gertie Long never testified again; she does not appear again in the indexes of the *New York Times, New York Tribune,* or *New York Evening Post.* Police officers Schick, Zimmerman, and Durrigan appear in print as police officers for many years in the future.

———

The Sunday saloon crackdown only grew tighter for the poor. The private clubs—on the advice of their attorneys—decided to ignore it. The issue was polarizing the city, with temperance, women's rights, and church groups staunchly supporting Roosevelt; and Tammany Hall, immigrants, and thousands of men opposing.

More than 20,000 members of the Catholic Total Abstinence Union converged on the city for its annual convention, selling out Carnegie Hall on Wednesday, August 7. Archbishop Corrigan and other high-ranking religious officials shared the dais with the mayor and dozens of officials including Roosevelt.

The bland meeting took a sudden turn when one-armed state senator T. C. O'Sullivan (Democrat) had the nerve to enter the lion's den and criticize the city's Sunday crackdown. He complained about the Puritans' gloomy Sunday in New York, which he claimed discriminated against the poor. He was hissed. He analyzed the law and the police's rigid enforcement. He was hissed. He painted a scene of poor men now buying bottles of hard liquor and "on Sunday in the presence of youth and innocence, the home becomes the scene of a debauchery darker by far with iniquity than the disorder which before flourished at the saloon or in the streets, within reach of the law."

Throughout the speech Roosevelt grimaced in anger and bobbed his head, restless to respond.

The catcalls and hisses grew so loud near the end of the speech that the archbishop called for a song to restore calm. All rose to sing "While We Are Marching for Temperance" to the tune of "Marching Through Georgia."

Roosevelt was introduced next. With his staccato gestures, he delivered the pithiest points of his stump speech. He said he would rather fail enforcing the laws than succeed by ignoring them; he praised the Catholic Church for its work for temperance and for decent observation of the Sabbath. "Never in the memory of any man have the saloons been closed as we have closed them."

He painted a rosy future for dry Sundays in New York. "I hope to see the time when a man shall be ashamed to take any enjoyment on Sunday which shall rob those who should be dearest to him and are dependent on him of the money he has earned during the week, when a man will be ashamed to take a selfish enjoyment and not to find some kind of pleasure which he can share with his wife and child."

The 7,000 people in the hall erupted in cheers that lasted five full minutes.

Commissioner Parker rushed over and shook his hand, as did the bishops. Women climbed onto their seats and "howled" with praise. "Never in my life did I receive such an ovation," TR enthused in a letter to Lodge.

———

Although Roosevelt repeatedly tried to declare victory in the Sunday shutdown, several newspapers, notably the *World* on Monday, August 12, claimed any New Yorker and most tourists could easily find a drink at about three-quarters of the city's 8,000 saloons on Sundays. "Individual members of the police force in every precinct admitted that the Roosevelt experiment had failed." The newspaper claimed the city was "as wet as before Commissioner Roosevelt snapped his teeth." It said bar owners manned side doors, scrutinized for regulars, and did a quiet thriving business. The *Washington Post* chimed in with a similar story, quoting "Copper Jim," a New York policeman. "The saloons and the hotels, raked in more long green and shoved more red liquor across their bars last Sunday than any day except Patrick's in the year."

———

Roosevelt decided to find out for himself.

He cut short his weekend escape and returned on Sunday, August 18, from Sagamore Hill, taking the ferry from Long Island City to 34th Street and arriving at 10 a.m. Roundsman Michael Tierney was waiting for him and had a closed carriage with a top-hatted driver ready. Inside sat Jacob Riis, who as a "personal friend" had agreed to write up the tour "at Roosevelt's request" for the *New York Evening Sun*.

The trio embarked on a whirlwind inspection. Beyond whirlwind. They would spend seven and a half of the next nine hours inside the vehicle, traveling from as far north as 71st Street to the southern tip of the Battery and zigzagging three times east and west, driving by 728 saloons.

Roosevelt and his companions first headed north along First Avenue past the slaughterhouses where butchers were sawing carcasses to deliver fresh meat for Monday. Riis, who relayed Roosevelt's opinions in his *Evening Sun* article, noted that butchers were supposed to be brawny men and "proverbial beer drinkers" but the saloons there were shut tight. Instead, the three observers "everywhere encountered a contented good humored crowd." Riis said when Roosevelt was recognized, he received mostly "respectful and admiring glances" with some occasional good-natured kidding.

They drove to Louis Gobhardt's saloon at 999 First Avenue and Roundsman Tierney thought the woman and child on the nearby stoop might be lookouts. Before the carriage reached the end of the block, they saw men entering a side door. TR dispatched a message to the precinct to send an officer.

Roosevelt came armed with the names of three saloons in the brewery district he wanted to check: Smith's at 69th Street and Second Avenue, Rooney's at 70th Street and Second Avenue, and another at 71st Street and Third Avenue. All three seemed a little suspicious, with crowds nearby, and TR had extra officers sent to walk there.

The carriage stopped at the 21st Precinct house at East 35th Street. As the sergeant "prattled" on about the effectiveness of the men, Roosevelt noticed the captain's Sunday saloon report on the desk. It stated: "From personal observation, together with the reports of the patrolmen on various posts and from the men I have detailed in citizen's clothes I find the law was uniformly enforced and well-observed." The report was dated Monday, August 19. The current time was Sunday, August 18, 11:55 a.m. Roosevelt took the "premature" update and didn't smile while the sergeant pointed out the blank lines remaining to note violations.

During the tour, TR exited the carriage to visit eleven station houses, got out to try the doors of three saloons, and ate lunch at Mike Lyons.

Roosevelt especially sought out several saloons that had promised to fight the shutdown: Murphy's on 23rd Street and First Avenue and another Murphy's on 20th Street and Second Avenue. The first Murphy's, its doors wide open, gave out free ice water. The second was shut tight. Tompkins Square, ringed by saloons, was crowded "with mothers and their babes . . . men sat and smoked on benches."

The Roosevelt carriage rolled on south into Devery's old 11th Precinct, where Polish and Russian names abounded, where overcrowding would create the most thirst. "Small beer saloons fairly teem among the tenements," noted Riis. He and TR—neither shy of hyperbole—found that the poor people "seemed never so happy or content as on the one midsummer day in their experience when the saloons were closed."

Roosevelt saw the clearing of Mulberry Bend with the buildings leveled to make room for a park; he saw an Italian selling watermelon and gelato. The group swung down through Chinatown and Roosevelt ordered the driver to stop in front of Mike Callahan's saloon. He alighted and tried the door, put his ear to the wall, and walked around to ensure that Mike was not doing business. He was quite pleased.

Roosevelt viewed the hundreds of closed Sunday saloons as an "unconditional surrender" by the saloon keepers and reveled in seeing "the raising of their blinds everywhere in token of submission."

In conclusion, Riis stated that peering out the window, they found 684 of the 728 saloons "shut tight," 41 open to "possibly doing business," and saw men enter only three drinking joints during the entire trip; they observed only one drunk and saw no one carrying liquor through the streets.

"The stories printed by some of the newspapers about the general failure of the police to close the saloons on Sunday have been comically untrue," TR later commented. He ate dinner at 689 Madison that Sunday night with Edith and Riis and burly roundsman Tierney. They relished what they had seen. Roosevelt had been *very privately* leaning toward supporting some kind of limited Sunday saloon opening, maybe four hours a day, but he changed his mind. "I have now begun to think that we ought not to have the saloons open on Sunday," Roosevelt confided in a letter to Lodge, "and that all we need . . . is to alter certain of its provisions so as to make it easier to enforce." He was considering lobbying the legislature to require saloon curtains to be drawn open on Sundays.

———

The Liquor Dealers' Association concocted a devious new strategy to fight Roosevelt; they would exercise their legal right to demand a jury trial for each of the hundreds of pending excise cases, shifting them out of the Court of Special Sessions.

At the new venue, a grand jury would have to be convened to review each case and opt whether to indict, a jury would have to be empaneled, the case would be tried, and then Recorder John Goff—elected in the 1894 reform tidal wave to replace Tammany's Smyth—would have to pass sentence on the convicted. The process was hugely time-consuming, and usually reserved for serious crimes such as murder. "Cleopatra's needle will have crumbled and the bones of the violators will be dust before they could all be heard," sniped the New York World, with undisguised admiration. The backlog totaled 7,000 excise cases.

Recorder Goff called this flood-of-cases strategy an attempt to undermine the legal system and, with his usual flinty contrariness, vowed to fight back. He said he would open his courtroom Monday, August 19, from 9:30 a.m. to midnight and do so every day as long as needed.

Goff, with a jury conviction already in hand, sentenced Dennis Mullins, owner of four saloons who had refused to pay excise fines for his bartenders, to thirty days in the Tombs city prison and a $250 fine—and if he didn't pay it, he would have to spend three months in a state penitentiary such as Sing Sing. That was an opening shot, like a loud warning before a blast. Judge William Travers Jerome, whose court was the one being bypassed, still had some cases in the pipeline, and he and his two fellow judges intended to inflict harsh sentences.

The judges were clearly ready to slam down the gavel. "As soon as we begin to send a few of these recalcitrant saloon keepers to jail," gushed an assistant district attorney, "the accumulation of excise cases will rapidly cease."

Later on Monday, two liquor dealers—with Mullins's harsh sentence fresh in their minds—stood before Recorder Goff, waived their right to a jury trial, and pled guilty, meekly vowing never to break the excise law again. Goff, enjoying their contrition, fined them only $30 each. The lawyer for the Liquor Dealers' Association, Frederick B. House, also contrite, informed Recorder Goff there was no conspiracy to inundate his court calendar but that 90 percent of his members faced bankruptcy and were desperately trying to avoid fines. (Mortgage records indicated that the previous week marked the biggest weekly borrowing by saloons—$434,941 by 277 saloons from breweries—ever recorded.)

Lawyer House approached Judge Jerome and Recorder Goff about a deal. It was a game of chicken and the judges had shown they were ready to send liquor men to prison even if they had to keep their courtrooms working triple overtime. Fred House offered that the liquor men would stop demanding jury trials, that they would plead guilty, hoping for lower fines, and would promise to cease selling liquor on Sundays after September 1,

1895. The association represented about half the saloon owners in the city; they also expected the police to crack down on the nonmembers. The judges refused to specify the fine amount ("dignity of the court") but promised to inflict much harsher fines and prison terms after the deadline. The police agreed to crack down and follow up on any leads provided.

The Central Liquor Committee met at the law office of Friend, House, and Grossman on Thursday night, approved the deal, and scheduled it for a vote at a mass meeting on Tuesday, August 27. The saloon men—fearing TR's hounding and the judges' sentences—voted aye.

When TR was informed, he cried: "I am deeee-lighted. I'm really deee-lighted." (This marks an early instance of his irrepressible catchphrase.) TR went out of his way to thank two judges: John Goff and William Travers Jerome.

On Friday, August 30, the final day when excise violators could plead guilty, Justice Jerome set up a "Bargain Day," allowing them to pay a fine of $25 to clear their cases. Newspapers noted the courtroom that day more resembled a bank, as almost 500 liquor dealers jammed in and waited on long lines to plead and pay. The *World* reporter saw so many men fishing out small stacks of dollar bills and waving them about, he said the room took on a "distinct greenish hue." Coins jangled, piles of greenbacks grew mountainous. The court collected a one-day record $8,050 in small fines.

Judge Jerome, amidst the din, loudly and repeatedly promised $200 fines and three-month prison sentences for violations after September 1. Judge Goff mentioned up to $1,000 and one year in prison.

Just as the deal was going down, Pulitzer's *Evening World* pulled one last yellow journalism stunt, perhaps hoping to derail the saloon owner Sabbath surrender. It ran a piece about an unnamed mother trying on Sunday, August 25, to buy a five-cent chunk of ice to cool the fever of her seriously ill child. And as the unnamed iceman was handing it over, an unnamed policeman arrested them both for violating the Sabbath and hauled them off to an unnamed precinct house. The bluecoat dismissed her excuses about a sick child.

> She hurried back to the tenement where she lived. She ran upstairs and entered her room. "I was kept away and couldn't get back sooner, darling," she said. "I couldn't get the ice because . . ."
>
> Suddenly the words died on her lips. She knelt down by the bed

and took a little wasted hand in hers. Then, raising her face, she gazed up with dry eyes that yet saw nothing and whispered: "Thy will be done, O God! Thou knowest best!"

For the child was dead.

Roosevelt later read the story and was appalled by the fraud and dishonesty of the newspaper. The writer deserved the severest punishment, he said. Nothing would sully the righteousness of the reform movement's Sunday saloon victory. "I am doing my best to . . . manage [the police force] in accord with the Decalogue [Ten Commandments] and the Golden Rule," he told a political gathering. "Be assured that the principles of public honesty and public decency will win in the end."

After all the hyperbole and fireworks, Sunday, September 1, had truly ranked among the driest in New York City history. This sudden resolution of the excise battle marked a huge victory for Roosevelt.

Others around the country were observing him as well. "Undeniably Theodore Roosevelt is the 'biggest man' in New York today, if not the most interesting man in public life," enthused the *Chicago Times-Herald*.

"You are rushing so rapidly to the front that the day is not far distant when you will come into a large kingdom," wrote Henry Cabot Lodge from London, "and by that time I will probably be a back number and I shall expect you to look after me and give me a slice."

THE ELECTION

Elections loomed two months away, and would mark yet another crucial test for Police Commissioner Roosevelt. Although his name was not on the ballot, his strict policies dominated the political discussion. Would New York City voters on Tuesday, November 5, 1895, elect reform-minded candidates for the legislature and for key judgeships? Would they elect Republicans? Or would they miss their Sunday beer and stampede back to Tammany?

This local election—although the mayor would stay in office for two more years—would reveal whether the voters wanted to continue high-minded reform or preferred to backslide toward seamier, more tolerant ways.

Publicly, Roosevelt wrote in articles and repeated in forceful speeches that his law-and-order crackdown would rally voters away from Tammany. But very privately, to the likes of Cabot and Bamie, he expressed his doubts.

___

In mid-September, Republicans from every corner of New York State boarded ferries and trains and horse carriages to flood into the racetrack town of Saratoga, New York, for the convention.

One politician looked poised to dominate the September 17 event, and that man had decreed that Theodore Roosevelt be banned.

Thomas Collier Platt, a former elected official and currently the president of a shipping company, was the Republican party boss for New York State. Though largely forgotten today, Platt was matter-of-factly identified in the *Boston Daily Globe* in May of that year as "one of the half dozen best-known men in the United States." Joked a Tammany man: "When Platt takes snuff, every Republican sneezes." He was a rainmaker who by controlling New York's various representatives could sway national politics.

As American political bosses go, Platt, then sixty-two, certainly did not fit the back-slapping, domineering stereotype. His limp, damp handshake surprised well-wishers; his shy demeanor, subtle smiles, and whispered suggestions earned him the nickname "Easy Boss." But Platt had the ear—and interests—of the plutocrats of the age such as J. P. Morgan, whose contributions helped bankroll his power. Skeletal and stoop-shouldered, the former Yale divinity student from Owego, New York, made so many crucial decisions on Sundays in a corridor of the Fifth Avenue Hotel, where he stayed, that it was dubbed "Amen Corner."

Reverend Parkhurst found Tammany's boss Richard Croker an unapologetic rascal but he called Platt "such a mixture of good and bad that nobody ever knows where he stands."

Issuing orders from Cottage number 9 of the U.S. Hotel in Saratoga, Platt dictated to his minions that the name of Roosevelt should not be uttered and that the issue of Sunday excise laws should be ignored. They obeyed.

This election, like so many in the Empire State, was shaking out to be two elections: New York State races and New York City races. With its capital parked in a relative backwater, a former fur-trading post called Albany, the state in broad strokes—with the exception of upstate cities such as Buffalo and Syracuse—broke down into the homogenous churchgoing native-born upcountry folk versus the two-million-strong ethnic stew of Manhattan.

Upstate, Republicans looked poised to keep both houses of state government, although the Democrats saw an outside chance. In New York City, Tammany Hall Democrats hoped for a comeback, riding a wave of anti-Roosevelt feeling.

Since the Republicans appeared heavily favored to win statewide, Boss Platt chose to orchestrate a cautious platform packed with safe platitudes: kudos for the Republican governor, Levi Morton, darts for the Democratic president, Grover Cleveland, and . . . don't forget to blame the recent state tax hike on the cost of caring for *New York City's* vast population of mentally deficient vagrants.

Platt was convinced that Mayor Strong had reneged on preelection promises to appoint Republicans, and he dismissed Roosevelt as a strong-willed reformer.

Republican senator Henry Cabot Lodge, Roosevelt's friend and mentor, had hoped that Platt would embrace Roosevelt and Sunday saloon laws "but [Platt] is singularly lacking in political sense of the large kind." One political observer summed up Platt's philosophy as: "Whoever pushes you up the apple tree is the boy to share the apples with."

Saratoga was packed with party faithful dressed in their Sunday best, entering the hall under canopies of fall foliage. Small-town lawyers jostled big-city full-time politicians. By noon on the second day of meetings, the delegates had reached their seats for the main event. At 12:15 p.m. Platt, walking alone and slowly, entered the convention hall to band music and sustained passionate applause and foot stomping. The convention, which the *New York Times* labeled "tame, thin, indifferent," briefly flickered to life. Then it settled back into Platt's low-key script. The *World* compared Platt to a puppeteer.

A few hours later, when the topic of the party's platform—already written in committee—was brought up for ratification, half a dozen men clamored for the attention of the convention chairman, Senator Clarence Lexow. (Platt had rewarded him for his namesake committee that had helped topple Tammany the year before.) Lexow ignored them. They shouted demands to read a minority report complaining that the Sabbath and Sunday excise laws—in their view, the most important issues in the state—were being back-burnered.

Lexow, following Platt's commands, ordered the minority report tabled and was moving swiftly forward to the next item of business. The hubbub filling the hall seemed to be subsiding when from the very back, a stout mustachioed man began bellowing something, demanding to be heard. The voice of former U.S. senator Warner Miller eventually pierced the din. "There should be no gag law in this Republican meeting," he shouted.

A bit flustered, Chairman Lexow hesitated, then said there would be no gag law and granted the man the floor. Hundreds of heads swiveled toward the back. Warner Miller—a longtime supporter of temperance and the Sabbath—abruptly recited a brief resolution to add to the party platform. "We favor the maintenance of the Sunday law in the interest of labor and morality."

The puppets were rebelling against the puppetmaster.

Platt, earning his reputation as "Easy," whispered to Edward Lauterbach, the chairman of the New York County [i.e., City] Republican Committee, and Lauterbach—a Jewish corporate lawyer from New York City—stood and endorsed the resolution. "That is the sentiment to which I am sure every Republican will subscribe." Lauterbach's nickname was "Smooth Ed." (He was as anti-Roosevelt as Platt but equally pragmatic in a crisis.)

Warner Miller, an upstate churchgoing man, took the Lauterbach endorsement as his cue to make a speech. He stressed it was key for the Republican Party not to retreat from its historic values of enforcement of the law and observance of the Sabbath.

And he explained that the Democratic Party was backing an "infamous" brand of personal liberty. "That kind of liberty is opportunity to evade the laws, liberty to levy blackmail, liberty to make contracts with certain men if they support Democracy and Tammany Hall."

He drew his biggest ovation when, with more than a hint of xenophobia, he singled out the foreigners of the City as clamoring for change. "The people who come into our country must recognize our laws and our customs. The demand for liberties for these people such as they had abroad cannot be considered by the American people. We have a Sabbath that all recognize." The hall erupted in cheers.

Another Platt crony, Hamilton Fish of the platform committee, leaped to his feet and endorsed the plank. He claimed—implausibly—the committee had steered away from the issue because they thought it pertained only to New York City.

Chairman Lexow put the plank up for vote by acclamation. The convention in one full-throated voice, with plenty of foot stomping and hand clapping, added the Sunday enforcement plank to the platform. WARNER MILLER STAMPEDES PLATT'S STATE CONVENTION ran one headline.

Somewhat surprisingly, when Roosevelt learned of the doings of the convention, he was a bit disappointed. In letters to Lodge, he couldn't stop fuming over Platt trying to bury him, and though he was pleased with Warner Miller, he considered it an "ill drawn and ill considered" resolution. "I have the courageous and enthusiastic support of the men who make up the backbone of the Republican party but I have no hold whatever on the people who run the Republican machine."

With genuine distance, Henry Cabot Lodge, an astute political observer, drew quite a different conclusion. Lodge, then traveling in Europe, interpreted the Saratoga convention as the New York State Republican Party courageously defying the boss to endorse Roosevelt. In very prescient words, Lodge explained: "You do not realize how you have impressed the popular imagination and that means getting what you want."

Lodge was genuinely enthused. He knew that his friend had languished a bit in the backwaters for six years as a civil service commissioner; he knew TR currently served as a high-ranking appointed official in the nation's largest city, but Lodge judged it time to dangle the bigger prizes. "There are to be two Republican Senators from New York soon—one very soon. There is a good chance for you to get the first one if you put yourself at the head of the element which forced your issue on the convention. I do not say you are to be president tomorrow. I do not say it will be—I am sure that it may and can be. I do say that the Senate, which is better, is well within reach. Stump the State. Get to know the people and insist everywhere on the vital importance of electing a Republican legislature to choose a Republican Senator." (The New York State legislature chose U.S. senators until 1914.)

––––––

Back in Manhattan, Roosevelt persevered with his reform agenda. Judge Jerome kept his word about tough excise verdicts after September 1, and sentenced widow Mary O'Hearn, who ran a small saloon (140th Street near the East River), to three months in the penitentiary for a Sunday violation. Sundays would be dry through the election.

The reform board continued trying to weed out bad cops; in four months, it had fired thirty-five and would tally eighty-eight dismissals by year's end, which might seem few, but that dwarfed forty-one the previous year or eleven the year before that. The board dismissed Edward Hahn for drinking in uniform; it dismissed his brother Frank for living in and aiding a brothel at 70 Eldridge Street; it also axed twelve-year veteran Edward Rothschild, after Lena Bendiener, twenty-two years old, holding her baby, testified that the officer had seduced her with promises of marriage. She said that they had set up house together on East 6th Street and he came home most days to eat and every fourth night to sleep. The biggest impediment to their happiness was that Rothschild was married with three children.

––––––

Hiring new cops, however, hit a snag. The new higher standards tripped up reform's effort to fill 325 vacancies for patrolmen. Of the first 1,497 applicants, more than half were rejected for being either undersized (less than five feet eight inches and 140 pounds) or medically defective (from flat feet to foreskin phimosis). Then only one-third of the survivors, that is, 148 recruits, passed the inaugural police civil service exam—"Multiply 252 by 504 and divide the product by 378"—and twenty-five of these men were excluded, some for cheating on the exam, others because the commissioners found "their personal characteristics or their antecedents" objectionable. ("Antecedents" presumably referred to close relatives convicted of crimes.)

Undaunted by the delays, Roosevelt in an interview described the ideal kind of police recruit. First and foremost: excellent character. "He must not be a drinking man," Roosevelt told the *Herald*. "He must not be a man of loose habits of living." Roosevelt expected the man to be a good son or a father; he must not have "evil" companions; he would prefer a man of great courage, someone alert, obedient, and with good judgment. He categorically denied all men who had ever worked in saloons.

The *Washington Post* said he was looking to hire "saints."

———

A little after midnight on the unseasonably hot Sunday, September 22, four friends, including a circus acrobat named William Coleman, who had spent the day outside of "dry" Manhattan, were walking west on 34th Street after disembarking from the Long Island ferry. One was boisterously telling a story that involved mentions of "this officer" and "that officer" when two strangers suddenly confronted him: "Who you talkin' to?" said one. Coleman sassed back: "Not you!" The stranger didn't like Coleman's tone. "That's a fresh duck; a good kick wouldn't do him any harm."

The words escalated, and they began fighting. During the fracas, one of the strangers fell hard onto the pavement. (He would never regain consciousness.) The two strangers, it would also turn out, were plainclothes cops working undercover excise.

The surviving officer asserted that his partner Delehanty had told the young men to be quiet but that acrobat Coleman had bull-rushed Delehanty and hit him hard with a sandbag (a small leather sack of sand) and tossed it away. It was never found. (A bystander would later testify he saw no sandbag, nor did Coleman's friends.)

Officer Delehanty was carried to nearby Bellevue Hospital. Coleman was arrested. The police version of events, of an officer brutally attacked with a sandbag, was quickly relayed to headquarters and spread through the force.

The following day, Monday, a messenger arrived with a note from doctors that, despite surgery to relieve pressure on the brain, Delehanty was dying. The Police Board rushed into an "executive session" closed to reporters and voted immediately to bring back the nightstick, which Superintendent Byrnes had banned three years earlier in favor of a smaller lighter billy club.

This sudden reintroduction of the symbol of the old days of "Clubber" Williams surprised many reformers.

The New York Police nightstick—a fearsome weapon especially effective during riots—measured twenty-four inches long and one and three-eighth inches in diameter; it was carved of hard locustwood and carried in a socket outside the coat. Chief Byrnes's billy club—or day stick—measured fourteen inches, tapering out from a one-inch handle to one and five-eighth inches at the business end, of granadilla wood, and could be slipped into a special pocket in the seam of the trousers.

"The skull-crushing, bone-breaking night club is not needed in any American city," opined one newspaper. "The policeman who cannot make an arrest without making a deadly assault on the citizen is not fit for the force." A veteran sergeant in the 1890s explained to then rookie Cornelius Willemse that once an officer gets a reputation for hammering crooks with his club, they'll avoid his turf. "There's more religion in the end of a nightstick than in any sermon preached to the likes of them," explained the sergeant. "That doesn't mean you've got to beat up drunks and boys, but when you're dealing with real criminals, let 'em have it. It's the only language they understand." Lincoln Steffens discovered that some cops also played a cruel game with the big club: they tried to levitate a sleeping vagrant with one swat, hitting both feet simultaneously and sending a shock up the spine. "That bum rose, stiff like a stick," one cop fondly reminisced to Steffens, "didn't bend a knee or move an arm. I think he didn't wake up. He just rose up running."

Roosevelt—later known for his "speak softly and carry a big stick"—never wavered on this decision. In his autobiography two decades later, he wrote that he "consistently encouraged" the men to be polite to citizens and to use force on violent lawbreakers. "Of course where possible the officer merely crippled the criminal," he added.

Roosevelt told reporters on September 24 that if Delehanty had carried a nightstick, he could have "easily overpowered" Coleman, with or without a sandbag. (In his eagerness to reintroduce the weapon, Roosevelt overlooked the fact that *undercover* cops did not hide twenty-four-inch clubs on their person.) TR noted that the nightsticks would first be given to officers in the 35th Street precinct, then gradually distributed citywide, roughest neighborhoods first.

———

Throughout September, private clubs were still flouting the excise law and serving members on Sundays. (Their lawyers argued that clubs were exempt.)

During the summer Roosevelt had announced a crackdown on "rich as well as poor," but then had uncharacteristically backed off. Police Chief Conlin waffled and an assistant district attorney lamely announced the impossibility of gaining admittance to gather evidence. *Town Topics* advised TR to go undercover at his own Union League. "He can hang about the clubhouse, hide in the toilet room or the cellar and burst forth like an official cyclone" or he can follow the "modern police policy of inciting the crime." The society weekly explained: "He can cordially invite [members] to 'take something' with him and arrest them if they accept."

———

The Democratic convention took place September 25 in Syracuse. Unlike the Republicans the Democrats spotlighted Sunday laws. After giving a respectful nod to "honest enforcement of the law" and to "orderly Sundays," the Democrats shrewdly endorsed a "local option" solution, that is, a vote by individual cities to determine their own Sunday excise laws. "Shrewdly" because Democrats did not control either the New York State Assembly or Senate, and even if by some far-fetched miracle they gained narrow control of both houses, they would never have enough votes to override the veto of a Republican governor. Nonetheless, despite its dismal prospects, "Local Option" delivered a better rallying cry for the Democrats than "Drink Up and Violate the Law!"

The pundits touted Tammany as poised for a comeback.

That prospect deeply infuriated Roosevelt. He repeatedly confided to Lodge that he expected to be blamed for the defeat. The irony galled Roosevelt. He was running a strict law-and-order Police Board as an antidote to decades of corrupt city politics and now his stern enforcement might bring the most corrupt hustlers of Tammany back to power.

———

Tammany Hall, the local Democratic clubhouse, at the time ranked as one of the most dominant, most lucrative urban political machines in the nation. The secret to Tammany's success was no secret: favors on a grand scale equal loyalty. *Give me your vote to elect my pals and I will help you.* The organization divided the city down to the door frames of the poorest shanty. Its ward heelers stood ready, especially eager to help the flood tides of immigrants.

Tammany had started innocently enough in 1789 as a patriotic club with faux Indian rituals; the members were still called "braves," wore head-dresses occasionally, did war chants. It had grown successful with the waves of immigrants, and had even survived the Boss Tweed scandal of the 1870s. Overweight, shaped like a pear on toothpicks, bald-headed, Tweed ranks as the most famous politician ever felled by a cartoonist. Thomas Nast's wicked caricatures in *Harper's Weekly* kept the scandal alive until the *New York Times* began printing city expense reports in 1871. The building of the three-floor New York County Court House cost $12 million, which vaguely translates to $240 million in twenty-first-century currency. One accounting item listed "brooms, etc." for $41,190.95.

Tweed, a onetime U.S. congressman, had skimmed millions in kickbacks on inflated city contracts. He also bribed Democratic *and* Republican state legislators to frame sweetheart deals. One judge described pending legislation to authorize an additional $10 million in Erie Railroad Stock for Jay Gould and others as "a bill legalizing counterfeit money."

Tweed's crimes had horrified New York, or so the newspapers said. However, within two years, New Yorkers reelected Tammany Hall politicians to top offices when the new boss, "Honest" John Kelly, ran an anti-Tweed campaign for Tammany. In 1886, Richard "Dick" Croker replaced Kelly. This boss fell more into the central casting mold of a boss. Bearded, gorilla-like, he rose from running an East Side tunnel gang. His fierceness was proven when he was accused of murdering a rival during an Election Day brawl. After a hung jury, the case was never retried. (Reformer Carl Schurz wrote: "some old-fashioned people considered [the killing] an objectionable feature of his career.")

Croker—in the mold of modern Mafia bosses—demanded absolute loyalty. Over time, he developed an understated but menacing demeanor; he had no interest in food, wine, music, or theater. He generally preferred the company of horses and dogs, this "mild-mannered, soft-voiced, sad-faced, green-eyed chunk of a man," as one magazine writer put it.

Croker, who grew up in a shanty, had amassed at least $3 million by 1894, and owned a magnificent home amid the swells at 5 East 74th Street, built of Meadow Grey Stone with a window looking out to Central Park.

For this upcoming election, Croker had returned from his racing stables in Ireland (and self-imposed exile during Lexow) to run Tammany Hall.

He welcomed the rise of Roosevelt and the shuttered saloons as an opportunity.

In forty-one days, New Yorkers would decide whether to reembrace Tammany Hall and Croker. Roosevelt—ever the knight-errant—saw it as a battle of good versus evil, of law enforcement versus crime. "I do not think we have impaired our chances of victory in the least," he wrote to Lodge, angling for a more upbeat tone. "There was risk either way; and only one way leads toward honesty."

———

On the same afternoon as the Democratic convention, a workaday Wednesday, September 25, the thirsty Germans of New York City engineered an extraordinary tribute to beer and liberty. More than 30,000 marchers, most native Germans or German Americans, almost all carrying small American flags, joyfully paraded up Lexington Avenue, along with musical bands, glee clubs, costumed bicyclists, and horse-drawn floats. "What a jolly saucy procession it was, to be sure!" assessed the *New York Recorder*. "How it flaunted the foaming glass or amber colored bottle in the face of the spectators! How it waved the American flag and yelled for liberty, personal liberty—the liberty to buy one's beer on Sundays and to drink it at one's pleasure!"

The Agitation Committee of the United Societies for Liberal Sunday Laws had sent police commissioner Roosevelt an invitation but probably more as a taunt or a joke. Though relentlessly demonized in the city's German-language newspapers, Roosevelt decided to take Carl Schurz's advice and attend.

Accompanied by roundsman Michael Tierney, the commissioner reached the reviewing stand at 86th Street at about 3 p.m., well ahead of the paraders.

TR was escorted to a place of honor, front row center. The parade arrived around 3:20 p.m. and gradually word spread among the marchers that Roosevelt was there. He never stopped smiling and waving. When a parader lifted a glass or bottle to him, he shouted back, *"Prosit!"* (There was no "open container" law in that era.) When one uniformed veteran of the Franco-Prussian War hollered in a booming voice: "*Wo ist der Roosevelt? Ich würde ihn sehen*," he leaned forward in the reviewing stand and shouted back, "*Hier bin ich*." The crowd erupted in cheers. Roosevelt had spent five months in Dresden at age fourteen.

The passing paraders by the hundreds reacted to TR. Many smiled; some cheered (they might have thought his attendance meant a sudden endorsement of their cause). Roosevelt, who doffed his hat and kept a perpetual smile on his face, was the center of attention in a reviewing stand of Teutonic elite.

Interspersed amid the marchers were horse-drawn floats, such as Lady Liberty in mourning. A beautiful young woman, in a red-white-and-blue dress, wore a floor-length black veil. But even she couldn't resist nudging the veil aside and peeking out and smiling at Roosevelt.

Another float, a simple horse-drawn delivery truck with a large banner, WORKINGMAN'S SUNDAY, showed three men—in blue overalls and colored shirts—inside a simple wooden cage, sadly passing around an empty "growler" (a bucket for carrying beer home from the saloon). Every attempt to gulp some beer ended in a miffed discovery of emptiness.

The highlight of the floats, the biggest crowd pleaser, was the Millionaires' Club. Four men in elegant black suits, with red silk handkerchiefs "and other signs of swelldom . . . sat around a marble topped table and quaffed champagne between puffs at large fat cigars." One of them seemed a dead ringer for Roosevelt. At the other end of the float, a policeman was arresting a bartender who was just then filling two beers for a couple of dockworkers. The rich drink; the poor suffer.

The commissioner smiled relentlessly, even at this float, calling it the "best of all floats . . . an excellent conceit."

Near the end of the parade, a man came by the reviewing stand and waggled his banner—ROOSEVELT'S RAZZLE-DAZZLE REFORM RACKET—within a foot of TR's face, drawing a big laugh. TR suddenly asked the man if he could have the flag, and the fellow somewhat sheepishly agreed. Roundsman Tierney jumped down and broke the long handle off and rolled up the banner. A little while later, TR saw SEND THE POLICE CZAR TO RUSSIA and asked for that one too. "Tie those up, Tierney, and I will take those away with me as souvenirs."

Roosevelt had warned the organizers that he would have to leave in time to catch the 4:45 p.m. train to Oyster Bay. "Good bye, it's been great fun," he told his hosts, rushing off to the 34th Street ferry to Long Island City. "I never had a better time in my life . . . I'm glad I saw it but a hundred parades wouldn't swerve me from my duty in enforcing the law." He apparently loudly repeated that last line to several of the dignitaries within earshot of several newspapermen.

With his infectious grin, Roosevelt had charmed some of the German marchers and dignitaries and most of the reporters, who liked the "Daniel in the lion's den" angle, but the real proof would be in the election results.

———

The local Republican Party was taking no chances. The top men were convinced of Roosevelt's unpopularity. So, "Smooth Ed" Lauterbach, the Republican leader in New York City, with Platt's blessing, decreed that no Republican organization, from the smallest club upward, should invite Roosevelt to speak in any of the campaigns . . . not for judges, assemblymen, state senators, county clerk, secretary of state, not anything. Roosevelt would thereby be banned from all the massive rallies as well. Lauterbach also issued an unequivocal statement that the "Republican party was not in any way responsible for Rooseveltism."

While the city Republicans tried to cast off Roosevelt, they embraced that retired policeman and poster boy for graft and excessive force, Alexander "Clubber" Williams. Piling up the irony, the Republicans, who had championed the Lexow Committee, which had exposed Williams's misdeeds and ill-gotten wealth, were now touting him for state senator in the Twelfth District. With great difficulty, Roosevelt muzzled himself regarding Williams, struggling to honor his vow to Cabot *not* to criticize the Republican Party. "Smooth Ed" Lauterbach was a worthy adversary for TR. Born poor on the Bowery, he had risen as a corporate lawyer; he was especially refined in his tastes in the arts, fluent in French and German. His wife often hosted musical soirees at their elegant home at 2 East 78th Street. Clever, witty, five feet six, with a pointed black beard, he was portrayed by cartoonists as a glad-handing Mephistopheles.

Roosevelt was deeply irritated by Lauterbach's renunciation of so-called Rooseveltism and planned on lashing out against him, at least after the election. (Lodge would later frantically try to talk him out of it. "Mr. Lauterbach looks important in N.Y. City—he is pretty small in the State and absolutely unknown outside of it. You are known all over the country and known as a Republican. What Mr. Lauterbach says is of no consequence. What you say and do is of vast consequence.")

Never one to back down, Roosevelt refused to disappear, as the Republican machine so clearly desired, but instead accepted dozens of invitations from a ragtag collection of church, temperance, and reform groups, speaking sometimes two or three times a night. He even spoke at a Harlem Democratic club. Up in Boston, the *Massachusetts* Republicans allowed him to speak. His own party in New York was cold-shouldering him, in the hopes of winning the city.

In late September, Reverend Parkhurst returned refreshed from two months in the Swiss Alps. He found the Republicans and Good Government groups and independent Democrats all at loggerheads, each making noises about fielding its own slate of candidates.

With Sunday shutdowns and Roosevelt in the picture, Parkhurst would need to practice some rare political alchemy to create a Fusion ticket, blending all the anti-Tammany forces.

Roosevelt analyzed the problem for Lodge. "The cowardice and rascality of the machine Republicans; and the flaming idiocy of the 'better element' have been comic and also disheartening," he wrote. "The Republican Machine men have been loudly demanding a straight [Republican] ticket, and those prize idiots, the Goo-Goos, have just played into their hands by capering off and nominating an independent ticket of their own." Many reformers belonging to the Good Government clubs (i.e., Goo-Goos) were wealthy and had a reputation for adopting uncompromising stances that guaranteed high-minded defeat at the polls.

Parkhurst approached the Chamber of Commerce and other top-tier citizens to form a Committee of Seventy to broker a broad Fusion campaign. "A bomb exploding in Tammany Hall would not have caused more consternation among the braves," proclaimed the *New York World* on the front page on October 2.

Parkhurst landed fifty wealthy prominent citizens—Gustav Schwab, Charles Stewart Smith, Joseph Choate, Elihu Root, J. P. Morgan—for the committee; they began negotiating with the Republicans and others to form a Fusion ticket. When compromise talks faltered, Parkhurst issued a statement threatening to run a campaign: "Down with Tammany. Down with Platt. Death to machine politicians in the city of New York."

A mini-Fusion ticket finally emerged on October 7. The Republicans and the anti-Tammany State Democracy Party agreed to band together. Needing the skill of a circus contortionist, they tried to concoct an excise plank to satisfy all constituents, especially the Germans. The platform began ambivalently enough: "We insist that every citizen is entitled . . . to enjoy the largest measure of personal freedom, consistent with the welfare of the community, and not in conflict with the moral and religious convictions of his fellow citizens."

The three-paragraph plank had enough "on the one hand, on the other hand"s for an eight-handed Lord Shiva. It culminated with an endorsement of the "local option," but it also included a Republican plank encouraging the Republican legislature and governor to promptly revise the excise law, without specifying the revisions.

Now came the crucial tests: Would the Germans join the mini-Fusion ticket? Would the Goo-Goos switch course and join mini-Fusion? Would the GARUs (members of the German American Reform Union) and the influential *Staats-Zeitung* newspaper back the cause?

On October 8, the Goo-Goos' meeting at the United Charities Building voted down Fusion, 63 to 47.

The GARUs met at Maennerchor Hall, 56th Street and Third Avenue, and voted by a shockingly large majority to endorse . . . Tammany Hall. "I'm no Tammany man," said Herman Ridder of the *Staats-Zeitung*. "I never voted for Tammany in my life. But I will and we all will this time, so that there may be no more blue laws." Key community leader Oswald Ottendorfer said he hoped the election of Tammany would send a strong message to the Republicans and Commissioner Roosevelt.

However, a faction of reform-minded German GARUs couldn't squeeze their nostrils tight enough to embrace Tammany; so the splintering continued further as Carl Schurz helped organize the German-American Citizens' Union, dubbed the GAZOOs.

The situation was hopelessly, ridiculously muddled. Although Roosevelt soldiered on with his combative style and big smiles, he was chafing more and more privately. "The attitude of the Germans has caused a regular panic among our people, from Platt to Strong [to] run away from the issue." He added: "It is almost comic to see the shifts of our State and City party managers in keeping me off the platform."

Roosevelt was feeling increasingly isolated. "I can't help writing you," he wrote to Lodge on October 11, "for I literally have no one here to whom to unburden myself; I make acquaintances very easily but there are only one or two people in the world, outside of my own family, whom I deem friends or for whom I really care."

The newspapers didn't tire of blaming Roosevelt for the fractured election that would probably boost Tammany.

Roosevelt was truly banned by his own party. On October 15, the Republicans held a massive rally at Cooper Union, a sprawling building at 7th Street and Broadway. Some State Democrats and GAZOOs joined the Republicans on the platform.

The festive well-dressed crowd of several thousand, including only a handful of women, cheered on Republican causes. Then the keynote speaker, Warner Miller of Herkimer, New York, blindsided his New York City hosts. He hammered home with absolute clarity that the Republican Party wanted the "saloons to be closed on Sundays." (He had turned down the local party's request to "blue-pencil" his speech; he in effect defied Lauterbach and Platt.) Ample-bellied, mustachioed, dead earnest, Miller said Sunday excise had grown into the biggest issue in New York State. "The Republican Party had to meet it or run away like cowards," he stated. Someone on the platform shouted: "You're no coward!"

Miller praised the police commissioners for their successful efforts and opined that the State of New York supported them. The comment drew pockets of passionate clapping, scattershot hisses, a low rumble of tepid applause. The reaction was decidedly mixed.

Miller, occasionally pounding his right hand down on the lectern, informed the crowd that a citizen's personal liberty should hold little weight in "great moral questions" such as observing the Sabbath.

Voters should never receive a "local option" vote for the "Sunday saloon," or for "gambling" or the "social evil" or for "every crime that breaks the Decalogue." The audience was warming to his theme.

He played once again on xenophobia. "We welcome every good immigrant to our shores, but we are a mature people, with fixed habits and customs, to which those who come here are expected to conform. They come here to escape the tyrannies of monarchial governments. We claim that as an American government we must ask all who come here to become Americans and be Americanized."

The crowd erupted in its first foot-stomping all-out cheers of the night.

He called the saloon "the rendezvous of every evil element of the community" and said that having it open six days a week was enough. He even wondered aloud whether the Germans who joined Tammany might not be anarchists or socialists. By the event's end at 11 p.m., half of the mostly Republican crowd had drifted out; the other half surged forward to congratulate Warner Miller on his speech.

Under a headline SUNDAY BEER FOR NONE, the *New York Times* stressed that Miller had championed the very points that the local Fusion ticket was trying to avoid, so as to woo the Germans. "Not only was [Miller] not 'bottled up' but he fairly spouted cold water," commented the paper with uncharacteristic playfulness.

The following day's *Times* headline was REPUBLICANS IN GLOOM. The *World* ran a front-page cartoon of the Tammany tiger standing with a paw on Roosevelt's head to get a boost over the wall. The caption read: " 'I don't care a rap for the consequences.'—Theodore Roosevelt."

A few days later, Roosevelt sat down for a long interview with a *New York World* reporter. He was asked if a Tammany victory in the election "will be due to the rigid Sunday closing under your administration?"

Roosevelt demurred: "Why, of course, it would not be due to that. If the Sunday closing brought about a defeat of the reform party the defeat would be due to those reform politicians and reform newspapers which have departed from the issue and have encouraged the forces of evil by taking the position that one set of law breakers are entitled to immunity at the hands of the police because they are politically powerful. If the men who believe in honest government had stood straight up to the issue of honesty in public office we would have won this fall hands down. I think we are going to win anyway. If we do not, why, all I can say is as I have said before, that I would rather lose on the issue of the honest observance of the law than win at the cost of a corrupt connivance with law breakers."

Around this time, Mayor Strong called Roosevelt in for a meeting. He tried to reason with him about letting up on enforcement; he tried to order him; finally he made a veiled threat of dismissal.

Roosevelt wrote Lodge of the incident. "[Mayor Strong] was terribly angry; but when he found I would not change, and the crisis came, he was more afraid of me than of all the Germans who were pushing him from behind; and he said he would do nothing until after election. I care very little what he does after election."

Roosevelt followed Lodge's advice and muzzled himself regarding his own party but his spleen spilled over regarding the Goo-Goos. In a published letter, he compared their ticket to a "crank vote," that is, a futile protest carried out by campaigning for an *unelectable* slate, such as the Socialist Workers Party. "In the case of the Good-Government people, it is the conscience vote gone silly." He called them the "best allies of Tammany Hall." He was deeply disappointed because he was a member of a Good Government club and regarded their work as very important.

Roosevelt again and again confided in Cabot Lodge, his father confessor.

"It has been an awful struggle, and I have been very lonely. I have not had one political friend of any weight from whom I could get a particle of advice or of real support. Now it seems as though, through no fault of mine, we are to meet defeat in this City."

Coincidentally, Lodge wrote to TR that same day from Paris, delivering a very perceptive, though obviously partisan, précis on New York City's 1895 election.

"The Germans behave very badly. They prefer beer to principle. What amazes me most about the [Republican] machine is not their being wrong but their utter stupidity. The issue was their chance and they neither rejected you nor sustained you. Anything more idiotic I have never seen. The Goo-Goos have behaved as they always do. I am amazed at what you tell me of Strong. Meantime the substantial victory is with you. The convention stood by you, you have a good Fusion ticket and even the city Republicans did not dare officially throw you over. You are strong with the people, you have their ear, your party standing before the country is unimpeachable, you are right and you have made a very big national reputation. All this will bear fruit besides being worth while itself."

Lodge's letters helped sustain him, but the strain of the election was finally catching up to Roosevelt. His wife, Edith, worried about his health. Even TR admitted to his sister: "Thank Heaven there is only one week more." As the election approached, Roosevelt, buoyed by all the enthusiastic crowds in the small venues, sensed a subtle changing of the tide; he allowed himself a sliver of optimism. He also had an ace in the hole. He believed a police crackdown on voter fraud would hurt Tammany far more than the Republicans.

————

The police department, through its own bureau of elections, handled the regulation of the polls. In recent years, the Tammany police work—to put it nicely—was purposely sloppy.

Though he received much less publicity for it, TR decided to put as much effort into ensuring fair elections as he did into closing Sunday saloons. "I have made the police force work like beavers to prevent fraudulent registration," TR wrote to Henry White (an American in London) on October 28, "and in consequence the Tammany registration in the worst wards has fallen off nearly a third." Purge the rolls of enough Tammany repeaters, prevent bullying near the polls, and the Fusion Republicans just might snatch victory.

Roosevelt also raised the standards for the 11,000 Election Day poll workers provided by the two dominant parties. He wrote in an article for *Cosmopolitan* timed for release before Election Day that the police department had rejected almost 1,000 poll workers on either intelligence or moral grounds. He instituted a literacy test. Elsewhere, he joked that this year "two plus two" would not equal "minus one."

Officials expected about 250,000 registered male voters in a city of 2 million men, women, and children to cast ballots on Tuesday, November 5. Roosevelt started early to make sure each and every voter was legitimately registered.

The first day of voter registration was October 8. All that basically was required was for a man to go to a polling place and swear to his name, his citizenship, and his place of residence. In this age before photo I.D. or hologram logos, double-checking a man's identity could prove difficult.

The hotspot for voter fraud was the lodging house. Men would be paid in cash, liquor, or cigars to wander all over town, use multiple fictitious names, and claim to reside at various lodging houses. Then on Election Day those men or others would vote under those names.

Tammany's Paddy Divver, a former alderman, could deliver hundreds of such votes through names registered at his seamen's lodging, and so could Mike Callahan with his Progress joint on Chatham Square. Big Bill Devery's uncle, Stephen Geoghegan, admitted during a congressional investigation that he invented voters and assigned them to various mud hovels on Dutch Hill in the East Forties, and that 25 percent of votes in his district were fraudulent.

Roosevelt shrewdly ordered the police in all precincts to go to the lodging houses on the three nights before October 8 registration. The patrolmen tramped up the dank stairs and copied down the names scribbled on the ledger. Anyone not on the lists who tried to register from those addresses would be arrested. He later bragged to Lodge about cutting down the "mattress vote." Roosevelt also directed the police to check on any address that claimed more than one registered voter. Patrolmen again walked to the buildings and demanded to see the persons registered or made inquiries about them.

The *New York World* reported on October 28 that voter registration had fallen by 30,000 names from the last election and that 23,000 of those lay in Tammany strongholds below 14th Street.

On October 29, Chief Conlin announced the long-rumored shakeup of the police force; he reassigned more than 200 men and transferred several captains "for the good of the service." In addition, the captains assigned many men on Election Day to polling places *outside* of their usual precinct. This juggling of men was designed to nix too-cozy relationships.

The law called for two officers to be stationed all day at each of the 1,392 polling places, a law that had previously been rarely honored for all ten hours from 6 a.m. to 4 p.m. It dawned on many of the 2,784 policemen that they would be unable to vote. (Tammany, recognizing its constituency, was not pleased, and hired a lawyer.)

Roosevelt defended the assignments, ultimately stating that the fulfilling of the election law for the whole city trumped the rights of the individual policemen. Commissioner Grant suggested hiring 2,800 temporary polling guards for three hours to spell the officers so they could vote. But the Police Board rejected the suggestion as too expensive and likely to cause chaos through the hiring of untrained men.

On Monday, November 4, at 6 p.m. Roosevelt called Chief Conlin and gave him the surprise order to enforce the Election Day excise law closing all saloons within a quarter mile of a polling place from 6 a.m. to 4 p.m. Tuesday. In a densely packed city such as New York, this would shutter almost all the saloons, the traditional gathering places for repeaters and fraudsters.

The order was given so late that Conlin had to send telegrams to all the captains ordering them to come down on Monday night to 300 Mulberry. General orders were repeated: two officers must patrol within a 100-foot radius of the polls and make sure no electioneering or bullying occurred inside that circle. Roosevelt and Conlin promised that any bad behavior that day by policemen would be severely punished. Every man—except 115 on the sick list—would be on duty: 2,784 at the polls, a skeletal staff of 276 in the thirty-eight precincts, and 100 emergency policemen at headquarters, with horses and patrol wagons ready to ferry them. Each of the four inspectors would hire a hansom cab and rove the city looking for problems.

Conlin also ordered the men to crack down on boys setting patriotic bonfires, a pastime that had blossomed into a New York City Election Day tradition; last year the fires had caused $12,000 worth of damage to brand-new asphalt.

———

At dawn on Tuesday, November 5, the city staggered to life as usual. The sun glinted off Diana's thigh. Drowsy workmen hoping to start the day with an eye-opener at their local saloons encountered oddly closed doors. Hundreds of veteran policemen, unused to the dog shift, found themselves tramping up and down near polling places, chatting with their partner, preparing for the very long day.

The 21st Precinct police discovered that the Slimy Back boys' gang had filled a vacant lot at 34th Street and Second Avenue with huge stacks of cast-off wood, barrel staves, cracked kegs, and firkins. The Slimy Backs' last election bonfire had roared so far into the night sky it damaged the tracks of the El; the gang had also rolled a stolen wagon into the fire and "danced the war dance of the great eastside." Now, before Election Day, the boys showered stones down onto the seven policemen loading their wood onto a rented wagon; they chased the laden truck, trying to ambush the driver and leap aboard to rescue the wood. A policeman collared one red-haired boy and dragged him kicking and screaming into the station house. "The sergeant gave him a lecture, and his father appearing and promising to spank him, he was allowed to go home." Policemen confiscated wood all over town.

The mild temperatures favored a large turnout. The front-page "Weather Prediction" called for "fair and warmer," with few clouds and mild south-westerly breezes. Roosevelt voted early. But thanks to Roosevelt, many fewer people voted *often*. Observers would later call this perhaps the cleanest election in New York City voting history. Roosevelt, in the name of fairness, had negated two of Tammany's weapons: voter fraud and strong-arm election-eering.

Roosevelt spent much of his day defending the board's decision to assign cops to new precincts and schedule them for the entire Election Day with no break to vote. Tammany lawyer Blumenthal claimed this violated the state law requiring all employers to grant at least a two-hour break so employees could vote. The judge, though sympathetic, decided that the problem didn't rate court interference. It could be handled by the legislature after the election.

Women, though deprived of the vote, tried to help at the polls. Mrs.

Mary Hall in the Tenderloin handed out glasses of milk for "soberin'-up" and gave a meal ticket to all men exiting the polls. Mrs. Stephen King, up in new Little Italy on 110th Street, handed out cigars, food, and lead pencils for marking ballots. Tammany doled out $70,000 in small bills to get out the vote, while reformers ponied up about one-tenth that amount.

In that era, the police counted the votes at 300 Mulberry. Far and away, election night ranked as the building's busiest hours of the year, with the floors lit from top to bottom and men clattering up and down the stairs.

First, the local election district counted the results and ran them over to the nearest police precinct house, which then relayed that rough unofficial tally by telephone or telegraph to police headquarters. Then policemen rushed the sealed satchels full of votes to police headquarters. Downtown, mounted policemen galloped with the bags; in uptown neighborhoods, policemen boarded the El trains and a troop of officers waited on horseback at the Houston Street station of the Third Avenue El and the Bleecker Street station of the Sixth Avenue line to race the ballots the last few blocks.

The first sack of returns reached police headquarters at 4:50 p.m. and votes flowed in steadily from then on; hundreds of winded patrolmen tramped up the front steps.

Bald-headed chief clerk William Kipp, with twenty-six accountants to aid him, tabulated the results in the trial room. Usually on election night, the room was packed with greater and lesser dignitaries but this year—either due to the reform board's earnestness or the nearby cordoned-off streets around a fire on Houston Street—plenty of seats remained vacant. The commissioners including Roosevelt mostly stayed in their offices, and messengers from Kipp brought handwritten updates.

At 5:20 p.m., a reporter caught Roosevelt for a quick comment. "It looks as if the godly are on top," he said excitedly, "and I am of the godly."

In that era before radio or television, tens of thousands of New Yorkers filled the streets foraging for the latest election results. Newspapers dashed off quick "Extras," but people wanting to know first swarmed down to so-called newspaper row on Park Row, which housed the buildings of the great papers. The major dailies then stood alongside the colossal tower of Pulitzer's *World*, which at 309 feet ranked as the city's tallest skyscraper. The barroom joke ran that *World* reporters could lean out the window and spit on the *Sun*.

The *New York Times,* capitalizing on Edison's inventions, draped a large canvas across the lower floors of its building and projected images of political cartoons, photographs, and updated election results. The operators even did a sequence of rapid-fire colored comics "in which the characters were made to perform absurd feats." This herky-jerky proto-animation proved especially popular.

One cartoon showed a German Hamlet in lederhosen holding two full steins of beer in one hand and nothing in his other hand, with a caption saying: "Two beers or not two beers?" The *Times* also delivered on its promise to its advertisers that it would intersperse copies of print ads.

Inside the news buildings, telegraph operators wrote down results on a piece of paper, shoved it into a container, and slid it down a wire to the men handling the projectors.

The *Times* drew a big enough crowd to awake the sniping of the nearby leviathan *World*, which peckishly rated the *Times*'s display as "a kaleidoscopic jumble of stale cartoons, advertisements and photos of utterly incomprehensible figures from everywhere in the Union." The *World* claimed that thousands of people migrated from the *Times* over to the Pulitzer Building, which had separate bulletin boards, organized to display updated results from each of the important races—and, in addition, announced results spelled out in lightbulbs in the dome.

At 7 p.m., Theodore Roosevelt said: "Really, the returns as yet are not unfavorable. I still predict a Republican success."

Over the next half hour, the votes of more than 300 election districts were tabulated and spread via "special" telegraph to the executive offices of Tammany Hall, to Republican Party headquarters, to Gilsey House, where the wealthy Fusion "Committee of Fifty" gathered, to a storefront on Broadway where the Good Government men and their wives waited.

And the news, district by district, showed an inexorable Tammany march forward, a bubbling up of the big Democratic machine. The reform police commissioners and their friends in various offices made quick grim tallies on backs of envelopes and notepads.

By anyone's math, Tammany Hall, thanks to the strong right arm of the Germans, was carving out a landslide victory in the city. The satchels of votes—unsealed and counted—showed it on pace to elect all the judges of the supreme court and the Court of General Sessions, ten out of twelve candidates for state senate, and thirty of thirty-five for state assembly.

At around 7:30 p.m., a suddenly deflated Roosevelt conceded the election to Tammany. His words were spelled out in lights around the dome of the *World*. The commissioner avoided the press for the rest of the night by sitting in the office of Frederick Grant, his fellow Republican on the board. The usually voluble Roosevelt was tight-lipped.

Lodge had sent TR a telegram from Europe pleading with him to avoid bad-mouthing Republicans on election night. TR obeyed but he couldn't resist taking a potshot at the Goo-Goos. He blamed defeat on "the folly of the Good Government Clubs in running a ticket of their own and compelling the Fusionists to run alone."

As Tammany's victory was becoming clear, the *Times* showed a Sunday saloon cartoon of TR in a policeman's keystone helmet, swinging a nightstick and dancing a jig while shouting "I did it!" The crowd found it hilarious. A reporter overheard someone mutter sarcastically: "Tammany ought to do something substantial for Roosevelt."

Over at Tammany Hall itself on 14th Street, the braves were celebrating with a very open bar and a mood of "riotous hilarity." A fellow named McGoldrick, who often bellowed out the returns, interspersed the numbers with snide comments aimed at Roosevelt, the Goo-Goos, GAZOOs, and various other losers. The crowd loved it. A regiment band "tooted and blared."

The *Tammany Times* later gleefully reported: "Teddy Roosevelt was at Police Headquarters watching the returns; he became bewildered at the figures for Tammany and it is said that an ambulance was called to take him to his home." The paper added: "However, at the hour of going to press, he is convalescent and in all probability will confer with William Strong in reference to closing the park this Sunday."

Town Topics, that soused society weekly, interpreted the election as being a victory of the "thugs" over the "quarreling psalm-singers," and an indication that New Yorkers prefer to be "crazy and reckless" than "crazy and religious." They dubbed Roosevelt "Idiot Boy."

To cap the indignities, the city also elected the most recent Tammany Grand Sachem, Frederick Smyth, as a supreme court judge for a fifteen-year term at an annual salary of $17,500. (Judge Smyth would deliver key rulings on the reinstatement of "Big Bill" Devery.)

Tammany also defeated Clubber Williams, who blamed the lies of Lexow.

Outside the city, however, in the rest of New York State, the Republicans achieved a solid victory, gaining 80,000 more votes than the Democrats in most statewide races. This marked a ringing vindication for Warner Miller's Republican strategy trumpeting law-and-order and sober Sundays. The party retained its absolute control of both the state assembly and senate; it promptly announced that liquor laws would be made stricter. "Smooth Ed" Lauterbach immediately declared the local Republican party would abandon the Fusion platform plank of "local option."

———

On election morning-after Wednesday, every newspaper in New York City, to some degree, blamed Roosevelt for the local defeat of Fusion and the defection of the Germans. "But for the exasperating effect of Mr. Roosevelt's uncalled for, unjust, harsh and oppressive execution of the Sunday excise law, a union of all the anti-Tammany forces would have been as easy and as triumphant as it was last year." So stated the *World*.

The *New York Tribune*, a staunchly Republican paper, ran a letter from a longtime Republican, hoping to use a "gigantic foghorn" to implore TR: "Do your duty, Teddy, and keep your mouth shut."

Local Republican politicians loudly hinted of a movement afoot to legislate Roosevelt out of office by changing the configuration of the Police Board. "It will be argued that Roosevelt has risen from a municipal sensationalist to a national mischief-maker and that another year of his Puritanical administration will increase the Tammany majority so that NY State will be lost to the Republicans."

Roosevelt tried hard to ignore it all, to keep a brave face; he requested that Chief Conlin gather the police captains on Wednesday as well as the men running the Election Bureau. They crammed into his office at headquarters; many entered smiling. He praised them highly for administering a "most orderly and honest election." He said civilian complaints were way down from previous years. His tone was quiet and earnest; the flamboyance of the election was gone.

"Now, in conclusion, I wish to say some things that I don't think it necessary for me to say but which I wish you, Chief, and you, the Inspectors, and every Captain and Acting Captain, to hear. The board will not tolerate the slightest relaxation in the enforcement of the laws, and notably of the excise law, and the board will hold to the most rigid accountability any man in whose precinct any such relaxation occurs. I know that that is needless for me to say. I know that you gentlemen understand it thoroughly already. Good evening."

At TR's request, Friday's board meeting was moved up to Thursday morning, and by Thursday night TR was out at Oyster Bay, to spend a rare four consecutive days there, recuperating. That Sunday, TR wrote to his sister Bamie that "every single [newspaper] has attacked me" and that the comments "do not affect me in the least." He said he was enjoying "riding, chopping, walking with Edith and the children to the full."

For the next week, politicians and pundits treated Roosevelt as a political piñata.

The following Sunday he wrote to his sister. "The political outlook is rather discouraging; it is entirely in the cards that I shall be legislated out of existence in a couple of months."

CRACK UP . . . CRACK DOWN

C hallenged, cornered, beleaguered, implored to lighten up, Roosevelt cracked down further.

The police—after notching a tentative victory in the saloon war—were devoting more manpower to suppressing the other main recreational vices: prostitution and gambling. The newspapers reminded readers that Roosevelt had told a sympathetic crowd in Boston just before the election, "I have got the screws on pretty tight now, but if we get whipped, I shall take another twist." TR's very strong right arm was now twisting; the Germans and others found the extra quarter-turn vindictive.

Some police captains—to curry favor with the board president—began arresting poor peddlers selling flowers in the streets on Sundays. The *World*, milking the outrage, cited the case of a father unable to buy roses to put on his child's grave. Selling flowers on Sunday was clearly illegal unless a buyer ate the flowers, which then might qualify for the "confectionary" exemption.

In addition, since apparently no law existed to license bootblack stands on the sidewalks, some patrolmen began threatening to arrest anyone—Italians mostly—shining shoes for a few cents. The head of the bootblack association hoped the officers were kidding, "as the police belong to a humorous race [i.e., Irish] prone to look upon the Italian as a 'dago' and as such the proper object of practical jokes."

This mid-November post-election gust of repression led to rumors that young girls would no longer be allowed to dance in the streets to organ-grinder music. Roosevelt found himself in the awkward position of wanting to postpone some of the crackdowns—on, say, flower sellers and bootblacks—without admitting to selective enforcement.

Roosevelt was working eight to ten hours a day at police headquarters—interviewing job applicants, fielding citizens' complaints, arguing with the press, handling his share of disciplinary hearings—and he was also devoting himself nights and weekends to finishing the fourth volume of *Winning of the West* by year's end. Toss in a two-hour daily commute. In stressful times, he often worked harder, chopped more wood at Oyster Bay.

Sometime late in the week of November 18, in the post-election doldrums, TR dined with an old friend visiting from Boston, the very perceptive doctor and Asian art collector William Sturgis Bigelow. Eight years older than TR, Bigelow, a fellow alumnus of Harvard, fit that vanishing breed of Victorian aristocrat scholar. The two men enjoyed each other's company, dined together every other month or so, and visited each other's country homes in the summer.

After this most recent New York meal, Dr. Bigelow wrote a very concerned letter to their mutual Boston friend Senator Lodge, part diagnosis, part prescription.

> *Theodore Roosevelt dined with me the other night. He has grown several years older in the last month. He looks worn & tired, for him, and has lost much of his natural snap and buoyancy. At this rate it is only a question of time when he has a breakdown, and when he does it will be a bad one.*
>
> *He is in a wholly false position & ought to be got out of it. Those cusses put him in there in order to shield themselves, behind his reputation for absolute integrity, against the charge of not doing the impossible. To the amazement of everybody, friends & foes alike, he has met the situation by doing the impossible. The result is that New York City is about the only Democratic spot on the map & he gets all the blame.*
>
> *The Sunday liquor law is a dead letter. You might as well try to enforce the law against smoking in the streets in Boston. More than that, it was never meant to be enforced. It was a blackmail law from the start. And the New Yorkers would rather be blackmailed than give up their Sunday beer. That's the whole story.*
>
> *Roosevelt ought to have a solid rest of several months. They can't remove him. He can't resign without putting himself in the light of giving up, beaten, which he will never do till he drops. The only thing is to get him shifted, somehow to an easier place that he can hold till the next Presidential year when he ought to have anything he wants. The State will agree because it is with him. The City Rep[ublican]s*

*will agree because they will be glad to get rid of him. If he keeps on
with this job he will break down, & we shall lose one of the very few
really first-class men in the country.—Think this over.*

Lodge did think it over, and he soon had an opportunity briefly to spend
some time with TR at the dock as he passed through New York when he
returned from Europe. Lodge sent a worried letter to TR's sister Bamie,
whose wedding he had recently attended in London.

*[TR] looks very well, but yet I am anxious about him, not from
physical but mental signs. He seems overstrained & overwrought—
That wonderful spring and interest in all sorts of things is much
lowered. He is not depressed but he is fearfully overworked & insists on
writing history & doing all sorts of things he has no need to do. He has
that morbid idée fixe that he cannot leave his work for a moment else
the world should stop.*

—————

On November 26, the Tuesday before Thanksgiving, Roosevelt called the
board meeting to order. One item topped the agenda. The board—after
waiting out preliminary court appeals—was now ready to vote on the guilt
or innocence of Captain Joseph Eakins. The reform board had invested
much time and effort. Commissioner Grant requested permission to read a
10,000-word legal brief defending Captain Eakins. (Eakins's lawyers had no
doubt written it.)

Impatient, frazzled, TR abruptly refused him, snapping out: "Call the
roll."

Chief Clerk Kipp intoned: "Are the charges proved?" Roosevelt—along
with commissioners Andrews and Parker—sang out "Aye," deeming Eakins
guilty of neglect of duty for failing to shut numerous brothels and tryst-
ing places. Commissioner Grant, with unaccustomed firmness, boomed out
a "No," the lone vote for acquitting the twenty-nine-year veteran. Besides
the public disgrace, Eakins would not now receive his half-salary pension of
$1,375.

Roosevelt, or a clerk under him, collected newspaper clips for a police
scrapbook. The person with the scissors and glue pot often pasted in the
most rabidly anti-TR articles, almost as though Roosevelt—just as he had

collected the "Czar" banner from the parade—were dead set on being amused by his foes. Dead set, teeth gritted, damned amused.

The *New York Mercury* called the verdict "as gross an act of injustice as was ever seen at a Massachusetts witch burning . . . Roosevelt is one type of American—the blue-blooded Knickerbocker Puritan gone to seed. Thank God they are fast dying out . . . Grant is another type of American, sturdy, magnanimous—the generous, justice-loving American of today, who is fast becoming the noblest type of man like his father, Ulysses . . . No Roosevelt was ever President; no Roosevelt ever led an army to victory—and none ever will."

In the legal brief that Commissioner Grant later handed to newspapermen, the writer argued that the Parkhurst Society case against Eakins was more of an ambush than a genuine attempt to clean up vice. The Society had informed the captain of alleged brothels on May 15 and the charges they brought against him specify conditions existing from January 1 to May 17. In other words, Eakins had two days to correct five months of problems. Grant's main point was that in order to gather evidence against brothels that was admissible in court, police officers had to perform morally reprehensible masquerades, paying to watch sexual performances. (The officers couldn't burst in without a search warrant and spot couples engaged in fornication or adultery, since neither act was illegal in New York State.)

"The board is striving to attract to the ranks young men of ambition, of wholesome clean minds, of temperate habits, of truth, of honor, and self-respect. What parent would be willing that a son should engage in such work? What wife would not seek separation from a husband whose regular business was to drink in low saloons with black and white harlots of the streets, to accompany them to their resorts, to witness their shamelessness and then tell of his conduct in open Court?"

Grant's genuine outrage reverberates here (and he would eventually quit the Police Board over this issue). Eakins's lawyers vowed more court appeals.

————

For his part, Roosevelt, president of the board, never shared any public or private doubts about the Eakins verdict. Though he was generally reticent on the topic of sex, TR did finally elaborate his views on policing prostitution in his autobiography, written almost twenty years later.

Roosevelt endorsed the novel idea of treating men and women alike caught in raids; he also wanted harsher punishment for brothel owners: "they should never be fined; they should be imprisoned." His disgust with the "infamous" men who coerced unwilling women into the trade was so great he thought they should be whipped. "The only way to get at them is through their skins." He also wanted to publish the names of any owners whose property was proven to be used for prostitution. He strongly opposed any stopgap approach such as cordoning off red-light districts.

While TR allowed that stingy employers paying inadequate wages to women contributed to the problem, he regarded morality as the more decisive factor. Girls who are "strong and pure" will resist while "girls of weak character or lax standards readily yield." Girls "who crave cheap finery and vapid pleasure" are "always in danger."

Ultimately, his fix for vice was simply virtue. Roosevelt saw the solution in the American home and American marriage. He envisioned virgin brides and virgin grooms, and faithful husbands and faithful wives, and a contented marital bed.

————

The day after the Eakins guilty verdict, Reverend Parkhurst advocated passing a law that would make it mandatory to dismiss any captain in whose precinct—or any patrolman on whose beat—brothels, streetwalking, or gambling joints flourished. "If this intention were put into effect," the *New York Recorder* dryly noted, "it would remove three-quarters of the present force."

Roosevelt's private views on prostitution—communicated discreetly to acting chief Conlin—as well as Reverend Parkhurst's more public views, seemed to be fostering a new attitude on the police force toward the world's oldest profession. The marching orders were not to look the other way but to arrest. The policemen and detectives started casting a much wider dragnet, and, as any fisherman will tell you, there are sometimes surprises when you cast a very wide net.

————

Saloons dotted the run-down German and Irish neighborhood around 1st Street, a couple blocks east of the Bowery. On the blustery cold night of December 4, streetlamps cast feeble pools of light onto cracked sidewalks. Around 10 p.m., a young woman, perhaps eighteen years old, climbed the stoop at 16 East 1st Street and inquired if the Dittmeyers lived there. She was dressed in a long skirt and long-sleeved shirtwaist with a high collar, a typical outfit for a shopgirl, but she had no coat or wrap. Thin, almost frail, she was also quite pretty, with blue eyes and a small delicate mouth.

The Dittmeyers didn't live there, someone yelled down to her. She walked around that dark neighborhood just north of Devery's dangerous old 11th Precinct for a while trying to figure out what to do; she wondered if she had jumbled the address, so she tried to rouse somebody at 11 East 1st Street. Knocking, stage-whispering, and more knocking finally led her to discover the Dittmeyers didn't reside there either, but a tenant thought the name sounded familiar.

A bit panicked, she accosted a stranger and asked him if he knew the Dittmeyers. The man ignored her and kept walking. A little while later, she accosted another man and asked him if he would go into a nearby saloon and ask if anyone knew Henry and Rose Dittmeyer, her uncle and aunt. She was fairly certain her uncle drank there. The stranger agreed, and since she had no coat, she waited in the doorway of the building next door. She was tired, scared, and shivering.

The man came back and, standing with her in the doorway, told her that someone in the bar thought Henry Dittmeyer lived in the *rear* tenement at 16 East 1st Street. They kept talking as they stepped out into the cold wind on the sidewalk.

Just then, a big blue-coated policeman grabbed her by the arm and ordered her to come along. She shouted, "Don't, don't!" and tried to explain but Officer Reagan twisted her arm, treating her like a typical streetwalker. With her free hand, she grabbed an iron railing; then she went jelly-legged and refused to walk. Reagan blew his whistle three quick toots for backup.

Amelia Elizabeth "Lizzie" Schauer frantically resisted the officers over the four blocks to the East 5th Street station house; she kept telling them that she was merely asking directions. She repeated that to the sergeant and the acting captain, neither of whom were impressed. They consigned her to a cell; in the morning, Officer Reagan hauled her before Police Magistrate Mott at the Essex Market Court House.

"I'm a good girl, judge, and it is all a terrible mistake," she told Judge John O. Mott, a short, bearded, bespectacled sixty-six-year-old recent Republican appointee. The arresting officer, Reagan, testified he saw her talk to two strange men but admitted that he couldn't overhear the conversations. She defended herself, saying she was trying to meet a friend and got lost; she said she lived in Brooklyn. Magistrate Mott, with his usual gruffness, judged her guilty and observed: "No respectable woman should be on the streets at night unaccompanied." He decided to show some leniency, though: he offered her a choice: three days at the workhouse or at the House of Mercy. "For god's sake, let me go home, Judge," she wailed. "I've done nothing wrong. I only lost my way and had to ask someone."

The following morning, before Lizzie departed for the workhouse, a lawyer hired by Lizzie's outraged aunt and a former employer convinced the judge to reconsider. Mott kept the teary women waiting four hours while he tried other cases. (Her aunt, Mrs. Osterburg, was holding her six-week-old baby in the courtroom the whole time.) They testified on her behalf and came armed with a letter of good character from Lizzie's doctor. Officer Reagan repeated his story but added the detail that she had cursed them out. Officer Oppenheimer, who had helped bring in her but had not testified at her first hearing, stated that he had seen her talking to an Italian earlier and he had confronted her. He said she had told him that the man would take her home or to a hotel but that the Italian had blurted out "Me no see her home" and walked off. Lizzie absolutely denied seeing Officer Oppenheimer earlier that night or having had any conversation with him.

Magistrate Mott believed the police officers. He lectured her that she should have asked directions from a policeman. He said it was confirmed that she was talking to a stranger in a hallway at 11:30 p.m. "for what purpose I don't know and can only assume that she was walking out in the night and a street walker." He reaffirmed the sentence of three days at the workhouse for disorderly conduct.

The following morning, Saturday, December 7, Lizzie Schauer, sobbing, was loaded with other convicted women, some of them drunks, vagrants, and streetwalkers, into a large barred police wagon. A matron slammed the door shut and padlocked it. The stench of sweat, liquor, and vomit from the veteran offenders filled the closed space. Two horses pulled the wagon about a mile over the asphalt and cobblestone streets to the East River pier at 26th Street; the driver waited, then guided the locked wagon onto the steamer *Thomas Brennan*. The ship handled the strong currents to reach Blackwell's Island. The crew lowered a ramp and the driver rolled the police wagon to the courtyard of the workhouse. The door unlocked, the women stepped down, blinking at the bright sunlight. A matron grouped the dozen women in pairs and marched them to a changing room. There, she ordered them to strip naked. Each one was weighed, measured, and examined for identifying scars. They entered the bath house next door for the mandatory bath to remove vermin and slow the spread of disease; they dressed themselves in rough heavy blue-and-white-striped cotton dresses. Lizzie was locked up with a grizzled elderly drunk.

By that time, the press had uncovered Lizzie's story and were championing her cause. INNOCENT LIZZIE SCHAUER ARRESTED AND RAILROADED TO PRISON—HER CRIME ASKING AN ADDRESS—IT WAS AFTER DARK WHEN MR. MOTT SAYS RESPECTABLE WOMEN CANNOT BE ABROAD ALONE (*New York World*).

Newspapers such as the *Herald* played it as a Victorian narrative of a pure maiden foully maligned and struggling to regain her good name. They charged that the reform police, wanting to shake Roosevelt's hand, were so overzealous they were hauling off innocent girls who asked directions.

The Saturday that Lizzie arrived at the workhouse happened to be the same day that the Police Board, after six months' probation, appointed Peter Conlin as chief of police, officially dropping "acting" from his title. On his first day in this job he had long coveted, he found himself besieged with complaints and editorials against the excessive powers of police.

The department and the district attorney's office decided to fight back. They released records of two earlier incidents involving the supposedly pure maiden Lizzie Schauer. An assistant district attorney stated that Lizzie's stepmother, also named Elizabeth, had filed charges in March against her for being "wayward and incorrigible" and in the complaint had accused Lizzie of "immorality" starting at age fifteen and of having a venereal disease; the stepmother in September had then accused Lizzie of cohabiting with her uncle, Henry Dittmeyer.

The police and the two branches of her family started a brutal tug-of-war in the newspapers over Lizzie's honor. The unspoken question: Was she virginal or not?

———

Peter Conlin—stinging from criticism over the Lizzie Schauer arrest—decided he would follow through on a suggestion made two months earlier by Commissioner Roosevelt. The chief would do the unthinkable: he would raid one of the most famous brothels in New York City, a place untouched by the police for thirty-five years. No one could say that respectable women lived there. He (and Roosevelt) would recapture the moral high ground.

Grove Street sits in a little oasis of elegant older buildings in the Greenwich Village section of the city. Number 39 Grove Street, a three-story brick building, is half secluded by two elm trees. Every day and night, elegant carriages rolled to a stop before the railed steps, and well-dressed men sauntered to ring the electric bell. The brothel—one of the most expensive in New York City—was an open secret. Owner Millicent Street strictly guarded access, and apparently paid for protection. No policeman had set foot inside for decades.

Not even when one of Vermont's leading citizens, General William Wells, died of a heart attack in a room there three years before, during a visit to the city with his wife in April 1892, did scandal threaten the place. A family friend explained to the newspapers that the general had collapsed while walking and had been carried to the nearest house.

When some of the well-heeled neighbors complained, Mrs. Street calmly informed them that if she moved, she would erect a double tenement "and fill it with negroes at $5 a month." The complaints died down.

Conlin had assigned acting inspector Brooks to infiltrate the house. He in turn had assigned two of his best undercover men. They staked out the building and one afternoon followed a pair of tipsy gentlemen back to their offices on Wall Street. With a few well-placed inquiries, they found the men's names and employers. The two undercover cops then sought out the men at a nearby bar and posed as out-of-town businessmen—in "hat manufacture" and "real estate"—up from D.C., looking for a good time. They bought some drinks; they shared some "wine suppers" until after one long night the two Wall Street men invited them to go with them to 39 Grove Street.

As guests of these regular clients, the two officers—Kemp and McConnell—entered the elegant townhouse. Plush silk settees stood under European paintings. Gas jets cast a warm glow. They bought rounds of champagne served in cut crystal. The place was so pleasant and high-toned that it didn't seem odd that the two men spent three evenings there without going upstairs with any of the beautiful young ladies. They gathered enough evidence of excise liquor violations to get a search warrant.

At 5 p.m. on Saturday, December 7, acting inspector Brooks pressed the buzzer at 39 Grove Street. A "colored maid" answered the door. He wedged his foot in before she could shut it. Brooks, with Kemp and McConnell and five uniformed officers, rushed inside. The maid screamed, another maid came rushing forward. She screamed. Various other females began screaming and for a while the police experienced an ongoing comic operetta with off-cue females hitting high pitches on various floors. Millicent Street, the fifty-seven-year-old proprietress, did not scream; she sat in a back parlor, deeply indignant at the intrusion.

No one escaped.

The police explored the house and rounded up Miss Street, her two servants (Martha Jones and Cassie Carter), eight extremely attractive well-dressed young ladies in their late teens or early twenties, and three men, who all happened to be bald. Roosevelt had given general instructions to haul in the men as well, and Inspector Brooks had followed orders.

The police loaded all fourteen, including regally lovely "Lillie Belmont" and sealskin clad "Cora Brown," into a paddy wagon and trotted them over to Mercer Street station for the night. Inspector Brooks was "jubilant," as were Conlin and Roosevelt, when informed.

The arrest record contained fourteen names but the police suspected most of them were fictitious. (Snooping reporters later discovered that one impressive, florid white-haired Englishman who gave his name as "Henry Harcourt" was a sixty-two-year-old physician visiting from London and staying at the Windsor Hotel.)

About half the prisoners made bail that night.

The following morning, Sunday, Magistrate Simms presided at the Jefferson Market Courthouse, that orange castle-like Victorian confection with a conical tower overlooking Sixth Avenue. The judge—after listening to testimony from the two undercover officers about prior evenings—set bail for Miss Street at $1,000 for maintaining a disorderly house and $200 for excise violations. He set bail at $200 for each of the maids who had served the drinks.

The judge then asked what evidence the inspector had against the eight well-dressed young women and the three men. (He first required all the women to remove their veils; he told the shiny-domed men to stop hiding their faces with their hats.) Inspector Brooks replied that he had no evidence of disorderly conduct.

Magistrate Simms was about to release them all when he decided that he would keep the two youngest under the new law that allowed judges to commit women over age fifteen who were found in a brothel to a religious home of their denomination.

The pair of nineteen-year-olds selected, "Elsie Eskin" and "May Daly," began to weep.

Lawyer "Manny" Friend of Friend & House pleaded with the judge that Elsie Eskin was a seamstress, sent by Mrs. Josephine Sanford of 210 West 54th Street to deliver some garments. Elsie, described as a "decided blond" (apparently, as opposed to a "bottle blond") with cascades of yellow hair under her hat, fainted suddenly with a loud thud to the floor. Her head hit the step up to the witness box, breaking her glasses; blood oozed from a cut on her face. Attendants clustered around her; she was eventually revived.

The judge decided to investigate further while they waited for an ambulance to take her to Bellevue.

Plainclothes detective McConnell testified that during the raid he had found Elsie in a waiting room by herself wearing street clothes and a winter coat; he said he had informed her that "the house was pulled." She replied to him that if he touched her, she would scream. McConnell told the judge he thought she was "fooling."

Miss Eskin explained to the court she was a lady's maid who had fallen very ill and needed an operation. (Her lawyer handed over a doctor's statement.) She now supported herself sewing for a Mrs. Sanford. She had arrived at 39 Grove ten minutes earlier and had never been there before. She fainted again.

The judge released her but he refused to release May Daly, who didn't look nineteen years old. The newspapers described her as "pretty and graceful" with "large brown eyes." Lawyer House said she came from a respectable family in Hoboken and was trimming a hat in the basement at the request of Cora Brown. When informed that she couldn't leave with the others, May threw a fit, weeping and shaking and screaming; the police called for another ambulance, this time from New York Hospital.

The three men and seven women left. Miss Street and the two servants made bail and left. Elsie Eskin had already left. The court attendants carried May Daly out to the ambulance. Yet another *possibly* innocent girl was in custody in Roosevelt's New York.

———

The key witness in the tug-of-war over Lizzie Schauer's innocence and purity was her Brooklyn physician, Dr. Jonathan T. Deyo, who had tested her virginity twice: during an earlier court case and again for an adoption recommendation.

The doctor and several relatives and friends told the newspapers as much as they knew of her life story. Lizzie's mother had died when she was two. Her alcoholic father had remarried a much younger woman, who happened to be both a devout Catholic and a binge drinker. She had demanded strict obedience. She beat Lizzie often; she once tied her to the bedpost, once drunkenly slashed at her with a knife, leaving a large triangular scar on her hand. The stepmother convinced her husband to make the child quit school at age thirteen to work.

Lizzie had worked as a live-in servant for several families in Brooklyn; she worked eighteen months for a Mrs. Evans, who called her a good pure girl. Two years ago, Lizzie's stepmother convinced Catholic Church officials that Lizzie was promiscuous and had her committed to the Sisters of Mercy. The Sisters, however, found her behavior exemplary and released her after three months.

Her most recent employer was Mrs. Joseph Rapp. "I can stake my life on Lizzie Schauer's character," Mrs. Rapp told a reporter. "Like other girls of her age she was fond of company but she seemed to care most for girl friends."

This past March, while Lizzie was still working for Mrs. Rapp, Lizzie's stepmother, with Lizzie's father's approval, had gone to the police and accused the girl of having sex with her boyfriend/fiancé, and stated that Lizzie was a "common streetwalker" with "a loathsome disease." Since the stepmother told authorities that her stepdaughter was not sixteen (i.e., still a minor), the official charge against Lizzie was that she was "wayward and incorrigible."

Lizzie and her aunt, Mrs. Osterburg, and Mrs. Rapp had attended the hearing in March at Monroe Street Courthouse in Brooklyn; the judge, weighing the favorable testimony of these character witnesses, offered to allow the women to take Lizzie to a reputable doctor to be physically examined for signs of promiscuity or venereal disease.

Dr. Jonathan T. Deyo of 9th Street, Brooklyn, inspected her. "The Justice on reading [my report] immediately discharged the young lady from custody . . . saying it was a most convincing vindication of her character and most fully disproved all the charges made against her."

Dr. Deyo chose not to reveal the "substance" of his report to the newspapers, but clearly he had found Lizzie to be a disease-free virgin.

In the 1890s, doctors routinely performed virginity tests to reveal the moral character of a young woman, although medical science had long judged the test not to be foolproof. "In all of medicine there is nothing more difficult to determine than virginity," Dr. Nicolas Venette cautioned in his oft-reprinted medical treatise. And Dr. Venette compared interpreting the telltale signs of vaginal penetration to "tracking the course of a ship on the sea, an eagle in the air or a snake on a rock."

Love manuals abounded with tricks that women might use to mimic virginity after its loss, including powders such as alum.

All that notwithstanding, Justice Tighe accepted Dr. Deyo's report and freed Lizzie in the spring. Then, on September 15, 1895—around the time of Roosevelt's victory over the liquor dealers—her stepmother brought new charges against her. Lizzie had traveled into Manhattan to spend the night with her other aunt, Rose Metzger Dittmeyer, at 16 East 1st Street.

Her stepmother suspected the worst and made accusations to the police that the Dittmeyers were encouraging Lizzie's immoral conduct, her uncle possibly participating; the authorities brought a charge of "abduction of a minor" against Mr. Dittmeyer. The stepmother and two police officers had shown up at 10 a.m. and arrested him; Lizzie was sent to the House of Detention to be kept as a witness at Dittmeyer's trial. For two weeks, she refused to testify against him, calling it all lies. During an interrogation, she stated she was eighteen years old; a birth certificate was found and thus the "abduction of a minor" charge was dropped, and she was released.

Dr. Deyo had recently had another opportunity to probe Lizzie. Three weeks earlier, he had examined her "character" again, to determine whether to write a letter of recommendation to Lizzie's paternal aunt, who had offered to let her come live with her in Germany. He wrote the letter.

But now, during the newspaper frenzy over the arrest of a supposedly innocent girl, Stephen J. O'Hare, the assistant district attorney who had handled the abduction case, leaked to the press that during her incarceration back in September Lizzie had confessed to him and to Judge Cowing she was of "unchaste character" starting at age fifteen. Lizzie denied ever admitting that and said the A.D.A. was confusing her stepmother's words with her own. Judge Cowing, when contacted, did not recall any such confession by Lizzie. The tug-of-war continued: cunning vamp or long-suffering virgin?

———

On Monday morning, December 9, Lizzie boarded the barred police wagon at 7:30 a.m. for the steamer trip back to Manhattan. She had served two days of her sentence but a supreme court judge had granted her lawyer a writ of habeus corpus and scheduled a morning hearing to review Magistrate Mott's decision. She waited at the Tombs prison, a massive, vaguely Egyptian-looking building, under the care of the so-called "Tombs Angel" Mrs. Foster, a society woman who for years made it her special cause to shepherd girls through prison and the courts. (Her most recent protégée was Maria Barberi, a pudgy Italian seamstress who had slit bootblack Dominic Cataldo's throat after he had repeatedly refused to fulfill his promise to marry her.)

Lizzie sat with Mrs. Foster at 10 a.m. in the packed courtroom of the supreme court as they waited for the arrival of Judge Charles Andrews. Lizzie's father, Casper, and her stepmother squeezed in on a bench nearby and began talking in loud voices.

"Her stepmother denounced her as a brazen streetwalker and told those about her that the girl was bad," according to the *New York Herald*. "The father left his daughter not a shred of reputation."

The judge got quickly down to business; he said he had reviewed the testimony and that it did not prove the charge of disorderly conduct. He said there was no evidence she was a "nightwalker," or had loitered for evil purposes, or that her conversation with strange men was for evil purposes.

"Putting the worst construction on the testimony given before the City Magistrate against this defendant I consider the evidence is not sufficient to warrant her conviction and therefore I order that she be discharged."

The courtroom erupted in cheers and scattered hisses. In the hubbub, Mrs. Foster wrapped her arm around Lizzie's shoulder and hustled her out of the building by a side exit. She wanted to keep the girl away from her stepmother and father and from Uncle Henry Dittmeyer, still angry over his arrest in September. Mrs. Foster, dressed in black, took her by horse cab outside the city to Mrs. Foster's own "Retreat for Young Women."

Most of the newspapers celebrated the freeing of an innocent.

Commissioner Roosevelt—after reading a report by acting captain Woodruff—defended the arrest. "If the officers arrested her without cause, I should have them punished," stated Roosevelt, "but from present appearances I believe the police were justified in making the arrest."

———

On that same day in another courtroom, the respectable parents of very pretty "May Daly," alleged courtesan/hatmaker's apprentice at the Grove Street brothel, arrived from Hoboken to vouch for their daughter. "Oh mama, you don't believe the charge that has been brought against me, do you?" sobbed the girl as she clung to her mother's shoulder. Her father stood by, blinking back tears. "I was always a good girl," she said.

Fighting her emotions, May haltingly testified to Judge Simms that one of the women of 39 Grove, Minnie Ross, had met her and asked her to come to the house to trim a hat. She was in the basement adding velvet to the crown of a chapeau when the police arrived. The judge agreed to release her to her parents and also abided by the lawyer's request not to ask their true family name. However, he gave a short lecture. He was convinced "May" had been invited into the house as a subterfuge to recruit her to work in the brothel. "I have taught her a lesson that she will not soon forget," said the judge to her parents. "It will keep her away from houses of this sort in the future."

—————

On Wednesday, December 11, Roosevelt awoke to a *New York World* front-page cartoon of the Statue of Liberty under arrest for being an unaccompanied female out at night.

CHRISTMAS: ARMED AND DANGEROUS

In his tortured mood in December, Roosevelt offered to join a military expedition attacking Canada if Great Britain's border dispute with Venezuela over British Guyana continued to escalate. "If it wasn't wrong, I should say personally I would rather welcome a foreign war!" he would soon write to his sister.

Early that month, he discovered the Republican boss Platt was cheating extensively over the voter registration for the Republican primary—even borrowing names from Tammany rolls and from street signs—but Roosevelt, with great exertion, muzzled himself, honoring his vow to Lodge not to publicly criticize the Republican Party. TR also ran headlong into Boss Platt over the selection of the next Republican candidate for president. He wanted to back Thomas Reed, Speaker of the House, but the boss was ordering all loyal New York State Republicans to support their favorite son, Governor Levi Morton. Making matters worse, Morton's signature on a Police Board bill could ultimately determine whether Roosevelt still had a job or not.

TR found himself boxed in on all sides.

In this feisty frustrated mood, he learned that a race-baiting anti-Semite who had just arrived from Germany on a crusade to crush the Jews in America was scheduled to speak at Cooper Union on December 12. Herr Hermann Ahlwardt, a member of the Reichstag (Parliament), chose the second night of Hanukkah for his message of hate.

In the late nineteenth century, a wave of anti-Semitism was surging both overseas and in vast swatches of America. The pogroms in Russia were chasing out hundreds of thousands of Jews; stereotypical Shylock portrayals of Jews as greedy moneylenders abounded. The Grand Union Hotel in Saratoga Springs refused admittance to the Jewish financier Joseph Seligman in 1877. The Union League, which had counted Jews among its founding members, decided to ban Jews, such as Jesse Seligman's son Theodore, in 1893. The famed Belmont family of New York found it convenient to convert away from its original name of Schonberg. Joseph Pulitzer so thoroughly hid his Jewish roots from his children that his son, Joseph Jr., didn't discover his father's past until he was a teenager.

Pulitzer was trying to thrive in a society that increasingly ostracized Jews. The widely read trade publication *The Journalist* called him "Jewseph Pulitzer" and described him as combing his hair with his devil claws: "In the multiplicity of Nature's freaks, running from Albino Negroes to seven-legged calves, there is one curiosity that will always cause the observer to turn and stare. This freak is a red-headed Jew."

Even in Roosevelt's former D.C. circle, economics philosopher Brooks Adams dreaded the rise of Jewish bankers and gloomily predicted a "gold-ridden, capitalist-bestridden, usurer-mastered future."

In this climate, with anti-Semitism on the rise, it was feared in many quarters that Herr Ahlwardt, a chubby, articulate former schoolteacher, might find an enthusiastic audience on these shores.

Jewish leaders approached TR at police headquarters and asked whether the commissioner would allow such a Teutonic hatemonger to address a mass audience in this great metropolis. "He has a perfect right to speak so long as he infringes no law," Roosevelt told them matter-of-factly. "If you choose to speak against the Gentiles, you are at liberty to do so at any time, upon the same condition." But the commissioner vowed the Cooper Union speech would be orderly and he told them that he refused to make a martyr out of Ahlwardt, either by some rioter harming him or by the police denying him his rights.

Soon after the Jewish committee left his office, Roosevelt lit on a remarkable and provocative strategy: one he called "purely American," one he judged feasible only in New York of all the world's cities, one that he would proudly recall later in life.

On the afternoon of Thursday, December 12, the day of the speech, Roosevelt told his roundsman, Michael Tierney, to go find a Jewish police sergeant. (Some accounts state it was Otto Raphael, but he was a rookie patrolman at the time; others state it was a "lieutenant," but that rank did not yet exist in the New York police department.)

"Pick out about forty good, true intelligent Jewish members of the force, men whose faces clearly show their race and order them to report to me in a body," he told the unnamed Jewish officer. "I want them to keep order at this Ahlwardt meeting tonight."

Roosevelt had a plan that he believed "could undo much of the mischief which [Herr Ahlwardt] was trying to do."

The Jewish officers assembled that afternoon for the commissioner, and the group comprised "full forty of the longest beaked noses on the force!"

Roosevelt told them: "I am going to assign you men to the most honorable service you have ever done . . . the protection of an enemy, and the defense of religious liberty and free speech."

Roosevelt was not in the least surprised that he could find—on such short notice—so many Jewish officers. TR estimated that Jews comprised the fourth leading "strain" on the force, after the Irish, Germans, and American-born Christians. According to Jacob Riis, Jews accounted for about 250,000 of the city's nearly 2 million residents in 1895.

In a later article, "The Ethnology of the Police," Roosevelt briskly waded into ethnic generalizations commonplace in that era (Irish "fight well"; Germans are "thrifty"). "The great bulk of the Jewish population, esp. the immigrants from Russia and Poland, are of weak physique and have not yet gotten far enough away from their centuries of oppression and degradation to make good policemen; but the outdoor Jew who has been a [cable car] gripman, or the driver of an express wagon, or a guard on the Elevated, or the indoor Jew of fine bodily powers who has taken to boxing, wrestling and the like, offers excellent material for the force."

TR added the Jews are "very intelligent," at least equal in smarts to native-born Americans.

Many New Yorkers feared Herr Ahlwardt's Jew-bashing speech might spark riots. In the hours before the 8 p.m. start, a raucous, mostly antagonistic crowd gathered outside the large squat Cooper Union building at 7th Street and Broadway. The throngs thinned as word spread that the Institute—famed for its free classes in the arts and sciences—was charging a hefty fifty cents admission to hear Ahlwardt.

At some point, Ahlwardt slipped into the building. "Down the main aisle passed the agitator between two rigid lines of Semitic profiles . . . those clean shaven helmeted Hebrew officers in mass like some ancient bas-relief on an Assyrian tomb . . . majestic in their bearing." Forty Jewish policemen in blue uniforms guarded the back and sides of the stage, as well as the entrances and exits of the great hall. The New York Times reporter doggedly counted the audience: 150 men and three women barely filling the first twenty rows; that same reporter would later decide that almost one-third of these spectators were plainclothes detectives, basing his estimate on the fact that those stone-faced men never stood up, never cat-called or applauded.

The *New York World* also did the math. "Rector Hermann Ahlwardt, the noted anti-semite, spoke in Cooper Union last night to an audience made up mainly of police."

Promptly at 8 p.m., Herr Ahlwardt, "round, fat, good-natured, shiny-faced," wearing a monocle, strode out across an empty stage to the lectern. No one introduced him. The *Tribune* estimated the paying audience of non-policemen was equally divided between Jews and Jew haters. The hisses drowned out the tepid applause.

Ahlwardt delivered his speech, "The Essence of Modern Judaism," in German. Hecklers shouted in German. (The only English heard that night came from policemen.)

Ahlwardt traced the history of the Jews as parasites. "In the Old Testament can you find a single Jew who worked? If you can find a single working Jew in those 4,000 years I am surprised." He analyzed how Jews in Europe reaped the labor of workers until they controlled all wealth and industry.

"Work is a curse for them," said Ahlwardt.

"Go down to the eastside and see if we don't work," shouted someone.

Ahlwardt pressed on with his theme. He explained the Jew's loyalty goes to his religion over his country.

As he spoke, at times, a Jew here or there would rise up and shout something or laugh hysterically. Each time, a uniformed officer or a detective would confront the heckler until he stopped. "The crowd yelled 'Pfui' instead of 'Rats,'" observed the *New York Sun*, "and their multi-syllabled [German] profanity rumbled like the final roll of the kettle drums in a Wagnerian opera."

About fifteen minutes into his speech, Ahlwardt moved away from the lectern and walked to the front of the stage. A man in the second row jumped up and with a "roar of rage" fired an egg at Ahlwardt, then hurled two more in quick succession. Ahlwardt, despite his pudginess and dress shoes, nimbly dodged all three, which cracked onstage, leaving yellow streaks. The police pounced on the man—Louis Silverman, it would turn out. Ahlwardt shook his finger at Silverman and yelled at him in German as a phalanx of New York's Hebrew "Finest" hauled him off.

"Gentlemen, do not allow this to disturb you," said Ahlwardt, quickly regaining his composure. "I had allowed myself fifteen minutes to show you the differences between the Aryan and the Semitic races. This man has shown you the whole thing in a moment. No other man but a Jew could have done this."

A drunken voice from the back yelled: "Anyone else would have thrown straight."

The *Sun* reported that even a few Jews laughed. Ahlwardt, with frequent interruptions, spoke for two hours. He mentioned that he had walked the East Side of New York, and that after seeing all the street signs in Hebrew, he wondered why the city wasn't called "New Jerusalem." Loud boos filled the hall. Ahlwardt maintained his composure; he mentioned that the messiah Jesus was the first Jew baiter. "I am neither afraid of Jews nor of rotten eggs."

After his prepared remarks, Ahlwardt asked if anyone had comments or questions: all over the hall men stood up (except the detectives). Several angry New York Jews made speeches in defense of their race and religion, which Ahlwardt coolly answered. He even hinted at something that sounded more like a Final Solution than Zionism. "I'm here to do a certain work. God wishes to get all the Jews into one country someday."

When the meeting ended at 11 p.m., six burly Jewish policemen encircled Ahlwardt and convoyed him out.

The police had squelched any riot, and had admirably handled the night. Editorialists citywide denounced Ahlwardt. Many New Yorkers were quoted uttering tolerant comments. Industrialist Gustav H. Schwab commented: "Some of my most intimate friends, some of the finest people I know, are Hebrews." (Ahlwardt's hate crusade petered out the following year in rural New Jersey, in a flurry of assault charges stemming from several fights.)

But Roosevelt's clever and humane strategy of setting Jews to guard a Jew-hater went largely unnoticed and unreported.

———

Four days after his leadership gem went ignored, Roosevelt woke up to read a devastating front-page article in the *New York World,* the largest-circulation daily. Pulitzer's paper charged that many of the nation's elite professional criminals were flocking to New York because the police were tied up enforcing petty laws and guarding Sunday saloons. The piece—MECCA OF OUTLAWS— which covered half the front page and spilled over to page two, featured sixty biographical descriptions and twenty drawings of dangerous burglars, con men, bank robbers, and forgers, now "at large" in the city.

The paper printed detailed drawings of these criminal masterminds—whose ordinariness made them more frightful—from bank thief Horace Hovan to swindler Colonel Alexander Branscom. "Scarcely a man of them would have been permitted to walk the New York streets in the old days."

The paper also charged that a shifting of manpower was putting the city at risk as detectives formerly stationed at ferries and train stations "who know the face of every notorious thief in the country" had been reassigned. It said convicts were bee-lining to the city from prisons such as Sing Sing, euphoric at opportunities to plot in secret since Byrnes's stool-pigeon network had been dismantled. The article cited the previous week's "Pope murder," the "Brentano mystery," and "the Harlem shooting" as crimes of "professional burglars or highwaymen." It tallied 143 crimes against life and property, 19 murders, 39 felonious assaults, 9 incendiary fires, 13 highway robberies, 62 burglaries in the past ten weeks. And it rehashed a grisly five-week-old unsolved "umbrella murder," in which a robber plunged the tip of an umbrella into the victim's right eye.

The *World* assured readers that a "most careful investigation" led to this exposé. "It is not to be doubted that Mr. Roosevelt will instruct those under him to find out the plans of these men nor is it to be doubted that he will want to know why he did not know of the presence of this galaxy of criminality before."

———

The following evening, on Tuesday, December 17, Commissioner Roosevelt attended a posh dinner that he expected to be a celebration of the reform movement's remarkable year. Instead, it turned out to be something of a Roosevelt roast.

Herbert Booth King—a socialite and advertising executive—hosted a dinner at the Waldorf for the mayors of New York, Brooklyn, and Boston. This A-list affair featured sixty guests, all male, the cream of local politicians, especially of the reform movement, including judges, district attorneys, parks commissioners, former mayors, senators, assemblymen, and police commissioners Roosevelt and Grant.

They sat at a horseshoe-shaped table in a private banquet room. A Tyrolean orchestra featuring virtuoso mandolin players performed as "choice viands and rare old wines" were served. Waiters hovered to keep glasses filled.

Around 10 p.m., Mayor Strong, smiling affably, rose to give an after-dinner talk about his first year in office.

Deciding to lighten things up for the holiday season, Mayor Strong recounted how a bevy of society ladies had cooed him into appointing eccentric colonel George E. Waring from Providence, Rhode Island, as sanitation commissioner. At first, during the snowstorms, everyone had been convinced Waring was a failure, but then they were shocked to discover that Waring was actually able to clean the formerly filthy, ash-strewn, muck-clogged streets and stop the overnight parking.

"After that, I thought I would have a pretty easy time, until the Police Board came along [in May] and tried to make a Puritan out of a Dutchman. I tried to convince some of the Commissioners that it wasn't possible but you know how it is when a man has got his commission . . . I went away on my vacation and when I got back the Police Commissioners were more than mayors in New York."

When the laughter died down, he continued: "I believe we have laws on the statute book for giving New York the best government any city ever had, if we only enforce them. If anything we have an *excess* of good laws."

He soon launched into an anecdote about whiskey. "A friend asked me how long since my grandparents were immigrants. I said about 1650. 'Well,' he said, 'don't you know that your ancestors left Scotland because they could not get a glass of Scotch Whiskey on Sunday?' That friend advised that I toss out the police commissioners."

The *New York Recorder* reported that "[Roosevelt] laughed louder and longer than any one else at Mayor Strong's first thrusts but as it became painfully apparent that the Mayor meant everything he said, the president of the police force became silent, then flushed, and finally paled with anger."

The mayor, basking in the laughs, blithely continued: "Why, a man wrote to me from Little Falls the other day, asking if I couldn't spare one of the Police Commissioners to stop the sale of ginger ale up there. I told him I couldn't, because all four of them were busy watching the girls who sell flowers and the poor devils who sell ice on Sunday."

Roosevelt squirmed in his seat, very impatient to reply in front of this esteemed assemblage, but he was forced to wait more than a quarter hour until Mayor Strong finished, and then Mayor Curtis of Boston delivered some brief remarks.

The commissioner rose; he might have been aiming for banter but his tight lips and chopping hand gestures belied him.

He informed these titans of reform that in addition to being a "Dutchman" he was also part Irish and that in any case, he was pleased the Puritans had come to these shores because they possessed two wonderful traits. "They were essentially moral and essentially manly." His remark drew applause, not laughter from the chastened crowd.

Roosevelt said the mayor was too busy to investigate every tale but that the story about the police cracking down on a poor ice seller on a Sunday was false. The "Czar's Minions"—as he sarcastically referred to his own policemen—had arrested a man selling policy (illegal lottery) tickets and that fellow, trying to avoid jail, had pretended to be an iceman. The press had mixed up the two stories.

He also stated with a distinct edge in his voice that he had no sympathy for law-breaking liquor dealers and would continue to shut them down.

Then, not satisfied with debunking only genial Mayor Strong, Roosevelt attacked the *New York World* for its "Mecca of Outlaws" article.

"The *World* printed a list of criminals, who, it said, were at large," he enunciated. "Many of them are dead and some of the others are in prison." He paused. "There was about two or three per cent of truth in the story, which is an unusually large percentage for the New York *World*." The audience—many with a drink in one hand and a cigar in the other—laughed very hard.

Roosevelt didn't realize just how right he was about the lack of truthfulness in "Mecca of Outlaws." Pulitzer's reporters had apparently thumbed through a copy of the decade-old *Professional Criminals of America* (1886) written by former police chief Thomas Byrnes and had borrowed eighteen of its first nineteen profiles. The theft bordered on plagiarism at times, such as this item for Edward Dinkelman, alias Eddie Miller, pickpocket/hotel thief: "Dark hair, dark eyes, dark complexion, round face, nervously quick in his movements" (*New York World*); "Dark hair, dark eyes, round face, dark complexion; dresses well and is very quick in his movements" (*Professional Criminals of America*).

The next day's wave of peacemaking by the mayor and commissioner didn't sway too many. "The mayor is just sick of Teddy," said one veteran Republican, "and hits him over the head with a bungstarter [the mallet to loosen corks from barrels] and tries to apologize now by saying he was jesting . . . these reformers make me tired."

———

Roosevelt planned on spending the Christmas holidays out at Oyster Bay with his large, boisterous family, children to the right, to the left, and underfoot. He delegated five straight days for enjoying the snow, the sleigh riding, the winter vistas. However, too much time not working sometimes led him to unpleasant introspection. On day two, he wrote a letter to Henry Cabot Lodge and noted "rather gloomily" that this would mark the first Christmas dinner not eaten at the Lodges' home after five consecutive years together.

Roosevelt complained about being tantalized but ultimately denied the chance to go to the Republican presidential convention by the local party leaders. He groused that even the stalwartly Republican *New York Tribune* now ran only anti-TR pieces since he had denied them their boodle in political advertising during the last campaign. He expected the mayor to criticize him in his upcoming annual address, and had heard that the Platt machine was luring Governor Morton to agree to sign a bill ousting the Police Board by telling him that TR planned on backing Congressman Thomas Reed of Maine for president instead of him.

Henry Cabot Lodge—troubled by TR's dour letters—rushed two upbeat missives in reply, stressing Roosevelt's national accomplishments. Roosevelt, already back at work by December 27, admitted he was grateful for the boost. "Don't imagine that I really get very blue. Every now and then I feel sullen for an hour or two when everybody seems to join against me here but I would not for anything give up my experience of the last eight months. I prize them more than any eight months in my official career."

———

Roosevelt's downhill slide sped up.

On Friday, December 27, thieves stole the Burden family diamonds and other jewels worth $60,000 (approximately $1.5 million in 2012 dollars). As word of the robbery spread on Saturday, Roosevelt was in Philadelphia giving a speech on the revitalization of the New York City police.

The townhouse of Isaac Burden—the very wealthy iron-ore millionaire—overlooked Madison Square Park. From his front steps, he could see Delmonico's; every morning, the tower of Madison Square Garden threw his yard into shade. It marked a prestigious address, fit for an elite family, one of the city's famed Four Hundred.

On Friday night, the husband and wife attended *Romeo and Juliet* sitting in their usual box at the Metropolitan Opera, bringing along two female servants and their coachman and footman, and leaving eight servants in the house.

Mrs. Burden arrived home from the opera just before midnight and went to place a necklace in the safe in her bedroom. She screamed when she discovered the safe door open and jewels missing, including a magnificent five-strand diamond necklace, with a center diamond the "size of a hazelnut." She yelled to a servant to press the "message alarm" and two boys raced over from American District Telegraph, nearby at Broadway and 26th Street; she sent them running to the 30th Street police station to alert Captain Pickett, who rushed over with several officers.

Detectives searched the three-story townhouse and the basement, yard, and stables. Mrs. Burden staunchly defended her servants from suspicion even though acting captain O'Brien suspected an inside job. At one point, a detective, ransacking the kitchen, removed a large ham from the icebox; several servants teased him, asking if he was very hungry and wondering if there was anything he wasn't going to search. The detective put the ham back. (Four months later, it would be revealed that the thieves, with the help of a maid, had stashed the jewels inside that ham.)

The sensational robbery seemed to confirm the *World*'s and other newspapers' charges that crime was once again rampant in New York. With Roosevelt in Philadelphia, Commissioner Parker took a rare lead in speaking to the press: he promised a crisp investigation and he adamantly denied that the reform police had gone soft on criminals.

The police department assigned massive manpower to searching the house, combing the neighborhood, and grilling second-story men and other burglars. The detectives cabled Scotland Yard; they sent "hundreds of postal cards to the police of other cities giving a description of the lost property."

However, in the days following, even the pro-reform *New York Times* joined the general bashing of the police: "The Burden robbery . . . means that the police system has permitted the existence, in point of comfort and security from arrest, of dangerous thieves who have been free to watch, plan and succeed in a center of this civilization."

The *Washington Post* took special delight: "Ted Roosevelt is going about the country lecturing on the efficiency of the New York police force, while that town is overrun with thieves and crooks and big diamond robberies are becoming a daily occurrence."

On Sunday, Roosevelt returned by train from resounding waves of applause at that municipal reform dinner in Philadelphia and headed straight to Oyster Bay. He unburdened himself to his sister.

We are having a good deal of anxiety with our detective bureau.
Under the old system certain classes of criminals were protected,
partly for blackmail, partly on condition that they should betray
and spy on certain other classes. Now we have stopped blackmail
and protect no criminal, and in consequence, the war we wage is
very hard indeed.

Roosevelt had always found the "stool pigeon" system morally repugnant—for the police to pay *some* lawbreakers in cash or in indulgence of their crimes for information leading to the arrest of *other* thieves for *other* crimes. He lobbied hard and convinced Parker to join him in eradicating it entirely.

Abe Hummel, a defense lawyer with several decades' experience, observed in a book on New York City crime:

Ninety-nine out of a hundred cases are worked through the squeal
of some thief, or ex-thief, who keeps posted on the doings of others
of his class in the city. He knows some officer intimately; goes to
him and tells him that the night before One-Thumbed Charley
turned a trick on Church street, and the stuff is "planted" at such
and such a place. Acting on this information, the officers visit the
place indicated, and just sit around and wait till their man shows
up. Lots of ability about that, isn't there? Some people have an idea,
you know, that after a burglary the detectives visit the house where it
occurred, and, after examining certain marks on the window where
the man got in, immediately say: "This is the work of Slippery Sam;
he is the only fellow who does this sort of work in this particular
style." Nothing of the kind.

The *World*, which never tired of twitting Teddy, interviewed some convicts at Sing Sing. One of the nation's highest-profile bank robbers, John Watson, serving nine years for his latest caper, said that without stool pigeons the police have no way of learning details about crimes. "They are just as much in the dark as any other citizen of New York."

———

On New Year's Eve in nineteenth-century fin de siècle New York, boisterous crowds massed not in Times Square, which didn't yet exist, but around Trinity Church on Lower Broadway, overflowing into half a dozen nearby streets, eventually toppling police lines and shutting down the streetcars. The people, ushering out 1895, waited for the famed church bells to peal in the New Year with a dozen-tune hourlong medley starting at 11:30 p.m. and climaxing with "Happy New Year" at midnight.

The church steeple was flanked by a full moon that night; gusts of wind racing off the water whistled through the canyons of buildings, chilling the tens of thousands who stared at the steeple and waited for the bells of Trinity to signal the New Year. Peddlers sold five-cent tin trumpets as long as a man's arm, and penny kazoos and Dutch watch rattles and slide whistles and drums and shrill horns called "laughing hyenas." With temperatures dipping to freezing and crowds crushing in on each other, people tooted and shouted and banged so much that no one could hear the long-awaited church bells. "The sweet-tongued orchestra in the belfry was drowned out, smothered, silenced in the din of 50,000 instruments of torture," reported the *World*.

Gangs of teenage hoodlums pulled little pranks, such as tipping over drunks. And Good Samaritans rescued mothers foolish enough to bring their babies into the throng, shepherding them into doorways. Liquor bottles were passed since no law prevented public consumption.

At the stroke of midnight, the world-famous chimes-man played "Happy New Year to Thee" and then later added "Yankee Doodle Dandy" and "Home, Sweet Home."

———

The holiday season did nothing to calm Roosevelt's jangled nerves and left him even more convinced that he might lose his job soon. "I don't see what else I could have done," he wrote to his sister. "I take things with much philosophy and will abide the event unmoved. I have made my blows felt at any rate."

I AM RIGHT

Roosevelt had heard the rumblings and rumors long enough. Sometime during the first two weeks of the New Year, he tried to arrange a meeting with Boss Platt, the Republican backroom titan. Platt's corrupt manipulations of voter registries during the recent primaries had guaranteed his dominance over New York's congressional nominations and the delegates heading to the national presidential nominating convention in late spring.

Roosevelt failed in his first few attempts to wangle an interview. So he reached out to one of his first mentors, the tough East Side Irish Catholic Joe Murray, who had seen potential in the loud twenty-three-year-old Harvard grad back in 1881 and had boosted him for assemblyman in the Twenty-first District.

Murray, a rough man, a classic machine Republican, who fondly participated in election brawls and rewarded loyalty, was now an excise commissioner at $5,000 per year. He agreed to set up a meeting with Platt.

On Sunday, January 19, 1896, big Joe Murray walked Roosevelt over to the Fifth Avenue Hotel and guided him in to see the sixty-two-year-old Platt, the wizened low-key orchestrator. Presidents such as Grant, Harrison, and Hayes had walked that same carpeted hallway to sound out Platt.

The two men were a caricaturist's daydream. Roosevelt, though stressed, was still all sturdy vitality with his steady gaze and quick smile; Platt was a world-weary, almost disappearing presence, with an immaculate fine suit hung on a skeletal frame. Roosevelt opened with the ostensible reason for his visit, to ask Platt his plans regarding the upcoming presidential election.

Platt was trying to be a kingmaker, throwing his support to the governor of New York, the machine Republican Levi P. Morton, but what if Morton faded early at the nominating convention—what would Platt do?

Since Roosevelt preferred Reed of Maine over Governor McKinley of

Ohio or Morton of New York, he hoped to find out something that he could report directly to Senator Lodge and to Reed, both of whom he would be seeing the following week in D.C. Authentic information about the nation's most populous state was political gold; Reed would be grateful. Platt was quite shifty in his response but TR did learn enough to decide that backing any breakaway movement by reform Republicans in New York State would at this time be a waste.

Roosevelt then asked if he could pose another question and Platt nodded his assent. Conventional wisdom now had it that the New York City Police Board would be abolished by a massive rezoning of the city plotted by the upstate Republicans. The Greater Consolidation of New York would meld the various counties such as Kings (Brooklyn), Queens, and Richmond (Staten Island) into one massive city—with combined police, fire, and sanitation departments—joining the current New York of Manhattan and parts of the Bronx. The bill's passage was a foregone conclusion if the Republicans stayed in power because consolidation would dilute Tammany's Democratic stranglehold. The creation of America's greatest metropolis would happen—to a large extent—because of gerrymandering and petty politics.

Pundits pegged consolidation as at least two years away (i.e., January of 1898), but now fresh rumors swirled that the Republican powers, exasperated by Roosevelt's policies, were planning a supplemental police bill that would allow the governor to fire the New York police commissioners immediately.

"I asked him if we'd be legislated out of office," Roosevelt later recounted of their succinct exchange. "He said: 'Yes.' I said: 'I'd fight.' And he said. 'Oh, certainly, that's alright.'" Platt spoke in an earnest voice barely above a whisper.

The state boss quietly predicted that the Police Board would be out of work within sixty days. As TR rose to leave, Platt asked Roosevelt a question: Did he agree that Commissioner Parker was a "very able man"? TR praised Parker and said he was working well with him. Platt then asked if Roosevelt was interested in being reappointed to a new Police Board along with Parker. Roosevelt declined the offer.

In a letter to Lodge that night TR characterized his meeting with Platt as "entirely pleasant and cold-blooded." He also promised his mentor that he wouldn't break with the Republican Party because "the presidential contest is too important." (Roosevelt didn't specify whether it was "too important" only for the country, or also for his future job prospects; he had shown himself elastic in presidential politics, resigning himself to Republican Party choices, such as Blaine in 1884.)

Roosevelt also wrote that Sunday to his sister of his "likely" ouster. He expressed no regrets, calling the year "perhaps the best spent of my life." He also vowed: "I wish to leave the force with our work practically done so as to make it as difficult to undo as possible."

He clearly intended to make his "blows felt."

————

The next day Roosevelt tried to eviscerate his enemies. He delivered a speech full of belligerent broadsides to a convention of Methodist ministers. He painted, more emphatically than ever, the image of a corrupt greed-driven world conspiring against the pure crusader and he depicted any legislature—even a Republican one—as being openly corrupt if it legislated out the pure crusader.

He identified almost all the major players in the political life of the great city and one by one accused them of backing criminals and lawlessness.

The next day, the *World,* in its coverage, devoted almost one-third of its front page to a massive cartoon. Flanked by the giant words "I AM," a pint-sized Roosevelt stood, with his back arched, his oversized head spewing saliva and words. And the caption read:

Judge Cowing is wrong in talking of the carnival of crime in New York—Magistrate Flammer is wrong in opposing my child spies—Public is wrong in saying crimes of violence are increasing—Newspapers all wrong—Old Police Board was wrong—Judges of General Sessions are wrong in imposing such light sentences—Legislature is wrong—And he obviously meant his hearers to understand **"I alone am Right!"**

And for once the *World,* so relentlessly criticized by Roosevelt, had delivered a news report, even a cartoon one, that was absolutely accurate . . . that is exactly what TR meant.

This was Roosevelt's greatest strength, and his most lampoonable trait: his utter righteousness, his zealot's self-confidence. It would lead him over a lifetime to notching world-changing victories but also to humbling, almost incomprehensible defeats.

In this speech to the annual meeting of Methodist Ministers at 150 Fifth Avenue, Roosevelt lumped together newspapers, politicians, bankers, merchants, crooks, gamblers, saloon keepers, proprietors of disorderly houses, and small shopkeepers, all "knitted" together to the corrupt old system, which had "thrived and fattened through dishonesty and favoritism."

He said the board had infuriated several powerful newspapers by ending the practice of handing out a fat advertising job for publishing election polling places and instead had put it out to the lowest bidder, saving the city $42,000. He dismissed Judge Rufus B. Cowing's speech to a grand jury describing an increase in crime, and pointed to a spike in arrests for homicide, burglary, and robbery for eight months of 1895 over the same period in 1894.

He blamed judges for causing crimes through excessive leniency, citing several notorious thieves with mug shots in the Rogues' Gallery who had recently received only two- or three-month prison terms.

He complained that after a policeman used an eleven-year-old boy to help get evidence against a "scoundrel" saloon keeper selling liquor to minors, Magistrate Flammer, "incredible as it may seem," reprimanded the police for using "child spies." TR indignantly pointed out that the youngster had a long arrest record, that selling liquor to ten-year-olds was heinous, and that the police used this sort of tactic only about once every six months.

Taking a new tack, he touted the Sunday saloon crackdown as honoring the legislature's goal of giving all workingmen—including bartenders—an "opportunity to rest and innocently enjoy" themselves on the Sabbath.

He took a direct jab at Platt without naming him. "In closing I wish to say one word as a Republican to the Republicans in control of affairs at Albany. I earnestly hope they will not permit any action to be taken in the interest of the lawbreakers and the spoilsmen and against the interest of decent men . . . For weeks, every corrupt politician, every tool of the lawbreaking liquor seller, every friend of the semi criminal classes, every man, rich and poor, who leads a vicious life, has been announcing with glee that the present Legislators under one pretext or another would get rid of the Police Board." Roosevelt warned that politicians voting them out would have to deal with the wrath of "plain law-abiding citizens of the state."

The commissioner achieved a righteous rhythm by the end. The *Sun* reported the ministers bathed him in applause and peppered his speech with cries of "Good, good," and "Amen."

The influential ministers' group passed two resolutions, one supporting the Police Board in its "just warfare against crime," especially illegal drinking, and the other imploring the legislature not to pass any law removing the "faithful" commissioners.

Roosevelt had previously aimed the brunt of his attacks at Tammany or Sunday saloons or the *New York World*, against vice lords or crooks; he had now thrown down the gauntlet to his own party, to more newspapers, even to judges.

———

The night of his speech, in a mood of utter hang-it-all defiance, Roosevelt—despite the slushy snow—decided to take a midnight tour with Jacob Riis. His faithful guide was going to help him assess the problem of vagrants and bums on the streets. Complaints about boozy panhandlers had been flooding into headquarters, and in the great metropolis, the ragged men and children seemed an eyesore and an embarrassment. A frequent theme of that judgmental era called for separating the unfortunate *worthy* poor from the shirkers and freeloaders.

Bundled up for warmth and disguise, Riis and Roosevelt wandered in the desolate southwestern regions of Manhattan island. A light snow mixed with rain fell; they visited a couple of precinct houses and then ventured not far from the deserted Cortlandt Street piers where travelers caught the steam ferry to the Pennsylvania Railroad Depot (Penn Station), then still located in Jersey City, New Jersey. (The station, larger than Grand Central, generated enormous daytime traffic of travelers heading west to St. Louis and Chicago and south to Washington.) At two in the morning, they saw a few tramps huddled in doorways, some sleepy watchmen guarding warehouses, and an occasional cop risking frostbite to walk his beat.

A cold damp wind gusted off the North River. The duo walked under the Elevated Railroad on Greenwich Street and headed toward the dim green globe lights of the Church Street station house and then up the steps. They entered and a grim-looking sergeant glanced down at them.

Riis knew the place all too well. A quarter century earlier, he had spent one of the worst nights of his life there. As an impoverished young immigrant, he had come in out of a freezing rain and soon found himself fighting with the drunks in the basement, and then later, in the pitch dark, someone had stolen his last valuable possession, a small gold locket, from around his neck. When Riis had complained loudly, the police threw him out, and during the struggle, a doorkeeper had picked up Riis's adopted stray dog and had bashed the animal's brains out.

The *Evening Sun* reporter now led Roosevelt down the cellar steps. "It was unchanged," observed Riis. "Three men lay stretched at full length on the dirty planks, two of them young lads from the country."

And Riis recounted to the president of the board his horror story, how he had gone into a rage, throwing paving stones at the building before being roughly escorted to the New Jersey ferry boat stop. "Did they do that to you," Roosevelt asked, indignantly.

At the next day's board meeting, Roosevelt recommended that the commissioners explore closing the police lodging houses. He was convinced that many of the professional beggars and lazy vagrants harassing citizens were spending their nights in police basements. "The system encourages pauperism," he said. "It has no redeeming features." The board directed Chief Conlin to prepare a quick memorandum on the topic.

The idea of closing the police lodging houses was not new, but no police board over the past three decades had succeeded in shutting them down. The public perceived the basement rooms as the place of last resort for the city's neediest.

———

New York City in the 1890s had a shelter problem.

On any given night that winter of 1895/1896, in the great chaotic city about 20,000 poor people with no permanent home—from newsboys to widows—scrambled to find a place to sleep. Since the police rarely enforced the law against begging—only 340 arrests were made citywide in 1894—many of the destitute panhandled for coins. Revelers complained about encountering armies of beggars at night, especially in the Bowery. The *Sun* reported a New Jersey man was aggressively accosted *seven* times, not far from Roosevelt's route, while walking a handful of blocks from the *Sun* office to the Cortlandt Street ferry.

The leading private charity—the Charity Organization Society (C.O.S.), an umbrella group representing 500 Protestant churches and smaller charities and 1,000 of the wealthiest donor families—strongly discouraged giving directly to beggars. "On a cold night in a comfortable home, one is reluctant to turn such an applicant away," conceded Reverend Lyman Abbott, "but to give him money or clothing is to do him a wrong because it adds one more impulse to his vagrant and lazy propensities."

Charities stressed work as the cure-all for poverty.

Speech after speech from the pulpit and lectern complained about the influx of out-of-state or upstate "skulkers, loafers, outcasts and criminals" who came to New York City to hustle up loose change, guzzle beer, and sleep outdoors by summer or in the cheap lodging houses, missions, or police basements by winter. "The metropolis . . . attracts them in swarms . . . with the vague idea that they can get along here if anywhere."

To prevent the beggars from receiving multiple handouts, the C.O.S. compiled a dossier on recipients. A visit to any of its offices entailed answering dozens of questions like "Did you receive a coat last winter?" "Why do you not still have it?" "How long have you been drinking?" Critics sniped that the C.O.S. should be called "Society for Suppression of Benevolence."

The president of the organization wrote a letter to the mayor just after Christmas requesting a crackdown on the granting of peddlers' licenses to cripples. "We are satisfied," stated Robert DeForest, "from numerous investigations . . . that such persons are vagrants, that the goods which they display are commercially worthless, and that their deformities are exposed to the public gaze simply to excite sympathy, and as a means of begging."

Catholic charities tended to ask fewer questions; Tammany ward heelers doling out cash asked only one question: Can I count on your vote?

Last-minute opportunities for overnight shelter for the poor ran from the relative "high end" of twenty-five-cent-a-night flophouses like Callahan's Progress Hotel on Chatham Square with shoulder-high partitions separating the beds to ten-cent-a-night open dormitories with canvas hammocks. The destitute could also nurse a two-cent cup of tea and a roll at an all-night restaurant, or sprawl on the floor in the back rooms of bars.

Recently, twenty-four-year-old novelist Stephen Crane had spent a night at a seven-cent lodging house and recorded it in a third-person narrative in "An Experiment in Misery." In the vestibule of the building, he received his first impression. "There suddenly came to his nostrils strange and unspeakable odors that assailed him like malignant diseases with wings. They seemed to be from human bodies closely packed in dens; the exhalations from a hundred pairs of reeking lips; the fumes from a thousand bygone debauches; the expression of a thousand present miseries."

The clerk led Crane into a crowded room full of cots; a gas jet flickered a small orange flame. He glimpsed dozens of sleeping men—some still as tomb statues, others gasping heavily "like stabbed fish."

Crane stuffed his hat and shoes in a locker by his head and stretched out. In the dim light, the narrow lockers seemed to him gravestones and the sleepers the restless dead. Some contorted in nightmares; some shrieked, some wailed. But at dawn, he was amazed by the muscular fitness of many of the unclothed men who only after they added layers of shabby garments once again looked downtrodden.

For those without even seven cents, without any money, there were still options: a city shelter—recently built on the Bellevue Hospital pier at 26th Street—and various religious missions. The Charity Organization Society, that arm of the wealthiest Protestant families, completed the Wayfarers' Lodge and Wood Yard in 1893, and supported its worthy endeavor by selling lodging tickets to private individuals and businessmen, who then gave them to beggars; they entitled the recipient to a bath, two adequate meals, and a bed in exchange for three hours' labor chopping and sawing firewood.

But for someone seeking charity with absolutely no strings attached, the police lodging houses, mostly precinct-house basements, offered a wooden plank, no food, no bath, no clothes, nothing but a slab of wood in a crowded room. Making the bed meant turning the plank.

"Yet hundreds of men and women, every winter's night fight like tigers for the bare privilege of being allowed to sleep upon a hard board, or even to be granted the luxury of having a roof over their head," wrote Mrs. Helen Campbell. She and Josephine Shaw Lowell, arguably two of the city's most influential charity executives, contended that anyone who applied to the police for lodging was in effect admitting to being a vagrant ("no means of support") and should be sent to the city's workhouse on Blackwell's Island.

The anti-vagrant laws were so vague ("without employment," "not giving a good account of himself," etc.) that the police could arrest thousands of men and women a day, if they so chose. (The mostly Irish Catholic Tammany force mostly chose not to.) One magistrate observed that the city would have to build 100 more workhouses before he could begin sentencing all the vagrants.

During the month of January a year earlier, the police had given free lodging to about 310 homeless men and women each night, compared to about 11,250 people who paid during the same period to stay in cheap licensed overnight accommodations. All told in 1895, the police provided 65,556 "lodging nights."

At the board meeting, Roosevelt said he was galled by this "unwise philanthropy." He told the story of a woman on the East Side who was attacked and robbed by two beggars. "The professional beggars and vagrants should be gotten rid of."

————

The following week, on January 28, with temperatures hovering at freezing, Chief Conlin delivered his report. From his years as a captain, he clearly despised the comingling of beggars and "reserve" officers in the precinct house.

He informed the board that he considered 98 percent of the lodgers sleeping in the eighteen precinct houses to be "lazy, dissipated, filthy, vermin-covered, disease-breeding and disease-scattering scum." He contended the police were coddling a "small army of beggars" who annoyed and threatened citizens.

He cited repeated recommendations by the Board of Police Surgeons to close the rooms down, since the "huddling like cattle of a large number of drunken, dirty and oftentimes diseased wretches, contaminates the air breathed by patrolmen in the same building."

Chief Conlin regarded the basement planks as an unsuitable option for a respectable person out of work and out of money; he also recommended assigning four plainclothes detectives to wander the city to round up professional beggars and vagrants.

Roosevelt lofted a resolution to close the lodging houses in two weeks, on February 15; the police sergeants would then give tickets to the homeless to take to the Wayfarers' Lodge and Wood Yard (28th Street on the far West Side near the docks) or give them directions to the new shelter and barge run by the city's Department of Charities and Prisons (East River pier at 26th Street).

Commissioner Parker raised the only opposition; it was sometimes hard to tell whether Parker opposed something merely to be contrary or whether he truly believed the punctilios or fine points of every law must be honored. Often, he seemed a prisoner of punctilios, the very opposite of Roosevelt's riding roughshod forward. Parker cited Section 258 of the New York City code that required the police to offer housing to the indigent. He was swayed only when the others convinced him that the law did not specify exactly *where* the beds must be and that police would be sending the indigent to these other buildings. Parker cautioned, though, that if Wayfarers' Lodge or the City Charity Department's Bellevue Pier facilities closed or were overwhelmed, the police must be willing to reopen the basement rooms. The resolution passed.

Roosevelt's midwinter timing was probably not ideal, but the reformers were in a rush.

————

The *New York Times* reported that the Platt forces expected to legislate out the Roosevelt Police Board by June 1, at the latest. They would pass a bill that in the name of claiming to ease the transition to a Greater Consolidated New York City would create a new interim Police Board.

Roosevelt knew his time was short. The board unfurled a pile of innovations.

They voted to test out a revolutionary idea: cops on bicycles. For months Roosevelt teased the idea's originator, Commissioner Andrews, but the board eventually relented and agreed to a tiny experiment: a four-man bicycle squad. Their main job was to reel in speeding cyclists, or "scorchers." The bike squad, with eye-catching yellow leggings and blue nautical caps, had to wear long heavy police coats, since they were debuting in the middle of winter.

The four bike officers—all cycling champs—chased after drunk drivers as well, guided traffic to the right of the road, and protected female cyclists, even the ones in bloomers, from insults. "Skeptical" Roosevelt was later deeply impressed when sprint champ Henry Neggesmith caught up to a drunk speeder, fought off the man's whip, hoisted himself onto the wagon, and subdued the lout. Roosevelt savored the detail that Neggesmith, a big powerful German, "jounced" up and down on the prone drunk for the trip to the precinct house. Novelist Stephen Crane, however, later complained that it used to be more amusing to watch "fat policemen on foot trying to stop a spurt." The "scorcher" usually won, Crane wrote, and the crowd enjoyed the show because "a majority of the policemen ... could swear most graphically in from two to five languages."

The reform board also rolled out pistol practice for the entire force. Commissioner Andrews later recalled the impetus came from an incident when three police officers tried to kill a mad dog and "shot a passerby in the leg."

Back then, officers had to pay for their own guns, and an inspection revealed that more than half the men carried cheap unreliable handguns of varying calibers, despite a mandate from seven years earlier to carry .38 caliber revolvers. The men rarely cleaned their weapons or handled them properly. "Chances are you could tackle ten policemen before you would find one with his gun loaded," said acting sergeant William E. Petty. Most were rotten marksmen, as was soon revealed.

The Police Board authorized Sergeant Petty to set up a pistol range in the Eighth Regiment Armory at 94th Street and Park Avenue. Petty, a national revolver champion, demonstrated proper technique to the board, putting four of five pistol shots into a one-inch square from ten yards away.

The first policemen to arrive confirmed the board's worst fears and gave the *New York World* fodder. "Policeman O'Donnell raised his pistol and fired. Bang! The target's purity was unsullied." O'Donnell went on to fire fourteen more shots. "How did I score?" asked O'Donnell. "You didn't," replied Petty. Up stepped an officer named Sheehan next. Sheehan, using his own gun, scored a 2 out of possible 75. Petty explained about safely pointing the gun to the ground, about closing one eye for aiming, about justified shooting situations. "A trained marksman can disable a man where the bumbler might kill," he said. Petty also gave tips on using a pistol as a club.

Sergeants rotated patrolmen precinct by precinct through the 12 noon to 4 p.m. class over the months of the New Year. The range became quite popular; officers showed up off duty. More than 130,000 shots would be fired there in 1896. Men who scored 65 out of 75 formed teams of sharpshooters, an "incalculable value to the force," according to Chief Conlin. Some historians credit this pistol training as leading to the founding of the nation's first police academy.

Perhaps the most controversial reform was the one least visible to the general public. Commissioner Parker, after spending the fall analyzing the problem and auditioning men, rolled out a completely revamped plainclothes detective squad. Not only did he rejuggle the forty-man headquarters staff, but he decided to bring back "ward detectives," those plainclothes precinct detectives who had served as errand boys for the corrupt captains of the Tammany era.

Superintendent Byrnes and the old board, in the heat of Lexow's anti-corruption fervor, had banned "ward detectives" in 1894 but that meant there were no *local* plainclothes men assigned full-time to investigate crime. This ban could start to cause problems capturing criminals and gathering leads since the reform board had also banned stool pigeons. Roosevelt and Parker were adamant about not paying one-half the city's criminals to snoop on the other half.

So Parker created a plan to bring back the ward detective, but he intended to weaken the bond between this plainclothes detective and the captain to deter any shakedowns. With his congenitally complicated mind, he decided that the ward detectives (two per shift per precinct) would report regularly to Chief of Detectives O'Brien at Mulberry Street, but receive daily orders from their captains.

Parker's plan called for extraordinarily long shifts. The day men would work 8 a.m. to 10 p.m. and one of them would remain on reserve each night to help the 10 p.m. to 8 a.m. shift. He studied the past thoroughly and placed all the men under central office command to avoid what he had concluded was the biggest hindrance to quicker crime detection: "sarcasm and criticism" between precinct men and the fellows from headquarters.

The four-man board approved the plan. Since the chief controlled transfers, Parker was able to single-handedly overhaul this department, with little input from the other three commissioners. Bringing back ward detectives was either brilliant or naive or, as cynics later charged, part of Parker's devious plan to reintroduce shakedowns.

———

The deeds and motives of Andrew Parker often fell into those hard-to-parse categories. He seemed to be a passionate advocate of reform. He shared a law office on Nassau Street with an anti-Tammany reformer whose father served on the board of the Parkhurst Society. He was born in the northern stretches of New York City, a year after Roosevelt; his father was a chemist; he studied law at Columbia with William C. Whitney and served as an assistant district attorney until a Tammany D.A. dismissed him. He was not married and lived in a boardinghouse at fashionable 20 East 29th Street. Parker was a guest at Sagamore Hill and at several Roosevelt dinners; he shared the dais with TR on numerous occasions, giving speeches mostly at churches, reform groups, temperance societies.

Roosevelt wrote of Parker back in the summer of 1895: "He is dead game and very efficient. He is absolutely free from jealousy and can do many things which I cannot. He likes to work beneath the surface." Another time: "He has exactly the peculiar knowledge and ability and the temper of courage and ruthlessness needed for our task." And Roosevelt confided to sister Corinne that the other two commissioners "could be replaced with advantage by two high class clerks."

Yet, there was something off about Andrew Parker. TR once called him "queer as Dick's hat."

A meticulous lawyer, he could talk endlessly about the fine print of a contract while ignoring the larger issues. His stenographer noted that Parker included punctuation when he did dictation. "He detested a misplaced comma as though it were an infectious microbe," recalled Louis Posner. A friend of his wrote that though Parker was a nominal Democrat "his mind was so independent and logical that ... he [reserved] his efforts for the men and measures that were to his liking." He read several foreign languages, including French, German, Hebrew, and Latin. He developed a rapport with many high-ranking police officers, including Chief Conlin and Chief of Detectives O'Brien.

His feud with Roosevelt began in earnest in February 1896. Roosevelt—so deeply frustrated on so many fronts—would over time demonize Parker and assign to him the worst motives, branding him as deceitful, corrupt, and worse.

Fellow commissioner Andrews found a huge gulf between "the secret and evasive Parker and the open, direct emphatic Roosevelt." Judge William Travers Jerome later commented that Roosevelt was "very much impressed by Parker" at first but that Parker eventually tied Roosevelt "in a knot."

The battle began over promotions. Stickler Parker, rereading the records from Albany, had discovered that the method the board had chosen—in its first months—of assigning and promoting officers technically violated the New York state legislature's mandates.

Back in July 1895, Roosevelt, boyishly cherishing derring-do, had pushed a system that stressed rewarding heroics by creating a merit list of "men who have done special service at the risk of their lives in saving life, in protecting life and property, in putting down disorder and in arresting dangerous criminals."

The board would recommend heroic officers for promotion, and they would then take a pass–fail exam. Parker found the police civil service law required a *competitive* exam to rank the men. Parker also discovered the board had no right to promote patrolmen to roundsmen since that technically was not a separate rank (such as captain or sergeant) but a duty assignment controlled by the chief.

This change in method might seem obscure, but reforming the police department hinged on placing strong honorable men at the highest positions—breaking from the old patronage days. And the force at New Year's had openings for sixteen captains (i.e., half the precincts), for two dozen sergeants, and, most importantly, for the district inspectors and deputy chief, directly in line for the top job.

At first, Parker's discovery about promotions hadn't seemed too disruptive. (It was a tad ironic, though, that Parker was correcting former civil service commissioner Roosevelt over a civil service law.) The board—with Andrews taking the lead—created a new method that would respect "seniority, merit and [include a] *competitive* exam." Each of the four board members would rate a candidate on a scale of 1 to 65 points based on a long list of qualities: integrity, efficiency, zeal, personal character, gallantry, courage, detection of criminals. (In practice, the long list would allow a commissioner to justify almost any rating.) A competitive written exam on laws, police rules, and tactics would determine the other 35 points.

Each applicant would receive a numerical rating from 1 to 100; the board would vote on promoting anyone scoring above 75. Seniority would break numerical ties.

The law stated that this bipartisan board needed a unanimous vote to promote an officer or a three-to-one vote if the applicant was endorsed by the chief of police. Here's where the mischief began. One commissioner could gum up the works and there were bound to be disagreements among four men over several dozen promotions.

Parker began expressing "reservations" about three veteran officers with stellar reputations, all darlings of reform: Moses Cortwright for deputy chief, and Nicholas Brooks and John McCullagh from acting inspectors to full inspectors. All three were Republicans and would be in line for the job of Chief Conlin, who had health issues, including failing eyesight. Parker—the nominal Democrat—also demanded that several other captains be allowed into the running for these plum inspector posts. Roosevelt, Andrews, and Grant opposed him.

The feud escalated quickly from Parker's muffled qualms to an outright battle.

Citing a shortage of detectives for his pet project (so far fewer than half the precincts had new plainclothes precinct men), Parker suggested that all four commissioners give up their personal roundsmen, who acted as jacks-of-all-trades. For Roosevelt, this was a gut-wrenching decision. Four days into his new job, Roosevelt had hired thirty-three-year-old patrolman Michael W. Tierney; a decade earlier, when TR was captain of Company B of the Eighth Regiment of the National Guard, he had found Corporal Tierney to be "exceptionally able and trustworthy."

Over the last nine months, Roosevelt had probably spent more time with the beefy Irish Catholic from the streets of New York than with any other person, certainly more than with Riis or Edith or the children or even Andrews. The only near rival might be secretary Minnie, given TR's Niagara of dictation.

Tierney, a seven-year police veteran, had served as Roosevelt's guide to the inner workings of the police force and to its clannish traditions. TR made Tierney work exceptionally long hours. Several times Tierney had accompanied TR on midnight rambles; the commissioner had also sent him on stealth investigations and several solo rambles. Back in July (before Parker's discovery), Roosevelt had rushed through a promotion to make Tierney a roundsman so that Tierney had the authority to press charges against any patrolmen caught napping or gabbing. (It turned out a police commissioner didn't have that power.)

TR—always open to moral arguments about manpower—now reluctantly agreed to surrender Tierney in late January, but he did so knowing that he was secretly planning a plum reward for the loyal employee. Roosevelt days later suggested Tierney for promotion to sergeant, a scant six months after his rise to roundsman. Three of the commissioners rated him 60 out of a possible 65—Parker did not rate him for never-explained reasons—and Tierney scored 25 out of 35 on the written exam, putting him at 85, near the top of a long list of the sergeant candidates. At the meeting on Saturday, February 1, 1896, the board voted on promoting eleven men.

Without any warning or preamble, Parker shocked Roosevelt by approving the others but opposing Tierney, saying he had "reservations." Playing his cards close to the vest, Parker asserted that Tierney's police record had almost a dozen minor violations and one major one. But what Parker saw as a blemish, Roosevelt regarded as a badge of honor.

Half a decade earlier, in 1890, Tierney was suspended for twenty days for pulling a revolver and threatening to shoot a civilian during an after-hours saloon arrest. Tierney claimed he was falsely accused of being drunk and abusive during the incident because the saloon keeper was pals with a Tammany police commissioner.

The board, siding with the saloon owner and the man arrested, had found Tierney guilty.

Parker's vote against Tierney that Saturday galled Roosevelt deeply.

Snow fell hard on Monday, February 3, mantling the city in white. Commissioner Parker had told the other board members he would be in Brooklyn on police business during the Tuesday board meeting.

At 3 p.m. on Tuesday, Roosevelt called in the other commissioners, brought forward another group of names of roundsmen for promotion to sergeant and reinserted the name of Tierney. With Parker gone, anyone receiving three ayes would also require Chief Conlin's approval to be promoted.

Conlin was called to the boardroom. While his relations with Roosevelt had always been cordial, Roosevelt clearly treated him like an employee, lecturing him on duty, even though the chief earned $6,000 to TR's $5,000 and was granted key powers by the legislature. The chief looked over the list and said he could give his approval to all the names except Tierney. Roosevelt was again stunned. Was this Parker's doing? Roosevelt said that both he and Commissioner Grant remembered the chief saying he could endorse promoting Tierney. Conlin wasn't so sure about that. "Did you deceive your superior officer when you said [Tierney] was alright?" TR barked at him.

Roosevelt then added that Conlin had already delivered a *written* recommendation for Tierney. The chief again said he didn't recall doing so. Roosevelt had the promotion book brought to him; inside it, pinned to the pages of various officers, were brief signed endorsements from the chief, inspectors, captains. On Tierney's page was pinned a note signed by Chief Peter Conlin. Roosevelt jabbed his finger at the signature. Again he angrily asked whether Conlin had lied during this earlier written appraisal. Then he said that if Conlin had, then the chief might be liable to charges of insubordination.

Conlin muttered: "Since I wrote it, I'll stand by it," so he gave his very reluctant recommendation that Tierney be promoted. The men were all promoted to sergeant and received 33 percent pay increases to $2,000 a year. The following day, Conlin asked to see the promotion book; he examined the Tierney page. There was indeed an authentic Conlin recommendation pinned to it but it was advocating a *different* officer.

Conlin—generally low key—was quite irritated. TR had bullied him in front of the commissioners, he had been duped. (Roosevelt later said that Grant had organized that promotion book; in other words, that Grant had possibly misfiled the note.)

Sergeant Tierney was assigned to the Charles Street station. Later that year he named his newborn "Theodore Roosevelt Tierney."

Parker dated his falling-out with Roosevelt to the first week in February, when he had opposed Tierney and decided he could not vote for Brooks or McCullagh, two other Roosevelt favorites, as inspectors. The board had a heated closed session on February 15 but Parker would not budge.

———

Away from 300 Mulberry, the ridicule of Roosevelt continued. "Let us be just," opined the *Washington Post*. "By the mobilization of the thieves, thugs and murderers in New York, Mr. Roosevelt is giving the balance of the country excellent police protection."

The *World* ran a list of fifty days of New York City crimes.

Even the reform *New York Times*—with its daily circulation dwindling to 10,000 copies or 1/50th of the *World*'s—seemed to be poking a little fun at him with its February 9 piece "War on the Banana Skin." The *Times* reported that Commissioner Roosevelt had summoned three captains, along with all their roundsmen and sergeants, and "talked to them pointedly about the prevalence of banana skins in the streets on the eastside." He read to them the city ordinance that called for up to a $5 fine and ten days in jail for littering fruit or vegetables. And, he read a second ordinance that required the posting of the first ordinance in all places selling such items. Roosevelt wanted those laws enforced. He also told them pushcarts could no longer block traffic on market days on Hester and Rivington Streets. "This law will inflict much hardship on peddlers," said one captain. "Nothing must stand in the way of the enforcement of the law," replied Roosevelt.

———

It was becoming increasingly clear that Roosevelt was far more popular out of town than in it.

He traveled to Chicago to give three speeches on Washington's birthday. A thousand college students in Kent Theater at the University of Chicago greeted him in the morning with a foot-stomping chant:

Who is "Ted-dy" Roos-e-velt?
First in war, first in peace.
First to reform the New York Police.

Roosevelt's theme was the reform of municipal government. He told them he knew the politics of only six of the last fifty men promoted in New York. He told them he never made a decision with an eye toward an election. "My closing word to you is: be honest, upright, loyal, patriotic Americans, strong for the right and against all evil."

———

As the closing of the police lodgings loomed, Commissioner Parker, true to form, raised concerns—perhaps more legalistic than charitable—about the exact number of available beds. He convinced the commissioners to push the February 15 target date back to March 1, then to March 11, 1896, until the Department of Charities and Prisons finally finished retrofitting a double-decker barge for homeless men and women in the East River.

On that snowy, extremely windy night of March 11, hundreds of vagrants, their ill-fitting rags dusted white, showed up at station houses citywide and the desk sergeants told them to hike over either to the privately run Wayfarers' Lodge at 520 West 28th Street or to the new city-run barge and pier at 26th Street and the East River. From the Eldridge Street station—the most frequented basement—to the cavernous public waiting room at the East Side pier marked a two-mile walk. Five inches of snow fell by 8 p.m., followed by sleet and hail; winds hit forty miles an hour; the harbormaster hung a hurricane warning flag.

Those first hundred who had a C.O.S. ticket that night and tramped to the Wayfarers' Lodge entered a hive of efficient charity. The Charity Organization Society had purchased several lots next to a sprawling woodyard and two years earlier had built a twenty-five- by seventy-five-foot four-story brick building, with basement shower-baths and disinfection rooms and second-, third-, and fourth-floor dormitories, able to hold 100 men. No smoking, drinking, or cursing allowed.

The drill called for new arrivals to register, answer questions, go to the basement, strip naked, and be examined, while handing over all their clothes to be fumigated in a mesh bag, hung in a room heated to 250 degrees. Anyone found with *any* money would be told to leave; any weapons would be confiscated. Everyone must bathe, and sleep in fresh pajamas. Dinner 5 to 7 p.m.—mostly meat stew except Friday fish chowder; breakfast 6 to 8 a.m.—bread, coffee, and soup. As mandatory morning-after work, men had to either double-saw an eighth of a cord of firewood or split a quarter cord with an ax.

As for the tramps who trudged to the city's East Side pier and barge near Bellevue Hospital, they found municipal officials trying to duplicate that Protestant charity's efficiency. On March 11, that first night, 363 men and women slept in beds either on the barge or in the building, with the overflow slouched on benches in the waiting room on the pier. They too had to register, strip, bathe, be examined, have garments fumigated. They must wake up at 5:30 a.m. and after an ample breakfast work three hours "to redeem themselves and earn their self-respect" as Charity Commissioner John P. Faure put it. If Faure ran out of tasks, he said he'd have inmates wheel barrels of coal up and down the lawn of the hospital. Again, anyone with money would be asked to leave. Faure stated the city did not want to compete with low-end lodging houses.

The next morning, March 12, attendants rousted the "Wandering Willies" at 5:30 a.m. and ordered them to shovel snow around Bellevue before breakfast; many offered to go seek work *immediately* but were not allowed to leave.

City officials, after the first few chaotic days, began asking more detailed questions and doing background checks, and discovered that at least one-third of the men had not been in New York City for the sixty days required to qualify for municipal charity, that 429 of the first 781 home addresses were false. Also, three-quarters were under the age of forty and were described as "able-bodied and strong" by a "physician who watched them as they bathed."

Josephine Shaw Lowell, former head of C.O.S., wrote that those statistics confirmed her suspicions about the bulk of New York's homeless; she contended that at least 200 of the 300 nightly sleepers clearly deserved the workhouse. Conveniently enough, that pier near Bellevue could take them there, if only the police would arrest them and judges convict them.

———

At the mid-March board meetings, Commissioner Parker refused yet again to approve the promotion of either Brooks or McCullagh. His logjamming of McCullagh was especially irritating to Roosevelt, who would repeatedly champion the man.

By many accounts, John McCullagh, born in 1845 in Ireland to Scotch Protestant parents, represented the beau ideal of a policeman: handsome, brave, a magnificent equestrian with a cavalry-trim dark mustache, a stickler for detail and discipline. Happily married, financially comfortable, with cousins who attended Yale, McCullagh was a fixture on the West End Avenue social scene. Absolutely incorruptible, this strict law-and-order Republican captain despised the likes of Tammany's Devery.

After joining the force at age twenty-five, McCullagh rose to captain in a dozen years; he helped break up many gangs. Roosevelt had the opportunity to hear an eyewitness account of McCullagh's bravery. When Riis was a young crime reporter, he was once walking after midnight along a deserted street when he bumped into the Whyo gang—"drunken roughs ripe for mischief." Riis recalled that "the leader had a long dirk-knife with which he playfully jabbed me in the ribs, insolently demanding what I thought of it." Riis, struggling to sound brave, hoped his voice wouldn't crack and answered: "About two inches longer than the law allows." The short *Evening Sun* scribe tried to shove the knife aside but failed. The thug leaned forward and the tip pierced the skin on Riis's chest.

The Danish newspaperman feared that one good thrust forward might kill him, and the cocksure goon was pushing. Riis quickly surveyed the Whyos surrounding him: "A human life was to them in the mood they were in, worth as much as the dirt under their feet."

At that moment, Captain McCullagh and his plainclothes detective happened to turn the corner. The two officers immediately attacked the gang. The Whyos dispersed and Riis found himself holding the dirk as a souvenir.

On Friday, March 13, Roosevelt tried a new tactic in the promotion wars; he officially requested that Chief Conlin deliver an evaluation of Brooks and McCullagh. He would force an opinion out of him. That night, though the board was fracturing, Andrew Parker attended a small dinner party at Roosevelt's sister's house, at 689 Madison. Other distinguished guests included Reverend Parkhurst and Joseph B. Bishop, of the reform *New York Evening Post*. Conversation apparently veered politely away from Parker and Roosevelt's tiff over promotions.

After the guests exited, Bishop, an admirer of TR, walked a few blocks with Parker. "I wish you would stop him from talking so much in the newspapers," Bishop years later quoted Parker as telling him. "He talks, talks, talks all the time. Scarcely a day passes that there is not something from him in the papers . . . It injures our work."

The veteran editor had difficulty suppressing a laugh. "Stop Roosevelt talking! Why, you would kill him. He has to talk. The peculiarity about him is that he has what is essentially a boy's mind. What he thinks he says at once . . . It is his distinguishing characteristic, and I don't know as he will ever outgrow it."

Over the weekend, Conlin decided that he would postpone indefinitely delivering any opinion on the worthiness of Brooks or McCullagh, in effect allowing Parker's veto to stand.

Roosevelt wrote to his sister in England: "Gradually and in spite of great difficulties with two of my colleagues I am getting this force into good shape, but I am quite sincere when I say I do not believe that any other man in the United States, not even the president, has had as heavy a task as I have had during the past ten months."

———

Though Roosevelt and Parker were fighting hard over these top-echelon promotions, they stood shoulder to shoulder in agreement on one type of candidate who should *never* enter the line of promotion for a shot at becoming chief of police. They both despised the prospect of a corrupt Tammany loyalist running the show. Parker had been fired from his assistant district attorney post by Tammany, making him a lifelong anti-machine Democrat.

On Monday, March 16, the disgraced captain William S. Devery, accompanied by his high-priced lawyer, went on trial for receiving a $100 construction site bribe, the last of the cases pursued against him. If affable Devery could beat the rap, he could seek immediate reinstatement, and Tammany would have a feisty popular brave back in the game.

DEVERY ON TRIAL

Out of uniform for eighteen months, heavier and paler, William Devery showed up smiling in a dark suit on the morning of March 16, 1896, in the courtroom of Judge Frederick Smyth. He found himself encircled by friends.

Seated upon the bench Devery saw supreme court judge Frederick Smyth, originally of County Galway, Ireland, who for the previous year had presided as Grand Sachem at Tammany Hall. Over at the prosecution's table up front, he recognized several more Tammany men, including the district attorney himself, Colonel John Fellows, a dependable Democratic speechmaker.

Milling among the dozens of current and former police officers in attendance, he spotted saloon owner Bob Nelson, who was especially pleased to see Devery, since he had put up bail. Acting as bail bondsman in a high-profile case marked a departure from Nelson's bread-and-butter business of collecting five-dollar bail from streetwalkers in Devery's various precincts; a reform pamphlet would later claim that Nelson was "so right with Devery" that he didn't have to give the customary kickback to the police desk sergeants.

But having so many Tammany men nearby did not guarantee a result in any courtroom, especially in a jury trial. This past year, Police Inspector William McLaughlin, another Tammany man, had been convicted on similar charges, of receiving a bribe from this very same builder, Francis W. Seagrist. McLaughlin and Devery were old pals; Devery had helped him avoid a night in the Tombs prison—while awaiting a verdict—and had snuck him into a Turkish bath last May 10.

Juries were fickle, and no one expected the well-respected sixty-two-year-old Judge Smyth or district attorney Fellows, to do anything ham-handed for Devery. (Something subtle, however, was not out of the question.) Both men were venerated and articulate pillars of the community, the so-called respectable wing of Tammany. Fellows had abandoned Tammany for more than a decade in the wake of Tweed and more recently, he had rallied a presidential convention with a stirring speech.

Judge Smyth, a veteran of the legal system, ran a tight courtroom. The *Tammany Times* crowed that Judge Smyth had been reversed on appeal only twice in fifteen years; the most recent, however, had been Charlie Gardner, the Parkhurst tour guide, ensnared by Devery but freed after serving one-third of his sentence. Reformers claimed the judge had always been biased in favor of the police.

Representing Devery once again was Colonel E. C. James, with his trademark halo of white hair and a large eye-catching white mustache. As ever, he exuded charm and confidence.

The newspapers expected jury selection to zip along; they were wrong.

Colonel James was taking no chances; neither—to all outward appearances—was the D.A.'s office. The A.D.A. read prospective jurors a complicated forty-nine-word legal question—on the topic of "hypothesis of guilt by circumstantial evidence"—and if the man was unable to translate the legalese into New Yorkese, the A.D.A. asked the judge to reject him for lack of intelligence. It was perhaps odd that the prosecution should want amateur legal scholars who might understand that the legal threshold for "extorting a bribe" involved more than the mere palming of a $100 bill.

The defense wanted no New Yorker who had followed the Lexow hearings.

The dueling lawyers diddled away three days to empanel a jury, leaving not enough time to open the case on Friday. Then after a man—claiming to be from the district attorney's office—came to a juror's home on Allen Street, asking the man's mother questions about his politics, Judge Smyth decided to sequester the jury at the Broadway Central Hotel.

They would be locked in a suite of rooms on the fifth floor, guarded by one Captain Lynch and four court attendants. The judge refused to allow any trips to theater or church but Captain Lynch took it upon himself to allow the fourteen men to take secluded supervised carriage rides in the park.

Sequestered, the jury men had little to do over the weekend but talk or read the newspapers, shorn of any Devery trial articles. Fortunately, they could follow the latest smashmouth installment of the Roosevelt versus Pulitzer feud.

———

The *World* had been running ongoing features on the crime waves plaguing Manhattan. In one piece, the paper listed the "Principal Highway Robberies and Burglaries of Fifty Days, as Reported by the Police and Newspapers" from December 1 to January 19.

In his embattled, aggravated state, TR decided to debunk Pulitzer. Despite his reformer's zeal for cost-cutting, he convinced the board and the shorthanded department to devote hundreds of police man-hours to reexamining forty-five separate cases to refute a two-month-old newspaper article that measured nine and a half by four and a half inches.

Roosevelt was on tilt. His official statement, endorsed by his fellow board members, sounds like a dinner party rant. "It would be quite impossible to catalogue and refute every false statement the *World* makes, because that would need the daily publication of a sheet very nearly as large as the *World* itself and most of its slanders are made so loosely that they can only be met by a general denial. But on January 20 the *World* was sufficiently unwary to commit itself to a definite statement. It gave, with date and place, what it called a 'catalogue of the principal highway robberies, and burglaries of the preceding fifty days' so as to prove that crime was increasing in this city and the police were inefficient."

He stated that only four of forty-five crimes cited by the *World* were "true." Roosevelt distributed to newspapermen a detailed double-columned list of each of the cases, presenting the *World* version and the "Actual Facts":

World	Roosevelt
DECEMBER 7 "Duncan Neil, an Anchor Line physician, assaulted and robbed of his money by highwaymen and found unconscious in West 28th Street."	"A pure fake. Dr. Duncan Neil was found drunk and insensible by a policeman, was arrested and brought to the station house; the next day he was fined by Magistrate Sims."
DECEMBER 16 "Michael Healy, 171 Perry Street, attacked by highwaymen, robbed of his watch."	"While drunk he got into a quarrel with a stranger, who struck him with an umbrella. He thought he had been robbed of his watch, but it turned out to be in the possession of his sister."

DECEMBER 27 "Burglars entered the house of Giuseppe Romano, 283 Mott Street, chloroformed eleven persons and got away with $400."

"No chloroform was used at all. The 'robbery' took place on the ground flat; all the people in the room had been on a spree and got very drunk, and certain of the party who were less drunk than the others took some money from them. How much is not known. It was simply the aftermath of a drunken orgy."

And so on. Roosevelt reminded readers of the fake "Rogue's Gallery" story in December, which he said contained what chemists would call a mere "trace" of truth; this list of crimes was 91 percent false with 9 percent true. TR called that an improvement for the *World*.

The commissioner paraded his own statistics: over the same fifty days from the previous year to this one, felonies dropped from 1,083 to 911, while felons arrested increased from 732 to 847. The commissioner said the police achieved these results despite the *World*, with its "extensive circulation among the criminal classes," encouraging thieves to move to New York City.

At the conclusion of his list, Roosevelt singled out Joseph Pulitzer, accusing him of paying his "reporters to lie" and of allowing his editors to grow too lazy to find even a glimmer of truth on which to base falsehoods.

Showing his Harvard roots, Roosevelt compared his opinions of publisher Pulitzer to British historian Thomas Babington Macaulay's take on a French Revolutionary aristocrat named Bertrand Barère. "He who has not read Barère's memoirs may be said not to know what it is to lie." Roosevelt added a caveat, though: "Of course, when Macaulay wrote thus of Barère's pre-eminence in his class [of liars], Mr. Pulitzer had not been born."

At this point, forty-eight-year-old multimillionaire Pulitzer—nearly blind—was largely an absentee publisher, running his empire via cablegrams relayed from his yacht and estates; he had offered $2 million to Columbia College in 1892 to found the nation's first school of journalism but President Seth Low and the trustees had snootily dilly-dallied on accepting the gift. And, William Randolph Hearst in the fall of 1895 had bought the *Journal* and soon dropped the price to a penny and in January deftly poached away the bulk of the *World* Sunday staff. The *World* (now one cent) and the *Jour-*

nal were engaging in a duel to one-up each other in outrageous commentary, acid cartoons, vulgar crimes, and extreme politics, a duel that would ultimately culminate in screaming headlines in 1898 leading to the Spanish-American War in Cuba. With its tower dominating the skyline, the *World*, however, was still the largest-circulation and most financially successful newspaper in the United States.

Rival newspapers, especially those financially supplanted by the *World*, feasted on TR's vitriol. The *New York Sun* ran a front-page headline that read: WORLD INFAMY LAID BARE: MR. ROOSEVELT'S CRUSHING EXPOSURE OF PULITZER'S ACADEMY OF CRIME. The editorial page of the *Evening Post* boiled with indignation at the *World* using fake crimes to try to hound the Police Board out of office.

The *World* fired back. With a certain shrewdness, it answered TR's tantrum with a calm report. The paper pointed out that the forty-five crimes were found in police reports and other newspapers. It noted that Roosevelt simply ignored eight of the most notorious crimes, such as the Burden jewel robbery, and in seventeen, by commenting on police action, he was admitting that the crimes were indeed "reported," which was all the *World* claimed. The original *World* list was topped by the words REPORTED BY THE POLICE AND NEWSPAPERS. So without straining, the *World* defended twenty-nine of the forty-five stories.

The *World* editors then pointed out that Commissioner Roosevelt was, in effect, lambasting *all* the city dailies by his criticism of this *World* article because the bulk of the stories ran in other papers as well. Roosevelt branded eighteen as "pure fakes"; the *World* noted that sixteen of those eighteen ran in the *Sun*, the *Herald*, or both, as well as in other papers. The newspaper also tracked down several crime victims whom TR had labeled as fabricators. Michael Healy, accused by TR of being drunk and wrestling an umbrella, said his watch was stolen and he hadn't seen his sister in three years. One victim, accused of lying, told the *World* he was mulling over suing Roosevelt. And on and on.

One senses that the police detectives dispatched to defend the department tried very hard to deliver a report that would please the commissioner. One also senses TR becoming increasingly unhinged at the prospect of losing his job. "I don't mind work," he wrote his sister that month. "The only thing I am afraid of is that by and by I will have nothing to do; and I should hate to have the children grow up and see me having nothing to do."

On its editorial page, the *World* pretended to take the high road. "We present a simple statement of facts to-day which must compel an apology on the part of Commissioner Roosevelt if he is an honest man or one who cherishes self-respect."

None arrived, of course.

On Monday, March 23, the *World* unleashed its harshest weapon of reprisal. It announced that Chief Conlin and Commissioner Parker were now running the Police Board. "The ego of the board [the *World*'s new nickname for TR] is in danger of eclipse." The *World* was soon echoed by many other papers including the respectable *Herald*, which reported that Commissioner Parker, "at first the least prominent of the quartet," had kicked over his "traces."

———

The Devery courtroom on Tuesday morning, March 24, was packed with the defendant's friends for the resumption of the trial and the start of the testimony. The jury, fresh from the Broadway Central, looked well rested and alert. Roosevelt did not attend, nor did any other board member.

The assistant district attorney, Austen Fox, laid out the prosecution's case. He accused Captain Devery of extorting a bribe from a man demolishing the American Surety building at Pine Street and Broadway. He explained that Devery did not make the demand personally—"like a highwayman who says 'Pay me money or I will arrest you' "—but relayed it through his plainclothes detective Edward Glennon, who had followed the captain during his previous two commands.

Fox traced what he called Devery's "long" but "pitiable" record as a police officer, emphasizing that investigations into prostitution in the 11th Precinct (by the Lexow Committee and Parkhurst Society) had led to Devery's being abruptly reassigned in November 1893 to the quiet 1st Precinct post of Old Slip station, not known for vice. But even here, the captain found a way to shake down a citizen, having Glennon try to pry $100 from a businessman wanting to skirt laws regarding construction sites.

The prosecution called its first witness, Charles Bissell. A pale young man walked unsteadily forward. A New Yorker did not cavalierly testify against the police. The judge would repeatedly ask him to speak louder. This clean-shaven office "timekeeper" for a demolition company, looking downward to avoid policemen's stares, testified that a police detective—whom he later identified as Glennon—entered the Seagrist offices on May 2, 1894, the day after demolition began. Glennon told him the police were receiving complaints about billowing dust and that he needed to see the boss. Bissell said the boss wasn't there. Glennon returned on three consecutive days, then threatened to shut the site down. Bissell said Glennon finally met with company owner Francis Seagrist on May 5, 1894.

The prosecution then called Seagrist. His demeanor and stride to the box contrasted sharply with his former clerk's. The forty-six-year-old demolition man, a lifelong New Yorker with prematurely white hair and a large black mustache over a receding chin, had been knocking down buildings and selling used lumber and bricks around Wall Street for more than a decade.

His testimony nine months earlier regarding fifty-dollar bribes had led to the conviction of Inspector William McLaughlin for acts committed when that Tammany man was captain of Old Slip in 1891.

The prosecution opened by showing the witness's vulnerability to extortion. Seagrist stated he had signed a contract on April 26, calling for the Pine Street demolition to be rushed and completed within twelve days, or he would forfeit $100 a day from his fee.

Seagrist stated that on May 8, Captain Devery arrived in person with Glennon—both in uniform—at the demolition site on Broadway. He quoted Devery as telling him matter-of-factly that he had received "a good many complaints" about dust and noise and that "you have got to come and see me." The captain even showed Seagrist a letter forwarded from Superintendent Byrnes's office. Seagrist knew exactly what that expression "come and see me" meant; he reluctantly agreed.

Seagrist stated he went the next day to Park Bank, cashed a check for $100, received a $100 bill, put it in an envelope, and walked to Old Slip station. He said Devery was not there in the morning but he found him in the afternoon and he shook Devery's hand, palming the envelope over to him, while saying: "I want you to treat me like a gentleman."

Those words might seem odd but Seagrist was trying to billboard to the court an important legal point—for his own preservation. He wanted everyone to know that with his $100 he was not buying illegal favors, merely courtesy. (In the earlier McLaughlin trials, the defense—also handled by Colonel E. C. James—had repeatedly stressed that if Seagrist paid bribes to violate demolition laws, then he too was liable to prosecution for bribery.) Seagrist also testified that the police *never* bothered him again on the site after his May 9 payment.

Wily Colonel James asked Seagrist whether detective Glennon did not indeed return on May 11 and tell him to send more water through the hose to keep down the dust. Answer: "I do not recollect."

The lawyer also asked the witness to recall more details about handing the envelope to Captain Devery. After looking at the bank check to refresh his memory, Seagrist stated he handed the money to Devery between 4 p.m. and 4:30 p.m. on Saturday, May 9. The word *Saturday* brought a smile to Colonel James's face. A calendar in the courtroom revealed that May 9, 1894, was a Wednesday.

After Colonel James completed his cross-examination, Colonel Fellows—the district attorney himself standing in for his minions—abruptly announced that the people rested their case. The court reporters were agog. This district attorney's office had had a year to prepare since the original grand jury indictment on March 20, 1895; the city officials had rested after less than an hour of testimony. Judge Smyth adjourned the case till the following morning. The staff of the Broadway Central welcomed the jurors once again to the fifth floor.

On Wednesday morning, the courtroom was again packed with friends in blue uniforms.

Colonel James began the defense, outlining Devery's version of events: first, the captain was out of town in the Midwest in early May, celebrating his victory in his last trial, when Seagrist claimed Glennon was hounding him to "come and see" the captain. Secondly, Devery was at a fire on May 9 at the moment when Seagrist claimed he was handshaking off to him a cash-filled envelope. "All of Mr. Seagrist's testimony seems to be a series of mistakes, to call them by no more offensive name," the lawyer pronounced.

The defense opened by calling local area workers—such as "elevator starter" Higginbotham of the Equitable Building—who testified that the police relayed their complaints and succeeded in forcing the demolition workers to keep down the dust clouds. The defense also brought to the stand some cops, a saloon owner, even the chief of the Fire Department to corroborate parts of the story, but this amounted more to window dressing.

The heart of the defense—the alibi—would be provided by three of Devery's closest friends: wardman Glennon (also at risk on these same charges), ex-inspector Alexander "Clubber" Williams (former superior officer, retired grafter), and Frank Farrell (neighbor, and rising Tammany sports gambling czar).

Thirty-five-year-old Glennon—smug, tough-looking, hooded sleepy eyes and a sport's black mustache with pointy ends curled down—took the stand. The sphinx spoke at last. He "glibly denied everything important in Seagrist's testimony," according to the *World*. No threats occurred, no meetings, no nothing. He grew indignant over the claim he had dragged Seagrist to a quiet spot by Trinity Church. He testified that the only time he saw Seagrist was when he went to the site in uniform on May 11 with patrolman Kiernan to tell the man to use more hose and water.

During cross-examination, the A.D.A. tried to chip away at Glennon's swagger.

Q: How long did you do this "Special Duty" [plainclothes work for Devery]?
A: From February 1893 to May 1894.
Q: And during that time you never made one single arrest, did you?
A: I think. (*pause*) I might have. (*pause*) I don't remember.
Q: You didn't do patrol work, you didn't do detective work. What did you do?
A: I did the precinct.

Loud snickers could be heard throughout the courtroom.

Glennon then explained that by that he meant he walked around the precinct ready to aid other policemen. Officer Kiernan subsequently corroborated Glennon's testimony regarding the May 11 warning to Seagrist.

The assistant district attorney did not probe Glennon's obvious incentive to lie and exonerate himself. The *New York World* viewed the district attorney's efforts as halfhearted at best: "So it drifted along. There was no sharp cross-questioning, no attempt to puzzle the witness, no efforts to surprise him, no objections from counsel."

Next up: ex-inspector Williams, tall, strong, lean, an impressive physical specimen. Despite his November defeat on the Republican ticket for the assembly, he still exuded cockiness.

Williams testified that he was an inspector on May 9, 1894, when he picked up Devery in a carriage at five minutes before 2 p.m. and carried him to the massive fire at Clyde Line pier at the foot of Catherine Street. They watched as drums of heating oil exploded and police fought to keep back the curious crowds.

When Williams left at five minutes to 4 p.m., he was "almost positive" that Devery was still there; a saloon keeper at 188 South Street testified that Devery was drinking seltzer just after 4 p.m.

Devery still needed another half hour on May 9 for a rock-solid alibi.

Frank Farrell supplied the crucial missing minutes. Farrell—thirty years old, slight of build, neatly dressed, low key, fond of derby hats—testified that he was a saloon owner. He failed to mention running any sports betting joints for Big Tim Sullivan or that he was a neighbor of Devery. He stated that he had sought the captain that afternoon at the station house but had been told to look for him at the Clyde Line pier. He asserted under oath that they had stayed together in the blaze area till around 5 p.m., then slowly walked to the Old Slip station house, arriving at 5:30 p.m., sitting on the stoop until 6 p.m.

Farrell explained he had called on Devery that day because he sought his advice on securing a liquor license for a hotel at 52nd Street and Third Avenue.

Devery's trio of chums had delivered the alibi . . . if the jury believed them.

Devery took the stand. He was "cool" and "calm" and "answered questions distinctly," stated the *Times* and *Sun*. He gave his age as forty, his home address as 327 West 28th Street. His lawyer guided him back over the days in question. Devery told the jury that in April 1894 he had been acquitted of charges brought by the Parkhurst Society and that he had requested and received a twenty-day leave of absence. He stated that he was vacationing in Chicago through May 4.

Devery emphatically denied ever receiving money from Seagrist. "I never saw him until I saw him on the stand in this court room," stated Devery in a loud, dramatic voice.

Cross-examination for the people was handled by former judge D. G. Rollins, his dome ringed with curly white hair, his voice "bland and solicitous." Somewhat oddly, Devery hesitated at an early softball question over how long he had lived at his present address. The *Herald* reporter viewed him as flushed and agitated. Devery stage-whispered to Judge Smyth, "what month is this?" before responding.

From then on, the cross-examiner Rollins "handled him gently and considerately" even when he forced Devery to admit he might have seen Seagrist for the first time at the job site and not in the courtroom.

Colonel James spent an hour and forty minutes making his closing statement. The *New York World* found the Colonel's tone confident and maybe overly calm. "The [spectators could] count the wrinkles in the back of Colonel James's neck and estimate the baldness of each lawyer in square inches. And they sleep without snoring, which is a concession to the dignity of the court."

Colonel James emphasized Devery's alibi; he stressed that Seagrist had repeatedly been fined by the police, which nurtured animosity in the demolition man. At some point, Parkhurst agent E. A. Whitney broke the unwritten rules of decorum and began snoring; court officers threw him out.

The judge sent the jury to deliberate at 9:40 p.m. that Thursday night, after explaining the exact definition of extortion—that the defendant made a "threat to do injury" and that Seagrist paid $100 to the defendant to "avoid that injury."

Devery walked up and down the courthouse corridors, smoking long black cigars and talking to friends. He looked animated and "hopeful." At midnight, the judge asked an officer to inquire whether the jury had reached a verdict; they had not. He ordered the twelve men locked in the small jury room, to sleep on the floor or chairs, with deliberations to resume at 10:30 the next morning.

He ordered Devery to the Tombs. Devery had been out on bail but the law required that if a jury continued deliberations overnight, he must spend that night in custody. Since Inspector McLaughlin had been caught going to a Turkish bath instead of spending the night in the Tombs, the sheriff's department couldn't risk letting Devery skip out. Deputy sheriff Kelly guided the former captain toward the "Bridge of Sighs" over Franklin Street to the Tombs prison. For half an hour, Devery lingered at the bridge's entrance talking to his lawyer's colleague Abram Elkus and to friends; then, finally, he bid them farewell and trudged into the covered walkway, a route taken by so many of New York City's most notorious criminals.

Devery would spend the night in cell number 3 on Condemned Row.

———

The *World,* waiting in vain for an apology from Roosevelt, found space—opposite a Devery trial story—to cover the arrest of a knapsack-toting peddler who was selling "Teddy Roosevelt teeth" tin whistles. The novelty item featured pressed-metal red lips flanking "abnormal," oversized, "dazzling white" teeth, with a whistle tucked behind. Acting captain John R. Groo arrested John Kennedy, who was hawking them for a nickel a couple of blocks from 300 Mulberry.

After passing the night in his suit clothes on a prison cot, Devery decided to avoid the Tombs breakfast and instead ordered "chops, eggs, rolls and coffee" from a nearby restaurant.

A deputy sheriff escorted him back to the courtroom. He learned from courthouse gossips that the first jury ballot was seven for acquittal, two to convict, and three blank. Devery paced. At 10:45 a.m., the jury, blaming irreconcilable opinions caused by two holdouts, sent a note to Justice Smyth asking to be discharged. A hung jury would extend Devery's exile and up his legal fees.

Judge Smyth sternly sent them back for more deliberations, saying he would hold them till they reached a verdict. At 11:30 a.m., the jury requested that the testimony of clerk Bissell and owner Seagrist be read aloud. That took an hour. At 1 p.m. the judge allowed them lunch back at Broadway Central.

Around 5:30 p.m. the jury sent a note that it had reached a verdict. Judge Smyth warned those in the courtroom that he would have the sheriff arrest anyone making an outburst.

The foreman, Anton J. Lehman, a manufacturer of canvas goods, announced: "Not guilty."

Devery's friends engulfed him; they "almost shook his right hand off." The judge thanked the jurors and told them their verdict was a "just and proper conclusion and no other result could have been reached." Devery lit up a cigar and inhaled hard, angling the long red fiery tip upward. He told the reporters he was too happy to talk.

A few minutes later, the Tammany Hall district attorney announced that the four bribery counts against Devery would be dropped.

Reporters rushed to police headquarters for a comment but could find only Commissioner Andrews. "[Devery] is not the kind of man we are making captains of," intoned the police reformer. "There is no reason why [Devery] should not be tried by the commissioners on any of the indictments that are now and have been pending against him."

Devery's last remaining hurdle was the bickering Police Board.

———

ROOSEVELT KING IN NAME ONLY, ran a headline in the *Journal*. HIS THE VOICE OF AUTHORITY BUT PARKER'S THE HAND THAT HOLDS THE ROD. And the paper explained that Parker had dug up "an old law that everybody had forgotten, giving the Chief of Police, backed by a single Commissioner, practically complete authority over the force."

Commissioner Andrews, a huge fan of Roosevelt, wrote a half century later in his unpublished memoirs: "It was a political shenanigan of a high order and put Roosevelt for the moment in the ridiculous position of an extremely vocal but wholly impotent figurehead."

SURPRISES

Amid all the quarreling and the twitting by the press, Roosevelt received what he thought was some very good news indeed.

The Republicans in Albany delivered on their promise to inflict stricter statewide liquor regulations. The Raines Liquor Tax Law, which went into effect April 1, granted Roosevelt his wish: saloons were now legally required to keep their curtains open on Sundays to give policemen an unobstructed view into the empty barrooms. The new law also stipulated that saloons *and* restaurants *and* clubs not sell liquor from midnight on Saturday to 5 a.m. on Monday. "[This] will effectively and promptly solve whatever remained of the problem of Sunday closing," predicted Roosevelt.

Many in Manhattan, from budget beer drinkers on the Bowery to swells sipping haut champagne at the Hoffman House, feared the worst.

The Raines Law, which ran to forty-five subsections, superseded all excise laws in New York State. It raised the drinking age from sixteen to eighteen years old; it banned platters of "free lunch"; it forbade bartenders from selling or giving liquor to "intoxicated persons," "habitual drunkards," or to "Indians"; it forbade pharmacies from dispensing alcohol-laced medicine without a doctor's prescription.

The Raines Law, dubbed High Excise, raised the annual taxes on all liquor-dispensing establishments in New York City to $800 from the $75 for beer-and-ale-only joints and the $300 for standard saloons. Experts expected the likely demise of 2,000 of New York City's lowest joints, the dimly lit, foul-smelling, rickety-chaired, stale-beer dives—meeting place of vagrants, shipless sailors, incompetent thieves, aging streetwalkers.

The bill's sponsor, Senator John W. Raines—tall, taciturn, with fierce blue eyes, the loner son of a Methodist minister—also aimed to sew shut the club loophole that had allowed the wealthy to drink on Sundays. Private clubs would henceforth be treated like saloons: they must pay the high $800 annual tax, display their liquor license in the front, and on Sundays make their *empty* barrooms visible from the street. This latter requirement seemed staggering. Would the barmen at J. P. Morgan's exclusive Metropolitan Club or at Roosevelt's Union League really pull open the curtains so passing beat cops or any gawker could peer in on Sundays? The 300 prominent clubs thrived on denying entrance; they promised privacy and unlimited collegial drinking.

Hotels with ten rooms or more, however, could still serve alcohol with a meal to guests all seven days of the week. (New York City then had about 300 hotels with liquor licenses.) No new saloon could open within 200 feet of a church or a school. Steep fines of $1,600 and a year in prison loomed for violators.

The new law would also create a "secret service" with sixty agents, a state-run enforcement unit forecast to become a patronage mill for Republicans in Albany. One paragraph of fine print appeared a potential goldmine. The Raines Law required that all payers of this excise tax take out a "performance bond" (i.e., an insurance policy) equal to double the amount of their tax. Henry B. Platt, son of the Republican boss, and Charles Raines, the son of state senator Raines, set up a "bonding" office for Fidelity and Deposit Company of Maryland, a floor below the New York State Liquor Tax Collectors in the Metropolitan Life Building. (Roosevelt, when first meeting Raines in Albany in the early 1880s, once privately commented: "he [has] . . . the same idea of public life and the civil service that a vulture has of a dead sheep.") Revenues for writing this two-page minimal risk boilerplate contract ($80 a saloon) were expected to hit $400,000.

Roosevelt's Union League Club announced it would close its bar on Sundays. On Wednesday, April 1, the police began enforcing the ban on "free lunch." Overnight, a catering industry that was supplying $15 million of food a year to bars, including more than two tons of potato salad a day, disappeared. The *World* grew misty over the departure of "hundreds of gallons of beef stew [that] sent its perfume like a benediction over the heads bowed in mid-day meditation of its mysteries." Word of the ban spread quickly among tramps and down-and-outers. The *Times* reported that "like a horde of locusts," they "alighted in a body on the pickled herring, potato salad and liver pudding, and devoured it in a jiffy."

That first Sunday in April, the police continued to enforce Roosevelt's saloon crackdown; in addition, a few clubs and most restaurants stopped liquor sales as well. The *New York World* punned in its headline on Monday,

April 5: RAINES MAKES A THIRST. The paper dubbed that Sunday the driest day of Roosevelt's reign. The police also began enforcing the "unobstructed view of the bar" law, and rowdy Mike Callahan hired men to remove a pane of frosted glass from his Chatham Square front window and replace it with clear. Even wives could now peer inside.

As predicted, some of the poorer bars failed to renew their licenses. Owner Charlie Reuss, after fourteen years sliding beers at 106 Eldridge Street in Devery's 11th Precinct, couldn't afford the tenfold tax increase. "I am going to Canarsie to see if I can make a living selling fishing tackle," he told a reporter. "What a cruel world it is."

———

Back in the police boardroom, the ugly bickering between "secretive and evasive" Parker and "open and emphatic" Roosevelt grew fiercer.

Their stalemate was ironic because Parker and Roosevelt agreed on almost all aspects of police reform—absolute honesty, harsh punishment, strict vice control, saloons closed on Sundays, no Tammany corruption. For months they had shared pulpit and lectern spreading the gospel of reform. But now, it was as though president of the board Roosevelt could not forgive Parker for defying him on those key top-level promotions.

The city's corporation counsel, Francis M. Scott, backed Parker's interpretation of the Police Board rules, which called for four ayes for a promotion. TR was one aye short of getting his way, and neither Conlin nor Parker was budging.

The corporation counsel also backed Parker's interpretation that the chief, without needing the board, could "detail" captains to be acting inspectors, just as he could install a sergeant as acting captain if a captain fell sick or went on vacation. Conlin settled the inspector squabble by "detailing" three captains to be acting inspectors and then assigning all six men. (Conlin happened to choose three captains favored by the board.) His one touch that might have borne the fingerprints of Parker was that he assigned John McCullagh to "goatville"—the sixth district, which included northern Manhattan, and parts of the Bronx and Westchester.

On April 1, the board agreed to throw out the promotion eligibility lists and start over. Roosevelt saved face by saying he thought leaving men dangling on a promotion list for too long might invite bribery or corruption, a not-so-subtle dig at Parker.

[BELOW] The Roman goddess Diana, atop Madison Square Garden at 26th Street, dominated the New York skyline; she was perched at 341 feet and towered over the surrounding buildings.

[RIGHT] This thirteen-foot-tall gilded copper figure by Augustus Saint-Gaudens, his only female nude, also served as spinning weathervane. The Edison lights made her seem to hover at night in the sky.

[TOP] A police raid on gambling. These gamblers were hauled by horse-drawn paddy wagons from a "pool room," the 1890s term for a place taking "betting pool" wagers on horse races. Note the size of the policeman; they often ate free in that era.

[RIGHT] The Bowery, under the shadow of the elevated train tracks, bustled at night with colored lights and cane-swirling barkers, in places such as the Lyceum Concert Garden. The joint then featured a minstrel show and cakewalk.

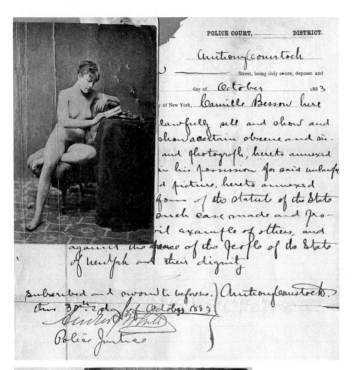

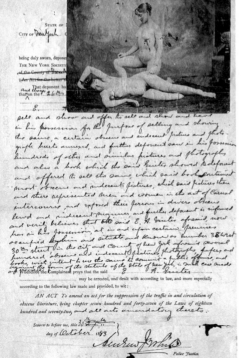

[TOP] Anthony Comstock's Society for the Suppression of Vice aided the police (who often didn't want their help) by tracking down sellers of obscene photographs. Comstock himself presented this evidence on October 30, 1883, against one Camille Besson.

[LEFT] Comstock agent J. A. Britton purchased this photo on October 26, 1883, from E. A. Ginter at his shop in the Tenderloin district at 38 West 30th Street. The agent stated Ginter offered for sale "several hundred" indecent and lewd items, including photos of "carnal intercourse."

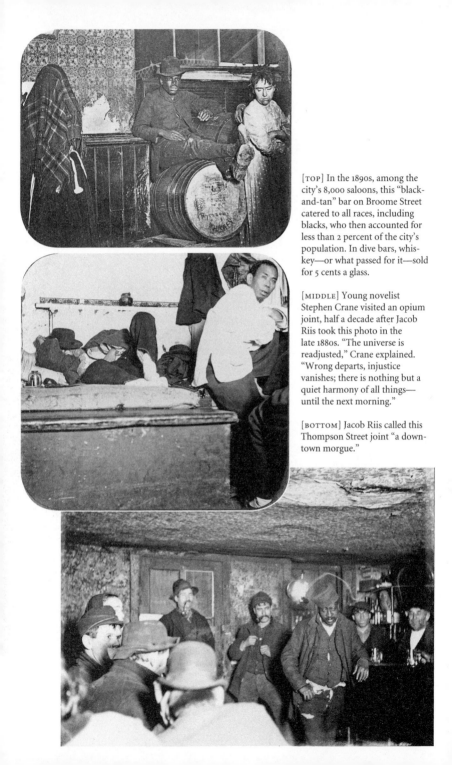

[TOP] In the 1890s, among the city's 8,000 saloons, this "black-and-tan" bar on Broome Street catered to all races, including blacks, who then accounted for less than 2 percent of the city's population. In dive bars, whiskey—or what passed for it—sold for 5 cents a glass.

[MIDDLE] Young novelist Stephen Crane visited an opium joint, half a decade after Jacob Riis took this photo in the late 1880s. "The universe is readjusted," Crane explained. "Wrong departs, injustice vanishes; there is nothing but a quiet harmony of all things—until the next morning."

[BOTTOM] Jacob Riis called this Thompson Street joint "a downtown morgue."

[TOP] Charles Parkhurst (1842–1933) delivered a sermon in February 1892 that sparked a crusade against vice and Tammany Hall. After being accused of knowing little about vice, he took a sin tour to explore brothels, saloons, even a transvestite club.

[ABOVE LEFT] Frank Moss (1860–1920), a deeply religious man and legal counsel for the Parkhurst Society, who dedicated himself to fighting corruption in the police department.

[ABOVE RIGHT] William "Big Bill" Devery (1857–1919) was a bartender and boxer before rising high in the police department. He called reformers "little tin soldiers" and would be suspended several times.

[TOP] This larger-than-life lush erotic painting, "Nymphs and Satyr," by W. A. Bouguereau drew tens of thousands of thirsty men to the elegant Hoffman House bar on 24th Street. The manager called it the world's greatest hotel advertisement. Women could enter only on certain "art"-viewing afternoons.

[BOTTOM] An 1899 guide-book describes this as "a dinner of society people at Delmonico's." The city's wealthy often dined here on Sunday evening, the tradi-tional night off for live-in servants.

[TOP] Strutting on Easter Sunday in 1897 alongside the Croton Distributing Reservoir at 41st Street and Fifth Avenue, the current site of the New York Public Library. In New York, extreme wealth and extreme poverty were often separated by a handful of blocks.

[BOTTOM] Jacob Riis called this Hester Street neighborhood "Jewtown" and judged it part of the most crowded square mile in the world. The Friday "Pig Market" drew huge crowds where everything was for sale, except pork. By law, pushcart peddlers were not to remain in one place longer than ten minutes; they paid off cops to survive.

[TOP] Theodore Roosevelt (1858–1919), sworn in as police commissioner on May 6, 1895, soon decided to try to enforce every law on the books and every rule for police conduct. "New York has never been so shocked and surprised in all its two hundred and fifty years of existence," commented one observer.

[BOTTOM] Theodore Roosevelt, seen here on January 12, 1895, a few months before moving to New York, with his large family: (left to right) Roosevelt, Archie, Ted, Alice, Kermit, wife Edith, and Ethel. (Portrait by C. M. Gilbert)

[TOP] The New York City police commission, as photographed for *Review of Reviews* May 20, 1895. (left to right) Frederick D. Grant (plodding son of late president, Ulysses S., whom TR called a "muttonhead"), Andrew D. Parker (canny lawyer who would defy Roosevelt), Theodore Roosevelt (elected president of the Police Board), Avery D. Andrews (Roosevelt's worshipful ally).

[MIDDLE] Thomas Byrnes (1842–1910), America's most famous nineteenth-century detective, was police chief when Roosevelt arrived. TR despised him for accumulating several hundred thousand dollars by doing favors for the wealthy.

[BOTTOM] Police Inspector Alexander "Clubber" Williams (1839–1917) was notorious for keeping order via crushing blows of his nightstick, and for corruption. Testifying before a committee, he recommended creating a red-light district and claimed he let brothels stay open because they were "fashionable."

[TOP] Mayor William L. Strong (1827–1900), a wealthy Republican businessman drafted to run for office in 1894. Jacob Riis said the mayor suffered from the "intermittent delusion that he was a shrewd politician."

[MIDDLE] Roosevelt quickly earned a reputation for his midnight rambles, hunting for lazy cops. Here, in the cartoonist's imagination, a pair of tramps cheer on the commissioner. Muckraker Lincoln Steffens reported that policemen amused themselves by trying to land the perfect blow on both feet of a bench-sleeping vagrant so that the shock went right up the man's spine and launched him up and running before he even awoke.

[BOTTOM] Newspapers began lampooning Roosevelt for enforcing long-ignored Sabbath laws and closing the saloons on Sundays, the workingman's only day off.

"Fanning" the Copper; or, the Tramps' Delight.

120   THOSE GOOD OLD DAYS HAVE COME AGAIN

NEW AMSTERDAM

BLUE LAWS
ALL CITIZENS
OF NEW AMSTERDAM
MUST BE IN BED BY
YE EARLY CANDLE
LIGHT

[TOP] A nineteenth-century New York tradition called for kids to "rush the growler," that is, fetch a pail of fresh beer home from the saloon for the family. Roosevelt opposed allowing anyone under the legal drinking age (then sixteen, raised to eighteen on March 23, 1896) to purchase alcohol.

[MIDDLE] Tammany Hall politician Mike Callahan bragged about never closing up his saloon on Chatham Square. When a Roosevelt cop tried to arrest him in June 1896, Callahan punched him in the face. (Note the sign for Callahan's "Progress Hotel" offering rooms at 25 cents a night; those temporary lodgers, otherwise known as voters, provided his political power.)

[BOTTOM] Brothers Theodore, then twenty-one, and Elliott, twenty, in September 1880, posing in Chicago before going on a hunting trip to celebrate Theodore's upcoming wedding. They killed more than 400 birds and upset a rowboat in Iowa.

[TOP] The place of last resort for a desperate homeless person in the 1890s was a "police lodging house," i.e., a room in a precinct house basement. Women at this one on Eldridge Street in the heart of the Jewish ghetto slept on wooden planks on the floor. Making the bed meant flipping the plank, Jacob Riis wrote. Cops often fumigated the rooms by smoking cigars. Roosevelt closed the police basements midwinter 1896 to steer the homeless to more hygienic shelters that required work, such as chopping wood or shoveling snow.

[MIDDLE] Roosevelt's longtime friend and mentor, fellow Harvard alumnus Henry Cabot Lodge (1850–1924) was then U.S. senator (Republican) from Massachusetts. TR wrote his most confessional letters to "Cabot," sometimes wondering how he had alienated almost every newspaper and mainstream politician in the city.

[BOTTOM] Thomas Collier Platt (1833–1910), the most powerful Republican Party leader in New York State in the 1890s. Roosevelt privately compared him to Boss Tweed, for corrupting the political process and picking the "worst" men.

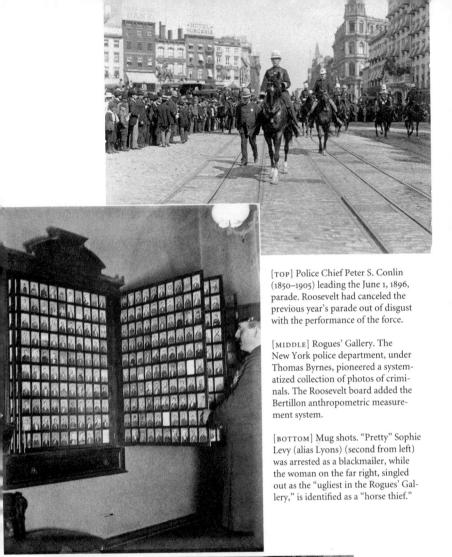

[TOP] Police Chief Peter S. Conlin (1850–1905) leading the June 1, 1896, parade. Roosevelt had canceled the previous year's parade out of disgust with the performance of the force.

[MIDDLE] Rogues' Gallery. The New York police department, under Thomas Byrnes, pioneered a systematized collection of photos of criminals. The Roosevelt board added the Bertillon anthropometric measurement system.

[BOTTOM] Mug shots. "Pretty" Sophie Levy (alias Lyons) (second from left) was arrested as a blackmailer, while the woman on the far right, singled out as the "ugliest in the Rogues' Gallery," is identified as a "horse thief."

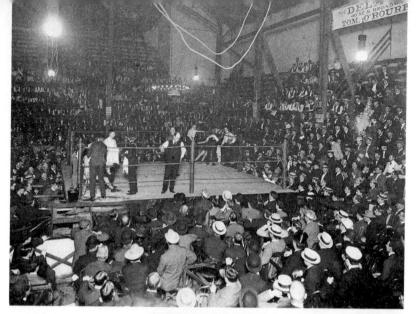

[TOP] Roosevelt never backed down from his love of amateur boxing. Police captains then often attended fights to make sure that laws against "prize fights" were enforced or to accept bribes to look the other way.

[MIDDLE] Roosevelt quarreled fiercely with "secretive" fellow commissioner Andrew Parker for more than a year. Roosevelt repeatedly called him a liar, and erudite Parker never seemed to care. The press delighted in egging them on.

[BOTTOM] Roosevelt lost his temper at a Tammany Hall politician during a meeting at City Hall and, in the heat of the moment, agreed to a duel. The joke going around was that the mayor William L. Strong (i.e., Willie) should either arm himself for protection or put Roosevelt out of his misery.

"WHY NOT DROWN HIM, WILLIE, BEFORE HE BITES?"

[TOP] To the drunk in the back row, the performer in neck-to-toe tights appeared nude (and the snake real). Theaters in the 1890s often featured "living statues" of women re-creating famous art works or mythical scenes. Roosevelt encouraged his officers to close down two skits featuring women in body tights.

[MIDDLE] Did Little Egypt dance naked at Sherry's for a drunken bachelor party in December 1896? Was Roosevelt there? A belly-dancing craze swept America after Little Egypt's performance in the midway at the Chicago World's Fair of 1893. (This collectible cigarette card was aimed to boost turn-of-the-century sales.)

[BOTTOM] Risqué stereoview cards were clandestinely offered for sale in New York. A special stereoscopic viewer made the image appear three dimensional. These cards—more often travel views and comic scenes—remained immensely popular from the 1880s to the 1920s.

[TOP LEFT] Co-owner Big Bill Devery throwing out the opening ball at a Yankees game at American League Park, April 14, 1910.

[TOP RIGHT] Big Bill Devery struggled to survive Roosevelt's repeated attempts to have him convicted of crimes ranging from accepting brothel bribes to aiding Tammany voter fraud. Devery advised cops to know "nuthin'" if they ever got caught, a bit of advice that served him quite well.

[LEFT] President Roosevelt, seen here in August 1905, still treasured the companionship of his newspaper friend and biographer, Jacob "Jake" Riis.

Commissioner Parker, who rarely gave a simple answer to anything, said that fair play demanded a larger pool of candidates—at least five captains—for the three inspector slots, whose appointees would be filling the pipeline to the top job of chief.

The cynical *Herald* viewed the deadlock as the same old struggle for patronage, Parker for the Democrats versus TR, who, "while scorning the idea of being influenced by politics, is desirous of promoting only Republicans."

Around this time, Roosevelt tried a bold new tactic to defeat Parker: change the rules of the game. With no subterfuge at all, he (with the backing of Andrews and Grant) appealed to the Republican-dominated legislature in Albany to pass a police bill that would allow promotions by a board vote of three to one, and would entitle the board—not the chief—to control all assignments and transfers, including roundsmen.

The *World* predicted the bill, if passed, would "spike Conlin's guns" and "slap" Parker. Pundits of all political stripes expected Republicans to pass it, since right now Democrat Parker and his "cat's paw" Conlin were holding up the promotions of two Republican inspectors.

On the overcast morning of Thursday, April 9, Parker and Roosevelt, both elegantly attired, traveled to cavernous Grand Central depot and boarded different cars of the same New York Central train to Albany, traveling as fast as fifty miles an hour up along the Hudson. The *New York Press* ran the headline LOOK FOR LIVELY FUN about the prospect of the fellow commissioners butting heads in the same committee room.

They descended five hours later at the Albany train station by the river and headed separately along Broadway and then up three stunningly steep blocks of State Street to the Capitol Building. The population of Albany, the state's fourth-largest city, stood at 90,000, less than one-twentieth the size of New York City. The elected representatives from picayune upstate counties like Oswego and Herkimer—despite drastically lower residency figures—could easily outvote New York City, which accounted for only 12 of 50 senate seats and 35 of 150 assembly districts.

Reporters, politicians, and sensation seekers packed the assembly committee room for the discussion of Bill No. 2,149. A family friend thought Roosevelt had a queasy, nervous look about him as he waited for Republican chairman George C. Austin to call him up. Austin flipped the usual order and allowed an advocate of the bill to go first.

Speaking loudly and forcefully, sawing the air and slamming the table several times, Roosevelt compared the bipartisan board approach to the parliament of Poland 200 years earlier that required a unanimous vote. "It was a comparatively simple matter to end such deadlocks, however, for it was usually done by killing the man who objected," said Roosevelt, mustering a thin smile. "But that method belonged to an earlier age," he conceded, turning to his fellow commissioner in the front row. "I would not like to kill Mr. Parker."

Roosevelt expanded on the accomplishments of the reform board, achieved before one lone board member began dissenting and before a reinterpretation of the rules granted the chief more power over the men. "I want the chief to be subject to the control of the board," said TR, shaking his fist. "I ask you gentlemen to put him in his proper place." With a master's tone, Roosevelt was making a scorched-earth request; what could Conlin possibly think of a board member who would refer to him that way? "The chief would have never done his duty . . . if he had not been compelled to do so by the Commission."

Icy and sarcastic, Parker argued that passing this bill would invite a return to corruption by overempowering the board and leaving the police chief powerless and forced to watch unqualified men rise. How could the chief be trusted to enforce the laws if he couldn't be trusted to pick the men to do it for him? *This* Police Board might be honest, but what about the *next* Police Board? Parker read aloud passages from the Lexow hearings, documenting how earlier police commissioners, who didn't need a unanimous, bipartisan vote, horse-traded among themselves to sell transfers and captaincies.

Roosevelt, unable to sit still, bobbed as Parker spoke, then darted more than once to the sleeve of Chairman Austin to demand rebuttal. Time was granted. Roosevelt repeated his earlier arguments, then, shifting to personal attack, accused Parker of missing meetings, of changing his position.

Roosevelt at one point blurted: "Emerson said that consistency is the hobgoblin of inferior minds." Parker shook his head.

ROOSEVELT: Oh, I can't accuse you of consistency.
PARKER: (*acidly*) Then you think I have a great mind?
ROOSEVELT: By Jove I think you've got a first class mind. Any man who can weave facts in and out in the way you can has a quick brain.

No debate judge stood by to score the combatants, but in any case Chairman Austin's committee, dominated by upstate Republicans, did as pundits predicted, and later in closed session voted favorably to send the Roosevelt bill to the assembly.

In the late afternoon, Roosevelt and Parker reprised their verbal joust before the Senate Committee on Cities. With Republicans holding an 8–4 majority, a positive vote for TR seemed a foregone conclusion.

Democratic senator Thomas F. Grady of Manhattan tried to come to Parker's aid by twitting Roosevelt about Election Day.

> GRADY: Your board transferred policemen so that they could not vote. You, however, voted before you went to your duties.
> ROOSEVELT: (*hotly*) But Judge Lawrence, a *Tammany Hall* Judge—
> GRADY: (*equally hotly*) Don't call Judge Lawrence a *Tammany Hall* Judge; he is a jurist; you should not bring him into politics.
> ROOSEVELT: Do you consider it a term of opprobrium?
> GRADY: No, but you used it as a term of opprobrium.
> ROOSEVELT: Not so, I merely used the word as descriptive. I wanted to point out that the Judge stated that our system of using policemen on Election Day was the best ever devised.

Edward "Smooth Ed" Lauterbach, the Republican New York City boss, walked in and out of the committee room several times. During Parker's final remarks, Lauterbach, Republican senator Ellsworth, and Roosevelt ducked out into the hallway to converse. (Reporters tried but failed to eavesdrop.)

Around 6 p.m., when the senate chairman recessed the hearing, Commissioner Parker, along with others, strolled out into the corridor.

Roosevelt, his face purple with rage, rushed toward the taller, bearded lawyer. Trying to control himself and keep his voice low, Roosevelt, clutching a handful of typewritten pages, held them out to Parker for inspection and enunciated to his fellow commissioner: "Mr. Parker, Mr. Lauterbach submits this statement to me as yours."

Parker bowed his head slightly, as though mockingly acknowledging authorship. TR hastily read a few lines aloud: "Never in the history of the force have Republicans been so largely selected. The list below will show this, and these selections, as the lists will likewise show, have been almost invariably suggested by Parker, and he has been the one who has [prevented] the

Democrats . . . In brief, if party selections are made the test, Parker has been a Republican and Roosevelt a Democrat."

For fans of comic opera and political intrigue, this was a masterstroke by Parker. Accuse Roosevelt—because of his proud municipal reform *non*partisanship—of not backing Republicans! Accuse Roosevelt, that high-ranking member of the stalwartly Republican Union League, of championing Democrats!

"Those statements are false," said TR, seething.

"They are all absolutely true," coldly replied Parker. Neither man wanted a scene in front of the newspapermen.

Roosevelt turned abruptly away and told Lauterbach he would send him a detailed reply on the following day. Too agitated by "so heated a wrangle," TR canceled a long-planned social call at the home of family friend Fanny Parsons.

The senate committee returned and went into closed session. The chairman, Republican senator Nevada N. Stranahan (Oswego), backed by Republican senator T. E. Ellsworth (Niagara), recommended that the committee report the Roosevelt police reform bill favorably, but five Republican senators—all part of Platt's Republican machine—voted against it, as did one Democrat. The final tally was 6–2 against, with one abstention and three absentees. Chairman Stranahan told reporters he hoped to bring the stalled measure up again.

On the train ride south, Roosevelt carefully read the eight-page typewritten letter. For almost a year, he had been walking a tightrope, trying to be a loyal party Republican on *national* issues and a staunch nonpartisan reformer on *local* issues. His attitude had deeply irritated Boss Platt and Lieutenant Lauterbach. TR had not handed a single patronage position to Republicans, not even a doorman or an elevator boy.

Parker's ambush pinned Roosevelt into a corner. If TR defended himself by stating he had backed more Republicans than Democrats, then his tens of thousands of well-applauded syllables about nonpartisanship, about the end of politics and pull, would deflate as empty platitudes.

The letter, with Parker's usual precision, analyzed the promotion of twenty-one acting captains, and found thirteen Republicans and eight Democrats. Going case by case, he cited the likes of "Walsh, *Dem.* strongly espoused by Roosevelt for promotion to captain, and opposed by Parker till longer probation is had."

Just after Roosevelt descended from the train, he learned that his thirty-seven-year-old first cousin, Dr. James West Roosevelt, born the same year as TR, had died. "West" was the family physician, had an Oyster Bay home nearby, and his children played with the Roosevelt children. Roosevelt found it difficult to concentrate.

On the following morning at 10 a.m., at the Friday Police Board meeting, reporters eagerly awaited the fireworks. Parker, uncharacteristically, showed up first. With stilted politeness, he and TR attended to mundane business. Commissioner Andrews tried to lighten the mood by recounting the mishaps of a rookie cop who got lost on his beat in the wilds of the Bronx, showing up an hour late for morning roll call. "The next time I get that post at night," Andrews quoted the patrolman as telling him, "I shall insist on being furnished with an ax to hew a path through the forest, with a locomotive headlight to illumine the way, and a dozen red sky rockets to send up for assistance in case I fall into some gully or get tangled up in the jungles north of 180th Street."

At the end of the open board meeting, TR commandeered Andrews and Grant into his office. Parker was not invited. The trio spent the next several hours drafting a long, detailed rebuttal letter to Lauterbach.

TR dictated it, Miss Kelly typed it, and all three signed it. "That statement of Mr. Parker that he is responsible for the bulk of the Republican appointments, and I responsible solely for Democrats is unqualifiedly false."

Roosevelt attacked each of twenty promotions in another double-columned presentation. For instance, TR devoted 203 words to rebutting Parker's claim of credit for advancing Walter L. Thompson, a Republican, to captain from his longtime perch as sergeant. TR explained to Lauterbach that Chief Conlin had first suggested Thompson to Commissioner Grant, who had endorsed him as "best" on a list of possible captains that he had forwarded to Parker, who had examined Thompson and concurred. "Meanwhile," Commissioner Andrews "independently" discovered Sergeant Thompson—a tough, spry five-foot-four-inch Civil War veteran called "Uncle Walt" by his men—and had suggested him to Roosevelt. Both Grant and Andrews encouraged TR to examine Thompson, whom he judged "a first class man." Roosevelt branded Parker's claim for sole credit as "undeniably false." The long letter is a testament to minutiae and bureaucratic anger. Sprinkled throughout are harsh words: "an absolute untruth," "an absolute falsehood," "untrue," "entirely untrue."

Roosevelt informed Lauterbach that the board made promotions based on merit, without regard to politics, that they *all* elevated thirteen Republicans, and Parker lied when claiming credit. But, curiously, he decided to reveal his votes for the near future, explaining "that the promotions the majority of the board were now anxious to make were, in the majority of cases, Republicans, as far as the board knew." He added: "I mentioned to [Republican politician Lemuel Quigg and an ally of Roosevelt] that I personally favor for inspectors McCullagh, Brooks, Vreedenburgh, Thompson and Sheehan." (Four of five were Republicans.) TR was walking a political tightrope.

———

That weekend, the Roosevelt clan gathered to cope with the sudden death of West Roosevelt. TR spent much of Saturday and Sunday trying to console his emotionally fragile sister, Corinne, who took the news hard, as did his wife, Edith, who still wore black from losing her mother eleven months earlier. Adding to the gloom, the family suspected that West's demise had been accelerated by alcoholism.

Roosevelt attended the funeral service on Monday morning at the Little Chapel on 20th Street and failed to come to 300 Mulberry that morning.

Someone sent him a letter bomb; this one had gunpowder.

A postal clerk tore open a corner of the package, which had no stamps, and saw a dozen matchheads. The superintendent of the post office, George Meeks, personally walked it to police headquarters but Roosevelt wasn't there.

A detective dunked it in a pail of water, then unwrapped it to discover red wallpaper rolled into a tube, with fine Chinese black gunpowder inside; at one end ten glued match heads lay opposite sandpaper attached to the wrapping paper. If opened quickly, it might produce a spark, which would set off the gunpowder. Chief of Detectives O'Brien said the explosion would not have killed anyone but might have caused severe burns or blindness.

When Roosevelt arrived after the funeral, he was told of the bomb. "If I had nothing worse than bombs to bother me," TR told a reporter, "my life would be a bed of roses." The *Journal*, without citing sources, added that the bomb was "very popular" at headquarters.

Roosevelt wrote and rushed at least two more letters to Lemuel Quigg, seeking advice on how to resurrect the police reform bill. Roosevelt wondered if the machine was purposely delaying it to force some concessions out of him—perhaps on Sunday saloons or specific promotions—but he vowed to Quigg he would not compromise.

———

Within days, the mischief-making, elfin lawyer Lauterbach leaked Roosevelt's embittered Parker-thrashing letter to the press, full of charge and counter-charge. The *World* promptly announced POLICE REFORM LOST, a sentiment echoed in other papers. Here was one reform commissioner (Roosevelt) loudly accusing another (Parker) of telling lie after lie after lie. "Roosevelt generally knew how to handle men who opposed him," wrote Commissioner Andrews years later, "but Parker's thick epidermis and his apparent indifference to accusations, which another would regard as a deadly insult, left Roosevelt sputtering."

Parker chatted briefly that day with reporters. "I regret that Commissioner Roosevelt should have seen fit to publish either his statement or mine, but, as we sportsmen say, 'the wounded bird flutters,' [and] some shaft must have struck deep."

TR complained to Lodge:

> *Lauterbach queered us before the Senate Committee . . . Andrews, Grant and I sent a letter to Lauterbach, taking [Parker's] statements one by one and denouncing them as falsehoods. Grant is a broken reed to lean upon, for Parker is continually playing on him and using him for his own purposes. I fear now that the bill will not pass but I am very glad to have got Parker in the open where I could nail him. He is a thoroughly tricky and despicable fellow but he is able and unscrupulous and it is not easy to catch him.*

The bill indeed died late that week in a (Republican-dominated) senate committee in Albany, and Roosevelt went to the circus on Saturday, where at least the clowns wore makeup.

———

Frustrated, TR needed help in his battle against Parker, something akin to a deus ex machina, when in Greek drama a god miraculously arrives to rescue the hero.

On Monday, April 20, Roosevelt received an anonymous tip; a letter writer stated that he had overheard two new officers, whom he named, at the West 47th Street Precinct bragging that they had bought their appointments through . . . Andrew D. Parker.

Roosevelt ordered the two patrolmen brought to him immediately. One forcefully denied paying any bribe; the other, a young recruit named Charles McMorrow, confessed.

McMorrow had worked the previous year as a night watchman at Everard's Brewery, but when he decided he wanted to become a policeman, he took the advice of a fellow Everard employee, James Coyle, to contact an officer at the Delancey Street station.

McMorrow approached James Devaney at his home at 353 West 53rd Street and Devaney said he could help him. He told McMorrow that he knew a high-ranking "clubman" at a Republican Club who controlled several places on the police. McMorrow would have to pay a $400 initiation fee to join the club. McMorrow told Devaney he had never heard of arrangements like that but Devaney assured him this was the best way to do it.

McMorrow agreed to the terms; he went through the normal application process, took the civil service exam, and was appointed a probationary patrolman December 17, 1895, and the following week he paid Devaney $200. He joined the force full time the following month, but balked at paying the balance.

Roosevelt asked McMorrow if any commissioner's name was mentioned. "It was to be done through Commissioner Parker." The board president then reinterrogated McMorrow in front of Commissioner Andrews; the confession was typed up and McMorrow signed it on Monday, April 20, 1896.

Roosevelt had a four-page signed confession implicating Parker.

Roosevelt allowed McMorrow, who was deeply frightened, to leave 300 Mulberry. One hour later, he summoned Officer Devaney of the Delancey Street station to headquarters.

Devaney stoutly denied everything. Roosevelt browbeat and lectured but to no avail. Devaney was a veteran cop and he knew how to stonewall. Roosevelt was banging his head against the blue wall of silence.

Very irritated, Roosevelt summoned McMorrow back to headquarters to identify Devaney; McMorrow stunned TR by saying he had never seen Officer Devaney before in his life and he denied that Devaney had ever threatened him. (One can only assume that in the hour that had elapsed, someone had a heart-to-heart conversation with McMorrow.) Flabbergasted, Roosevelt tried to summon McMorrow's fellow Everard employee Coyle, who had first suggested Devaney, but found out Coyle had died a month earlier.

———

Mayor Strong was often the last one to know anything. He was flighty, wealthy, and independent-minded enough that party politicians stopped pitching him. He was furious that neither Parker nor Roosevelt had sent their Lauterbach letters to him and he was tired of reading about the feud in the press.

On Tuesday, April 21, the mayor personally berated TR at a dinner at the Lotos Club attended by sixteen top-ranking administration officials. Roosevelt responded with what might almost pass for an apology. In this rarest of missives, Roosevelt wrote: "We did not suppose you would care to be brought into a personal trouble of this kind, in which the public at that time had no interest. I can assure, you, Mr. Mayor, there was no intention of being disrespectful. We will invariably consult you in advance about every step we take hereafter." He sent copies of both his and Parker's original letters and added copies of promotion memos from the police files.

Roosevelt also informed the mayor about the McMorrow bribe trail leading toward Parker. Roosevelt needed all the ammunition he could get to convince the mayor to start the process of ousting police commissioner Parker and replacing him with a new face who would give TR that fourth aye. (By law, the mayor could bring misconduct charges against a commissioner and then act as judge in a dismissal hearing.) "I had quite a time with the mayor last night," Roosevelt wrote his ally Andrews, "on the whole, rather friendly but for Heaven's sake be sure to try to see him and have a long talk over matters Friday or Saturday. I shall see him Sunday. We want to 'stay with him' as the boys say."

Even though Roosevelt wanted personally to pursue—with ultimate discretion—his investigation of the Parker bribe, he had no choice but to leave it for a week. He had two out-of-town speaking engagements, first in Columbus, Ohio, and then in front of 3,000 students at the University of Michigan in Ann Arbor.

When he returned the following weekend he wrote to his sister: "I cannot be sure of Parker's financial honesty and he is exceedingly able and adroit and as finished a liar as Talleyrand. I feel very uneasy lest he compromise us."

Roosevelt was convincing himself of Parker's guilt; he had already told the mayor but now he decided to send the written McMorrow confession to the mayor and to corporation counsel Scott. He certainly hoped this information might sway the mayor to start dismissal proceedings. The mayor and corporation counsel requested instead that TR tell no one else for now and not share the document with anyone.

———

All the Police Board turmoil and disagreement between Parker and Roosevelt was grinding down the fifty-five-year-old chief of police Peter Conlin, physically ill with rheumatism and mentally strained. He requested a thirty-day leave of absence and wanted to combine it with his unused twenty days of summer vacation. Parker and Grant both approved the move but TR and Andrews—both perhaps eager to put the chief "in his place" and provoke retirement—opposed it, citing an impending flood of important police matters. TR and Andrews suggested that they would agree if Conlin obtained a doctor's note but Parker convinced them demanding this would insult the chief. They relented. Conlin told reporters he planned to return in time to lead the police parade on June 1.

———

As April progressed, Roosevelt watched—in shock—as a pillar of his accomplishments, his Sunday saloon crusade, unexpectedly started to crumble.

The crackdown was working well when a handful of saloon owners—tired of sunning themselves on Sundays outside their closed joints—decided to try one last far-fetched gambit: convert their saloons to hotels. (The Raines Law allowed "hotels" with ten rooms and liquor licenses to serve liquor *with a meal* to guests *round the clock* in the restaurants or guests' rooms—just not in the hotel bar.) Florrie Sullivan, cousin of Tammany's "Dry Dollar" Sullivan, hired carpenters to chop up his second floor into ten hotel rooms. The workmen framed in the small rooms, applied the plaster and lath, hung the doors.

Sullivan for years had seen his neighbor Mike Lyons, with his famed restaurant (where TR had eaten at 3 a.m. during a midnight ramble), serve liquor round the clock, thanks to its hotel license.

Florrie applied to the exiting excise board (not replaced till June 1) and received a hotel liquor license. On Sunday, he sealed tight his barroom.

"There's no fake hotel about this place," he told reporters. "You fellows have got to eat those sandwiches or you don't get a drink. I won't have any funny business around here."

Florrie showed little sympathy for the fellow who complained that he had eaten six sandwiches and couldn't stand another; Florrie was collecting a dime for every beer and sandwich. A few blocks away on Canal Street, the owner of a ratty little bar was also packing in customers. He had rented the empty storeroom next door to serve as his "hotel" dining room and he struck a deal with the cheap lodging house above to deliver him ten rooms. A new "hotel" was born. Captain Kirchner estimated that forty new hotels opened in the first two weeks of April in Devery's old precinct.

Silver Dollar Smith, at 64 Essex Street, spared no expense the first Sunday for his "Silver Dollar Hotel." He threw tablecloths over the pool tables and charged every newcomer five cents for a ticket that entitled him to a sandwich. "Silver Dollar" himself pinned each guest with a boutonniere of violets. The *Times* called it "one of the busiest places in New York" with 500 guests before noon.

Bowery celebrity Steve Brodie, famed for jumping off the Brooklyn Bridge, was short of space in his building, and he told reporters he had to convert a basement coal bin to a hotel room. Barkeep Andy Horn—with a joint favored by Park Row newspapermen—sent carpenters to his attic to carve ten rooms, though in some only a midget could stand upright. Customers complained about "eggs boiled to an indigestible degree of hardness." Mike Callahan—Roosevelt's nemesis—grabbed ten rooms from his lodging house, and guided guests through a maze of stairways and courtyards to his "hotel restaurant," since he had to keep his massive barroom locked.

Tammany Hall building inspectors seemed ready to look the other way at shoddy construction.

As for the private clubs being forced to comply, lawyers for the wealthiest ones met at the Arion Club on April 2 to fight the new law. The nation's finest legal minds pored over the fine print pro bono, or for the good of the club's bar, whose liquor sales generally subsidized the rococo clubhouses and staff. Within a week, they found a judge who agreed that clubs did not "traffick in liquor" and therefore should not be subject to the Raines Law. The nitpick saved the millionaires from taxes and open window shades, and more importantly allowed them to serve liquor around the clock.

So now, in addition to the creation of new liquor-friendly hotels, new liquor-friendly clubs began springing up. Any bar owner too cheap or lazy to build ten new rooms could create a new "club" of loyal patrons such as "Knights of the Octagonal Table." Club incorporation applications would soar tenfold.

———

Just a week after the dire Raines thirst headline, the *New York World* trumpeted: DRINKS? ALL YOU WANT: "Five Hundred Places Sold Liquor Yesterday to the Thirsty; They Were all Called Hotels; Most of them However Were Very Backward about Renting their Rooms." A plainclothes detective arrested a bartender for selling him a beer and just a sandwich, but Magistrate Brann in Yorkville Court judged that a sandwich constituted a "meal" and another judge decided that a customer off the street qualified as a "guest."

By the following weekend, the *World* headline was RUM RULED THE CITY. And the reporter gleefully announced: "The Tenderloin glistened with its brilliant evil; the eastside wallowed in beer." Some joints served the same sandwich over and over. The city almost seemed giddy with its newfound freedom, especially in the sudden ninety-degree heat wave. Raines Law jokes were springing up.

> BARTENDER: We'll have to stop the drinks for a few minutes.
> OWNER: Why, what's the matter? Beer give out?
> BARTENDER: No. Nothing like that. Some idiot has eaten the sandwich and there aint another one in the whole block that aint in use.

The police force and the police brass were baffled by this sudden new development. They sent repeated requests for clarifications to the board and to the mayor's office. Roosevelt was outraged. "Ten beers and one hard boiled egg scarcely constitute a meal," he complained at the Tuesday board meeting.

Not unreasonably, Roosevelt expected a sane interpretation of the words *hotel* and *meal* and *guest*. He complained that the outgoing excise board was granting hotel licenses with "extraordinary rapidity." "The police have special instructions just now to be vigorously on the look-out for 'fake hotels' . . . Hotels must be bona-fide ones or they will be suppressed . . . The Health board will also see that its regulations are strictly and properly enforced." Roosevelt reported that the police had sent twenty-five cases against "fake" hotels, such as Mike Callahan's, to the district attorney, and he was confident that "no little schemes of the liquor sellers to evade the Raines law" would prove successful.

Parker, too, opposed this sudden free-for-all on Sundays. He suggested that Parkhurst Society agents could go to these so-called hotels in the middle of the week and request rooms. "Saloon keepers will soon find out that in order to be exempt from the salient limitations as to Sundays, they must keep honest and bonafide hostelries," he pronounced in his usual lawyerly manner.

With nothing to lose, hundreds upon hundreds of saloons raced to convert to hotels.

Max Hochstim, who had his finger in every lucrative vice, was especially proud of his new hotel's bridal suite, with a big fireplace and chromolithographs of Niagara Falls, overlooking the bustling street corner of Delancey and Suffolk. "Who says Max Hochstim aint running a genuine hotel?" he asked a touring reporter.

Hochstim borrowed (or swiped) fancy printed menus from Silver Dollar Smith and crossed out "Smith" and wrote "Hochstim." The canny owner even bought silverware but then had misgivings. "Can I get it with chains?" he asked the salesman, who gave him a confused look. "To fasten to the table," he explained. "I guess you don't know the people round my way."

Hotels, even these quick-start hotels, could now serve guests round the clock. And so could clubs. And Sunday, blessedly, was now the same as Monday. For New Yorkers, deprived by Roosevelt for almost a year, this seemed too good to be true, a drunken daydream, from which the Sunday revelers and barkeeps would soon awake with a horrible hangover.

The Police Board was perplexed. (At least the legislature in Albany had closed its four-month session without removing them.) At the Friday, May 1, meeting, Commissioner Parker suddenly interrupted the discussion of Raines Law issues to point out that the one-year term of board president Roosevelt expired on that day. The other commissioners looked shocked, and Andrews stammered something about needing to postpone any vote. Parker demanded that Chief Clerk Kipp verify the law on the length of the president's term. After a few minutes Kipp returned and confirmed that the term had expired. Commissioner Parker said he wished to make a nomination. He paused dramatically. "I nominate Theodore Roosevelt." The *Evening Post* considered it all a "practical joke" by Parker.

Still very perturbed over the Raines Law loopholes, Roosevelt on Sunday, May 3, decided to set out on a tour of the Tenderloin and the East Side to see the law in action. He rode in a carriage with a reporter from Hearst's *Journal* and was accompanied by his new "handy man" at headquarters, patrolman Frank Rathgeber. The patrolman would do the investigating, since Roosevelt was now too recognizable. (Though TR had relinquished Roundsman Tierney at Parker's request in January, he had added Rathgeber since his public spat with his fellow commissioner.)

The carriage rolled to a stop and Rathgeber, in plainclothes, alighted and walked to the side door of a famed saloon on Sixth Avenue. He tried to enter but a man asked for his club membership card. Without one Rathgeber was out of luck, since they didn't have a hotel license. Rathgeber returned to the carriage.

The next joint was a big saloon converted to a hotel. Rathgeber entered the crowded place; the bartender told him he must order a sandwich with his beer. He did, and described the sandwich to Roosevelt as "pretty bad, it looked like it had seen better days." He didn't need more food to get his second beer. (Rathgeber would drink enough beer and nibble enough sandwiches to wind up calling in sick the next day.)

At the following place, a hole-in-the-wall saloon, the barroom was closed but in a "dining room" upstairs near the "rooms," Rathgeber ordered a nickel beer. His sandwich was a "crust of bread" that looked like it had aired on the table for a week. (Playwright Eugene O'Neill once famously described a Raines Law sandwich as "an old dessicated ruin of dust-laden bread and mummified ham or cheese.")

Each time the policeman returned to the carriage, Roosevelt asked him many questions such as: Did you see any other food served than sandwiches? Did the place bear any resemblance to an ordinary hotel? Were you asked to register as a guest?

He clearly was gathering material for a legal challenge. Rathgeber said he saw many sandwiches but only one bed. He never registered. He never was asked to buy a second sandwich or even to eat the first one.

Roosevelt was also curious about a certain Avenue B saloon that he had heard was staying open on Sundays without pretending to be a hotel because the owner, William Fagan, was the brother of a police sergeant. Roosevelt told Rathgeber to knock at 205 Avenue B. The bouncer cracked open the door, took one look at Rathgeber's face and shoes, and allowed the patrolman inside; Rathgeber drank a beer from a keg in the back room. No food anywhere. Roosevelt, while waiting, saw a teenage girl come out carrying a "growler."

Roosevelt was so irritated by this blatant disregard of the law that he had the carriage driver head over to the *neighboring* precinct, the 14th, to find an officer to make the arrest inside the 13th Precinct. He wanted to make certain no local cops would tip off the joint. Roosevelt, with his zero-tolerance policy, soon had charges brought against 13th Precinct captain Theron Copeland, a well-respected thirty-nine-year veteran of the force without a single prior complaint, and against roundsman John Kirzinger and beat cop James Donnelly.

Several reporters the next day asked Roosevelt for his observations on the Raines Law. He said the law was in a "transition period" and he expected improvements when the state's "special agents" started their jobs on June 1. He also displayed a streetwise understanding of its impact. "The practical effect is merely to charge double [on Sundays] for the first glass of beer (ten cents). In other words, if a man will buy one sandwich for five cents, he can have all the beer he wants." He noted that the police had made arrests for that behavior "but the City Magistrates have discharged the prisoners in every instance, and the Grand Jury has refused to indict."

———

Bar owners and others citywide quickly began to realize this might be an "Alice in Wonderland" moment, a Mad Hatter's tea party where a sloppily written law aimed at repression would lead to wondrous new freedoms and cocktails for all, twenty-four hours a day, seven days a week.

Could the "hayseeds" have really bungled the new legislation that badly? Could Tammany clerks and judges of all stripes really interpret the law that way? Could glasses down and "last call" really be "bottoms up" and another round? Could New York really become the city that never sleeps?

Though Roosevelt certainly had not created the Raines Law, these events, especially the demise of Roosevelt Sundays, played out like a slap in the face of the commissioner. New Yorkers were drinking openly in "fake" hotels and "fake" clubs on Sundays and also at three in the morning. And they were not only drinking. The frantic conversion of hundreds of saloons into hotels was bringing thousands of cheap affordable beds within a drunken stagger of the bar, very convenient for couples on their fourth cocktail or for prostitutes. And unmarried young women—shopgirls and factory girls—who might never walk blocks to a sleazy hotel, might just stumble up the convenient barroom stairs to one of the ten Raines Law rooms.

Roosevelt, who for a year had delighted in describing sober workingmen picnicking with their families on Sundays, was not amused by any of it.

Volcanic Roosevelt finally erupted on May 5.

On that day, he attended a Board of Estimate meeting in place of Commissioner Andrews, department treasurer, who was vacationing in Texas. Representatives from various branches of government, such as sanitation or fire, often appeared at these meetings to deal with budget matters and pry loose funds tangled in red tape.

While other topics were discussed, Roosevelt waited his turn that afternoon, sitting at the rectangular conference table, to the mayor's left. Opposite him sat tax commissioner E. P. Barker and catty-cornered was comptroller Ashbel Fitch. Impatient, Roosevelt occasionally popped up and paced the room. Lawyers and reporters filled the gallery of the ornate chamber in the southwest corner of City Hall.

Frustrated over McMorrow, undermined by Parker on promotions, bereft of his constant ally Andrews, TR eagerly undertook the mission to land $9,000 in disputed allocations in order to replenish the department's depleted "contingency funds."

For six months, Comptroller Fitch, elected in 1893 (pre-Lexow) and the highest-ranking Tammany Hall Democrat in Mayor Strong's municipal government, had repeatedly denied the request. Ashbel Fitch was a short, dome-bald forty-eight-year-old Columbia College–pedigreed lawyer with an unusually thick black beard and flowing Teutonic cavalry mustache. The *New York Press* identified him as a "Tammany official who derives more joy from teasing reformers than from eating his dinner."

Roosevelt bristled over the fact that detectives had shelled out their own cash to pursue undercover gambling, brothel, and saloon arrests but had not been reimbursed; even Chief Conlin himself had peeled off $200 during a massive gambling sting. A jailhouse matron, earning a meager $1,000 a year, had reached into her own purse for several hundred dollars to provide dinner and breakfast to female prisoners and lost children—all unreimbursed. The department hovered on the verge of running out of money to pay for telephone service, telegrams, trial stenographers.

"Contingency funds" served as a catch-all budget term for "everything else," that is, "miscellaneous." In 1895, the police department had plowed through the $11,000 allocated for the year and racked up another $8,000 or so. Treasurer Andrews requested on December 10 that $7,500 in unused funds allocated in 1892 to build a new 9th Precinct station house be shifted over to contingency funds. It seemed a routine request.

Tammany's Fitch claimed such a move would be illegal, in effect, purloining money that should be returned to the city's general fund. When the Police Board countered that this practice had been pursued for years, Fitch slyly asked during a February hearing: "This [Police] Board is expected to be better than the old one, is it not?"

After that meeting, Mayor Strong said that Fitch had denied the police department request "out of pure cussedness."

Despite Fitch's qualms, the Board of Estimate had voted four to one back on March 4 (with Fitch dissenting) to approve the transfer of funds. Fitch, however, still refused to deliver the money, engaging in-house counsel to deliver a report showing the Police Board had acted illegally in spending money for unapproved items, and afterward demanding reimbursement. Could the police build six more station houses and demand reimbursement? Could the sanitation department buy 20,000 extra brooms? Where did it stop?

Of course, Fitch knew better—he knew that each department needed some wiggle room in its budget, but he mockingly chose to mirror Roosevelt's rigid enforcement of *all* the laws.

The previous month, TR had told reporters that Fitch was working "in the interests of the criminal classes" because detectives would no longer risk spending their own cash to pursue undercover investigations against brothels and gambling joints.

"[Roosevelt] is constantly saying that everybody in journalism, in office or in politics who disagrees with him on any subject is aiding the criminal classes," responded Fitch. "He probably honestly believes it is criminal to oppose him in anything."

Fitch had advised the Police Board to appeal the matter to the New York State Supreme Court and the board had replied it would. That's where the issue stood on May 5.

The mayor introduced Roosevelt, who reiterated the Police Board demands. While he spoke for ten minutes or so, Ashbel Fitch tilted his chair back and glued a smug smile to his face. Roosevelt looked straight at Fitch: "Remember you are keeping this money away from the poor policeman, not from us, and from the poor prisoners, who will starve if they are not attended to." For emphasis Roosevelt pointed his finger at Fitch, who, with exaggerated nonchalance, lolled further back and crossed his legs.

Then Fitch in a low calm voice asked why the Police Board had not taken his advice a month ago and brought the matter to the courts. "You characterized my course as a move in the interest of the criminal classes. Then you shut your mouth and we heard no more for a time."

Fitch said he had read that Commissioner Parker would go to the courts and get the money immediately. "But you started a public row with him and he forgot all about it," said Fitch, smiling at Roosevelt. "Your starving prisoners were not considered, were they? If anyone is to blame, it is you."

Roosevelt lost it. Newspapermen said he flushed deep red, balled his hands into fists, and with his eyes blazing under contorted brows, he pounded the table. "What you say is not true," he shouted. "You are the one to blame." Fitch, irritatingly calm as ever, replied with a faintly aristocratic accent: "I won't discuss this matter with you in this fashion."

The mayor interjected: "Gentlemen, gentlemen!"

Roosevelt was leaning in over the table toward Fitch, who said sarcastically to him: "Oh, go ahead, I know you are a fighter. You're always fighting. It appears to be your talent."

Roosevelt shouted: "You wouldn't fight! You'd run away!"

Fitch, slowly tipping his chair forward, replied: "I'd never run from you."

Roosevelt: "You daren't fight. That's your way."

Fitch, with a smug smile: "What shall it be? Pistols?"

Roosevelt was in a full rage; he banged the table; his voice hit a higher pitch: "Yes, pistols or anything you choose."

The mayor, despite his rheumatism and gout, slammed down his hands. "If this thing does not cease, I shall arrest you both." The corporation counsel, Francis Scott, confirmed the mayor had the power to do it. (Pundits later cited Section 235 of the New York State Penal Code: "Any person who challenges another to a fight or a duel or who sends a written or verbal message, . . . or who accepts such a challenge . . . is punishable by imprisonment up to seven years." They suggested TR arrest himself.)

Fitch couldn't let it go. "I have refused to pay this bill because you have infringed the law," he said to TR. "You have violated a statute and should be indicted for it." Before Roosevelt could reply, Corporation Counsel Scott jumped in again . . . this time with mock indignation. "I must insist that the administration gets its law from us."

Fitch, shifting easily to banter, asked: "Do you refer to me, sir?"

Then, both Roosevelt and Fitch agreed to let the courts and the corporation counsel decide the issue.

————

Still seething, Roosevelt returned to 300 Mulberry and finding no other commissioners there to pass any resolutions, he issued a long angry statement about how the department, deprived of funds, might soon be unable to afford telephone calls or go undercover. He vowed to continue fighting the comptroller's efforts to cripple the force.

Fitch kept his response playful. He said if Roosevelt "challenged" him, he would choose "Fighting Bob" Evans of the U.S. Navy as his second, and in any case, he was ready. He informed reporters that he had been a member of the elite fighting society Corps Franconia at the University of Heidelberg. The *Journal* advised its readers that Otto von Bismarck, a fellow member, had fought thirty-nine duels in three years.

The *Evening Sun*, the paper of Roosevelt's pal Riis, rated the would-be duelists: neither man was adept with a pistol; Roosevelt preferred "a magazine rifle with which he has often punctured grizzly bears"; Fitch opted for a sword "with which he was wont to slit cheeks and open foreheads at Heidelberg." The paper added: "If we really thought the gentlemen were fighting mad we should propose a meeting in the City Hall Plaza with fire department hoses at thirty paces, each combatant advancing as he fired the Croton [reservoir water] at the other."

The next day, Commissioner Parker walked over to Comptroller Fitch's office at City Hall, and they agreed to file the paperwork to let the courts decide the budget issue. "It was a matter easily arranged with any sane person," Fitch told reporters.

The *Evening News* ran a cartoon of Mayor Strong trying to restrain a snarling pit bull embellished with Roosevelt's head. Ran the caption: "Why not drown him, Willie, before he bites?" A friend of the mayor sent him a toy pistol for protection to carry to future board meetings.

The city was having a tad too much fun at Roosevelt's expense.

"Yesterday I lost my temper with Fitch," TR wrote to Lodge, unburdening himself, "which I should not have done, but he is such a contemptible lying little blackguard, and does so much mischief that I found it difficult to pardon him."

Roosevelt relentlessly lobbied Mayor Strong to dismiss Parker. The mayor arranged a meeting at his home on May 13 with Parker as well as several high-ranking municipal power brokers, but Parker never showed up.

———

Roosevelt's relations with the inscrutable Parker were only worsening.

Parker blindsided Roosevelt at the end of the May 15 board meeting with the announcement that he intended to issue a statement on the successes of the revamped detective bureau. Parker, alone among the commissioners, had overseen the makeover in the wake of Byrnes's forced resignation. The arrest numbers were startlingly good.

TR said the board would issue a statement.

Parker countered that he would do it.

Roosevelt, red-faced, flared that he found it highly improper for a "private member" to give it out.

Parker: "What is a private member?"

Roosevelt: "I meant a 'single member.'"

Parker in his irritatingly calm way pointed out that other members had given out statements, such as Andrews about the bicycle squad or Grant about steam launches.

"Am I to understand that it is improper for a Commissioner to express himself on a matter that is to the great credit of a most important bureau of the city?" asked Parker. "The telling of this report is an encouragement to the law abiding element and a menace to the criminal classes."

TR said it was permitted but he was preparing a report for the mayor that would include this same material. Commissioner Andrews, standing nearby and trying to be helpful, said to TR: "Your report would be stale then." Parker replied: "And that is just where the shoe pinches." Parker said he intended to issue the statement and Roosevelt could contradict his report if he liked.

With his tone-deaf ear for publicity, Parker issued a brief statement late Friday announcing that the reorganized detective bureau had arrested nearly double the number of suspects in the past year, 2,527 (up from 1,384), that convictions had led to total prison sentences of 1,102 years (up from 751), and that property recovered increased to $197,333 from $139,502. Newspapers gave these bravura statistics an inch or so at the bottom of the Saturday police roundups.

Parker was just adding one more bamboo shoot under Roosevelt's fingernails, as it were. Roosevelt wrote his sister, complaining about "endless petty rows with Parker & Fitch, very irritating because they *are* so petty."

————

Exasperated, Roosevelt decided to go on another midnight ramble on Monday, May 18, his first nighttime hunt for derelict policemen in months. He invited along his Boston friend Dr. William Sturgis Bigelow, who was briefly passing through New York and staying at the Holland House. TR also asked Commissioner Andrews to accompany him and to bring along his roundsman, John Tracy, whom Andrews had refused to relinquish to Parker.

Bigelow, a genuinely curious scholar who had penetrated the closed society of Japan, was eager to understand the clannish behavior of the New York police officer.

The party set out at midnight in a carriage from the West 37th Street police station. After driving around for an hour or so on the West Side, they were rolling along 42nd Street when they saw a large patrolman leaning suspiciously against a saloon side door between Eighth and Ninth Avenues. Roosevelt and his party alighted from the carriage just as the door cracked open and an arm suddenly emerged holding an oversized schooner of amber liquid. The policeman took the tankard, lifted it to his lips, and began draining it.

Roosevelt, in a kind of racing tiptoe, sped across the street, reached the policeman, and tapped him roughly on the shoulder, sternly saying, "Officer, give me that beer." The startled bluecoat, in mid-gulp, spritzed a geyser of foam and looked at the squat bespectacled man accosting him.

Just then, a hand emerged from inside the bar, yanked the glass, and slammed the door shut. The patrolman took one look at Roosevelt, teeth and spectacles glinting in the moonlight, as one paper put it, and the man sprinted off without saying a word.

Andrews by now had reached the scene and the two commissioners raced after the bluecoat. "Stop running, you fool!" shouted Roosevelt. About fifty yards away, near the corner, they caught him. Roosevelt demanded his name. "Ginger ale," he replied, gasping for air, "Ginger ale."

"Not what you were drinking," said TR to the doubled-over officer.

"Your name, man." Patrolman Joseph Meyers was ordered to come to Commissioner Roosevelt's office at 10 a.m. and as they left him, he kept muttering, "Ginger Ale, ginger ale." A conviction for drinking in uniform could cost a man his job.

The hunting party wandered in its carriage through seven precincts, including Devery's old precinct. They alighted occasionally to stalk but found only two more derelict officers, men who were seen talking to strangers for more than ten minutes.

The four hunters ate breakfast at 6 a.m. at a Bowery restaurant. Roosevelt later pronounced himself quite pleased with the improvement in the patrolling. He rested on his couch till 10 a.m., when the three officers arrived. Meyers stuck by his ginger ale claim and told TR he ran because he had heard an emergency call-for-help whistle. The commissioner told him the timing of the whistle—unheard by TR—was uncanny, coming just as a police commissioner tapped him on the shoulder. TR had Tracy lodge misconduct complaints against all three men.

Roosevelt and Andrews showed up a little late around 10:30 a.m. for the regular Tuesday morning board meeting. Parker and Grant were not there. A roundsman found the two men in Grant's office talking and looking at newspapers. He informed them that the board was waiting and Parker said they were holding a "consultation" and they would attend shortly. On many occasions, Roosevelt met informally with Andrews and Grant in his office, excluding Parker, and clearly Parker in his meticulous way was playing tit for tat and returning the favor.

Impatient as ever, Roosevelt was at a full boil by 11:15 a.m. when he sent the messenger again. He was convinced the full board needed immediately to vote through an official request for salaries for 800 additional officers, or else the mayor would be unable to present the item to the Board of Estimate. (The governor had just signed the bill; Comptroller Fitch would be handling the transfer of funds.) Roosevelt stalked out of the room to go to City Hall, a few minutes before Grant and Parker sauntered in.

No board meeting occurred but reporters pressed Parker for a comment on TR's anger at his absence. He said Andrews had recently been away in Texas for days, that TR "goes away often to lecture upon what he has done for the police force in this city and to tell how he has suppressed crime." Parker added that perhaps Roosevelt was "irritable" because of his lack of sleep.

Roosevelt race-walked to City Hall, looking for the mayor to complain yet again—and even more loudly—about Parker. By befriending Grant,

Parker could now stop the board from doing even routine business that called for a majority vote. This new partnership marked an escalation in the war for control.

———

Ashbel Fitch, that "contemptible lying little blackguard" as TR had called him, now accused Roosevelt of paying for prostitutes.

Fitch instructed the comptroller's in-house counsel to shine a light on the piles of brothel expense vouchers that Police Board treasurer Avery Andrews had naively included in a transfer-of-funds request.

Although it was well known in police circles that plainclothes detectives investigated brothels, it was nonetheless quite stunning to see dozens of these expenses listed in cold type in newspapers: upstanding officers handing taxpayer dollars to soon-to-be-naked demimondaines. Fitch's charge boiled down to Roosevelt secretly using city money to finance orgies for policemen. Each police officer's request for reimbursement, in its terseness, did read somehow like an aide-mémoire to a night on the town.

Detective Henry Hahn, thirty-six years old, filed a slip that read:

- cab hire from R.R. station to Mrs. Clemens' house of assignation in Kingsbridge: $6
- paid May Williams and Gussie Rous for exposure of person: $10
- bought 5 pints of wine at $2.50 pint: $12.50

A pair of patrolmen in the Tenderloin, Thomas McGuire and Paul Gallagher, explored a high-end brothel on East 35th Street and filed these expenses:

- hire for dress suit, shoes and hat: $5 (McGuire)
- paid for woman: $7.50 (McGuire)
- paid for wine: $15 (McGuire)
- woman: $7.50 (Gallagher)
- drinks: $4 (Gallagher)
- cigars: $1 (Gallagher)

Newspapers such as the *Sun* and the *World* filled column inches with these itemized accounts of nights of carousing, from the bargain prices of the East Side up to the high-end Tenderloin.

Included in the stacks of papers was an endorsement by veteran detective Hahn: "The prices are fair and reasonable, and no greater than those charged to ordinary customers and such claim is justly due." (It's unclear if Roosevelt knew that during the Lexow investigation Henry Hahn had been accused of shaking down brothels in Devery's 11th Precinct, or that both of his brothers had been tossed from the police force: Edward Hahn for drinking in uniform, Frank Hahn for secretly running a brothel.)

The comptroller's counsel read aloud many of these vouchers during a May 19 supreme court hearing before Judge Roger A. Pryor, a Tammany appointee, who called the expenses "monstrous" and "preposterous." Seemingly deeply shocked, Judge Pryor wondered aloud how any city official could possibly audit and approve these types of bills. The career of this sixty-seven-year-old jurist had taken some sharp turns: he was a former Confederate general who had barely escaped hanging before reinventing himself in New York as a Tammany Hall Democratic lawyer, and now judge; he had ruled favorably on a key Devery appeal back in May 1895.

Anyone in city government knew that the police spent money in brothels, gambling joints, and illegal saloons to gather evidence. It was deliciously ironic that Fitch accused Roosevelt's Police Board of immorality. Roosevelt's board was unapologetically prudish.

Recently, for instance, two high-ranking police officers, with Roosevelt's backing, had investigated the wedding-night scene in a Broadway show called *Orange Blossoms.*

Acting inspector John J. Harley and Captain Patrick H. Pickett had attended a performance of the play in the company of Mrs. Elizabeth Grannis of the Social Purity League, the trio sitting in the orchestra seats of the Gaiety Theatre on Broadway north of 28th Street.

This packed 800-seat theater, which had debuted as a minstrel hall, generally served up a Tenderloin evening, a bit racier than the legitimate theaters but not as lowbrow as the Bowery. But the performance that night, and for the weeks preceding, had out-of-towners buzzing: a long scene of a young bride undressing for bed on her wedding night. (She has just told her parents good night; the groom yawns and points to his watch, indicating it is time for bed; she asks him to give her a few minutes alone.)

Petite French actress Mlle. Pilar-Morin played the bride. Later in a courtroom, she described her performance:

"I first take off my wedding dress, and then remove my corsets and undo my petticoat strings. When they are off, I scratch myself to show my relief at having the tight corsets off. Then I make a screen with my skirt and [behind it] take off my shoes, stockings and garters. I have my stockings pulled on over a suit of thick tights. Then I slip on a night dress and get into the bed. A property man knocks and then I say 'Entrez!' "

Her silhouette was distinct throughout but only her bare arms were actually exposed. The police officers found the striptease "filthy, lewd and scandalous." Mrs. Grannis—attending to uphold the "sacredness of marriage"—said she thought she saw the actress, while standing in just her chemise, fluff the light garment out and then glance downward at her own nudity in a kind of bemused, eye-rolling way. (Pilar-Morin denied that.)

The police officers brought a charge of offending the public decency against theater manager John B. Doris. Abe Hummel defended Doris and pointed to Shakespeare's *Othello* as having far more scandalous scenes. Many pillars of the theater testified on Doris's behalf in the Court of Special Sessions on Monday, May 18, including playwright David Belasco, who found the pantomime "highly moral." The police captain admitted, on cross-examination, that he could not see any more of the form (i.e., the naked body) than at the opera.

Police magistrate Hinsdale, however, ruled against *Orange Blossoms*. He explained the nudity was not excessive but the context changed all. "The pantomime sketch is an invasion of the sanctity of the nuptial chamber." He fined the stage manager $250, or thirty days in jail. Roosevelt later called the performance "one of the most flagrant ones" and thanked the judges for "their hearty co-operation."

———

Roosevelt opened the Wednesday morning papers to discover more columns full of Fitch's mischief, detailing the brothel expenses with rows of policemen's names and items such as "Paid for Woman: $10; Wine: $20; Cigars: $2." One wonders how these notices played out with the officers' wives. Ran a typical editorial: "Cab hire, dress suits, patent-leather shoes, opera hats, large amounts of wine, 'women', fees for peculiarly indecent behavior, constitute the bulk of these charges. It seems that the spy paints the town red at the expense of the community. He creates crime for the purpose of arresting unfortunate women. And the Police Board, under the Roosevelt management, audits his bills!" The *New York Recorder* added that if these charges had been made against a Tammany Police Board, "all decent citizens would have felt the [board members] ought to cool their heels in Sing Sing."

Roosevelt rushed to reply to Fitch, to Judge Pryor, to the delighted editorialists.

Rocketing from one point to the next in a seven-page statement dictated to Minnie Kelly, he called Fitch the best advocate ever for the brothel industry. He said the police for years had been spending money going undercover into brothels and that judges recently had been demanding two eyewitnesses before issuing warrants. He stated that no other means existed for making these cases.

Roosevelt pegged this crackdown on "illicit sexual intercourse" as "one of the least pleasant [duties] of the police." He called it a "disagreeable task to get evidence against houses of prostitution" but said the job must be done, just as a surgeon must "undertake an operation for some loathsome disease."

Roosevelt proudly noted that over the past year, from May to May, the number of convictions for "keeping houses of prostitution or assignation" had more than doubled to 403 from 172 previously, with another 207 cases pending.

"The case of the 15th precinct [of former Captain Eakins], which includes Wooster, Thompson, Greene and West 3rd Streets and Minetta Lane, etc. may be taken as one in point. It was formerly infested with vice from one end to the other. Within six months between forty and fifty houses in this precinct have been closed, not one of which could we have closed save by procuring testimony of the kind to which the Comptroller objects. The 15th Precinct is now a reputable part of the city. What the precinct was, the whole city would become if the Comptroller's desires in this matter were carried out."

———

On that Wednesday, May 20, the mayor sent a private letter to Parker asking for his resignation. Strong did not inform the press. He told Parker that when he appointed him, he expected him to have "at heart the best interests of the city [to] work out a complete reformation in the department." He wrote that he felt at the time Parker would "add greatly" to that prospect but that now, over the past four months, Parker has lost his influence with both the public and fellow board members. "I would like your resignation on receipt of this note," he demanded.

Roosevelt soon found out and his mood measurably improved in his letters. He wrote almost giddily of staying in town one night and dining at the Claremont with the mayor and his closest advisors. "I am on pretty good terms with the old boy now," TR wrote to Bamie. The request for Parker's resignation, though still a secret, was reinvigorating Roosevelt.

A week later, Parker sent a combative private letter back to the mayor, refusing to resign. He recounted that almost a month earlier, he had offered to answer any questions. "It was the most courteous and proper method that I could conceive," he averred. "Notwithstanding you never sought from me a particle of information."

Parker stated that after hearing additional hostile remarks, he again offered to talk to the mayor alone or with other gentlemen. He reminded the mayor: "[You] fixed the evening, and were to fix the hour and place and to send me word. I have never heard a word from you since."

Mayor Strong, experiencing the slipperiness of the man, wrote an irritated response. "You can judge my astonishment," he stated, reminding Parker that on Monday, May 11, they had set a definite meeting time of Wednesday evening, May 13, at the mayor's home with two reform power brokers and the city's corporation counsel. "And we had a very pleasant evening waiting for you until 11 o'clock."

Mayor Strong reiterated that he expected Parker to resign. "It would save you a great deal of trouble and me a great deal of trouble and the Police Department some severe criticism." He added it is "in your own interest that you should step quietly down and out." That last line smacked of a threat; the mayor was clearly referring to the bribery allegations that Roosevelt had whispered in his ear.

But Parker knew nothing of the McMorrow bribery confession, and when confronted that week by the press with the rumors of his resignation, he told them that he was not "the resigning kind." And he added: "If the mayor thinks I have been guilty of any dereliction of duty, he can prefer charges against me and I shall await them with the utmost serenity."

BACK IN BLUE

Under all the acrimony, Parker and Roosevelt still agreed on many aspects of reform, especially on *not* letting Big Bill Devery back onto the police force. Reverend Parkhurst had contacted Roosevelt and Andrews, and offered to help build a new case. After hurriedly sifting through files, Parkhurst Society counsel Frank Moss had sent a note informing them he was free to meet "any forenoon" the last week in May.

But the offer of help came too late.

The district attorney announced he was dropping the remaining indictments against ten police officers, including Devery, due to lack of evidence. The D.A. cited a judge's ruling that the testimony of 11th Precinct brothel keeper Rhoda Sanford—based on entries such as "$1.50 to man shark" in her ledger—was not credible since she had contradicted her own words under oath at the Lexow hearing.

The district attorney's office had failed to convict almost all the policemen accused of crimes during the Lexow hearings; the city had spent $50,000 trying twenty-three men, including ten captains, and had landed three: one on a reduced sentence via a confession and two convictions, both under appeal. The trial results—to many New Yorkers—spelled vindication.

On Tuesday, May 26, the board, with the utmost distaste, under legal constraints because Devery had been twice acquitted and was not under pending indictment, restored him to duty. They also restored Eddie "The Sphinx" Glennon.

Since Devery could not be demoted, Chief Conlin assigned him to be captain of the West 125th Street precinct, an increasingly thriving German and Italian community.

Devery's return came less than a week before the massive June 1 police parade. (The board—after much soul-searching—had deemed the New York police department sufficiently reformed to earn the right once again to strut through the streets.)

Chief Conlin, recently back from his European vacation, fine-tuned parade assignments. Pistol range practice was curtailed in favor of marching drills; horses were groomed and re-shod; mustaches were trimmed.

Big Bill paid for rush alterations to his dress blues. He told friends he planned to celebrate his return by marching up Broadway. Two days after his reinstatement, Devery reported to the Twelfth Regiment Armory at 62nd Street and Ninth Avenue for parade drill practice, but the presiding officer, Captain Anthony Allaire, informed Devery that he had orders from head-quarters that the captain was not permitted to participate in the parade. No record has survived of Devery's exact verbal response. He returned to his precinct house at West 125th Street.

Word spread quickly through the police force that the popular, funny, resilient officer—despite his full reinstatement—was banned, while Captain Max Schmittberger, who had testified against several fellow captains in exchange for immunity, was marching at the head of a company in the same battalion.

The irritated hum of whispers regarding Devery grew so loud they made the papers, with the *Times* and *Herald* confirming much "ill feeling" among the rank and file that the "well-liked" and "persecuted" captain would be forced to stand on the pavement, a mere spectator.

Chief Conlin, a week back in uniform, claimed that Devery's exclusion occurred only because the captain had not drilled with his men and had been in limbo when assignments had been handed out. Conlin made these statements two days before the Monday, June 1, parade.

Final marching orders were issued: gather at 1 p.m. at the Battery far downtown; final reminder: no gum chewing. At the very last moment, Chief Conlin, for reasons he never shared, decided to allow Captain Devery to march at the head of his precinct's men.

On a sunny breezy Monday, under a blue sky flecked with a few clouds at 2 p.m., a handful of Andrews's bicycle officers led the way uptown, riding upright to avoid "bicycle hump." Enthusiastic crowds jammed the five-mile parade route that stretched from the southern tip of Manhattan up Broadway to 23rd Street, then east to Madison Avenue, up to 41st Street, then back south along Fifth Avenue to the reviewing stand at Madison Square Park, opposite the Worth Monument.

Roosevelt, in black frock coat and silk top hat, arrived at the V.I.P. seats with Mayor Strong in a calèche drawn by two "prancing bays," attended by a liveried coachman and footman. The two grandstands filled up early and policemen refused to let dozens of ticket holders through the barricades. (Reverend Parkhurst waved his ticket and two policemen promptly turned their backs on him.)

The grandstand was chockablock with senators, generals, commissioners. Grant and Andrews arrived before Parker, which led to whispers about Parker's resigning, but Parker showed up a few minutes before 4 p.m., the slated arrival time of the paraders.

More than 2,000 police officers, in dress blues, marched eighteen across nearly in lockstep. The patrolmen in single-breasted, long-belted coats swung their arms in near unison, and the pair of brass buttons at the sleeve glinting in the sun formed a steady mesmerizing arc. First came a marching battalion of police, then a military band playing martial music, then another battalion, proud, smiling, an idealized vision of the city's protectors. The higher-ranking officers, mostly mounted, with more brass buttons and more gold braid and stripes, dazzled even more.

Along the route men cheered and women, especially in the politer uptown neighborhoods, waved handkerchiefs. Chief Conlin, looking "buoyant and beaming," deftly led the parade on his fine horse, "Prince." The parade, after a year hiatus, marked a triumphant return to respect for this police force, humiliated by the Lexow revelations and also buffeted by relentless reproofs from Roosevelt.

The cheers had indeed abounded all along the parade route, except for one undercurrent of resentment. Reporters heard onlookers, block after block, pointing out Captain Schmittberger and some shouted catcalls of "squealer" and worse. The tall athletic German captain kept his eyes mostly rigidly forward or downward, appearing "uncomfortable." At the parade's end at Madison Square Park, within earshot of Roosevelt, just as Schmittberger marched by, a dozen or so men and women began twirling wooden rattles, and the crowd gradually mounted a "storm of hisses" described as "deafening."

In stark contrast, any reinstated captain who had survived Lexow and defied reform was loudly cheered. And Captain William "Big Bill" Devery, leading the second company of the fifth battalion, received repeated bursts of loud applause and shouted well wishes. The *Tribune* reported that the captain (and former bartender) "swaggered along with a defiant look, as if he meant to say, 'What if I did blackmail people? They could never prove it.'"

Roosevelt and the city had inadvertently tossed Devery a very nice welcome-back party.

But, before the Tammany officer could bask in the resumption of his lucrative eighteen-year police career, friends at headquarters whispered to him that the board, in rare unity, was seeking new disciplinary charges against him.

PARKER TRIAL

On the day after the police parade, Roosevelt and Andrews collaborated on formulating official neglect-of-duty charges against Commissioner Parker. The most potentially damning charge of corruption—that is, of accepting the McMorrow bribe—had melted away, probably under the scrutiny of lawyers. They wrote up the detailed charges in a June 3 letter to reform Republican lawyer Elihu Root, who had mentored TR's failed mayoral bid in 1886 and now served as private counsel to Mayor Strong.

Root relayed them to the mayor, who on June 8 officially accused Parker of missing thirty-four of sixty-four board meetings, of ignoring 156 citizen complaints in November, of failing in his Pension Committee chairmanship duties to oversee a single pension, of delaying nineteen police misconduct verdicts, and finally of failing for a week to grade exams of candidates for captain.

In a private letter, Roosevelt called Parker's neglect of duty "very much his least but also his most easily proven sin." Roosevelt was playing for keeps. If he failed to force out his fellow commissioner, he would have to continue to work right alongside of his inscrutable, unflappable, unswayable colleague.

Parker, too lawyerly to say too much too early, gave very brief rebuttals in the press to all five charges, and pronounced the sum of them "trivial, mere rot." He called the last charge "petty . . . a schoolboy complaint."

The endless Police Board squabbles were finally coming to a head.

No more backstabbing, the stabbing would now all be in an open hearing room.

In an oddity of municipal governance, Mayor Strong, who had demanded Parker's resignation, would now act as his impartial judge. The mayor—a business tycoon who had never played judge before—would preside in a trial that would wind up lasting for eight hearings, spread out over a month. At its end, Roosevelt would call it "really very nearly as much a trial of me as of Parker."

———

At first, city pundits expected the mayor to rubber-stamp a conviction after dozing through a kangaroo trial; they expected Republican governor Morton to affix his needed signature on the dismissal papers; they expected the canny lawyer Parker to spend a year or so appealing the verdict in the courts.

Nothing played out as expected.

The trial opened on the morning of Thursday, June 11, in the mayor's office at City Hall. It was a Who's Who of political affairs. The mayor, corporation counsel, lawyers, police commissioners, various city officials, politicians, and gawkers crammed into the large office with windows overlooking the four-acre park and landmark fountain. Former police chief Thomas Byrnes even made a surprise grand entrance. He was wearing "a light summer suit, a broad smile and he looked as happy as a big sunflower," according to the *New York World*. Byrnes advanced slowly through "a siege of hand-shaking."

Roosevelt rushed in at the last minute and absentmindedly occupied the vacant seat next to Parker. He quickly switched places with Grant.

TR got settled, looked up, and was stunned to see who was representing Commissioner Parker: Roosevelt's longtime friend and sometime family lawyer, high-ranking Republican general Benjamin F. Tracy. White-bearded Tracy, a decorated Civil War hero, was Republican royalty; he had recently served as secretary of the navy under President Benjamin Harrison.

"Rather to my surprise, General Tracy turned up as [Parker's] counsel and my assailant, though he knows Parker's shortcomings well and has heard from me all of our troubles," Roosevelt later wrote. "It strikes me as a not very honorable course but it is just the kind of thing that [Joseph H.] Choate does and that most lawyers seem to regard as in accord with their peculiar code of professional ethics."

The mayor chose Elihu Root, another powerhouse Republican lawyer, to handle the prosecution. Fourteen years older than TR, Root often found himself trying to tamp down Roosevelt's impulsiveness. (He remained enough of an intimate to tease Roosevelt; years later, he sent the then president of the United States a birthday telegram: "I congratulate you on attaining the respectable age of 46. You have made a good start in life and your friends have great hopes for you when you grow up.")

Waggle-eared, with a push-broom mustache over a weak chin, fifty-one-year-old Root knew sixty-six-year-old Tracy well; they shared the dais at many a Republican banquet and sat at nearby clubroom tables at the Union League; they were rainmakers. Both were known as extremely intelligent, with a genial wit that could turn caustic.

Root opened the proceedings by numbingly walking the Police Board's dour bald-headed chief clerk, Colonel Kipp, through the facts of the charges about Parker's attendance, pension duties, and responses to citizens' complaints.

From the outset, Roosevelt, though merely a spectator, was, by his own admission to his wife, extremely nervous. Throughout, he scratched frantic notes in pencil onto a tablet and had trouble sitting still.

General Tracy, on cross-examination, tried to lighten the tone. Alluding to the citizens' complaints, which Parker had supposedly ignored throughout November, General Tracy elicited from Clerk Kipp the information that Parker had actually forwarded them all to Police Chief Conlin, who had in turn handed them to the appropriate captains, who had answered them. So, Parker's "grave omission," stated Tracy, ladling on the sarcasm, was that he "failed to give the complainants a notice which they had already received from the police captains?" "Yes," replied the earnest clerk Kipp.

The room erupted in laughter. Roosevelt, not smiling, scribbled more furiously. He and Andrews sat near the corporation counsel and repeatedly whispered suggestions.

As for the attendance at board meetings, Kipp revealed that most board decisions—except promotions and retirements—required only three commissioners and that agendas were often informally discussed beforehand.

On the issue of Parker's delaying police misconduct verdicts, Kipp stated that Parker had affected only nineteen verdicts out of more than 3,000 cases that had crossed his desk.

By any yardstick, this first day had not gone swimmingly for Roosevelt. He had difficulty sleeping that night and on successive nights, Edith later confided to her sister-in-law.

On Friday, day two, the hearing room was less packed; ex-chief Byrnes had bailed; the corporation counsel assigned an assistant. Root was clearly avoiding fireworks. Parker appeared confident and well rested.

Root recalled Kipp and plodded through placing on the record many of the citizen complaints not personally answered by Parker, also many of the pension cases not personally handled by Parker. General Tracy interjected at one point when the mayor's eyes kept involuntarily closing from boredom: "That kind of evidence is laughable." Shot back Root: "Then you may spend your time laughing."

Commissioner Grant made a request to testify immediately since he would be leaving that evening to go to St. Louis for a week as a delegate to the Republican National Convention . . . the fact that Grant would miss the board's next two meetings did not bolster TR's case against Parker on attendance.

Root called Grant for the prosecution but the affable man, his combed-over locks plastered to his dome, did not seem to relish taking sides. He answered questions simply and tersely.

Root focused on the pension cases—Parker and Grant comprised the entire Pension Committee, with Parker as chairman. Grant claimed no pensions were paid later than normal. General Tracy on cross-examination asked Grant if he could cite a single instance when Parker's absence stopped the board from acting on an important matter; Colonel Grant scrunched up his face and tried to conjure up the hazy memory of perhaps one retirement vote a year ago.

Then General Tracy asked Grant about the other commissioners' absences and summer vacations. "Did Roosevelt leave on Thursdays and come back on Tuesdays?"

Elihu Root objected to the question. "I have no doubt you prefer to try Roosevelt," snapped Root. "My friend has just betrayed the secret of this trial," replied General Tracy, affably. Amid the laughter, the mayor sustained the objection.

Roosevelt was not enjoying the show. "President Roosevelt displayed considerable nervousness as the trial went on," stated the *New York Tribune*, the paper of the mainstream Republican Party. "He established a [patrolman's] beat back of the counsel table, and walked it uneasily during much of the session, occasionally stopping to drop some comment into the ear of his colleague Commissioner Andrews."

Testimony continued. Grant confirmed that he knew that many of Parker's absences were due to work Parker was doing for the committee on the Greater Consolidation of New York. General Tracy kept trying to hammer away about Roosevelt's attendance but the questions were not allowed. The

World estimated that the mayor sided with the prosecution nine out of ten times.

Around 6:15 p.m., Grant asked how much longer the cross-examination would take. He had to catch a train, specifically the "Special Train" of the McKinley League of New York State. When told "four hours," he asked to be excused. The mayor abruptly adjourned the trial.

———

Roosevelt rushed out on Friday night to Oyster Bay only to find out that Edith, in a mixup, had already headed into the city. He spent the night alone. She and the children then boarded an early Saturday morning train and reached Sagamore Hill in the swirling rain. "Today we are having a terrific storm and I am glad, for Theodore is fit for nothing but to sit quietly with a book," she wrote to her sister-in-law, Bamie. "This trial has been a terrific strain."

Roosevelt also did what he usually did in times of Police Board strain; he focused in his letters on international and national politics. He knew that the convention that week would crown taciturn McKinley as the candidate, and not his original choice, Thomas B. Reed of Maine.

"While I greatly regret the defeat of Reed, who was in every way McKinley's superior . . ." he wrote to his sister, "McKinley himself is an upright and honorable man, of very considerable ability & good record as a soldier and in congress."

Roosevelt wished he could be at the Republican convention in St. Louis but instead he returned to Manhattan, to City Hall, to find himself once again in a brutal conflict, with the whole town watching. The *Herald* called the mayor the "stage manager" and opposing counsels, Root and Tracy, "two rival stars of comedy."

Roosevelt showed up at Friday's Parker hearing wearing an oversized McKinley-Hobart button, with clear color portraits of the candidates, bigger than a silver dollar. Newspapermen and politicians clustered around to view it, and TR remarked that it was the first of its kind to reach New York City. By design or not, Roosevelt briefly shifted the spotlight away from the stumbling prosecution.

Everyone expected Root to call Roosevelt to testify but instead he recalled Colonel Kipp for a run-through of yet more of the mind-numbing citizen complaints.

Even these did not go well on cross-examination.

General Tracy spotlighted the notes of Mrs. Josephine Shaw Lowell, wealthy founder of Charity Organization Society of New York. She had complained in November about a Sunday saloon illegally thriving in her neighborhood. Parker's assistant had forwarded her complaint to Chief Conlin, who had assigned Captain Martens, who found the complaint groundless. Mrs. Shaw Lowell considered Martens's reply inadequate, so she complained again, but not to the Police Board per se. Tracy cleared his throat, then slowly began reading the opening of her letter aloud: "My Dear Mr. Roosevelt." The lawyer turned theatrically to the mayor and said, "Your honor, we cannot admit Mr. Roosevelt's private correspondence as testimony into this official investigation." He paused. "This letter, as I read it, refers to a 'pointless communication received from Mr. Roosevelt's Department.' We are not responsible for Mr. Roosevelt's 'pointless communications.'"

The mayor laughed and the letter was not admitted.

TR could do little but scribble furious notes and remain mute.

———

Matters were not faring any better in his attempts to right the mounting Raines Law fiasco. That week, Magistrate Cornell dismissed a hefty stack of "Raines Law hotel" Sunday violations brought by the police; he stated the New York Supreme Court had ruled that a sandwich, no matter how small, did indeed constitute a "meal." The Roosevelt police—after months of Sunday victories—were now striking out in sobering up the city on the Sabbath.

However, over on the vice front, the police, with help from crusader Anthony Comstock, scored a significant victory, the culmination of a two-year Comstock manhunt for "The Voice." Within months of the invention of a workable camera in the 1840s, someone had experimented with photographing nudes. Now, with Edison's invention of the phonograph, someone was recording wax cylinders with smutty stories and jokes, to be played through ear tubes for a nickel a listen in saloons and arcades.

Comstock and his agents had confiscated some particularly offensive cylinders but had never found the producer. One featured a stage actor mocking Shakespeare: "To pee or not to pee, that is the question, whether it is better in the flesh to suffer the stings and smarts of this outrageous clap or to . . ."

The "Voice" also told profane jokes: "What did Adam do when he discovered the difference between himself and Eve?" Answer: "He split the difference, raised Cain and did it again when he got Abel."

But many of these recordings were neither tame nor highbrow; on one, a couple mimicked the frenzied escalating heavy breathing of intercourse. Another featured a labor union meeting of New York "whores" hosted by "Ophelia Openhole, President" and "Sarah Broadass, Secretary" in which the pair tried to establish minimum rates.

- "Common old fashioned fuck" [man on top]: $1
- "Rear fashion": $1.50
- "Back scuttle fashion" [anal]: $1.75
- "Pudding jerking" [a hand job: French *boudin* or blood pudding is a kind of fat squishy sausage]: $2
- "Tasting French" [oral]: $2.50
- "French fashion with use of patent balls" [elaborate oral]: $3.50
- "All night, with use of towel and rose water": $5

On June 24, Comstock's agent, George Oram, acting on a tip, found thirty-one-year-old actor Russell Hunting at 45 Clinton Place on the East Side and bought wax cylinders from him for $1.50 each; Hunting bragged he had just sold fifty in Coney Island. Armed with a warrant, Roosevelt's police later seized three phonographs, fifty-three cylinders, and stacks of promotional literature. Magistrate Kudlich of Jefferson Market Courthouse soon sentenced audio porn purveyor Hunting to three months in jail.

———

Over the weeks in June, Parker attended board meetings regularly and, surprisingly, was now working efficiently with the rest of the board toward delivering another round of promotions of captains and sergeants. Written tests had been scheduled and graded, eligible lists fine-tuned. The topic of promoting inspectors was avoided.

The rumor mill had it that the mayor was considering dropping the Parker charges to prevent Parker and General Tracy from humiliating Roosevelt and Andrews on the stand. The rumor mill was wrong.

The trial resumed on Monday, June 29. General Tracy called Grant back to testify. Grant freely admitted many meetings were rescheduled to accommodate his travel plans or those of TR or Andrews. "You have got enough evidence out of me to convict me already, I guess," said Colonel Grant, chuckling. (Roosevelt, in a letter to Cabot Lodge, speculated whether a "fool" such as Grant or a "knave" such as Parker could cause more damage to a good cause.) Elihu Root completed his redirect questioning of Grant, then he shocked almost everyone in the room: he rested the prosecution's case, without calling Roosevelt.

General Tracy then asked the mayor to dismiss the charges. Tracy promised that if the mayor convicted Parker, he would appeal to the courts even before the governor made a decision on whether to sign. He pointed out how odd it was that the prosecution never called Commissioners Andrews or Roosevelt, and that Grant had essentially played out as a defense witness.

The general scoffed at the main charges, especially the pension issues. "I say all these [pension] cases were properly attended to." Mr. Roosevelt shook his head vigorously as though dissenting. General Tracy stared at Roosevelt, then remarked: "I see my friend shakes his head, but there is nothing in it."

Moments later, when the mayor refused to dismiss charges, Roosevelt exulted. "He jumped around like a tin monkey on a stick," sniped the reporter for the *World*, "grinning with delight and nodding his head first to one friend and then to another." Parker and Tracy reacted as though they had expected just such a ruling, and were now quite prepared to bring on a very vigorous defense.

––––––

On Wednesday, July 1, dozens of police officers crowded into the mayor's office. The defense planned to call as many as forty men who currently worked in the police department, from Chief Conlin and Inspector Moses Cortwright down to elevator operators and doormen. Common sense dictated that anyone saying anything excessively positive about Parker risked earning the wrath of board president Roosevelt. Career men with families, men hoping for promotions, would have to make hard choices.

Inspector Moses Cortwright—a respected veteran with twenty-nine years on the force—took the stand and said he consulted Commissioner Parker more than the other commissioners, especially on legal matters. He added that Parker could easily be found at headquarters, since he was usually the last commissioner to leave the building, after 7 p.m.

Captain Stephen O'Brien—the outspoken forty-five-year-old head of detectives, originally trained by Byrnes—testified that Parker single-handedly reorganized the detective bureau, spending a solid month investigating the records and traits of 500 officers to find 100 detectives. "He found out things I never knew," said the police department's current spymaster. O'Brien asserted that Parker made himself available on nights and weekends, and frequently pleaded the department's needs with district attorneys and judges.

The highest-ranking witness, Chief Peter Conlin—resplendent in gold epaulettes and sleeve bars—took the stand. After establishing the chief's credentials, Tracy asked several questions about working with the Police Board. "I was most frequently in consultation with Mr. Parker, because the other members of the board seemed to refer everything legal to him," stated Conlin. "They deferred to him so much that I concluded he was the master spirit of the board."

Roosevelt had been scratching out a note. He dropped his pencil.

"I consulted with Mr. Roosevelt once or twice but he referred me to Mr. Parker."

The utterance seemed to hover in the air. The usually voluble Tracy spoke not a syllable for almost a full minute.

He tried to follow up by asking Chief Conlin to compare the various commissioners but the mayor ruled the questions inadmissible. But back on the topic of Parker alone, Conlin responded that he spoke to Parker almost every day "and made no important changes without consulting him." If he couldn't find him, Parker encouraged Conlin to come to his house, even as late as eleven at night.

General Tracy slipped in: "Did you consult the other commissioners as much?"

"No sir!" came the ringing reply before Root could raise an objection.

Why? "Because I understood Mr. Parker was more in charge than the others; because he knew more about it, could give better suggestions, better advice, better criticisms than the others."

The mayor—who seemed to slouch lower in his high-backed rocking chair as the day progressed—announced that he wanted to finish up the trial so he could head to his country home at Richfield Springs for the Fourth of July. He seemed to want desperately to leave.

———

Testimony resumed on the morning of Thursday, July 2—the sea of blue still filled the room and Chief Conlin climbed back into the witness chair. Conlin's frankness, along with these slaps at Roosevelt, brought renewed crowds, overflowing the room. The muggy summer weather made the mayor's office, despite its many windows, "as stuffy as a lower east side hall bedroom when the breeze is cut off," according to the *New York Times*. Men in starched collars sweated.

The defense tried to bring out that Conlin was no puppet and refused to accept some of Parker's suggestions for captain. Eventually, Conlin's testimony wound down and General Tracy said, "Thank you, that is all, Chief."

Conlin, however, remained in the chair. "I want to say right here that before this little trouble the board was all a unit, working together for the good of the force. They worked hard and well, and did all they could do to uphold my hands, for which I am grateful. I think the people of New York ought to be grateful to them too. Colonel Grant is an energetic untiring worker. Mr. Andrews too has his heart in the work and I think his inauguration of pistol practice was an excellent thing. As for Mr.——"

Root interrupted: "Oh, stop. How is this relevant?"

"Why did you stop him before he reached Commissioner Roosevelt?" asked General Tracy sharply.

Root: "Was this all prearranged?"

Tracy: "I would have liked to hear about Roosevelt."

TR could stand the comedy no longer. "I don't care to get certificates of good character from my subordinates," he snapped in a loud voice.

Conlin then left the stand without saying another word.

The rest of the morning's testimony was anticlimactic. The elevator operator revealed that Parker had been at police headquarters on both Thanksgiving and Christmas, which might say something about his dedication or about his lack of a private life. (Parker was the only bachelor on the board.)

———

In the afternoon, one of the two main combatants finally got a chance to testify. Parker took the stand. General Tracy started slowly by letting Parker recount how he had worked his way up from being a stenographer in the corporation counsel's office at age seventeen. Parker said he had belonged to no political party for the past ten years, except for a few months with a Democratic reform organization. He was an Independent.

How did he, such an outsider, land the job as police commissioner?

Parker replied that he never sought the job but was called in out of the blue by the mayor. He was told that if Elihu Root approved of him, he would be appointed.

The newspapers reported that Mr. Root smiled at this moment.

Parker said Root approved of him and the mayor appointed him.

Parker described the early days of the board, how he and Roosevelt worked intimately together to handle the easing out of Chief Byrnes, and remained cordial and cooperative for nine months right through February 4, when Parker voted against Brooks and McCullagh and Tierney. Even after that, Parker went to dinner at Mr. Roosevelt's home, and prior to the split, Roosevelt had repeatedly commended his work to large audiences.

As for his absences, Parker said he informed Roosevelt of them in advance and always revealed his views, and that he never missed a meeting requiring four votes. Parker added that Roosevelt even encouraged him to miss some board meetings to go to Albany and consult on the Greater Consolidation bill. Why? He wanted "inside tips" on the police supplemental legislation. Or, as General Tracy put it, "on whether Mr. Platt was going to turn you all out of office?" Parker replied, "Yes." Many of the politically savvy in the audience laughed. Roosevelt scowled fiercely.

The mayor confided to friends that he was deeply disappointed by the prosecution's case so far, and vowed aloud not to let this trial interfere with his annual monthlong summer nursing of his gout at Richfield Springs.

Compelled to return 215 miles to the city just for the trial, he advised the participants to finish in two marathon sessions, on July 7 and 8. Around now, Roosevelt somehow convinced Root to call him as a rebuttal witness; clearly Root had been trying to keep his ignitable young friend out of the verbal reach of General Tracy.

Roosevelt took the stand on the afternoon of July 7. Witnesses said he looked almost electrified.

"I have always been nervous before a contest," Roosevelt told a family friend, "although I have not a particle of nervousness when once the fight is actually on, and indeed rather enjoy it. In the old days I was always nervous before a boxing match or polo game, or even a hard day with the hounds; after killing my first grizzly I recollect the hunter who was with me telling me that from the way I looked just before I went into the thing he would have believed if the bear had happened to get away that I had been afraid of it."

Indeed, once Elihu Root began asking questions, Roosevelt answered without any nerves or hesitation. The *New York Times* compared his power and directness to a strong-armed archer firing arrows. The *World* added the observation that he appeared determined not to lose his temper.

Root was now perhaps the more nervous one because he kept Roosevelt on the stand for only about thirty minutes. The prevailing notion among Root, Edith, and Lodge was that TR could be a loose cannon. Root lobbed straightforward questions about Parker's attendance and minimal input on hiring new recruits. TR said Parker did not attend meetings to abolish police lodging houses, the Broadway squad, or the steamboat squad, or to initiate pistol practice.

Root: "Was the business of the board postponed because of Mr. Parker's absences?"

Roosevelt: "Yes, scores of times."

He said Parker "habitually" reached the building in the late afternoon but refused to commit—when TR offered—to have board meetings at 4 p.m. instead of 10 a.m.

Roosevelt accused Parker of delaying the appointment of patrolmen whom Parker had originally recommended, a vague charge that implied corruption, of Parker's waiting for another payoff. Mostly, he accused Parker of neglecting board work for the past six months. "It was a wonderment to us what he had been doing."

Root abruptly turned to General Tracy. "You can have the witness." The *Tribune* and the *Herald* judged Roosevelt "disappointed" at the sudden stop.

Tracy began aggressively; he tried to trace all of TR's complaints as surfacing only after Parker refused to vote for Brooks and McCullagh, but Roosevelt denied it.

TR dated his first disagreement with Parker to months before that. He said a realization slowly welled in him that Parker might be "double-dealing and untrustworthy." He found that Parker covertly criticized their decisions over promotions to the editor of the *Evening Post*, who relayed Parker's words to him. All the while, Parker was pretending he had no problems with their approach.

Roosevelt said he found in early fall in the raucous runup to the election—when Republican machine men and Germans begged the police to lighten up on Sundays—that Parker had been secretly bad-mouthing the board's excise crackdown. Roosevelt said he confronted Parker about it in front of the mayor.

General Tracy, without missing a beat, then asked: "Didn't Parker then tell the mayor he endorsed strict excise enforcement? And didn't you say to him, 'You are a bully fellow to stand up for a colleague in that way. If only the other fellows were like you'?"

Roosevelt's fuse was lit. It hadn't taken long. "What?" he shouted. "Parker stand up for a colleague! No." TR calmed himself down. The question was repeated. "I may have said the first part of the sentence," TR conceded.

General Tracy walked Roosevelt through statement after statement of praise he had been quoted as giving Parker. Were his praises of Parker's speeches "false and insincere"? General Tracy cited a Renwick Hall appearance on October 12, 1895, when Parker spoke first and received a long ovation, and then Roosevelt came to the podium and said: "He is just as good a commissioner as he is a speaker."

Tracy cornered Roosevelt into admitting that he was deeply upset by Parker's letter to Lauterbach, in which Parker claimed that Roosevelt championed more Democrats than Republicans. "I thought worse of Mr. Parker than I ever deemed it possible," stated TR, looking directly at his fellow commissioner.

Then General Tracy tossed what appeared a softball question at Roosevelt. Why should Parker be removed? Roosevelt unspooled his pent-up anger. Parker should be ousted for "mendacity, treachery and double dealing" and for "demoralizing the force." TR said Parker refused to act with them on promotion, refused to make concessions regarding Cortwright, that he had held up Steinkampf, that he had forced the other commissioners to fix their merit marks and then submit them to him "so that I had to make concessions to him until I was perfectly ashamed that I yielded to him—I yielded to no other man like I did to him."

GENERAL TRACY: That was the real secret, you had to yield.
ROOSEVELT: Gracious me! If he had only been right I would like to have yielded to him.
GENERAL TRACY: You enjoy yielding to a man?
ROOSEVELT: By George, I do. Now that is a fact.

The room erupted with laughter. Long laughter. Waves of it. TR looked deeply uncomfortable.

General Tracy showed no mercy. Roosevelt mentioned that Parker held up "scores" of patrolmen's appointments. General Tracy asked for a single example. Roosevelt could not furnish one. Roosevelt claimed Parker held up the pistol practice. Tracy asked if Roosevelt did not recall a handwritten endorsement from Parker on the bottom of TR's typewritten note on the topic. Roosevelt did not. "Why is it that Parker recalls these events more clearly than you do?" The mayor mercifully called a dinner recess at 7 p.m.

————

Their bellies full but their appetites for mischief apparently unslaked, Parker and Tracy decided to zero in on the promotion to sergeant of TR favorite Michael Tierney.

General Tracy's cross-examination, extending from 8:30 to 11 p.m., picked at Roosevelt's role in browbeating Chief Conlin to defy Parker and promote Roosevelt's protégé on February 4.

Roosevelt praised Tierney as an "exceptionally able and trustworthy" corporal when he had served under him a decade ago, but Roosevelt admitted that he knew little about Tierney's activities for the past four years.

General Tracy wanted to know whether Roosevelt realized when he waved the promotions notebook in Chief Conlin's face and pointed to a memo of endorsement in Tierney's folder signed by the chief himself that it was a mistake, a misfiled document?

"No," answered Roosevelt.

TRACY: And that the chief had never written any such thing about
    Tierney?
ROOSEVELT: No.
TRACY: Have you heard of it?
ROOSEVELT: The chief told me so two or three days afterwards.

TR confirmed that he gave Tierney a merit rating of 60 out of a possible 65 even though the officer had a dozen police misconduct convictions, including a twenty-day suspension for attacking a civilian. Roosevelt reiterated that he had interviewed a police surgeon who had disagreed with the board's judgment on the suspension.

Tracy probed more about Tierney. Roosevelt snapped, "Some of the best men we promoted had infinitely worse records."

General Tracy immediately looked shocked. He solemnly asked the mayor to strike that line of testimony out of the record "to save a little reputation for these gentlemen." As he said it, he gestured toward the half dozen police captains in the audience.

Since the trial focused on Parker's delays, Tracy tried to spotlight Roosevelt's reckless speed. He showed that Roosevelt had once returned to Parker a pile of half a dozen cases, totaling more than 300 pages of testimony, in less than half an hour. TR had simply accepted Parker's verdicts. Tracy also brought out that Roosevelt could recall few details from the 1,500 cases he had judged.

————

On July 8, the final day of the trial, the mayor pronounced himself ready to go all night to finish up. The porch rocker and sulphur baths of the Spring House at Richfield Springs clearly beckoned.

General Tracy homed in on Roosevelt's attendance; he came armed with every TR speaking trip or vacation. The travel log included: September 11, Roosevelt "law and order" speech in Buffalo; September 25 in New Haven to address Yale graduates; November 8, postelection recovery at Oyster Bay; December 30, Roosevelt in Philadelphia; February 22 in Chicago; April 22 to 27 in Michigan and Ohio. All these board meetings were rescheduled and Parker was cited for missing half of the new "special meetings." Then asked Tracy: "You rescheduled to suit your own convenience then punished Parker for missing?"

Tracy wound down his cross-examination by focusing on promotions and how TR and his colleagues could fix the deck by giving a candidate a 40 or less for "merit." Then, no matter how high the officer scored on the civil service exam (worth up to 35 points), he could not earn the 75 points needed to make the eligible list. Roosevelt conceded the narrow point, but strongly disagreed that this power would lead to promoting the wrong men.

Roosevelt left the stand.

The mayor called a dinner recess, and at this point, the perspiring sixty-six-year-old General Tracy pleaded fatigue and asked to be excused to catch a train to Bar Harbor, Maine. So Andrew D. Parker gave his own summation for the defense, a dense, detail-filled, two-hour-long speech, tackling point after point.

He was, as ever, tone deaf to everyone's exasperation and exhaustion but maybe he calculatingly delivered the speech to list key points for a future judicial appeal.

Parker couldn't leave the topic of Tierney's drinking alone. He said he informed Roosevelt the man had a "still" on him and drank at headquarters, but one day later Roosevelt reported back to Parker that he had investigated and determined that Tierney *never* drank. "I laughed at that," said Parker. In the hot stuffy room, lit by bare electric lightbulbs, Parker asked for the charges to be dropped.

The mayor whispered back and forth with the assistant corporation counsel and then stated that he was "reserving judgment."

The next day, even the sympathetic *New York Times* stated: "It has by no means been made clear that Commissioner Parker was a negligent, inefficient or unfaithful commissioner." The "reserving judgment" was a slap at TR.

Roosevelt, however, with his uncanny ability to wear blinders when needed, interpreted the events contrary to the newspapers in the city. In a letter to family friend Fanny Parsons, Roosevelt wrote: "In the trial before the Mayor I scored a complete victory over General Tracy in a very hard six hours cross-examination and had the satisfaction of stating under oath to Parker, who was not six feet distant, all that I thought worst in his moral character."

He repeated almost the exact words writing to his sister Bamie, adding, though, that he had "forgiven" General Tracy for representing Parker since the lawyer had delivered to him the "satisfaction of telling, under oath, with Parker not six feet distant, just what I thought of [Parker's] mendacity, treachery and duplicity."

Wife Edith hoped her husband could now start to relax. "Thank goodness the Parker trial is over. I enclose part of Theodore's examination. It has been a dreadful strain for him. He is physically well though sleepless and nervous."

Around this time, Roosevelt began hinting heavily in letters to his friend and mentor Senator Henry Cabot Lodge that in "six or eight months," he would have finished "all that I have to do" at police headquarters, which seemed to mean he would be ready for a new job. By sheer coincidence, that time frame would fall just as the newly elected president would be making appointments to his cabinet. If Republican William McKinley of Ohio won, might there not be some place in his administration for the law-and-order crusader from New York?

But first Roosevelt would have to convince the Midwestern governor that he had abandoned his longtime love affair with Reed of Maine and was now a loyal McKinley man.

The mayor spent weeks at Richfield Springs, refusing to deliver a ruling on the Parker trial or to pin down when he might decide. Roosevelt needed a quick guilty verdict and the governor's swift signature, and the court system's rejection of any appeals. He didn't get any of it.

And every day for the foreseeable future Roosevelt and Parker would work side by side as commissioners, in this most dysfunctional Police Board family.

RESTLESS SUMMER

In mid-July the squabbling Police Board finally succeeded in promoting eight men to the exalted rank of captain. All were talented department veterans whom the board was convinced had not been tainted during the Byrnes years. Robert Young of the Elizabeth Street station spoke some Chinese; Daniel C. Moynihan had excelled during a horse-car strike. They each received a gold shield, and a pay raise to $2,750.

They reported to their new precincts at 8 a.m. on Thursday, July 16. That afternoon, Roosevelt summoned the new captains to headquarters for a lecture. (There was always a King-Arthur-addressing-his-knights feel to these chats.) He stressed courage and honesty; he implored the men to root out all bribery in their precincts, to be brave during riots ("cowardice . . . will no more be tolerated than it would be in the army"), and especially to crack down on vice. "Keep up a continual and unending warfare against crime, and especially that vicious sort which is carried on behind closed doors— pool-rooms, disorderly houses, and violations of the excise law. Keep that up to the handle." He warned them if they failed to stay honest, "no influence on earth can save you."

It's fascinating and somewhat uncanny that despite one of the most concerted efforts in the history of New York City to crack down on whoring, gambling, and after-hours drinking that all three somehow thrived.

Although TR and Parker squabbled over promotions, they agreed completely on suppressing vice, as did Chief Conlin and the inspectors and several well-placed captains, including Chapman of the Tenderloin. Yet vice thrived. Suppressed in one place, it emerged elsewhere. Police hit at street-walkers and known brothel locations, but the city was now embracing Raines Law hotels, and prostitutes were also taking apartments in tenement buildings. The police shuttered gambling palaces and the kingpins created private clubs with easy membership. Acting captain Groo had just raided a betting poolroom and offtrack betting parlor on Bleecker Street catering only to women. Comstock chased nudity on the stage but the new Olympia roof garden featured massive nude statues and risqué skits. Pushcart peddlers hand-sold penny cards of French nudes; bookseller Herman Stoll offered *Bride's Confession*, *Stolen Sweets*, and *Fanny Hill*; and although "The Voice," Russell Hunting, was temporarily in prison, others were standing up to the microphone to warble dirty songs and jokes.

The same night that TR gave his speech to the captains, yet another Tenderloin crowd tried to rescue yet another pretty woman whom a plainclothes officer accused of streetwalking. She claimed her only mistake was replying "Good evening" to the man's "Hello" as she walked in front of the Metropolitan Opera House at 39th Street. "Bertie" ran to the cellar entrance of the Park & Tilford Grocery, yelling that a man was "insulting" her. As the crowd tightened around him, the man showed his badge. Revelers were unimpressed and called him "dirty sneak" and worse; someone ran to Soubrettes' Row and twenty sporting women rushed to the scene to try to free their comrade. They circled Officer Saubel, cursed him, threatened him, enticed him, but he refused to let "Bertie" go. When the horses of the patrol wagon galloped off, the crowd followed shouting and the next day's headline ran: BROADWAY TO HER RESCUE.

Over and over, New Yorkers chafed at the purity crusade. It was as though the spirit of the city—some inarticulate force of hundreds of thousands of European immigrants mixed with locals, all of it long marinated in Dutch tolerance—refused.

————

The inconclusive Parker trial—twinned with the mounting Raines Law fiasco—seemed to mark a turning point for Roosevelt. He had served fourteen months as commissioner.

Besides hinting to Lodge about his need for a new job, TR began taking three-day weekends at Oyster Bay; and he decided to spend almost three weeks out west in late summer, including a long stay at his ranch in the Badlands of North Dakota.

Roosevelt's restlessness was getting the best of him. He rushed three long letters on three consecutive days to Henry Cabot Lodge at the very end of

July, complaining about his frustrations with the police job and longingly analyzing presidential politics.

Roosevelt had recently met with gruff personable Mark Hanna, Ohio mining magnate and McKinley campaign manager, and TR enjoyed relaying it all to Lodge. He told him that he advised Hanna to contact Lodge and Massachusetts Republican State Committee chairman George H. Lyman for "money help," which he needed in the Northeast. Hanna had replied that Lodge topped his list of people to consider, both now and after the election. "Of course, I can only tell you what he *said* he would do, not what he *will* do."

TR also wrote that Platt—still smarting from his New York presidential candidate's demise—refused to reach out to Hanna, and awaited an invitation. TR was enlisting an intermediary to send Platt a message to drop the "point of punctilio" and contact Hanna.

Roosevelt met a second time with fifty-eight-year-old Hanna, long known as a champion of moneyed interests. "He is a good natured, well meaning, rough man, shrewd and hard-headed but neither very far-sighted nor very broad-minded, and as he has a resolute imperious mind he will have to be handled with some care."

Roosevelt, insightfully, suggested that Lodge throw a "small" dinner party for Hanna, as the man hated pomp and fuss.

The end of the week found TR bickering viciously with Parker again over the promotions to inspector. Roosevelt, Grant, and Andrews had banded together and vowed to consider only Brooks and McCullagh. Parker promised a fight. "No spoils politician ever dared to do in this department what these men have done," he told the press, comparing the actions to a Tammany fix for a favorite.

———

Amid the battles over promotions, the board remained united against vice, and yet it couldn't gain much traction in its fight. That week the police tried to shut down Hope Booth for her striptease, "Ten Minutes in the Latin Quarter; or, a Study in the Nude" at the American Roof Garden.

New Yorkers, in the un–air conditioned summer heat, flocked to half a dozen gargantuan roof gardens for the cooler fresher air, overpriced drinks, and easy, playful entertainment.

The "Latin Quarter" skit, which looked like the hit of the season, was a pantomime showing a French painter holding auditions for nude models;

first, he rejects one (clothed) woman as too fat, another as too skinny, then he allows a young female (Hope Booth) who arrives in beggar's rags to pose. (Remember the craze of that era about Trilby, a poor pretty model transformed by a hypnotist named Svengali.) Hope Booth goes behind a large red Japanese umbrella on a darkened stage to remove her tattered garments; she tosses them aside one by one; the umbrella rolls away as high-beam calcium lights flash on to reveal her wearing nothing but a long silk cape about her shoulders. To the drunks in the back rows, she appears naked. (An astute reporter for the *Sun*, however, stated that she had on an "exceptionally thin covering of flesh-colored stockingnet.")

The Police Board contacted Chief Conlin, who sent acting inspector Harley to investigate.

When Harley went, accompanied by a roundsman, on Tuesday, July 21, he found the roof garden's entrance jammed, scalpers hawking tickets at triple the price; the program listed the sketch as last in the lineup, to allow "spare time to buy drinks."

The next day, the two policemen pronounced themselves "shocked" and Harley testified at Jefferson Market Court House that he had never seen "as much of the female form before during any theatrical performance."

At the hearing, Hope Booth shrewdly handed into evidence a pair of "double thick" shoulder-to-toe tights. She stressed their uncommon thickness. Magistrate Deuel refused to convict on public indecency; the district attorney brought the case to the grand jury, but it too refused to indict.

Roosevelt announced to the press that he was deeply disappointed by the verdicts, and also over the likelihood that Hope Booth would reprise her role. So was *Town Topics*. "Where she ought to be slender, she is too thick; above all, her ankles are ponderous," complained the editor. "I protest again she ought not to be allowed to reappear upon the stage unless submerged in bloomers and shoulder-of-mutton sleeves." "Latin Quarter" returned and helped launched Hope Booth's long career.

Frustrated by Parker and permissive judges, TR raced to Oyster Bay late Friday, July 31. His houseguests that weekend were Mr. and Mrs. Bellamy Storer, close Ohio friends of candidate McKinley.

———

The clannish Roosevelts did not invite houseguests cavalierly. Two Sundays earlier, TR had hosted Jacob Riis; the previous weekend, fellow commissioner Avery Andrews. TR also mentioned a friend of his late brother Elliott, a "conscienceless adventurer with no morals of any kind," fresh from Nyasaland in Africa, "but of such a varied past as to be rather entertaining for twenty four hours."

The Storers were presumably welcome for the entire weekend or longer.

Bellamy Storer, two-time congressman from Ohio, had stood in D.C. as godfather to Roosevelt's son Archibald ("Archie"), born April 9, 1894, when TR was still a civil service commissioner. The Storers hovered on the edge of that clever D.C. circle of the Lodges and Roosevelts, historians Henry Adams and John Hay, and British diplomat Cecil Spring-Rice. Lawyer Bellamy Storer, age forty-eight, had impressive bona fides, having attended Boston Latin and Harvard (class of '67), but his political career did not flourish until he married Maria Longworth, a clever, entertaining, and very wealthy widow.

Roosevelt knew well that very few people in Ohio had more influence with McKinley than the Storers. When McKinley had lost his fortune three years earlier and scandal loomed, Mr. and Mrs. Storer had quickly volunteered $10,000 to help save him and his political career. A friendship was cemented; McKinley supposedly cried on hearing of the financial pledge. The Storers, leviathans in Ohio, were looking forward to visiting the Roosevelts in the weeks following the presidential nomination of their state's circumspect governor. "The [Roosevelts'] life [at Oyster Bay] was ideal in its simplicity and nobody could be more amusing than the host—one never knew what he would say next."

Maria later remembered TR as being especially edgy during that summer of 1896 but she said they also found him very funny; they laughed a lot. "His vituperation was extremely amusing and he had a most extraordinary vocabulary." TR, selecting a Storer, took Maria out for a row on the bay. She recalled feeling a tad nervous as Roosevelt was rowing "spasmodically and sometimes absent-mindedly." Their conversation drifted to his current job, and she recalled that TR sounded "much depressed." He expected the political machine to force him out soon. "I don't know what I shall do next," he told her. "I have no future; I shall be the melancholy spectacle to the bunnies [the Roosevelt children] of an idle father writing books that won't sell."

A steam vessel passed them and the wake almost capsized the small boat. "Please row back," Maria told him. "We can talk better on dry land."

As the two walked toward Sagamore Hill, Roosevelt told Maria that one job did appeal to him but "McKinley will never give it to me, I should like to be Assistant Secretary of the Navy." Roosevelt added that McKinley did not like him; Maria later conceded she knew that to be accurate but she opted at the time *not* to confirm TR's suspicions. She promised that she and Bellamy would both directly ask McKinley, if elected, to appoint him to the post.

Days after the weekend visit, Roosevelt wrote Bellamy that "it would be well for me to accept Assistant Secretary of the Navy in the very improbable event of it being offered" but that first the Storers must land a cabinet post for Bellamy. He added a postscript: "Need I say how we enjoyed your visit?" To Maria, he wrote that he had personally lobbied Mark Hanna for Bellamy. "He listened attentively, spoke very warmly of Bellamy, but said that at present he was considering nothing but how to elect McKinley."

———

While the Roosevelts enjoyed the offshore breezes at Oyster Bay, a ferocious heat wave rolled in slowly and relentlessly, stifling the city.

Four people died in Manhattan from heat prostration on Wednesday, August 5. The "heated term," as Roosevelt called it, began as the typical muggy miserableness of August in New York City but then day followed day with no breeze, no fresh air, no rain; the unpleasantness metamorphosed into a kind of suffocating blanket draped over the sweat-soaked city.

New Yorkers slept on roofs, on fire escapes; they camped out on piers and snuck past policemen into the parks. The deepest suffering occurred in the overcrowded tenements where four families sometimes shared a handful of rooms. After a while, it was hard to breathe indoors. "The heat did not reach 100 degrees at any time during this period," explained one contemporary observer. "It was rather the continuance of it night and day, the absolute stagnation of the air and the oppressive humidity, that made these days so trying to all and fatal to so many."

Roosevelt, his vacation two weeks away, remained in the city out of a sense of duty night after night and explored the misery. He watched horses dying in the streets and horse carcasses rotting in a welter of flies and maggots; he wrote it gave the city "a genuine flavor of pestilence." Roosevelt later in his autobiography recounted that a dray carrying eleven horse corpses collapsed in front of a shop. The owner repeatedly begged city officials to come cart away the pile of rotting oozing horse flesh. Finally after several days he implored the police to "remove either the horses or his shop, he didn't care which."

The heat crept up on the city . . . everyone daily expected relief that never came; hospitals became overwhelmed. The initial death count rose to forty-five on Sunday, August 9, then seventy-two on August 10. The death toll kept rising. (More than 900 people would die in New York from the heat.) Police shot dozens of mad dogs; more than the usual quota of New Yorkers went insane; several died by sleeping on overcrowded roofs and rolling off the edge.

Officials rushed offers to relocate the poor to homes in rural areas upstate but almost no one took the opportunity. To spare sanitation workers from the sun, their work hours were shifted to start at 2 a.m. The public baths, including the floating swimming pools in the rivers, were switched to staying open round the clock with the women's hours greatly expanded. The Moderation Society operated several ice-water wagons; the sign read ONE QUART PER FAMILY.

Exhausted horses bruised their flanks crushing toward the single large trough at Greeley Square at 34th Street. Down on the Bowery, no public troughs existed, leading shrewd saloon owner Steve Brodie to offer free water to horses of any teamsters. An eleven-year-old was caught swimming nude in Rutgers Square Fountain on the East Side; a vagrant was caught sleeping nude in Central Park. The sanitation department, after sunset, opened the fire hydrants of one neighborhood after another, and exhausted half-naked men, women, and children crowded into the streams in the streets.

Eight policemen passed out. The oldest animal at the Central Park Zoo, an eighteen-year-old buffalo, died and its body was carried to the Museum of Natural History to be stuffed.

The weather forecast remained bleak.

————

All this heat spelled disaster for a barnstorming presidential candidate.

On August 12, day seven of this horrific heat wave, Democratic hopeful William Jennings Bryan was scheduled to give a speech at Madison Square Garden. Pundits had long marked the date as a prime opportunity for the Nebraska orator to spread the spark of his populist message and make key inroads in the Northeast. (Republican McKinley, on the other hand, was choosing to stay in Canton, Ohio, and let others do the talking for him.)

Thirty-six-year-old Bryan had not even been expected to win the convention in July over Richard Bland, but his fiery "Cross of Gold" speech had captivated blocs of delegates; horse-trading had done the rest.

The organizers of the Bryan event in New York expected a tidal wave of support; the Garden would have to add extra seats to near-double its capacity to 15,000; perhaps an equally large crowd would gather outside. Bryan could ride this throng and the coverage of the hoopla to gain momentum.

The presidential contest seemed to be shifting from the candidates themselves to the fiscal policy planks of their message. Bryan supported the silver standard and McKinley endorsed gold. Strong opinions on the topic fractured the nation.

Roosevelt, dubbing the election the most important since the Civil War, grew rabid in his letters about the silver craze. "Not only do [Bryan supporters] wish to repudiate their debts, but they really believe that somehow they are executing righteous justice on the moneyed oppressor." He then condescendingly analyzed the psyche of Bryan's supporters. "They feel the eternal and inevitable injustice of life, they do not realize and will not realize how that injustice is aggravated by their own extraordinary folly, and they wish, if they cannot lift themselves, at least to strike down those who are more fortunate or more prosperous."

Thomas Beer, author of *The Mauve Decade*, had a more *Town Topics*-style take on the bitter fiscal divisions. "It was now understood that some numerical incantation known as the silver standard would either make everybody sixteen times richer or would ruin the United States. Few minds were strong enough to comprehend the reasoning of this process but a plain case of the people against the wicked rich had been made out."

Roosevelt, surrounded by loyal Republicans, expected the Northeast to back McKinley but he still worried about the appeal of Bryan. "[He] is a personally honest and rather attractive man, a real orator and a born demagogue, who has every crank, fool and putative criminal in the country behind him, and a large proportion of the ignorant honest class."

Though wilting under the oppressive heat of August 12, New Yorkers by the thousands flocked by streetcar and El toward Madison Square Garden. The organizers had decked the north end of the arena with two enormous portrait banners of Bryan and Arthur Sewall. Workmen added seats; they draped red-white-and-blue bunting; bands practiced patriotic songs.

In the sweltering heat, the New York police were key to it all going smoothly; they would have to control the immense crowds of perspiring Democrats. The police assigned 400 men for crowd control. The police plan—not well coordinated with the Garden officials or the campaign heads—called for the officers to cordon off a block-wide protective buffer around the Garden long before the 8 p.m. start of the speech.

The police that evening let through thousands—perhaps enough to fill the Garden—and then sealed the barricades at 7 p.m. when the Garden opened its doors. The massive flaw was that many of the ticket holders, including many of Bryan's most passionate supporters and more than a few important members of the press, were locked on the wrong side of the barricades. No cajoling or browbeating swayed any police officers, and several indignant dignitaries were arrested trying to bullrush the gates. Patrolman Charles Becker arrested lawyer J. Brownson Ker, who was carrying a "Special Invitation" and refused to stop.

Inspector Cortwright, a Republican, who was overseeing all in Conlin's brief absence, called for mounted police to charge the surging crowds at several places, eventually forcing the masses into Madison Square Park. Acting inspector Brooks commanded inside the building; acting inspector McCullagh fought the toughest crowds on Fourth Avenue. Both happened to be loyal Republicans, as, of course, was Roosevelt.

The headlines the next day regarding the runup to the speech would complain: INEFFICIENCY OF TEDDY'S RECRUITS. A *New* York *Sun* editorial would dub it "the most remarkable exhibition of mismanagement seen in this city in many years." An article in the *New York News* would call the riot police "as utterly useless as a row of tin soldiers."

The *World* estimated that one-quarter of ticket holders were turned back into the howling, sweating, swirling mob on the fringes of Madison Square Park. The Democrats could see nude Diana but they couldn't get under her and into the building. The *Sun* gauged the police as "remarkably adept at letting gate-crashers in and keeping ticket-holders out."

The Garden was full by 7:30 p.m. A *World* reporter pulled out a thermometer; the inside of the Garden, despite open windows and roof ventilation, stood at ninety-seven degrees, with 2,000 electric lights aglow.

The nearly 14,000 men in the perspiring audience almost immediately began removing their coats and vests until the Garden seemed a sea of ghostly white, except for the occasional woman's bonnet. Men smoked cigars. Tall, strong-looking Bryan, the youngest presidential candidate ever of a major political party, strode to the lectern, and the crowd, hats and handkerchiefs waving, engulfed him in an eight-minute tidal wave of ovation. Passionate enthusiasm emanated from the young crowd, mostly under thirty.

Then Bryan began to read his speech. The "Orator of the Platte," who had mesmerized the Democratic convention in Chicago, was not moving his arms or modulating his voice or showing his passion. The man who had delivered the memorable "Cross of Gold" speech was reading a detailed, complicated diatribe on the silver standard; the mesmerizer was droning on in the kickoff speech of his campaign.

Some in the soaking-hot upper galleries began to leave, then an occasional person below. "The filling of the Garden was in fact very bunglingly done," observed the *New York Times* in an arch editorial.

> But it is a pleasure to be able to say that the emptying of it was accomplished without any danger or confusion . . . The managers of the meeting accomplished this perfectly. They employed for this purpose an expert, in the person of William J. Bryan of Nebraska . . . After Mr. Bryan had been talking about ten minutes people began to go out quietly without haste or crowding. As he continued, the stream of outgoers gradually increased . . . It was a steady gradual dispersion that endangered nobody's life nor even made anybody uncomfortable. It took Mr. Bryan nearly two hours to complete his task but when he ceased speaking he had reduced the crowd to dimensions so moderate that the remnant could disperse at once without any danger.

Bryan showed some life in the last few minutes of his speech but by then the Garden was half filled.

As Roosevelt gleefully wrote to Lodge: "Bryan fell perfectly flat here."

On the day after the Bryan fiasco (now day eight of the heat wave), various heads of the municipal government of New York City held an emergency meeting to devise ways to help the heat-prostrated masses. Among other ideas, such as soaking the Tenderloin, the Board of Estimate approved an emergency fund of $5,000 to buy ice, to be distributed to the poor by the police.

Roosevelt resisted the temptation to spend nights in the breezes of Oyster Bay and remained in the sweltering metropolis to observe and make sure ice was indeed distributed. The city quickly purchased ninety-three tons of ice at four dollars a ton. Horses hauled wagonloads of it. Hundreds lined up at sunset at the station houses to collect a free ten-pound chunk of ice.

(Police captains were authorized to buy extra axes to chop the ice.) Roosevelt visited four nearby precincts: Oak, Liberty, Madison, and Mulberry, and estimated that about 1,000 persons received ice.

Most families sent children to collect the ice since the police would be less likely to accuse the family of being too well off to qualify. "What does your father do?" the officers would typically ask. The children began lining up at 4 p.m., carrying tin pails and buckets and pots for the 6 p.m. delivery. When the wagons failed to come on time to the Madison Street station, the children there began banging on the pots, creating a deafening din.

The Board of Health was also sending out eighteen wagons to haul away dead horses, seven carcasses per trip. They also sent out smaller wagons to spray disinfectant. The most fast-paced city in the nation was slogging forward in slow motion.

The heat wave finally broke on August 14 as cooling showers and light breezes lifted the stinking wet blanket off the city. The temperature dropped ten degrees.

In the newly merciful weather, Roosevelt personally oversaw preparations for that evening's Republican "Sound Money" speech on the gold standard at Madison Square Garden by Bourke Cockran; doors would open at 6 p.m. instead of Bryan's 7 p.m.; no one without a ticket would be let in. That night, an overflow crowd of 12,000 was smoothly handled. No complaints for this Republican event. Cockran delivered a rollicking speech that had the audience cheering wildly. The euphoria was relayed to McKinley in Canton.

The Police Board called a "special meeting" for Thursday, August 20, to address the contentious issue of promotions to inspector. Roosevelt was leaving the following morning for an extended vacation out west.

The *World* would later say of the meeting: "Prize fights have been conducted in a more orderly manner." The *Herald* headline was WAR IN THE BOARD. Andrews stormed out of the meeting; Roosevelt shouted at Parker; Parker calmly and maddeningly talked on, refusing on technical grounds to approve the promotions of the the two Roosevelt favorites, Brooks and McCullagh.

———

The following morning Roosevelt rode by carriage with his luggage to a Hudson River pier to catch the ferry to Jersey City. He boarded the train heading west. His trunks contained at least one new rifle.

To some, the Badlands were bleak; to Roosevelt, they were a wide empty grassy place, filled with cattle, magpies, hawks, sheep, and the occasional cowboy, where he went to repair his soul and to recalibrate his nervous system.

Camping out under a sprawling mantle of stars, galloping after antelope, hunting, Roosevelt would shed the grimy police department and distance himself from New York City. He would also find time to campaign for McKinley.

CAMPAIGNING FOR McKINLEY AND HIMSELF

When Roosevelt returned from his three weeks out west, he looked ruddy and sunburned. After getting over the initial disappointment of discovering his cattle herd thin and sickly, he had spent the next twelve consecutive glorious days "riding over the great plains and sleeping in the open at night." He especially enjoyed testing out his new toy, a smokeless Winchester rifle, featuring cutting-edge half-jacketed .30 caliber bullets.

Newspapers around the country picked up the *Omaha World-Herald*'s feature on TR the cowboy, delivering that widely appealing image of a Knickerbocker heir, a member of the Harvard East Coast elite, riding and broncobusting with the last heroes of the frontier. "Roosevelt cannot see a dozen yards away without his glasses, but he can do some fancy [rifle] shooting that would win applause at a Wild West show."

After expanding his lungs with prairie air, Roosevelt had found time to squeeze in two days at Republican headquarters in Chicago, scrutinizing reports from throughout the region. He analyzed Republican prospects state by state for Lodge ("affairs are very much demoralized in Michigan but we shall win," "in Iowa the defection has been *very* great"). He personally checked the leanings of the ranchers and cowhands in his own desolate neighborhood. "The Dakotas are a little against us but with proper care, I believe there is at least an even chance of carrying them," he wrote. "There is a great need of money to spend in an entirely legitimate way for educational purposes."

With the clarity from his weeks in the Badlands, Roosevelt seemed now to be even more committed to exploring his options *outside* the police department. He would never admit surrender or retreat—his personality forbade it—but he began to write more often of having "done nearly all I could do." While his letters finesse the topic of exiting, his actions over the fall show him missing numerous meetings and traveling again and again to deliver campaign speeches for McKinley.

In mid-September, Henry Cabot Lodge relayed to Roosevelt the stellar news that the Massachusetts senator had convinced the New York State Republican Party to allow TR to accompany him on a series of joint campaign appearances upstate. The only catch was that Roosevelt must go meet several high-ranking local Republicans to confirm the assignment. TR instantly replied that he was "overjoyed" and would do so.

The meeting was bound to be awkward because the New York Republican machine—run statewide by Thomas Collier Platt and citywide by Edward Lauterbach—had not forgiven Roosevelt for his Sunday liquor crackdown that had boosted Tammany and capsized the local elections a year earlier. They also resented that Roosevelt stuck by his credo to be a *nonpartisan* city official and refused to fight outright for Republican appointments, a point that Parker had tried to exploit.

Roosevelt, like a schoolboy taking his medicine, recounted to Lodge his visit to the "gentlemen who have been endeavoring to get my scalp for the last year or two." He relayed: "We greeted one another with hilarious politeness."

He added candidly, "The lovely Lauterbach was prominent among them; I never can help being amused with that graceless sheeny." (The published volume of letters states "graceless person"; a "sheeny" was a mildly derogatory term for a Jew.)

Roosevelt had already given one campaign speech in New York City at a "Sound Money" luncheon on Friday and apparently impressed the highest-ranking Republicans with his take-no-prisoners tone. He had sawed the air, he had used props such as oversized silver and gold coins, he had spewed venom. At that luncheon, TR accused Bryan's "Free Silver" supporters of violating the Commandment "Thou Shalt Not Steal." He called farmers "the basest set in the land." Roosevelt was discovering that audiences preferred his harshest rants—which were so extreme that they were amusing—to his attempts at reasoned discourse.

A star pit-bull campaigner was born.

The committee decided to forbid Roosevelt from appearing with Senator Lodge and Governor Black at the opening salvo in New York City, where his popularity had waned. Instead, they approved him to join Lodge for an upstate swing past Utica and on to Buffalo, all conservative strongholds. Roosevelt and Lodge left the city on September 28 on a specially reserved railroad train and spent the next three days zigzagging through the fall foliage, giving whistle-stop and big hall speeches. Roosevelt reported to his sister that standing-room-only crowds followed them and Cabot made "remarkably good speeches." He rated himself as doing "well enough." In Utica, TR called Bryan's ideas "silly and wicked enough to fit well in the mouth of an anarchist leader"; in Gloversville, New York, Lucius N. Littauer, the nation's largest glove manufacturer, introduced him and he spoke to an overflow crowd of 3,000 persons at the Kasson Opera House.

In addition to this jaunt through western New York, Lodge invited TR along to pay a flying visit to McKinley in Canton. That posed a small dilemma for Roosevelt. He had promised the Storers that he would not visit Canton without them. He wrote a note to Bellamy apprising him that he *might* swing by Canton with Lodge but he left further details vague.

A steady parade of supplicants was marching up Canton's patriotically festooned North Market Street. A delegation of 300 farmers from West Virginia and 600 railroad workers from Ohio and Illinois had just hit town, and their leaders were preparing to make speeches. Since both Lodge and TR had supported Reed of Maine for president literally for years—even once backing him over McKinley to be House Speaker—they now had to convince McKinley of their newfound allegiance.

The campaigning duo arrived past midnight on October 1 and clerks at an overflowing hotel had to squeeze the senator and the police commissioner into "a garret room." After a few hours' sleep, they prepared to walk to McKinley's home but three days of rain had reduced the candidate's lawn to mud, so they were told to go to a place called the Tabernacle. They talked with McKinley, a confident, clean-shaven fifty-three-year-old Civil War veteran, on a day when callers included three congressmen and two sons of former presidents: Harry Garfield and Rutherford Hayes.

Roosevelt could genuinely embrace most of McKinley's platform, especially the key economic tenets, although the New Yorker was more hawkish in foreign policy. "McKinley is bearing himself well," he wrote to Bamie. "He was entirely pleasant with us, though we are not among his favorites." Roosevelt's frank assessment jibed with Maria Storer's candid opinion.

Despite the bland McKinley welcome, Roosevelt had certainly enjoyed his stumping tour; he enjoyed almost any activity away from 300 Mulberry. He gushed to Lodge that "it was simply delightful to be with you for the five days."

Roosevelt, however, never saw Bellamy or Maria Storer in Canton, and several notes have survived in which he tried to finesse the slight. The Storers apparently did not respond to the first. ("Did you get my note about the Canton incident?") He later added: "I was more sorry than I can say that we failed to get together there, as I did not much care to see our President-to-be except with you for various reasons."

———

Back in New York, although Roosevelt's two main priorities were hiring 800 new recruits and ensuring a fair election, he also found time to aid Reverend Parkhurst in his Captain Ahab–like pursuit of "Big Bill" Devery.

Big Bill's command of the 125th Street precinct for the past four months had been uneventful; he had maintained order and was already popular with the men. No civilian complaints marred his record.

Parkhurst, however, with no desire to forgive or forget, contacted Roosevelt about bringing new charges against Devery. Roosevelt's right-hand man, Commissioner Andrews, introduced a resolution at the Wednesday, October 7, board meeting to hire Frank Moss, Parkhurst Society lawyer, as special counsel to reinvestigate various cases against Devery. Moss had overseen the original Parkhurst investigation of Devery (1892), had defended Charlie Gardner when accused of extortion by Devery (1893), and had acted as Lexow interrogator of Devery (1894). No man knew Devery's delinquencies better than Moss. The resolution passed.

Roosevelt then instructed Chief Conlin to aid Frank Moss and to turn over the 11th Police precinct blotters from 1893 to him. Conlin forwarded the order to the precinct and Moss gathered the oversized daily blotters. Someone at Eldridge Street leaked word to the press.

Devery was furious when he found out. He unleashed a torrent of wounded outrage to the *Herald*.

"I have been nineteen years in the service and have never had a citizen's complaint against me. I have been tried in the courts and have been honorably acquitted of the charges this [Parkhurst] Society brought against me. This man Moss has been a witness against me and now he is to be my prosecutor and the books of the department have been placed at his disposal . . . I arrested their agent Gardner for blackmail and since that time they have persecuted me . . . Who is my counsel? I have none and no money to employ one. They have already robbed me of eighteen years of my savings." Then he added, under his breath: "They have taught me enough to be my own lawyer."

The *New York World* twitted TR over meddling in the case. "It is remarkable that lawyer Moss, a private citizen, should be allowed to go to a police station and carry away the blotters for inspection," carped the *World*. "No other citizen would be allowed to do such a thing." Several newspapers tried to roast Roosevelt but the board president took the time to investigate the Devery specifics. He "most emphatically" denied any persecution of Tammany's Devery. He pointed out that the courts had overturned Devery's dismissal in August 1894 on procedural grounds because the board had tried him in absentia and not allowed him an illness delay. Roosevelt contended that that sort of technical reversal "left the case exactly where it was in the beginning" and open for a new hearing.

He also claimed—not very convincingly—that hiring Moss was a simple matter of manpower. "No one Commissioner would be able to go over all these cases and sift them." Devery was back in the crosshairs.

———

Roosevelt, that October, in any case, was far more interested in a different prize, the upcoming election. Oddsmakers by the middle of the month had McKinley as an overwhelming favorite at four to one, but some change of sentiment and heavy money on Bryan from the West was starting to shift the odds to three to one. The *World* reported that a Montana silver king offered $100,000 against $300,000 if Bryan won but found no takers at Republican headquarters. Man-to-man election bets were legal then (and are still legal now).

Newspapers reported a straight-up bet of $6,000 was offered at Hoffman House and Delmonico's that McKinley would not win New York State by more than 150,000 votes. Two New York bookies took the bet and the money was placed at the Second National Bank.

Some Republicans, in their darkest moments, feared that Bryan might squeak out a victory, rallying the West and the South and snatching some extra states in the Midwest.

———

TR reached Chicago to speak on Thursday, October 15, at the massive Coliseum under the auspices of the American Republican College League. A rollicking enthusiastic crowd of 13,000 awaited him.

McKinley remained on his Ohio porch with his ill wife. The Republican campaign planners were sending out a battalion of surrogates to plead his case for leading the country back from the fiscal miasma of 1893. Mark Hanna and the top men apparently appreciated Roosevelt's performances so far because they gave him this plum assignment of addressing huge rallies in Chicago and Detroit and of traveling in Illinois and Michigan in the footsteps of the Democratic candidate himself, Bryan.

TR's letters around this time reveal a renewed vigor; he clearly was enjoying these national political battles.

Around 7 p.m. on a Thursday night in Chicago, the Second Regiment Band began playing patriotic songs as the bunting-draped hall filled up. The crowd neared a fever pitch of enthusiasm when Abraham Lincoln's son, Robert Lincoln, introduced his fellow Harvard graduate Theodore Roosevelt. The jacketed college men chanted "Teddy," "Teddy," "Teddy" over and over and applauded for long minutes.

Roosevelt, riding the fervor, gave an impassioned speech, one that so impressed the *Chicago Daily Tribune* that it printed the text word for word starting on the front page. "I let myself go and I hit at the [Silver Democrats] as hard as I knew how," he later wrote to his sister.

Roosevelt lumped Bryan with other dangerous demagogues, such as Socialist Eugene V. Debs; he compared him to Robespierre and other guillotine-wielding fanatics of the French Revolution. He claimed the Bryan campaign was waging a war against "morality and ability," a campaign against "men who pay their debts and obey the laws."

Roosevelt was rewarded again and again with thunderous applause.

"Instead of a government of the people, for the people and by the people, which we now have, Mr. Bryan would substitute a government of a mob, by the demagogue, and for the shiftless and disorderly and the criminal and the semi-criminal."

The audience cheered and stomped their feet. Arriving armed with various props, Roosevelt now held up two loaves of bread, a small one that he called a "five-cent loaf," the other one, twice the size, an eight-cent one. TR said under Bryan the five-cent loaf would cost more than nine cents because Bryan opposed a fat dollar, and therefore under Bryan's "lean dollar," all items would cost more.

The two-hour speech marked a huge success for Roosevelt and perhaps a turning point in his public speaking. His new formula: entertainingly demonizing the opposition and waving the flag. "I made a success of it and got in good form and spoke to immense audiences, who always listened attentively and sometimes as in Chicago and Detroit, went mad with enthusiasm."

———

McKinley won in a rout. He drew about 5 percent more of the popular vote but crushed Bryan 271 to 176 in the Electoral College. The states had fallen mostly as Roosevelt had predicted, with Bryan's strength limited to the West (except California and Oregon) and the solid South. The orator from Nebraska carried just one fewer of the forty-five states than McKinley but unfortunately for him Texas then had fifteen electoral votes and Florida four compared to Pennsylvania's thirty-two and New York's thirty-six. The local bookmakers scooped up $6,000 when McKinley clobbered Bryan in New York State by 270,000 votes, grabbing almost 60 percent.

Roosevelt, in the final frantic days leading up to the polls, had worked hard to guarantee another fair election. Tammany once again would not be stuffing any ballot boxes or registering vagrants on his watch. He again raised the standard for poll watchers and ordered interviews of hundreds of candidates for the low-paying job. He ensured that police would be allowed to vote, while still assigning them to distant precincts.

Newspapers universally acknowledged a well-run election. The only slight quirk was that the Raines Law forbade the sale of liquor in saloons but allowed it in hotels on Election Day. Since New York City barkeeps had converted 1,500 saloons into Raines Law hotels, voters did not have to wander far for a drink. An inebriated electorate apparently didn't harm Republican chances.

Roosevelt was beyond ecstatic at the McKinley victory. He called it a "triumph of patriotism." The Republicans toasted themselves in a series of lavish dinners at New York's prime venues. Roosevelt rewarded himself by going to a boxing match on November 16.

The election won, Lodge importuned McKinley again on Roosevelt's behalf, and the pair weighed another trip to Canton. This time, Roosevelt strove mightily not to offend the Storers. He wrote Bellamy Storer on November 18 and 19, ultimately concluding that he would prefer to avoid the trip altogether.

TR instead agreed to attend an event close to the Storers' heart, a lavish dinner in Cincinnati, which the couple hosted for the local New England

Society on December 22, celebrating the Pilgrims landing. (A year earlier, he had turned it down.)

He pretzeled himself linguistically in a postscript trying to please and appease the Storers. "I should rather have you speak in my behalf than anyone in the United States, and I think you could do most good; but I rather hate to go there [to Canton] with you, for, somehow, it does not seem to me that it would be a good thing for you to speak for me before me."

Roosevelt tried to pull his weight in the job-hunting game; he wrote a letter to McKinley pushing Bellamy Storer for a high cabinet post or a plum diplomatic assignment.

Just before Thanksgiving, the Storers visited McKinley at his home. They ran into Police Commissioner Grant, who was pitching himself for secretary of war, and Maria served up to TR a (now lost) anecdote of Grant's bumbling self-promotion. At some point during their chat, Maria steered the conversation to the subject of TR and made an impassioned plea for him to be the next assistant secretary of the navy. She wrote Roosevelt and, treading delicately, suggested that he come to Canton to dispel McKinley's final reservations. "He saw me when I went there during the campaign," Roosevelt replied, "and if he thinks I am hot-headed and harum-scarum, I don't think he will change his mind now."

Hackles up, TR added that he did not want to appear "as a supplicant" because he was convinced he would do "good work" for the U.S. Navy. (When word later leaked of his job quest, the rarely-friendly-to-TR *Washington Post* pointed out that Roosevelt had written a well-respected book on the War of 1812, was a lifelong student of the navy, and could easily decipher arcane reports on vessel displacement and armament.)

McKinley around this time extended another invitation to Henry Cabot Lodge, who visited on Sunday, November 29. Lodge reported that he chatted for two hours with the president-elect, mainly about foreign policy, especially Cuba. (McKinley hoped to avoid war long enough to repair the U.S. economy first.) Then Lodge broached the subject of Roosevelt's appointment.

"[McKinley] spoke of you with great regard for your character and your services and he would like to have you in Washington. The only question he asked was this, which I give you: 'I hope he has no preconceived plans which he would wish to drive through the moment he got in.'" That question implied that the battle-hardened major feared TR might be too belligerent in foreign affairs, too overeager to build a massive fleet. Lodge, without hesitation, replied that Roosevelt would strictly follow administration policies. To portray headstrong Roosevelt as an obedient bureaucrat took a practiced poker face and decades of Boston Brahmin breeding.

Lodge discussed other topics with McKinley but then as he was preparing to leave, he added: "I have no right to ask a personal favor of you but I do ask for Roosevelt as the one personal favor." McKinley replied that he carried no hard feelings from TR and Lodge supporting Reed. "You have a perfect right to ask a personal favor and I understand what you want." He did not say he would grant it; he said he understood it.

A few days later back in D.C., Lodge ran into Bellamy Storer, confided "my influence is nothing compared to yours," and asked him to keep "steady pressure" on McKinley. Bellamy then—for the second time—invited Lodge to attend the Pilgrims landing banquet in Cincinnati on December 22 but Lodge begged off, explaining that his younger son was returning from Cambridge.

Supplicant Roosevelt had no choice regarding the banquet invitation. Maria asked him to come out a day early, but he pleaded police commission business. She asked him to stay a day late, but he pleaded—as he had from the beginning—that he had to attend the Cove School Christmas Tree lighting in Oyster Bay on the morning of December 24.

———

TR wrote again and again to thank Lodge. "The main reason why I would care to go to Washington is to be near you," he penned once. TR added elsewhere that Cabot and wife Nannie were the "only people for whom I really care outside my own family."

Lodge also met with New York State Republican boss Thomas Collier Platt on Roosevelt's behalf. Lodge quickly discovered that Platt's focus then was primarily on self-promotion. Riding the Republican landslide, Platt was jockeying to have his minions in the Legislature elect him as the next U.S. senator from New York. Lodge informed TR he must go to Platt and promise not to oppose the power broker's candidacy.

Unfortunately for Roosevelt, Platt's only rival for senator was Roosevelt's longtime Harvard friend and mentor Joseph Choate, who back in 1881 had helped launch Roosevelt's political career by championing him for assemblyman. TR made a painful but pragmatic decision. He showed up at the Wednesday night Republican banquet and backed the inevitable Platt.

In the reality of hardball politics, TR was discovering that he would need not only McKinley's blessing but also Platt's, since McKinley had decided that he could hand New York Republicans only so many plum appointments.

And at that moment, Platt would not lift a finger for Roosevelt, except perhaps to toss him out of New York. Conveniently for TR, Washington lay 200 miles to the south.

BELLY DANCERS AND SNOW BALLS

The rumor that Roosevelt was at a private party at Sherry's with a nude belly dancer swept through the police department late on Saturday, December 19. Tammany cops were much amused. The story got even better when it was relayed on good authority that one of Roosevelt's favorite reform captains was on his way to raid the restaurant and that he *did not know* that Roosevelt was there. Captain Chapman had heard that Little Egypt was performing "table tricks."

A dusting of snow gave the Tenderloin that night a rare patina of purity. Bawdy women still bustled into the dance halls but they looked less garish bundled in snowflake-flecked winter coats, swathed in scarves. Band music, with more than a smattering of sentimental songs to suit the Christmas season, drifted out through the open doors.

Just after midnight, Captain George S. Chapman—a strict fifty-year-old officer, bald-headed with massive muttonchop sideburns—walked, wearing civilian clothes, from the West 30th Street precinct house over to Sherry's Restaurant at 37th Street and Fifth Avenue. He was heading to one of the most respectable, exclusive, expensive venues in New York City. Only in this reform era under Roosevelt could a captain even consider barging in there, on a tip of "indecent behavior" from a theatrical agent. In season, the cream of the city's youth attended Monday and Thursday "Dance Classes"—orchestrated by Mrs. William C. Whitney and dubbed "The Swells"; and on Sundays, the traditional night off for domestic servants, Sherry's Restaurant, along with Delmonico's and the Waldorf, attracted a very large following among the Four Hundred.

Chapman and two detectives found the building locked but saw lights on the second floor and faintly heard music through the closed windows. He pressed the buzzer but no one answered. A quarter hour later, Chapman, who considered it his duty "to drive out crime and iniquity without fear or favor," saw a couple rushing out of a door and slipped inside. He climbed to the second floor, heard voices, and entered a room. He was shocked.

Chapman, a straight-arrow nineteen-year police veteran who didn't "smoke, drink or chew," saw nine women in various stages of undress, and four men clustered nearby. He saw a voluptuous woman "standing in her underclothes," with one leg raised, rolling off a pair of tights; he saw a blonde with her "bosom exposed" and "no skirt" over her legs. He thought: "Orgy."

"It seems we are to have no privacy at all," shouted the most naked of the women, who added yet louder: "Get out!"

Chapman balled his fists; observers later said he turned white with rage. "You are a disgrace to your sex and you are not fit to call yourself a woman," he yelled. "I know what you are going to do in this room with all these men. You ought to be ashamed of yourself." He identified himself as a police captain.

The blonde ran behind some hanging tablecloths. Chapman turned to a young pretty brunette and asked: "Are you Little Egypt?" She indignantly said no.

An elegantly dressed twenty-five-year-old man, with hair parted down the middle, came up to Chapman, smiling; he thought Chapman was part of the evening's entertainment. His friend had threatened to hire a fake police officer to show up at midnight to "arrest" several guests. The man, host Herbert Barnum Seeley, thought Chapman, with bald head and abundant whiskers, was an actor hired to look just like vice crusader Anthony Comstock.

He very quickly realized his mistake.

Captain Chapman informed him that he had heard "immoral nude dancing" would be taking place here. Seeley, a grandson of P. T. Barnum, denied the accusation, pointing out to the captain that he had entered the *actresses' dressing room*. He said he was throwing a bachelor's dinner for his brother. Just then another guest, Horatio Harper, a partner in Harper & Brothers publishing house, rushed up to Chapman and grabbed him by the shoulder. He threatened to "toss him" out, even if he was a police officer. Harper was slurring his words.

Seeley tried to assure Chapman that a respectable show—banjoists, singers, dancers, monologuists—was going on in the *other* room, the dining room. He quickly introduced Chapman to a few of the celebrity performers, such as Minnie Renwood, who had played the ingénue Trilby for newfangled Vitascope moving pictures. Seeley added that the guests for this bachelor party were quite "prominent men"; did Chapman wish to meet them? The Captain angrily said he did not care how prominent they were.

He eventually agreed to walk with Seeley into the dining room, where the guests, who had been drinking for several hours, applauded. They too thought Chapman part of the entertainment. (Fifteen courses of food and drink and entertainment were planned.)

The dour Chapman quickly corrected them; he told them that his duty required him to investigate an accusation of "immoral" dancing. "A woman who would so degrade her sex to dance naked before a party of men . . ." his voice trailed off. "She is a direct insult to your wives and your mothers and your sisters," he said, staring at each of the men.

Harper tried to cut Chapman off but he refused to stop. He spoke of arresting any offenders. "I would not tolerate such a thing on Fifth Avenue any more than I would on Eleventh Avenue." A gray-mustached man (Seeley's father) rose and informed Chapman that no indecent behavior was planned. The others chimed in. (They were lying.)

Perhaps hoping to intimidate Chapman, Seeley introduced some of the guests, with names such as Edward Fish of the New York Stock Exchange and H. H. Flagler, the son of H. M. Flagler, a Standard Oil magnate and Rockefeller partner. (Roosevelt was *not* among them.)

They invited him to stay for the next act but he begged off, saying he had been awake since 7 a.m. and still had to tour the rest of his precinct. As he and his two detectives left through the dressing-room door, that first blonde, Cora Routt, who had been the least dressed, put her thumb to her nose and wiggled her fingers, and singsonged: "Good-bye, captain of the precinct." Chapman didn't reach his bed at the station house till 3 a.m. He thought the incident over.

———

Theodore Roosevelt was spending the weekend at Oyster Bay, frantically trying to enjoy himself and forget his frustrations. He "played bear" so enthusiastically with the children that he had an attack of asthma; he was chopping a dead tree for firewood when a heavy rotten branch crashed down on him; he was so energetically feeding logs into the roaring fireplace that he crashed his forehead into the stone mantel.

Amazingly in a city with more than a dozen active dailies, not a single newspaperman found out on Sunday about the Chapman raid. Word began trickling out Monday morning, creating a feeding frenzy just as Roosevelt arrived, banged up, at 300 Mulberry. Reporters descended on Herbert B. Seeley, on his father, and on Louis Sherry. All three expressed profound "indignation" and "outrage" over the "invasion" by a police captain "without a warrant," interrupting and spoiling a harmless private party at a preeminent venue. Restaurateur Louis Sherry huffed to the *Herald* that he catered to the "very best people in the city and no others."

Reporters rushed back to police headquarters and the Tenderloin precinct with these quotes and confronted the commissioners, Chief Conlin, and Captain Chapman, who all quickly realized that the coverage would be overwhelmingly hostile. "A perfect whirlwind of denunciation and invective has broken over the hapless head of Capt. George Chapman who made a raid and found nothing," wrote the *World.*

Had Roosevelt attended the party, he would have been labeled a hypocrite; instead, he found himself and his police force flayed for excessive zeal and Puritanism.

TR, one of whose great strengths was seeing all fights in black and white, found himself stuck in a decidedly *gray* fight. His lectures on morality and decency had led one of his captains to intrude on a possibly harmless private party and lecture the guests. Roosevelt uncharacteristically withheld judgment pending an investigation by Chief Conlin.

Complicating matters, TR had to leave in a few hours to honor his commitment to attend the Pilgrim dinner in Cincinnati for his patrons, the Storers.

———

With the Sherry's news breaking all around them, the Police Board tried to squeeze in a routine board meeting in the early afternoon before Roosevelt's departure.

Commissioners Parker and Grant officially complained that Frank Moss of the Parkhurst Society—despite being hired by the board—was refusing to turn over any evidence against Captain "Big Bill" Devery. Moss had brazenly told the two commissioners that he felt he could not trust them to weigh the material but not let it color their opinion at a subsequent trial. (An unnamed police official told the *Sun* the "amusing" part was that Moss feared prejudging while he and Parkhurst despised Devery "as the devil hates holy water.") Parker had retorted that if Moss didn't turn over something, then the Rules and Discipline committee would never bring *any* charges, especially since Devery's trial would cost the city even more than Eakins's.

The agenda turned to the board's bread and butter: promotions. The name topping the eligible list for sergeant was Commissioner Andrews's longtime helper, Roundsman John Tracy, the same man who had accompanied TR and Dr. Bigelow on a memorable midnight ramble.

Commissioner Parker—who had been amenable to the choices of Roosevelt and Andrews on more than a dozen recent captain and sergeant promotions—informed the board that he would vote against Roundsman Tracy. He claimed Tracy's long service at headquarters "unfitted him" for the sergeant's job at a precinct. Parker had originally agreed to a rating number that made the man eligible, but now he was blocking his promotion.

Andrews's thin waxed mustache vibrated with irritation. He and TR were furious. Colonel Grant—seemingly oblivious to the tension—smilingly suggested that the board jump around on the eligible list, that he had several other worthy candidates in mind.

Roosevelt snapped. He called Grant's suggestion "illegal" and stated that civil service rules required following the list in order. He also said he had read in a newspaper that a commissioner would try a ploy—jumping around the list—to promote men selected by the local Republican power brokers. (Days later, TR would write to Lodge: "That muttonhead Grant has suddenly gone in with Parker to carry out . . . the dictates of the Republican County managers, Lauterbach and Gruber; he is hoping to get something good from McKinley, and relies upon the backing of the local machine.")

Grant was flummoxed, but Commissioner Parker counterattacked for him. He once again accused TR of aiding Democrats. He said Tammany's "Big Tim" Sullivan had told him that Roosevelt had privately revealed the ratings for Big Tim's cousin.

The needle found its mark. Roosevelt, turning red in the face, denied the charge and said all he told Sullivan was that if he found his cousin worthy, he would back him with a good rating but that he could not reveal to Big Tim the ratings numbers or promote his cousin out of turn.

Then Roosevelt rose to leave. He said he had a train to catch. Apparently, Mr. and Mrs. Storer had prevailed upon him to leave Monday for his Tuesday night Cincinnati speech so as to give them more time together. He would be staying at their house in Walnut Hills.

Roosevelt, like Grant, was chasing a job in the McKinley White House.

Instead of cozying up to local Republicans about promotions, his patrons required a trip to the Midwest. During the next six days, when the Roosevelt reform police force would be flambéed over the Sherry's incident, TR would be at headquarters only the morning of Christmas Eve.

―――――

With Roosevelt gone by mid-afternoon, Parker took charge of the Chapman-Seeley investigation. Central office detectives quickly made a key discovery: belly dancer Little Egypt had indeed performed after Captain Chapman left. This was a bombshell. The "indignant" guests at the so-called innocent affair had possibly witnessed an indecent dance, if she performed fully nude. This fact, if proved, would provide complete vindication for the reform police raid.

The detectives tracked down Little Egypt to an apartment on Seventh Avenue and 50th Street where she was living under the name of "Mrs. Harper." They secretly brought her to headquarters in a closed carriage on Monday night, hustled her in the Mott Street back entrance away from reporters, and brought her to Commissioner Parker's office. Chief Conlin and his aide, Sergeant Flood, stood present in the small room as witnesses, along with a stenographer.

Little Egypt was really a Little Algerian. She said her birth name was Ashea Wabe; she refused to give her age but reporters later pegged it at around thirty-five. She was vivacious, petite, with long thick dark hair, and large dark eyes arced by heavy brows. She painted her lips deep garish red.

Dozens of women called themselves "Little Egypt" and it's impossible to know whether this Ashea Wabe danced under that name at the World's Fair in Chicago in 1893, but there's no doubt that Midwest performance in the midway set off a hoochie-coochie craze in America. Vaudeville marquees blazoned Little Egypts. The United States was playing catch-up to Europe's nineteenth-century fascination in art (harem paintings) and novels (Flaubert's *Salammbô*) with the sensual Near East.

Little Egypt sat in Parker's cramped little office; her eyes sparkled and she seemed to enjoy her situation at police headquarters, rather than dread it. Several times, she rose from her chair to demonstrate her dance movements. Once, she tried to draw "staid" Commissioner Parker's hands onto her body to show how the Seeley guests had touched her.

She spoke in North African French and heavily accented broken English, which the stenographer cleaned up into simple American phrases. She said her contract called for her to be paid $100 to dance two "nautch" dances. For the first, which she would dance on a stage, she would wear slippers and knee-high red stockings with no tights. "My thighs were to be covered with thin gauze from above the knees to the loins through which my body could be seen." (A modern couturier might call her outfit black diaphanous harem pants.)

Above her waist, she was to wear a small Zouave jacket that covered her breasts. Her midriff would be bare. She would wear a fez on her head.

For the second performance, her encore, to be done among the dinner guests, "I was to dance entirely naked except for silk stockings and slippers."

Basically, this little Algerian was admitting that she was *hired* to commit a crime.

She then told the story of what she actually did on Saturday night at Sherry's. She had arrived around midnight with her "colored maid." They were ushered to a private blue dressing room on the third floor and given champagne. An hour later, apparently when Captain Chapman was in the building, she was quickly hustled by two young employees to a small yellow garret room two floors higher.

She danced her first dance around 3:30 a.m. "I did not dance the [nude] encore as I was told there was danger of the police coming again." She said she repeated the first dance but did so off the stage and among the guests. She signed the affidavit "Egypt."

The woman was smuggled back out of 300 Mulberry. For a week, Parker and a very tight circle in the police department succeeded in keeping Little Egypt's confession a secret.

When the scandal broke for the public on Tuesday, December 22, most newspapers played it as the reform-crazed police violating the sanctity of Sherry's to fish for vice. Headlines blared: THE INVASION OF SHERRY'S (*Tribune*) and POLICE OUTRAGE (*World*). The *Washington Post* said the police treated New Yorkers as children, "to be watched, and guarded and punished for naughtiness." The paper blamed the "Roosevelt-Parkhurst combination" for inspiring Captain Chapman to the unimaginable effrontery of lecturing citizens mid-dinner and voicing his "shame" at their behavior.

Even the reform *New York Times* sniffed: "The bad taste shown by young men who degrade good victuals and drink by interpolations of vaudeville stupidities is a matter into which the Commissioners need not inquire." By the following day, it would call Sherry's "a house of entertainment of the highest character which is frequented every night during the fashion-able season by the wives and daughters of the best-known citizens of New York" and the paper would wonder about the quality of information that had prompted the captain to investigate.

The *World* tracked down the man who gave the tip to the police and found out that he was a rival theatrical agent, with a gripe over fees and lost clients.

Chief Conlin, Captain Chapman, and Commissioner Parker seethed at this portrayal of the police as bumbling intruders. (Roosevelt was in Cincin-nati.) All three were convinced that Chapman had courageously done his duty in investigating a possible crime at a public restaurant.

Parker gathered statements. He somehow convinced Herbert Barnum Seeley—a descendant of P. T. Barnum, the circus magnate, whose fortune totaled $3 million at his death—to admit that Little Egypt had danced. But he denied that she did anything lewd. "She proved so uninteresting and so unentertaining that at my request the manager called her off."

While the press harvested endless anonymous comments battering the police, none of the guests or the host or Louis Sherry brought formal charges against Captain Chapman. Very irritated, Conlin sent messengers with letters to all of the twenty-two guests asking them to give statements on Saturday, December 26. None of their names—besides that of Barnum Seeley—had appeared in print.

Clearly, none of the married or single dinner guests wanted this case to continue.

The *Herald* reported that on Wednesday afternoon some "brokers on the Consolidated Exchange" danced the "couchee-couchee" for twenty-nine-year-old bridegroom Clinton Barnum Seeley while someone sang, "She had never seen the Streets of Cairo / To the midway she had never been." The *World* reported the shady past of host Herbert Barnum Seeley, a West Point dropout who had apparently bilked a Newport heiress out of $900 in a race-track bookmaking scheme.

———

Roosevelt returned to headquarters the morning of Thursday, December 24; he had been guest of honor along with M. E. Ingalls, president of the Big Four Railroad, at the Ohio banquet. Bellamy Storer, having inherited the post from his father, was toastmaster.

TR arrived in New York and immediately tackled the issue that rankled him most . . . Parker's charge that he had helped Tammany's Big Tim Sullivan. Roosevelt met with Sullivan and issued a statement in Sullivan's name denying the charge. (Sullivan ducked out of the building.) Roosevelt stated that Parker had told "an absolute untruth."

Parker took a break from his Chapman investigations to issue a statement that Sullivan "in my room informed me" that Roosevelt revealed to him the rating given by each commissioner and Roosevelt had pointed out "that he had given [his] relative the highest rating of any of the commissioners."

TR left work early to start Christmas vacation. He didn't comment on the Sherry's raid.

———

The weather for the four days through the weekend was frigidly cold and bright, with dazzling snow everywhere; TR called it an "ideal Xmas." The family lit the candles on the tree and sang carols; TR, along with his oldest son, went skiing and chopped wood to feed the roaring fires. The children ate Ridley's striped candy canes before breakfast, and even Edith agreed to play a silly Parker Brothers game called Pillow-Dex that involved bopping balloons across a net set up on the dining room table.

On Monday morning, Roosevelt took the sleigh, train, ferry, and elevated car in from Oyster Bay. The commissioner arrived to discover that the investigation of the private dinner at Sherry's—of which he knew no details whatsoever beyond the newspapers—was rushing headlong toward a trial before his own police board. Roosevelt was furious.

Chief Conlin, wanting to resolve the matter, had already signed the paperwork to charge Chapman with entering Sherry's "without a warrant" and for "behaving in a rude, boisterous, insolent and arbitrary manner." Parker, as the sole member of the two-man Committee for Rules and Discipline who was not on vacation, had approved the charges and scheduled a trial for Thursday. (Grant was out west.)

An influential alderman, reform Republican Benjamin E. Hall, showed up at 300 Mulberry Street, as representative of Seeley and his guests, to protest against a trial. He spoke to Chief Conlin, telling him, in effect, that these powerful men, once disturbed mid-dinner, now wanted this latest disturbance to end, and he pointed out that Clinton Barnum Seeley's wedding was slated for Wednesday at Trinity Chapel. He told Conlin that none of them wanted their likenesses in the newspapers. "The higher the standing of the people, the greater the sensation."

The wealthy guests seemed dumbfounded that they would not be allowed to hurl charges of boorish behavior at the police department and then walk away. Conlin refused to drop the matter, said it needed airing at a trial. Alderman Hall walked through the building looking for commissioners. He spoke briefly to TR and made an appointment to see him on Wednesday. He found Andrews and made his case. Andrews climbed a flight of stairs to Roosevelt and the two conferred. They decided that the investigation was racing forward far too quickly, was being improperly handled solo by one commissioner (Parker), and that neither of them had been consulted.

They found Chief Clerk Kipp and called a "special" board meeting for 3 p.m. Commissioner Parker was informed in his office but he didn't go to the boardroom. A quorum of three was required, and Commissioner Grant was vacationing.

Roosevelt waited, then, rage mounting, with Kipp and Andrews trailing, race-walked to Parker's office, where they found him calmly reading. Roosevelt ordered Kipp to call the special meeting to order. Parker pointed out that they had recently passed a resolution—*in his absence*—that all board meetings must be held publicly in the boardroom. Nonetheless, Andrews, exasperated, shouted a resolution. "I move that the [Chapman] charges be referred to President Roosevelt for examination and that all proceedings in the case [including] subpoenas, be suspended for the present."

Parker calmly told Kipp to mark him "Absent" for this meeting, meaning they had no quorum. Andrews and Roosevelt started shouting. When they stopped, Parker offered to attend a board meeting in the public boardroom in five minutes. He showed up as agreed. Andrews brought the same resolution to the floor; TR and Andrews voted in favor and so did . . . the exasperating Parker.

Parker told the assembled newspapermen the board should hurry. "The papers have fiercely denounced the Captain, the Chief of Police and the Department, and we ought to learn the truth." Roosevelt and Andrews announced they would immediately begin their own investigation. (Neither man knew about Little Egypt.) The words *stalling* and *cover-up* sprang into the following days' newspapers. Adjudged the *World*: ALDERMAN HALL PULLS WIRES FOR HIS FRIEND AND CLIENT SEELEY: ROOSEVELT'S FINGER IN THE PIE.

Despite the Christmas season, relations between Parker and Roosevelt were hitting new lows. Parker's irritating precision, his marshaling of obscure facts, repeatedly pricked TR's passionate beliefs and bluster. Then on Tuesday up bobbed the ghost of McMorrow, the allegedly bribe-paying patrolman, to make matters even worse between the two commissioners. Back in April, TR's probe into the $200 bribe had fizzled, undermining his case against Parker. Mayor Strong had *still* not rendered a verdict about Parker's removal.

TR had left the investigation open for six months, and now the board was cleaning out a backlog of *all* untried cases. Commissioner Andrews presided over the hearing that morning. McMorrow's lawyer demanded to interrogate Roosevelt since Roosevelt had received the original confession, which formed the only evidence against his client.

During the course of the questioning, the lawyer noticed that parts of two pages of the four-page confession seemed to have been cut out. He asked Roosevelt about it. Roosevelt replied that McMorrow had said that he "understood" that his bribe money was headed to a commissioner's secretary but he had offered no proof. "I brought it before the board and at the request of the commissioner I cut the pages out."

The lawyer asked: "Have you any objection to revealing the name of the commissioner mentioned?"

Roosevelt: "Commissioner Parker."

The words lingered in the room; the lawyer seemed surprised that TR had answered the question. The day's headline in the *Herald* would be: PARKER'S NAME CONNECTED WITH CHARGES OF BRIBERY, and in the *World*: ROOSEVELT'S QUEER STAB AT PARKER. Since the charges hadn't panned out, Parker's name had never been made public.

Parker was, as usual, attending to business elsewhere but word snaked through the building to his secretary, Louis Posner, who relayed the information. Later that day, Parker issued an indignant statement harshly criticizing Roosevelt. He pointed out that he was the only commissioner to oppose McMorrow's appointment, because he had learned that the man had been fired from the Eighth Avenue Railroad. He said he didn't know—from April to November—that a *written confession against him* existed and he flatly denied asking Roosevelt to tear out or cover up any evidence.

The next day, the antagonists resumed the scuffle.

The board met at its usual time on Wednesday, handling ninety minutes of business. Roosevelt, resisting pressure from wealthy Republicans, voted along with Andrews and Parker to bring Captain Chapman up on charges, to allow him to clear his name or be convicted. As the meeting wound down,

Parker mentioned that he wanted a word with Roosevelt. Commissioner Andrews disgustedly requested permission to adjourn the meeting so he could leave the two men alone (with reporters).

Parker asked why Roosevelt had concealed McMorrow's written confession from him for so long. TR replied that he thought Parker had seen it.

Parker said he clearly recalled talking to Roosevelt about bribery cases. "We joked about it . . . I said the word was that you were the only commissioner not bribed because you didn't need the money."

Then Parker leveled the charge that Roosevelt didn't mention the confession because he was trying to "trap" him and bring that case to the mayor. Parker added that Lincoln Steffens of the *Evening Post* had revealed to him last spring that Roosevelt and Andrews were searching for crimes by Parker and "were greatly disappointed when McMorrow fell through."

Roosevelt slammed his hand down on the table and denied it. He demanded that Steffens be brought in and questioned.

Parker then brought up the cut-out pages. TR said he thought it was Parker's wish, to protect his young secretary. Parker asked if any copies of those pages still existed. Roosevelt thought that his secretary, Minnie Kelly, might have one. Parker said: "I should consider it a great favor to have it so that I can make it public."

They wrangled some more over Big Tim Sullivan; they wrangled over several newspaper quotes; they wrangled over the sergeant promotions. Along the way, something must have snapped in Roosevelt; he must have had some inkling of the fruitlessness of the endless bickering, or some faint memory of advice from Edith and Cabot Lodge.

He turned to his fellow commissioner and said: "Parker, I feel toward you as Tommy Atkins did toward Fuzzy Wuzzy in Kipling's poem after he had smashed the British square. 'To fight 'im 'arf an hour will last me 'arf a year.' I am going out of town to-night but I suppose we will have another row at the meeting next Wednesday."

Commissioner Parker laughed and replied, "I'll be glad to see you when you get back, Roosevelt."

TR tried desperately to enjoy New Year's at Oyster Bay. He was welcoming the onset of 1897 amid gorgeous snow, but the rite, this year as always, coincided with ending his season at Sagamore Hill and closing up the house. After January 1, he and Edith would be moving the clan back to Bamie's on Madison Avenue for at least the next four months.

Just two days into the New Year, Roosevelt unburdened himself to Lodge.

"Here matters are worse than ever," he wrote in a letter, inadvertently mis-dated January 2, 1896. "The [Republican] machine is really infamous. Not only do they back Parker, but they have induced Grant by the promise of their aid with McKinley, and he has openly gone in with Parker. I have said the latter is a liar a dozen times; I cannot shoot him, or engage in a rough-and-tumble with him—I couldn't even as a private citizen, still less as the chief police officer of the city."

This bleak portrait of his life as commissioner served as a not-so-subtle reminder to Lodge to please try to get him out of New York and back to Washington.

———

The same night that TR wrote to Lodge from Oyster Bay, a boxer fighting in Manhattan at the Broadway Athletic Club was knocked into a fatal coma during a police-sanctioned fight. Many in the press leaped to blame Roosevelt.

He had been outspoken on the topic less than two months earlier.

"When I was at Harvard and sparred for the championship I suffered a heavier punishment than any man there did. And I have been knocked out at polo twice for a ten times longer period than Choynski was knocked out for. I don't care very much for a professional sport of any kind but I thoroughly believe in boxing as I believe in football and other manly games."

TR noted to the *World* that thirteen people had recently died by drowning while ice-skating on frozen ponds but that didn't mean Americans should stop ice-skating.

———

The Chapman case took a sudden dramatic turn between the time Roosevelt left for New Year's vacation and when he returned. The *World* tracked down Little Egypt and somehow got a copy of H. Barnum Seeley's long statement to Parker. "Little Egypt's Own Story/She Was to Appear in Gauze . . . /Herbert Seeley Gives the Names of All His Guests . . . Parker Wins and Chapman's Trial Is Ordered."

Seeley was quoted as saying he didn't want a "Sunday school" but rather a "gentlemanly stag entertainment." He delved in great detail into his quest for performers. He complained that Chapman's intrusion, especially his lecture, "threw a great deal of damper upon the dinner and the spirits of the company could not be restored."

Many clubmen considered his voluntary revealing of the guest list as extremely bad form. Names included Marmaduke Tilden of Larchmont, New York; A. Gould Hamilton of South Orange; H. H. Flagler of Park Avenue; E. P. Delanoy, office at 1 Wall Street. Ten of the twenty-two guests were married; Wall Street dominated the occupations, though most were independently wealthy. Ages, besides the bridegroom's, ranged from thirty to fifty-five.

The *World* interviewed Little Egypt at her apartment on Seventh Avenue, and she reenacted the couchee-couchee dance for the reporter. In her broken English, she told him she loved to dance "in zee all-togezher" (i.e., nude) and could not understand what the "fuss" was all about.

Within hours, public opinion took an abrupt U-turn. The guests were no longer wealthy men at a harmless but tawdry dinner; they were deviants befouling Sherry's.

The Chapman trial began on Thursday, January 7. Commissioner Grant would preside, with Commissioner Parker at his elbow. Andrews and Roosevelt did not plan on attending.

Many people eagerly awaited the trial to hear under oath from the mouths of the vaudeville stars all the (sordid) details. *Town Topics* couldn't wait for the verdict so it delivered its own: "We find all the diners guilty but as all the married ones have doubtless by this time received adequate correction from their wives, the matter need go no further."

Oscar Hammerstein couldn't wait, either. The theater impresario, who had opened the enormous blocklong Olympia entertainment complex, with a music hall, restaurant, theater, and roof garden, at 44th and Broadway, debuted *Silly's Dinner*, starring Little Egypt playing herself. The whiskered police captain and one especially drunken guest, who dances while passed out on the floor, almost steal the show from Little Egypt's red stockings, which can be seen dancing suggestively below a carefully placed curtain. Roosevelt's police were now vaudeville comedians.

Spectators lined up at 1 p.m., two hours early, at 300 Mulberry Street to land seats for the Barnum-Seeley circus/trial in the police hearing room. (Commissioner Grant would ban female spectators on the second day.) Two top lawyers made surprise appearances. The Seeley guests had retained Colonel E. C. James (of the Devery trial) to help the police department with its prosecution of Chapman, and introduce every legal trick to keep the twenty-two blueblood guests off the stand. Little Egypt, who had blithely confessed to being hired to violate the law in her statement to Parker, retained florid, diamond-decked man-mountain William Howe of Howe & Hummel.

Close to 3 p.m., the vaudeville femmes fatales—all in elaborate hats and brightly colored theatrical dresses—began arriving; many of them were escorted by a stage-door Johnny. The dinner guests, impeccably garbed and sheepish, already milled in the hallway. Sometime after 3 p.m. a carriage rolled up and the acrobatic Algerian dancer slowly descended, bundled in layers under a hat "heavy with black ostrich plumes," accompanied by her maid.

Since witnesses were forbidden to hear the testimony of other witnesses, a court officer guided the dancers and singers to a large police classroom, called the School of Instruction. Just as the trial was called to order at 3:20 p.m., someone realized that the twenty-two Seeley guests were also "witnesses" and therefore must leave the hearing room. A clerk began shepherding the dignified men toward the room already containing Little Egypt and a half dozen beautiful young women. "Gee! I wish I was a witness," someone shouted. Commissioners Grant and Parker had trouble suppressing laughs.

Parker whispered to a clerk, who whispered to Captain Chapman, who walked to the School of Instruction and guided the female performers out of that room and up to the boardroom; he posted two guards.

The trial would occupy four and a half days, and the witnesses, with only minor discrepancies, would describe in detail the notorious night's entertainment. Herbert Barnum Seeley had auditioned and hired a male singer and half a dozen female vaudeville acts to perform during the gaps of a fifteen-course banquet. For instance, he booked the Leigh Sisters to do their famed umbrella dance—first, only one pair of legs can be seen behind a large umbrella, then a third leg emerges, then a fourth, often at surprising angles. Miss Lottie Mortimer would sing the saucy "Jusqu'a-Là" ("Down to There") describing an accident with her bathing costume while swimming in the Narragansett; Daniel Quinn, accompanied by banjoists, would sing "Put Me Off at Buffalo" and "Beer, Beer, Glorious Beer."

All the females wore costumes acceptable on the stage. Observers, however, agreed that the entertainment, in a handful of areas, veered toward the "indecent." The host hired plump and pretty Vitascope star Minnie Renwood to play an ingénue "Santa Claus Up to Date" and hand out gifts. He and a friend wrote out four signs to pin to her costume of mismatched tights and an army jacket. The *World* called the signs "bestial in the extreme" and refused to print them; that left half a million readers to wonder.

Santa (Minnie) also handed out twenty-two gifts, aptly selected for each guest, to be given while she recited some comic rhymes. Several newspapers called the verses "vile" and one paper judged the gifts "obscene . . . positively bestial for a man to receive from the hands of a woman." This self-censorship left readers assuming the worst: erotic statuettes, phalluses, Spanish fly ointment?

A century-plus later it is a challenge to understand the Victorian fuss. The four signs were eventually revealed: MILK BELOW, THE HEART OF MARYLAND, HELD BY THE ENEMY, and SECRET SERVICE. Barnum's grandson unconvincingly swore the placing of the signs on Minnie's torso was random. The twenty-two gifts included a toy piano, a drum, a box of blocks, a miniature cradle with twins, an ear syringe.

Also pushing propriety was one elaborate drinking toast. Seeley had hired Lottie Mortimer—an established vaudeville star with a prominent nose and oversized mouth, whose specialties were songs and "coon monologues"—to deliver it. No newspapers would print it; the *Sun* described it as "pure filth."

Miss Mortimer, who clearly had a gift for comedy, mentioned that several guests had requested pencils and asked her to repeat it slowly so they could write it on their menus. She referred to Little Egypt's trousers as "mosquito netting." She also recalled that during a break half a dozen impatient, tipsy banqueters had clustered around her and asked what would happen if one of the two straps of her clingy bodice broke. She told them, "Nothing" several times, but they didn't believe her. "Some of them felt something would happen and so they cut it." She paused. "Nothing happened."

Another Victorian point of honor was why four men were in the women's dressing room. One actress claimed the talent agent always sang out: "Ladies, I am coming through; put something around you." This drew an unexpected laugh.

Ultimately, the vulgarity of the night hinged on what the Barnum heir had hired Little Egypt to do, and what she had actually performed. She was, appropriately enough, the last headliner at the trial, on Tuesday, January 12.

Her larger-than-life lawyer, William Howe, was sporting diamonds on both hands, at both cuffs, and a robin's-egg blue tie; his gold stickpin—about two inches long—depicted a squatting devil with ruby eyes and an emerald tail.

Little Egypt, while taking center stage, opened her sealskin coat to reveal she was wearing a silver-and-blue-striped bodice that appeared as if she had been "poured into it." The press called her facial expression half defiance, half amusement. "She is a strange sort of creature, with a swarthy face that would be positively ugly were it not lighted up by a pair of big bright black eyes." The fifty spectators drank in her exotic appearance. They craned and tilted to hear better so as to try to decipher her mangled French-English accent.

She said the agent Phipps had asked her to dance for a "party of artistes" at Sherry's. She was supposed to do her dance and then "a leetle Egyptian pose on a leetle pedestal in zee altogether." She was asked to define "in zee altogether" (a phrase made famous by Du Maurier's massive best-seller *Trilby*).

Little Egypt replied: "Oh, monsieur, just a little pose in zee altogether, a leetle Egyptian slave girl, comprenez vous? The pose in zee altogether was for zee encore." She added she would only do what was proper for Art. She said Captain Chapman's arrival had nixed that part of her act; so instead she climbed down from the stage to dance.

LAWYER: Did any of the guests put their hands on you?
EGYPT: Oui, oui he just take me that way there on my leetle leg.
LAWYER: Did he pinch your leg?
EGYPT: Oui.

She was asked if the guests said anything to her. "Zee gentlemen zay: You no dance leetle Egypt. You a leetle black nun." No one was certain what much of her testimony meant, not even the translator. She had clarified "leetle" but soon after, the defense rested its case. The climax was a bit anticlimactic, which was probably how the Seeley guests felt that night.

Commissioner Grant adjourned the proceedings for the evening. Little Egypt and Cora Routt rushed over to the Olympia to perform in *Silly's Dinner*. The *Sun* stated that the trial had "occupied all the time of the police commission for nearly a week and . . . has been the principal topic of conversation in the city all of that time."

During the trial's final half day of lawyer motions and testimony by bit players, Commissioner Grant called a ten-minute recess so he could very briefly attend a Police Board meeting. Many of the reporters for the Sherry's trial trooped with him to the boardroom. With this press audience, board members indulged in a little stage-whispered banter. Roosevelt turned to

Grant, the judge: "Is it true that the Seeleyites [i.e., the guests] have been closeted in the School of Instruction with Little Egypt?"

Grant replied that they had been cooped together only briefly at the beginning. "Nothing is so laughable," chipped in Commissioner Parker, "as to see the regiment of disconsolate chappies filing through the courtroom after something to eat or drink." All three commissioners laughed. Roosevelt commented that he expected "the trial will have a healthy effect upon dinners of this kind in the future."

Grant walked back downstairs and resumed the trial. After Colonel James recalled the assistant manager at Sherry's and two theatrical agents— all denying any nudity—he rested his case. As the dozen lawyers and several dozen newspapermen and the participants began to file out, it was realized that the twenty-two Seeley guests and host had been forgotten. They had spent four and a half humiliating days waiting to testify and had never testified. A court official unlocked the door and let them out. They walked out of the building, refusing to comment but "smiling."

Protocol called for the commissioners to review the trial testimony, then render a verdict, which they would . . . in two weeks.

Captain Chapman, while awaiting his fate, did not slow his quest for moral purity; he started a new campaign to root streetwalkers out of the Tenderloin. On Monday, January 18, around 10 p.m., his policemen arrested twenty-four women. "This man," Eva McMonigal said, pointing to plainclothes detective Leazenbee, "came to me and asked me where I was going. I told him I was going home, whereupon he seized me by the arm and took me to the station." The judge—with great irritation—dismissed that charge and the charges against five others out of the two dozen arrested. This led the *Herald* to do some math and postulate that twenty-five of every 100 women arrested by Chapman's patrolmen would be innocent.

The newspaper warned that shopgirls couldn't return home alone, and wives with husbands working evenings couldn't visit friends or run errands because "unscrupulous" policemen wanted to "make a record" number of arrests. One woman wrote in: "Will it be necessary for a woman [wanting to walk alone at night] to obtain a permit from this crass executor of the law to prevent her arrest as a member of the demi-monde?"

Chapman vowed to keep arresting disreputable women in his precinct. He had come through the trial unscathed except for the revelation that he had exchanged photos with an eighteen-year-old dancer; he claimed he admired her purity. The *Herald* published a map of his precinct (14th to 42nd Street, Park Avenue to Seventh Avenue) alerting single women to the dangers of going there at night without an "escort."

———

The escalating war against prostitution, however, took a sudden surprising toll. The Parkhurst Society's lead investigator went insane. Arthur "Angel" Dennett, undercover crusader who had masterminded the brothel probes in the precincts of Devery and Eakins, began babbling about being the Count of Monte Cristo during a meeting with the mayor.

Dennett was a lanky, animated man from New Hampshire who rarely slept at night; his specialty was wandering the streets till dawn dressed as a gentleman looking for streetwalkers. He often lulled the young ladies into sharing details of their lives by warmly praising their beauty or offering them sympathy for their condition.

Reverend Parkhurst wrote an open letter to the newspapers, blaming the Angel's madness on the slack police department.

"We do not quite understand why the men on our staff should have to work day and night and grind themselves into insane asylums doing police duty for a city that is supposed to be equipped with a reform Police Board and a reform Chief of Police."

Parkhurst complained that he had expected widespread vice under Tammany but not under a reform administration. He targeted the "disintegration of the police board" for "demoralizing" the police force. "Speaking in behalf of an indignant community and in behalf of the blackmailed and persecuted, we demand that they should find some way out of their quarrel."

Chief Conlin testily denied any responsibility for Dennett's delusions, and pointed out that the police, especially the reform captains, had repeatedly cooperated with him.

The *World* found one of Dennett's most recent reports, and that document offered a huge hint as to the frustrations that might have tipped him over to madness.

> The streets of New York City are infested at the present time by throngs of women and girls of low character. Their number has increased greatly in the last few months, especially on Broadway in the vicinity of 34th Street, on Third and Sixth Avenues, and on 42nd

Street. The increase is startling and from personal investigation I am prepared to say that it can be attributed almost entirely to the Raines hotels.

He blamed not police corruption but that paradigm of unintended consequences, the Raines Law. The Angel stated that 95 percent of streetwalkers now used Raines hotels, and added that the even greater evil was that "semi-respectable" women would go there. He said he questioned 100 prostitutes on where they first "became vicious" (i.e., lost their virtue, trafficked sex for money) and sixty-eight replied that it was in "easy-going hotels" like these.

After acting violently during a sanity hearing, the Angel was committed to the Bloomingdale Asylum for the Insane.

————

Judgment came for Chapman. Although Colonel James submitted a long, well-argued brief defending the dinner guests' right to privacy, Commissioner Grant didn't bother to read it before the day of the vote, February 3.

Commissioner Andrews glanced at it and quoted the maxim "A man's home is his castle," but Grant cavalierly quipped: "Well, if a man uses his home for immoral purposes, I think the police ought to break into it." Subtle Parker then added: "That may be bad law but it is good doctrine . . . it is easy to raise a storm against the captain but Captain Chapman did what mighty few captains would do."

The commissioners were in harmony over a policeman's right to investigate an immoral performance in a hired room of a public restaurant.

They voted 4–0 in favor of acquitting Captain Chapman.

Roosevelt, though he said he wished Chapman had not exchanged photographs with one of the performers, hailed the verdict and the propriety of the raid. "If he erred at all," said TR, "he erred on the right side."

WHERE'S THE EXIT?

Roosevelt's quest to return to D.C. as assistant secretary of the navy stalled sometime during that odd four-month interregnum between post-election euphoria and the inauguration of a new president. Senator Lodge was working the room, along with several other senators, as were the Storers, but they all found the path blocked. Lodge unsuccessfully probed for concrete answers. Other names were bobbing up, such as Henry W. Raymond, who had served in the cabinet under Secretary of the Navy Tracy. TR began to downgrade his chances.

Meanwhile, the reform board moved to put Big Bill Devery back on trial, which would mark his fourth major legal battle in four years. Frank Moss of the Parkhurst Society had finally delivered the evidence to the Rules and Discipline committee of Parker and Grant, who approved moving forward. Chief Peter Conlin agreed to bring official charges of neglect of duty (i.e., not closing dozens of brothels in 1893).

Commissioner Andrews set Devery's trial for Friday, February 12.

———

Just as the ruckus over the Seeley dinner was dying down, a new banquet took center stage. "New York is now convulsed over the Bradley Martin ball, owing to that fool [Rev.] Rainsford having denounced it," Roosevelt wrote to his sister, still in Europe. "I shall have to protect it by as many police as if it were a strike."

Mr. and Mrs. Bradley Martin, at a time when thousands of men had recently lined up to earn fifteen cents an hour shoveling snow during a blizzard, planned to spend $100,000 on a gala historical costume ball at the Waldorf. The champagne would be 1884 Moet & Chandon Brut Imperial; courses would include Lobster Newburg, Baltimore terrapin, and canvasback duck.

"New York is credited by outsiders with being ostentatious, luxurious and unpatriotic," observed William S. Rainsford of St. George's Protestant Episcopal Church at Stuyvesant Square. "I think such charges are untrue . . . [but] the offering of any excuse to bring them should be avoided, especially now when there is so much suffering and so great a tendency to distinguish between the masses and the classes."

Editorial writers pointed out that the money spent on a single costume, even stripped of jewelry, could feed a New York family for years. Unlike the Astors, Theodore and Edith turned down the invitation, although his sister Corinne and her husband, Douglas, accepted.

Rumors floated of anarchists' bombs, of angry riots. Around 11 p.m. on Wednesday, February 10, carriages began rolling to the manager's entrance of the Waldorf on 33rd Street west of Fifth Avenue. As crowds gathered to gawk, the police decided to close 33rd Street from Fifth Avenue to Broadway.

Though at least 1,200 invitations were sent, the controversy whittled the attendees down to 700, with far more females than males. A profusion of Marie Antoinettes mingled with the rare Sir Francis Drake. Men in powdered wigs and silk ruffles wore high heels with diamonds in the buckle.

Mrs. Bradley Martin, as Mary, Queen of Scots, accompanied by John Jacob Astor, led the opening quadrille of honor at midnight, to a minuet; a Hungarian orchestra played hidden behind streaming vines of roses; the three quadrilles, of elaborate formality, preceded the two-hour dinner. The cotillion started at 3 a.m. and general dancing at 4 a.m.

Town Topics awarded its unofficial first costume prize to James H. Beekman for his Henry VIII and to Miss Kate Brice for her Spanish infanta after a painting by Velázquez. But *Town Topics* couldn't be all smiles. It slapped Otto Cushing of Boston for indecent exposure. Mr. Cushing was dressed as a sixteenth-century Italian falconer, wearing tights, a short leather vest, and a small cap. A stuffed falcon was perched on his shoulder. Despite the eye-catching bird, observers couldn't help noticing that his dance steps set certain southerly parts in motion. "The costume, what there was of it, was a faithful copy of an old picture but it was a little too historically correct for these modern and more Puritanical days," harrumphed the magazine.

Reaction to the ball ran the gamut. "The working people do not read the accounts of great fetes like this with bitterness in their hearts," wrote *Munsey's Magazine*. "The Country is still young enough for any American to believe that he or his son has the possibility to achieve anything."

But on the negative side, the police were almost universally criticized for closing a public street to protect a private party. A burly sergeant stopped an acquaintance of Roosevelt from walking west on 33rd Street. "Dear Roosevelt," he wrote in an open letter published in the *World*, "you have bitten off bear's heads and slung Indians forty feet by the scalp lock. What would you do if a man stopped you and forbade your passing through a public street in an orderly manner?" The fellow reckoned that Roosevelt "would make a fuss beautiful to behold."

TR found the issue irritating. "The complaint is such nonsense that it hardly deserves an answer," he told reporters, and added, not entirely convincingly: "Precisely the same course is followed when there is a clambake or a picnic on the East side, a fire or any gathering of any kind." This led pundits to envision the police protecting a ball in Hogan's Alley.

Roosevelt later delivered a bit more candid opinion of the whole event to his sister. He and Edith attended a dinner party at the Bronsons' that included the Bradley Martins. (Mr. Martin himself escorted Edith into the dining room.) "We were immensely amused by the intense seriousness with which they regard themselves and their ball."

———

Citing an excessive caseload, Commissioner Andrews rescheduled Devery's trial for the middle of March. This would also give prosecutor Moss more time to prepare.

The reform board, with the legislature back in session and possibly sharpening an ax, rushed to institute more innovations. Commissioner Andrews—fresh from his bicycle squad's success—wanted to follow the lead of Europe and adopt the Bertillon system of identification. In the 1880s, Alphonse Bertillon, working in the Paris Prefecture of Police, had pioneered an exhaustively thorough system of anthropometric measurements, as many as 243 per criminal, although as few as two dozen would suffice.

For instance, the technician used special calipers to do several skull measurements as well as gauging the length of each ear. Arm spread was recorded and trunk height while sitting; eye color was minutely described. The recording process could take forty-five minutes for each criminal, especially with uncooperative ones. (An experiment at Sing Sing prison, taking the Bertillon statistics of 1,500 prisoners, had found no two exactly alike.) The system, though time-consuming, was considered foolproof.

The board authorized Andrews to build a Bertillon measurement room and combine it with the police force's first in-house photo studio. Currently, detectives marched handcuffed prisoners two blocks through the streets to the public Norman Coe photo studio at Broadway and Bleecker. There, hardened criminals waited their turn among women and frightened children. Several copies were made; one was placed in the Rogues' Gallery, along with an accompanying card detailing height, weight, hair color, eye color, scars, tattoos.

Andrews ordered the equipment and oversaw the construction, and on Monday, February 15—after all the requisite gee-whiz articles on Bertillon in newspapers—Commissioner Andrews ordered Chief Conlin to begin sending criminals to the top-floor studio and measurement room.

Chief Conlin refused.

Andrews was furious. "The chief has not felt inclined to regard my instructions," he told reporters, "and as a result, the outside expenditures for photographing criminals, which amount to $15 or $20 a day, continue to go on, and the gallery with three or four men detailed there, is idle." He added ominously: "If Chief Conlin continues to disobey orders, something may drop on him."

Conlin said he took orders from the *entire* board and not from one individual police commissioner. His refusal wasn't cavalier. Andrews had staffed the studio with four men reporting to him, including a police surgeon who was very friendly to TR and Andrews. The head of the detectives, Stephen O'Brien, found it intolerable to have to bring criminals to get their photos taken by a unit controlled by two commissioners; he also regarded Bertillon as a big waste of time. (Veteran cops of that era, such as Thomas Byrnes and Detective Sergeant O'Brien, believed that the current system worked fine and that repeat criminals rarely fooled them with dyed beards or massive weight gain.) O'Brien had written two notes to Parker, who in turn had advised Conlin, who found himself yet again in the middle. "Roosevelt and I instantly recognized Parker's fine Italian hand," Andrews later surmised.

The story—with all its innuendo and backbiting—raced through the department on Tuesday, February 16. Sometime that day, the normally mild-mannered Chief Conlin snapped. He was already accused of being Parker's puppet, which he hotly denied.

"I dislike to be made use of as a missile to be thrown from one Commissioner to the other, or to interfere in any shape with their petty quarrels," he told a reporter for an evening newspaper. "I am expected to look after the rank and file and to protect life and property. The constant bickerings between men who know better, not only demoralize the force but interfere with me in the discharge of my duty."

At the regular Wednesday board meeting, Parker blandly asked Andrews for a report on the status of introducing Bertillon. Andrews refused. TR asked Andrews whether the board had not already voted to adopt the system. Andrews replied, "A year ago." Parker pointed out that the resolution authorized Andrews *only to purchase equipment.*

PARKER: We ought to know what has been done.
ANDREWS: I will not get into a discussion.
PARKER: No discussion is necessary.
ANDREWS: I would not get into a discussion with *you*, anyhow.
PARKER: Then you may continue in a state of semi-barbarism.

The board president reluctantly agreed to allow Parker a brief time to review the new Bertillon system before the board voted on whether to adopt it.

That night, Roosevelt—in limbo over his own job prospects—stewed over Chief Conlin's harsh comments and over his insulting refusal to follow Andrews's request. The next day, Thursday, which happened to be Roosevelt's turn as trial judge, he arrived early from his sister's house at 62nd Street. He reached Mulberry Street and barked out a command to a messenger to request Chief Conlin to come immediately to his office.

Conlin took the elevator up. Roosevelt asked Conlin point blank if he had indeed made those remarks about "petty quarrels" and "constant bickerings" among board members.

"I have no explanation whatever to make," Conlin brusquely replied.

"What!" exclaimed TR, "I insist, sir, that you make an explanation."

Conlin refused. "That is something that I must respectfully decline to do," he said, adding if the board passed a resolution requiring a statement from him, he would deliver one but that he could not be called upon to make statements to individual board members.

Agog, TR threatened to bring up Conlin's insubordination at the next board meeting. The chief departed.

Later that same day, Roosevelt was sitting behind the judge's desk hearing testimony about a policeman caught napping, when a mailman arrived with a letter for the commissioner. As the federal employee in his gray uniform approached to deliver the envelope, the complaint clerk shouted: "Take off your hat." The man ignored him and kept walking. Roosevelt echoed the command in an even sharper tone. "Take off your hat!" The man snapped off a fine salute. "Excuse me, we never remove our hats while on duty," he said calmly. "They are part of our uniform."

The letter carrier handed the envelope to the commissioner and then slid a memorandum book onto the desk for a signature. "Humph, I thought you were a witness," muttered TR, while signing. The man exited, head held high.

TR immediately called for his secretary, Minnie Kelly, and angrily dictated a letter, in front of all the accused policemen and reporters, to local postmaster Charles W. Dayton, inquiring whether hats were required to be worn at all times. He mentioned possibly writing to the United States postmaster general. After he finished dictating, he ordered the roundsman manning the door not to allow any more postal carriers to enter until this controversy was straightened out.

Newspapers raced to lampoon Roosevelt for his lordly ways. One cartoon revealed that the proper way for a letter carrier to approach "King Roosevelt" was to prostrate himself full length on the floor and look downward, while meekly reaching up to hand over the letter. Other panels showed policemen kneeling to him and citizens bowing deeply.

The *Washington Post* picked up the item and enthused: "A fight between Teddy and the United States would be quite exciting."

However, before any battleships could be launched local postmaster Dayton announced that, quite the contrary, letter carriers were expected to be polite, which included doffing their caps indoors. Badge No. 1626 was identified as a "substitute carrier" named M. F. Donovan, who became a folk hero in certain unreformable wings of the police department.

Chief Conlin, too, refused to prostrate himself. On Monday, February 22, the Bertillon room stood ready, painted white, packed with calipers, scales, cameras, equipped with wall-mounted sliding oak devices to measure arm span and trunk height. It was staffed with four men but not a single police officer brought in a single criminal to be measured. The marooned men practiced on each other.

Roosevelt and Andrews deeply resented the waste and the slight by the police chief, and they weighed their options. They quickly and surreptitiously consulted the city's corporation counsel, Francis Scott, and drew up three specific counts: insubordination, disrespect toward his superior officer, and conduct unbecoming an officer. The board's feud would now undermine the one high-ranking officer functioning fairly smoothly during all their caviling, quibbling, and head-butting.

All four commissioners attended the board meeting the next day. Commissioner Andrews slowly, with a certain gravitas, read the three pages of charges against Chief Conlin. TR and Andrews called Conlin's conduct "highly insubordinate," "subversive of discipline," and "totally destructive of . . . respect for authority." The typewritten charges described how Conlin "publicly" accused the board of "interfering with him in the due performance of his duties" and that Chief Conlin offered "no denial, explanation or apology" despite an "opportunity specifically given . . . [to him] by the President of the board."

The charges warned that if this conduct was condoned or overlooked, it could act as an "example for the 5,000 members of this Department" who "with equal impunity" might follow it. Conlin's behavior "deserves severe censure and increases in gravity with the age, rank and experience of the officer concerned."

As soon as Andrews finished, Commissioner Grant moved that the resolution be tabled to "lie over." Board president Roosevelt explained that the mayor's office had approved the charges, and he asked whether Grant meant he wanted to hold them "until the next meeting" for discussion. Grant replied, "No, I want to kill it."

Some newspapermen thought they perceived Parker smiling behind his fingers, as he abruptly called for a vote on the motion. The tally came down: two in favor of tabling the charges (Parker and Grant); two opposed (Roosevelt and Andrews). The clerk explained that though the charges were not approved or tabled, they could still be advanced again. Roosevelt said he reserved that right, possibly at the next meeting.

Had Grant, with his swing vote, chosen to approve the charges, Roosevelt might have had the leverage to negotiate Conlin's retirement. Conspiracy theorists at the newspapers thought perhaps job hunter TR wanted to oust the *Democratic* police chief and replace him with a *Republican* to curry favor with the local Republican party and Boss Platt.

But now, ironically, Conlin absolutely could not retire and still get his ample half-salary pension until these charges were resolved, one way or another. Conlin, ill frequently last year, had mentioned retirement to friends. If this was Parker's "fine Italian hand" again, the movement was well played.

Later that afternoon, Chief Conlin, who by law controlled transfers, not promotions, transferred the four officers in the Bertillon/photo studio into the detective bureau. Their new boss, Chief of Detectives O'Brien, ordered them to carry on their work.

The following morning, Thursday, February 25, a detective finally brought a crook to the new Bertillon studio on the top floor. James "Red" Sullivan, a thirty-seven-year-old ex-convict charged with robbing a drunken man of twenty-five dollars on Park Row, was the first criminal to be measured on Bertillon standards and first man photographed by the "Police Photographic Bureau." The officers took half an hour to fill in thirty-nine blanks in centimeters, from his arm span—1 meter, 65 centimeters—to his 14.2-centimeter head width, to his 6.9-centimeter right ear length. Under "eyes," the card stated: "areola, radiating, orange, tone dark, periphery, azure blue, tone medium." After all the minutiae was recorded, the examiner listed identifying marks, which included a tattoo—"J.S."—on the right forearm, all of which makes one suspect that Chief of Detectives O'Brien was smirking about the challenges of ever re-identifying ginger-haired James Sullivan.

"Red" Sullivan was already No. 3592 in the old Rogues' Gallery, but now he was B1 in the new Bertillon system. Officers wrestled three more rogues upstairs: John McGrane, wagon thief David "Hymie" Rosenberg, and Jimmy Jordan. In about two hours, all four had Bertillon cards. Commissioner Grant hailed the new system, saying the "custody of criminal records" would remain intact within the detective bureau, and not under the control of a single commissioner. (The cumbersome measurement system remained in use for more than a decade, until gradually replaced by fingerprinting.)

On Friday, March 5, Commissioner Andrews scheduled Big Bill Devery's hearing for the following week. That same night, with the blessing of embattled police chief Conlin, Captain Chapman organized what was the biggest vice raid to date in New York City history. It would also rank among the most knuckleheaded and ham-handed. Chapman was that rarity among veteran police captains, a genuine prude, and New Yorkers marveled to see him running the Tenderloin.

Just after midnight, about 200 men and women were dancing to the strains of a lively waltz at the Newmarket club on 30th Street and Sixth Avenue. A certain timeworn decorum prevailed. No high kicking allowed; no cheek-to-cheek dancing. No robbery; no profanity. The club occupied the site of the Old Haymarket, one of the city's best-known places for out-of-towners to come buy some cocktails, dance a few dances, and meet mercenary women of easy virtue. The dames asked the gents the eternal questions about wanting to have a good time, and the men departed with them. A reporter once tallied that among thirty-eight unescorted women who entered after 1 a.m. one night, twenty-nine left with a man within the hour. Drinks were bought but money rarely traveled from male to female hands inside the club. Thanks to securing a Raines Law hotel license, the joint didn't stop serving until the bartenders collapsed around dawn.

Captain Chapman had ordered his detectives to gather evidence about prostitution at the club, but a recent grand jury had refused to indict anyone. Chapman was undeterred. He approached reform magistrate Robert C. Cornell of Jefferson Market Courthouse, who decided to grant a warrant to pick up the owner on suspicion of running a disorderly house and also anyone there engaging in disorderly activities.

At midnight, when the sixty police officers reached the Tenderloin precinct station house after their shift, Chapman without explanation ordered them to form a double-file line; about fifteen central office men joined the parade. Chapman then ordered them to march double-time one block to the Newmarket. The bluecoats surrounded the building.

Chapman gave the signal; he and twenty other officers dashed through the front door and onto the crowded dance floor. The musicians abruptly stopped a "galloping waltz," as one newspaper put it, the violins in mid-scrape, with a spontaneous synchronicity that would have delighted any conductor.

Painted women shrieked in the sudden silence. Men, many with wives in far-off cities, scrambled toward the exits; Chapman ordered his officers to guard all doors and windows but quickly realized he needed reinforcements. The bushy-whiskered captain himself ran back to the station house and telephoned the West 20th Street precinct house for reserves.

None of the clubgoers understood the raid. Was it now against the law to dance? Were cocktails at midnight taboo? Captain Chapman arrested the alleged owner, Edwin B. Corey, and then announced that he would be arresting everyone else as well. Was it two hundred people? Three hundred? Three hundred fifty? Some men tried to fight their way past the burly policemen but none succeeded.

The police gathered everyone into the middle of the dance floor and formed a large ring around them. Patrolmen came and escorted a dozen or so at a time outside into a pair of horse-drawn police wagons waiting curbside. About a thousand-plus liquored-up onlookers, who found the raid more entertaining than the nearby Oasis or any of the other clubs, rained down hoots and catcalls onto the police.

The revelers, one by one, climbed into the wagon for the short ride to either the Tenderloin or West 20th Street precinct house. It took twenty-seven trips by two wagons to ferry all the prisoners. Three sergeants sat at the desk in the Tenderloin station house taking the "pedigree" of the 141 male and 60 female prisoners consigned to crowded holding cells.

Arresting officers told newspapermen they had turned down gold rings and cash and promises of favors. The richer among the prisoners sent messengers with scribbled notes to friends and attorneys to rush over and make bail. Before dawn, at least twenty men and twenty-five women produced enough money and paperwork to leave the building.

Court convened the following morning. Under the minaret-like orange tower of Jefferson Market Courthouse, each bedraggled prisoner, who had slept in evening clothes, was called to stand before Judge Cornell. The magistrate asked if Captain Chapman or his officers had witnessed this particular person commit a crime. Each time, Chapman said no. Each time, Magistrate Cornell released the prisoner. "Discharged." "Discharged." "Discharged." An assembly line of the hung over and exonerated.

The wait to appear dragged on so long that waiters from nearby restaurants delivered more than fifty breakfasts to the courthouse.

The only hitch, according the *New York World*, was that many of the men had given fictitious names when first arrested, and now couldn't remember them. Dozens of "John Smith"s failed to approach the bench. One fellow was impressively still drunk ten hours later and demanded an explanation as to why he had been arrested. Magistrate Cornell repeated that he was discharged and muttered, "Oh, go away." The man then confronted Captain

Chapman, who promptly arrested him for "drunk and disorderly" conduct and this charge stuck.

Two hundred times Magistrate Cornell discharged prisoners for lack of evidence. Only owner Corey was held. Editorials of outrage against the reform police popped up.

Just as Roosevelt's Sunday saloon crackdown had alienated tens of thousands of German voters, so did this raid irritate another bloc of voters who would never want to see another merger of Republicans and reformers.

———

On Sunday, March 7, the Republican power brokers decided to try to put the Police Board out of its misery.

One by one, they arrived in the ornate lobby of the Fifth Avenue Hotel at 23rd Street for a session with Senator Platt. Attending were congressman Lemuel Quigg, insurance commissioner Louis F. Payn (a close friend of the governor), city czar "Smooth Ed" Lauterbach, ex-postmaster Van Cott, and "Wicked" Gibbs.

The board's days appeared limited, no matter what the coven here concocted. The Greater Consolidation Act, which would merge Brooklyn, Manhattan, and Queens, was expected to go into effect in nine months on January 1, 1898, and it was expected to replace the local police boards with a new Greater New York Police Board to be appointed by the new mayor, elected in November.

But none of this was certain, and although Roosevelt was likely to lose his job in January (unless reappointed by the new mayor), several high-ranking New York City Republicans decided that they could not wait that long to be rid of him. Goaded by Lauterbach, they aimed to create a bill that would oust the current Police Board immediately and replace it with a new board appointed by the Republican governor Frank Black.

They argued that a board changeover would ease the eventual transition to a Greater New York police force. Cynics argued it would allow the Republicans to control the police and election machinery in the runup to the hotly contested election for the first mayor of Greater New York in November. At stake was the largest city spoils system in the nation, and the Republicans knew they would need every trick to defeat Tammany Hall in the wake of Roosevelt.

Newspapermen routinely camped out in the lobby when Senator "Easy

Boss" Platt took the train up from Washington, and word of the meeting leaked out, unleashing a geyser of commentary, from premature obituaries for the board to tepid defense. Commissioner Grant volunteered that killing the board might be the only way to achieve harmony; Roosevelt preferred that the legislature grant the mayor the power to remove and replace commissioners, without trial and without the governor's approval.

The *New York World* pointed out that if Roosevelt was appointed assistant secretary of the navy, that too might bring harmony to the board.

———

Senator Lodge, in the damp chill of March in D.C., called in every favor and tapped every shoulder. He incurred those implied debts that Roosevelt so scrupulously tried to avoid. Lodge updated TR in a very long optimistic letter (March 8, 1897) that read like a roll call of influential Republicans.

> *You have been in my thoughts day and night and your name has been on my lips daily and yet I have not written you. The simple reason has been that in this town of crowds and rush, with a dying Congress and incoming President, with struggling ambitions and an air filled with contradictory rumors it has seemed to me that it would be a useless annoyance to tell you all the phases and fluctuations and all I was doing in the campaign I am making for you—the only thing I care about winning out.*

Lodge recounted a very favorable meeting with the new secretary of the navy, John D. Long; he noted that Senator Wolcott, Republican of Colorado, would ask McKinley for Roosevelt's appointment as "his one personal favor"; Speaker Reed of Maine would write to McKinley and to Long. Judge William H. Taft, "one of the best fellows going," convinced a friend of McKinley's named Herrick to sing TR's praises. Vice President Garret Hobart unexpectedly approached Lodge and offered to help; Hobart happened to be meeting with McKinley that afternoon.

"You have, I think, a right to be proud of such support as that I have described and you have not raised a finger and it has all come voluntarily. All I have done is to mass and direct a little."

Roosevelt, under so much stress, reacted in a gush of gratitude. After Edith and TR read aloud Lodge's letter about his efforts for TR, he wrote he felt "a little like bawling." He searched for ways to articulate his appreciation.

Roosevelt added that Parker and Grant had so hamstrung the police force that "I hail this bill to legislate us out as a relief." He refused to count the navy job as a sure thing.

"I have no idea what I should do next," he very soon wrote to his sister, "but I should enjoy and should feel I deserved three or four months holiday at Sagamore; and surely there is something I can turn my hand to."

———

On March 12, Captain Devery walked up the familiar steps of 300 Mulberry Street and took the elevator. It was a shorter commute to headquarters than to his precinct on 125th Street. He glad-handed the boys.

Commissioner Andrews sat down at the desk in the hearing room and cleared some papers to one side. The day of reckoning for the Tammany brave, contemplated by the board for more than a year, was finally at hand. Just then a messenger arrived in the room and handed a document to Andrews. It was a "writ of prohibition" from New York Supreme Court justice Miles Beach.

Late the previous afternoon, Devery's lawyers, Colonel James and Abram Elkus, had argued before the judge that the bipartisan Police Board was not bipartisan and didn't fulfill the law's provisions: "No more than two members of the board can belong to the same political party or be of the same opinions on State and National issues." James and Elkus argued that at least three board members agreed on national issues of "opposition to the free coinage of silver, the maintenance of silver and paper currency at a parity with gold, the Monroe Doctrine, pensions for soldiers, sympathy with Cuba, tariff for revenue, admission of territories." At the state level, at least three agreed on the Consolidation of Greater New York, the liquor tax, and ballot reform.

Commissioner Andrews read the document and reluctantly halted the trial and announced he would forward the legal papers to corporation counsel Scott.

Speaking to reporters, Andrews said he wouldn't comment "off-hand" but then proceeded to do so, admitting that "no more vicious system" than a bipartisan commission existed. He also conceded that three commissioners, including him, agreed on many of those national issues. The *Tribune* explained it succinctly: Commissioner Andrews voted for McKinley.

Devery had slipped off the hook yet again. The supreme court judge chosen to review this temporary writ was onetime Tammany Hall sachem Judge Frederick Smyth.

———

The legislation to oust the Police Board was stalling in Albany. Upstate church-belt Republicans wanted to horse-trade a tightening of loopholes in the Raines Liquor Law for their support of the Lauterbach police bill that would terminate Roosevelt. Raines himself wanted all the thousands of new "fake" Raines clubs to be taxed heavily or disbanded; he wanted new hotel rules about room size and wall thickness to close the "fake" Raines hotels. "If the Republican party makes these amendments," sniped Republican Abe Gruber, "it couldn't elect a mayor of the Greater New York if the Democrats went to Sing Sing for a candidate."

The *Brooklyn Eagle* published an incisive editorial on its neighbor city's Police Board. Under the headline A DISORDERLY HOUSE, it wrote:

> The police board is not composed of two good men, Roosevelt and Andrews, one weak man, Grant, and one bad able man, Parker. It is composed of four men, full of faults, who, officially speaking, keep a disorderly house.
>
> Roosevelt is a good man in the most obnoxious sense of the word. He is about as unwise and whimsical as can be. Mr. Andrews sticks to Mr. Roosevelt with the tenacity and intelligence of a porous plaster [i.e., a Band-Aid]. Mr. Grant is a quiet methodical, ordinarily capable man. Parker is a shrewd, cool, keen character, with whom Grant prefers to act [instead of] following the vagaries of Roosevelt.
>
> The advantage which Parker has over the rest of the board is simply that which coolness, sanity and ability make for themselves over circumstances and men that disregard such qualities.

———

On Tuesday night, March 16, 1897, Roosevelt, the invited speaker, inched his way through the standing-room-only crowd of about 400 men and women at the cramped Social Reform Club on East 4th Street. (Edith was visiting friends in Philadelphia for a few days, and TR always seemed wound a bit tighter when he couldn't confide in her.)

He would later describe the audience as "many socialists and anarchists, both of the parlor and practical kind." That night, TR added a theme of social justice to his usual paean to reform board accomplishments. He spoke of how the police had almost banished local gang leaders who used to terrorize poor neighborhoods; he also spoke of the need to defeat clever, wealthy scoundrels who finessed the laws to steal whole railroads. But Roosevelt stressed that laws should not merely defend the poor and undermine the wealthy; laws should defend the honest and attack the criminal. The audience seemed to welcome the distinction.

The commissioner—among other police highlights—then spoke of the great restraint the police showed during the massive election rallies. "I did not hear of a single instance of clubbing," he said. "I beg your pardon," someone shouted. "I was poked in the ribs." Roosevelt, trying to control himself, said, "I saw 20,000 gentlemen who were not poked with a club. Of course *you* were poked in the ribs . . . and if you had not been kept back, you would not [be] here to raise objections."

Roosevelt received steady polite applause for his speech. The moderator then asked for any comments or questions from the audience. Up rose Moses Oppenheimer, a European Socialist who had emigrated after several arrests in Germany.

Oppenheimer, a skilled rabble-rouser, ambushed Roosevelt. He had prepared a speech, and had already handed copies to the press. He now blindsided Roosevelt, who was forced to sit on the stage and listen. Oppenheimer began by recalling the days when the police commissioners "were in the habit of visiting churches and friendly political clubs and telling everybody how painstaking and good and virtuous they were." The audience laughed loudly; TR sat facing them, unamused.

"Like clergymen, Mr. Roosevelt and Mr. Parker spoke from pulpits and would have no back talk. Tonight is the first opportunity for frank public criticism." He said public officials should not be allowed to judge themselves and declare victories, but rather should be judged by others.

We all know about the great anti-saloon crusade, the Haroun-Al-Raschid midnight rambles, the sensational handshakes; in those breezy and bustling days Mr. Roosevelt was in the habit of brushing aside every criticism with the accusation that the critics were criminals or the allies of criminals. Result—the Raines hotel, the speak-easy, and the people's verdict in the election of 1895. Then there was a crusade against what is called the "social evil." That is more rampant than ever.

The packed house responded with shouts of "That's right." Roosevelt looked extremely annoyed.

Oppenheimer continued that police officers were judged on the volume of arrests; witness Captain Chapman's recent Tenderloin raid in which hundreds of citizens were falsely arrested. "To deprive a peaceable citizen of his liberty, to haul him to the police station and to court, to put him to the trouble and expense for insufficient reasons may seem but a trifle to a man who sits comfortably in his office at Mulberry Street, but to the innocent victim it is no trifling matter," said Oppenheimer.

The German native claimed it was very difficult to bring a complaint against a police officer, with policemen creating fear and the Police Board strewing red tape. "Let us fight against abuse of power and official terrorism which no free community should tolerate." The hall erupted in cheers.

Roosevelt leaped to his feet. He said Oppenheimer had no idea what he was talking about, that he was ignorant of the facts; the crowd responded with hisses and catcalls. TR offered to repeat the statement. He said Oppenheimer was trying to bring back the corrupt days of Tammany Hall and that knuckling under to Oppenheimer's criticisms would transform New York City into such a cesspool of vice "as would make Babylon seem an Arcadia."

Roosevelt said no promotions were made for volume of arrests but all were made for "gallantry or merit." This was not actually true because of civil service rules. As for illegal arrests of women, he said he had personally investigated "every single instance" and found not one single innocent woman had been arrested.

TR said people were biased and couldn't let go of their image of the police as corrupt but that the police had indeed changed. "I have striven as faithfully as mortal ever did to be a servant of every man in this city, no matter what his creed or politics," he said, his voice quavering, almost breaking. "I have done all that in me lies to make the department honest."

The next day, Henry Cabot Lodge, who seemed to be finally swaying McKinley to select Roosevelt, opened his newspaper to see his friend portrayed as angrily debating a German Socialist.

Lodge dashed off two unusually frank letters to TR, basically counseling him, in effect, to shut up, and to refuse all public speaking engagements until the new job was settled.

"Edith got hold of the first [letter] immediately on her return from Philadelphia," TR informed Lodge, "and insisted on reading it aloud to me, and endorsing all the views it set forth with fairly rabid emphasis." TR informed him he had no more speaking commitments besides a Young Republican club in Brooklyn "where I cannot conceive of anything unpleasant happening."

He couldn't resist defending himself for the Social Reform Club tirade. Roosevelt said that nine out of ten times he won converts on the East Side, and that the club boasted respected members such as Mrs. Josephine Shaw Lowell and Dr. Rainsford, but TR admitted: "I appreciate fully the discredit attaching to what looked like a joint debate with an abusive socialist blackguard."

Roosevelt said the club set him up and that most newspapermen "of the Free Silver Socialist stripe" were tipped off in advance to come watch him being bludgeoned. But Roosevelt claimed his best option in "a bad business was to fight it out" and that although Lodge might find it hard to believe, "They cheered me and cheered me again and again, and thronged around me so to shake hands, and to tell me that they had changed their opinion, that I was not able to get away for half an hour."

He conceded, though, that among newspapers only "the utterly unimportant *Times*" saw it that way.

———

Mayor Strong dismissed Commissioner Parker.

On Wednesday, March 17, the mayor's secretary took the 4:30 p.m. train to Albany to hand deliver the mayor's verdict to the governor and to request his signature to finalize the dismissal. The document stated that the mayor judged three of the five charges against Parker proven—poor attendance, failure to handle pensions, and citizens' complaints. He added in a cover note that this one commissioner was paralyzing the board.

Parker, who had spent $3,000 on legal fees, had recently written a letter to the mayor demanding a resolution of the charges pending against him; he had probably not expected *this* resolution.

Roosevelt, newly chastised by Lodge about inflammatory rhetoric, gave little public comment; privately, however, he told Lodge that he doubted Governor Black would sign the papers because Boss Platt feared giving TR more power with such an important election coming up. In the meantime, Parker remained a full member of the fractured Police Board.

———

Roosevelt, in his irritable state, could not let go of the Social Reform Club incident. He refused to accept the private apology of club official E. W. Ordway, who explained that Oppenheimer had simply taken advantage of the "free discussion" period. TR countered that free discussion had nothing to do with an ambush or a joint debate, and that he would no more agree to debate Oppenheimer than he would anarchist Johann Most. He added that the club's applause for Oppenheimer's "lies" meant an endorsement of them.

Ordway forwarded one of the letters from the "gentlemanly and lamb-like Roosevelt" on to the club president, Charles B. Spahr. "As he virtually tells me I lie two or three times I suppose that settles it—it seems to be his method of argument. So I think the whole matter better be dropped."

On Monday, March 22, Colonel James argued his case for Captain Devery in the friendly confines of the chambers of supreme court judge Frederick Smyth. The witty lawyer framed his argument by taking the concept of a bipartisan four-man commission to its most absurd lengths. "If at any time in the six years in which a member holds office he comes to the same conclusion on State and National issues as two other colleagues, he then *thinks himself* out of office."

James stressed that the sloppily written bipartisan law was unconstitutional because it denied freedom of political thought.

Justice Smyth asked what the result would be if the Police Board were declared an illegal entity. Colonel James replied, "One result would be that it could not try this relator (pointing to Devery). With any other results we have no concern."

Justice Smyth said he would take these considerations under advisement and that for now the writ of prohibition would remain in effect. (Smyth would die before he would make a ruling.)

The *New York Tribune* later commented: "For a big man, Devery has crawled through some exceedingly small holes."

———

Roosevelt despised trading favors or recommendations; a man either believed in a candidate or a cause, or he didn't. Horse-trading was beside the point. So it must have pained him to write four letters to Republican congressmen from New York asking for help. To Murray Mitchell: "If you are at liberty to say a good word for me I should be very much obliged." To Sereno Payne: "If you are in any way hampered about this, just tear this note up without answer." More of the same to Philip Low and James W. Wadsworth.

Roosevelt wrote the notes, placed them in envelopes, and mailed them all to Lodge on March 25. He was clearly uncomfortable. "This is a new kind of business for me and I may have put the matter wrong or it may be unwise to send them."

Boss Platt cracked open the door. Word spread as far as Lodge in Washington that Platt might welcome TR leaving the state, if Platt could influence Mayor Strong's choice for a new police commissioner. Lodge telegraphed TR to investigate and he reported that the mayor hadn't touched the topic of a replacement yet. "You know the Mayor makes up his mind in a good many different directions . . . and he talks with even greater ambiguity than he thinks."

Roosevelt hastily began exploring a complicated stratagem to force out "weak and treacherous" Chief Conlin and have loyal Republican John McCullagh replace him.

———

On April 1, President McKinley offered a cabinet post to a New York police commissioner . . . but Colonel Grant turned down assistant secretary of war. He still expected something more prestigious or an embassy post overseas. The *Chicago Tribune* reported that had Grant accepted, that would have filled the administration quota of New Yorkers. This time, Grant's bone-headedness aided Roosevelt.

On Tuesday, April 6, at 6:05 p.m., TR sent a telegram to Henry Cabot Lodge: SINBAD HAS EVIDENTLY LANDED THE OLD MAN OF THE SEA.

President McKinley, bowing to the wishes of Secretary Long, sent Roosevelt's name that evening to the Senate for confirmation.

Roosevelt was overjoyed; he described himself as "astonished." He soon admitted that the police job had become intolerable. "I do not object to any amount of work and worry where I have a fair chance to win or lose on my merits; but here at the last, I was playing against stacked cards. Now that I am going, all the good people are utterly cast down and can not say enough of my virtues!" (His sense of humor was returning.)

Reverend Parkhurst called Roosevelt's departure "a municipal affliction" and a "personal bereavement." The *New York World* sounded as arch as *Town Topics*: "As Assistant Secretary of the Navy, Mr. Theodore Roosevelt will have to be obliged to leave New York for four years. It is hard to see how the Administration could have made a selection better calculated to please New Yorkers." When reporters informed Commissioner Parker that the Senate had confirmed Roosevelt, he laughed for a very long time; then, catching his breath, he said: "What a glorious retreat!"

That November, **Tammany Hall**—campaigning against the sour preachiness and enforced sobriety of reform—succeeded in electing its candidate, Robert Van Wyck, as the first mayor of Greater New York. And on May 21, 1898—within fourteen months of Roosevelt's exit—a new Tammany-dominated Police Board swore in **Big Bill Devery** as police chief. Big Bill—born on the tough Irish East Side, never convicted of a crime, Tammany's own—now commanded a police force of 7,600 men, the nation's largest.

The Tenderloin immediately erupted in celebration. "It has been a long time since the sporting man was in such good spirits as Saturday," declared the *Herald*. The paper ran a clever cartoon of a joyous Tammany tiger popping out of a jack-in-the-box with a demonic grin and a brimming mug of beer. The *New York Times*, citing Tammany's "utter unscrupulousness," predicted the city would be run "wide open."

Devery, on his first day, issued a most amusing policy statement: "I shall insist upon a fair and impartial enforcement of all the laws and ordinances, without fear and without favor . . . Gambling of all kinds must go. I will not tolerate it in any shape."

Lincoln Steffens would write: "[Devery] was no more fit to be chief of police than the fish man was to be director of the Aquarium, but as a character, as a work of art, he was a masterpiece."

The 250-pound chief knew that in a week he would be leading the first ever Greater New York police parade through the streets of Manhattan. So he borrowed a majestic bay horse named Bullet from the parks police and started brushing up his riding skills.

————

At almost the same time, **Roosevelt**, too, was practicing his riding—although more cavalry charge than parade step. Less than a year after landing his dream job as assistant secretary of the navy, Roosevelt defied his Republican friends and quit to volunteer to fight in the Spanish-American War in Cuba.

The expeditionary force, known early on as "Teddy's Terrors," then as the "Rough Riders," landed at a small fishing village, Daiquiri, on the coast of Cuba. Roosevelt was wearing a military uniform ordered from Brooks Brothers; he carried extra eyeglasses in a secret compartment in his hat. He climbed aboard an undersized horse called Texas, his blue neckerchief at his throat, providing a fat target for snipers.

United States Army troops, marching ahead, had slogged up a muddy path and captured a key hill; they then lay flat and waited for further orders. When Roosevelt arrived there with his recruits, he demanded that all the American forces fight onward through the intense Mauser rifle fire up to the summit. The army soldiers and their officers replied they would wait; two men—perhaps mockingly—trampled down a fence for him, and Roosevelt ordered his troops to follow on foot as he rode up into a hail of bullets.

His charge was extremely brave and reckless; eighty-nine Rough Riders would die that day. At one point, he shouted to his men: "Are you afraid to stand up when I am on horseback?" A bullet glanced off TR's elbow and scraped his horse's flank; he pulled his pistol and killed a Spaniard ten yards away. By mid-afternoon on July 1, he and his orderly stood atop a crest above Kettle Hill, victorious, soon swamped by back-slapping comrades.

He would later write to Lodge: "Three days I have been at the extreme front of the firing line; how I have escaped I know not; I have not blanket or coat; I have not taken off my shoes even; I sleep in the drenching rain & drink putrid water." (TR never sounded happier.)

His hunting pal Robert "Fergie" Ferguson wrote to Edith:

We've been having the devil of a fine time of it—shooting Spaniards and being stormed at by shot and shell—No hunting trip so far has ever equalled it in Theodore's eyes.

. . . When I caught up with him the day of his famous charge . . . T. was reveling in victory and gore—He had just "doubled up a Spanish officer like a Jack-rabbit" as he retired from a block house, and all the way down to the next line of entrenchments he encouraged us to "look at these damned Spanish dead."

He seldom uses such strong language.

Thanks to naval firepower, American forces and the Cuban rebels quickly achieved victory over Spain, just as yellow fever began to ravage the troops. Colonel Theodore Roosevelt arrived back in Montauk, Long Island, on August 15, 1898, hailed as a national hero. He readied his war memoirs for rapid publication. (Humorist Dooley would call them "Alone in Cuba" and recount how TR's single shot had killed the entire Spanish army and the archbishop eight miles away in Santiago.)

Within days, even Senator Platt was boosting war hero Roosevelt to run for governor to replace the scandal-scarred Republican then in office. Roosevelt, with little hesitation, agreed; the order instantly went out to manufacture thousands of campaign buttons. After intensive campaigning, he won the statewide election by a scant 17,000 votes, the slim margin due to losing still-irritated New York City by 60,000.

———

On Monday, January 2, 1899, Theodore Roosevelt was governor and Big Bill Devery was police chief.

Devery was fulfilling the reformers' worst fears, throwing the city "wide open" for vice. He blessed gambling, prostitution, and after-hours drinking all over town . . . for a shakedown price. The cops rediscovered curse words, quashed riots with a fierceness, and kept crime such as burglary and assault at about the same levels as in the Roosevelt years. Devery shipped squealer Schmittberger to "goatville," in the Wakefield section of the Bronx.

And Devery also began hanging out on a street corner at 28th Street and Eighth Avenue till past midnight, smoking cigars, leaning on a fire hydrant, meeting with Tammany politicians, underworld pals such as Frank Farrell, bagman Glennon, various police captains, ordinary citizens. He carried two fat rolls of cash in rubber bands and often treated at the oyster stand across the street or at Ruppert's saloon. One of his favorite expressions was: "When you get caught with the goods on you, you don't want to know nothin'."

The *New York Times*—finally resurrecting itself as an aggressive paper—published an exposé revealing that gamblers were paying a staggering $3 million a year for protection: 400 poolrooms at $300 a month, 500 crap games at $150 a month, 200 gambling houses at $150 a month, 20 elaborate casinos at $1,000 a month, and ten-dollar bills from hundreds of small "numbers" shops.

Devery, in response to the increasingly harsh criticism, decided to adopt a page out of Roosevelt's playbook and enforce the *letter of the law*, only in this case against . . . bandleaders in posh restaurants and hotels for playing music without a license. The big chief vowed to stop those lawbreakers from performing Schubert and Brahms to lunching ladies at Sherry's, Delmonico's, and the Savoy. None of the reformers seemed to appreciate Devery's sense of humor.

————

As for Roosevelt, his principled belligerence was once again infuriating New York State Republican power brokers and bumping him upwards. Governor Roosevelt, fine-tuning his reform agenda, imposed a corporate tax on public franchises such as railroads and was ousting corrupt administrators, both Republican and Democrat. "I have found out one reason why Senator Platt wants me nominated for the vice-presidency," Roosevelt wrote to Lodge on February 3, 1900. "The big-monied men . . . whose campaign contributions have certainly been no inconsiderable factor in his strength, have been pressing him very strongly . . . to get me out of the state."

Senator Mark Hanna, McKinley's right-hand man, deeply opposed the vice presidential "boom" for TR, still one of the nation's most popular heroes from the brief war in Cuba. "Don't you realize there's only one life between this madman and the White House?" Hanna told several high-ranking fellow Republicans.

In the runup to the November 1900 election, Police Chief Devery decided to refuse to cooperate with the voter fraud investigations overseen by the head of the New York State election bureau, Roosevelt's John McCullagh.

On Sunday, November 4, Devery officially ordered all 7,600 policemen to refuse to allow New York State inspectors to perpetrate "tactics and methods of intimidation upon respectable citizens." When informed at Oyster Bay, Roosevelt turned apoplectic with anger and threatened the Tammany mayor and district attorney with legal proceedings. He urged McCullagh to rush to the grand jury with Devery's "obnoxious order" on Monday morning, and the panel promptly indicted the chief of police for the felony crime of hindering duly appointed election officials. Chief Devery—whose first reaction was "They're crazy!"—surrendered in Recorder Goff's courtroom to avoid the shame of public arrest.

The McKinley-Roosevelt ticket won in a national landslide, although native son Theodore Roosevelt yet again failed to win over New York City, this time losing by 29,000 votes. "I hope you noticed how I called down

[Tammany Boss] Croker, [Mayor] Van Wyck and Devery when there threatened to be trouble in New York," Roosevelt crowed to Lodge. "I was glad Croker gave me the chance through his man Devery."

———

On September 14, 1901, after the assassination of McKinley, Roosevelt ascended to the presidency. He took the oath of office in a borrowed top hat, the youngest president in the history of the country, six weeks shy of his forty-third birthday. His pals Senator Henry Cabot Lodge and Dr. William Sturgis Bigelow sent him a giddy telegram: VIVE LE ROI [Long Live the King].

———

Two months later, the reformers in New York City, with Mark Twain campaigning and Roosevelt in the White House, finally won another election. The new mayor, Seth Low, in one of his first acts in office on January 1, 1902, fired Big Bill Devery. Soon after, the former police chief spent the extraordinary sum of $377,800 to buy a dozen buildings at auction in Manhattan, several in Hell's Kitchen, others in prime West Village territory. That purchase alone would place Devery's fortune on par with Theodore Roosevelt's. Devery also bought a share in a racetrack.

Tammany Hall, in the final desperate days leading up to the mayoral election, had abandoned Devery. Big Bill fought back and ran for mayor as an independent Democrat. "Elect me and I'll bunch Tammany and these reformers into the cage over there at 102nd street and drop them all into the river with the rest of the dogs." He lost, despite hosting lavish barbecues of 700-pound oxen, beer picnics, and boat excursions.

Devery and his bookmaker pal Frank Farrell bought a struggling baseball team in Baltimore for $18,000 and brought it north in 1903, defying Tammany's edict that the New York Giants of the National League have a monopoly on baseball in the city. That ball club, which had no official name, was soon called the "Highlanders" or "Hilltoppers" but would later take the name . . . the **New York Yankees**.

The partners had to fork over a hefty $250,000 to clear and build on a rocky hilltop at 165th and Broadway (today's Columbia-Presbyterian Hospital). Their hurriedly constructed stadium included 5,000 folding chairs and held about 15,000 fans; the contractors failed to fill in a pond properly in right field, the muddy gulley had to be roped off, and umpires judged balls hit there a ground-rule double.

The team, despite bringing in marquee stars such as Wee Willie Keeler, who had hit .427 in 1897, didn't win many games. An early-twentieth-century riddle ran: "What animal comes from the bushes, doesn't know what to do with a bat, cannot even catch a fly, and lives on goose eggs?" Answer: "The New York Yankees."

In 1909, Devery suggested introducing a new team logo, one that resembled an old New York police award badge and would become a sports icon; it featured the now classic interlocking *N* and *Y* and was placed on hats and uniform sleeves. (Louis Tiffany himself had designed this "valor" medal in 1877, and the commissioners had given it to a wounded policeman, John McDowell, right around the time Devery had joined the force.)

In 1915—four years *before* the arrival of Babe Ruth—Devery and Farrell sold the Yankees to brewery heir Colonel Jacob Ruppert and his partner, Colonel Tillinghast L'Hommedieu Huston, for $460,000.

————

President Roosevelt had a pretty good run over those same years, busting trusts, creating national parks, flexing the United States' muscles abroad, hosting Easter egg hunts at the White House. Some of his presidential success can be attributed to having intelligent, cautious advisors such as Henry Cabot Lodge and Elihu Root nearby, unlike his lone-wolf days at 300 Mulberry Street. TR never lost his astounding energy, confidence, or his desire to preach.

Underneath it all, Roosevelt never really changed; instead of being on an impossible four-man commission, he was commander-in-chief, a job title that suited him. The *Washington Post* had once presciently joked about Roosevelt being reluctant to share responsibilities with God.

Later biographers, enamored of Roosevelt's presidency, have donned rose-tinted glasses to view his two years as New York City police commissioner. In the most simplistic view, TR is credited with single-handedly reforming and revitalizing a deeply corrupt police force.

Much of that viewpoint seems to have come from Roosevelt's own self-assessment in the several magazine articles he penned on his stint as commissioner and in his autobiography, which are all characteristically positive. "Our [police] efforts were crowned with entire success," he wrote. "The improvement in the efficiency of the force went hand in hand with the improvement in its honesty. The men in uniform and the men in plainclothes—the detectives—did better work than ever before."

Contemporary observers were not so kind. Even the sympathetic *New York Times* weighed in that Roosevelt's "fanatical gusto" in enforcing defunct laws and ordinances "undoubtedly . . . interposed great obstacles to the political reform of the city."

Lincoln Steffens observed: "The New York police force . . . did not reform . . . and the Great city of New York, nay the Greater City of New York, called back Tammany and peaceful repose in easy corruption . . . New York is New York again, *vox populi, vox* of the devil."

———

In 1919, Theodore Roosevelt and Big Bill Devery both died.

Roosevelt's obituary filled front pages worldwide. The obituaries for Big Bill Devery, tucked inside local newspapers, were surprisingly kind. "Devery was always on trial for something or other and always being acquitted," opined the *New York Times*. "Devery's offenses against public decency were not light, but his humor and rough-and-readiness always disposed his adversaries to have a sort of liking for him."

A 100-piece police band led Devery's funeral procession in Far Rockaway, Queens; police commissioner Richard Enright ordered the flag at headquarters flown at half-mast for thirty days.

The final appraisal of Devery's estate—filed a decade later, in 1929—found the former chief insolvent at his death, and his wife, Annie, who had inherited all, had left only $6,218 at her death in 1926. "Devery's generosity was well known to all his associates," wrote one newspaperman, "as was also his fondness for [horse] racing, which made him almost a regular attendant at the races here and at Saratoga and elsewhere."

———

In most of Roosevelt's obituaries, his other exploits squeezed out all but a fleeting mention of his police commissioner days.

Over the decades, the **New York City Police Department** continued its cycle of corruption and crackdown, of palms greased, then wrists slapped. Criminals—many working in the gambling and prostitution rackets—continued to pay for the blindness of the men in blue, so as to satisfy the appetites of New Yorkers.

"I wish about forty police captains would die over night," a reform police commissioner told the City Club in 1908. "That is nothing personal. Neither do I mean it to their disadvantage. But they are no good."

The 1,500 Raines Law hotels, with cheap beds near shelves full of liquor, further corrupted the city; brothel madams noted that "by furnishing drinks or a good supper, a man can get a [shop]girl to go upstairs there," and the madams complained bitterly about the "Amateur Competition."

The weathervane statue of nude **Diana**, with her budding breasts, stood atop Madison Square Garden till 1925, while police officers—Irish, Italian, Polish—twirling their nightsticks, walked the beat below, sometimes keeping the peace, sometimes selling a turn of their heads, selling a wink.

The Mazet hearings (1899) were followed by the Curran Committee (1913), then the Seabury investigation (1932). And on and on, till the revelations of Frank Serpico and the Knapp Commission (1971), and then the Mollen Commission (1994).

The Island of Vice—with its reformers and its unrepentant, with its convicted and its not yet convicted, with its endless strivers—has seesawed back and forth over the years between tolerance and less tolerance, between cops who take and cops who don't.

"There are no better men anywhere than the men of the New York police force," Roosevelt wrote in his autobiography in 1913, "and when they go bad, it is because the system is wrong." And he blamed corrupt commanders, and singled out Big Bill as "one of the Tammany leaders, who represented in the police department all that I had warred against while Commissioner."

Ultimately, the job of police commissioner did as much for Roosevelt as Roosevelt did for the job. His two years there launched him onto the national stage; he honed his speaking skills; he even learned to silence himself occasionally so he could carry the Republican banner another day. He developed thicker skin and an intermittent sense of humor about newspaper attacks; he learned the impracticality of bitter feuds, the dangers of impulsive crusades. He saw brutal poverty close up. He earned a reputation as a reformer.

During his stint from 1895 to 1897, Roosevelt genuinely inspired the righteous among the police force; soon after, Big Bill helped give the rest of them their humor, their swagger, and their common sense.

As in ancient Rome, the vitality of New York City sometimes seems to come more from the crooks than the do-gooders.

ACKNOWLEDGMENTS

My greatest debt is to New York City.

My father's family came here in 1920, moving to Coney Island when he was thirteen. He rode the nickel subway and ate the nickel hot dog. He got caught selling bootleg liquor during Prohibition and bribed a cop two cases of Slivovitz to beat the rap. He worked in the Garment District and smoked a half dozen Bering Plazas a day into his late eighties. (I went to elementary school reeking of cigars.) And about a week before he died, he confessed to me that my grandfather, who ran a saloon, had rented rooms upstairs by the hour. "By the hour," he repeated. I got the point.

My dad once bought us sight-obstructed seats to a Yankees World Series and we sat behind a green-painted steel girder. We leaned apart on cue as Mickey Mantle and the rest of the hitters stepped up to home plate. In high school, I played blackjack in illegal East Side parlors that had key locks on both sides of the door. I was mugged seven times. What I am trying to say is that I am a New Yorker. I have walked the streets mentioned in this book and tried to imagine them car-less in 1895, in the last days of exclusively "live" entertainment when people wandered into concert saloons, dime museums, fancy theaters, into gambling joints and opium dens.

―――――

I came to this project a Roosevelt novice. Patty O'Toole, author of *When Trumpets Call*, gave me a box of TR books. I have kept them for six years. She is writing a Woodrow Wilson biography and probably needed them. Sorry.

I contacted Edmund Morris and he allowed me to come to his home in Connecticut to look over some of his notes. I outstayed my welcome. When I came back a second day, he sped my note taking by encouraging me to use a copier in his wife's office. I am deeply grateful and am in no way assigning him any responsibility for any mistakes. In fact, his thorough TR research has made me feel ever since like I've been climbing Cleopatra's Needle covered in grease.

I want to thank Mike Bosak and Tom Vasti, formerly of the NYPD, for making the cop's life come alive; I want to thank Kenneth Conboy, who wrote his master's thesis on TR and aided me over lunch at the University Club.

Big Bill Devery's relatives provided fine documents and leads: especially Sharon Alforque, Michelle Kelly, and Bill Cleary.

Librarians and archivists everywhere helped: Ellen Belcher at John Jay, Ken Cobb at Municipal Archives, David Smith at New York Public, and especially, Wallace Dailey at Harvard.

In five years, the debts mount. Paul Grondahl (who arrived via Mr. and Mrs. Smith) helped with the steep hills of Albany; Timothy Gilfoyle handled my overeager erotic queries; Jay Berman told the best story on the disappearance of the Roosevelt Police Board minutes (it involves boxes in the basement of the Tweed Court House and workmen in a rush to finish a demolition job). John Vella, the superintendent in a Union Square building where I have a room with a view, read some of my other books, and kept asking when the hell I would finish. Thanks for the impatience. And thanks to all the people who e-mailed and asked what was next. After a few years on this project, I started to feel invisible.

I want to thank Richard Williams, Terrence Brown, executive director of the Theodore Roosevelt Association, Laura Neely, Kathy Dalton, Kevin Baker, James McGrath Morris, Gary Marmorstein, Mark Epstein, Craig Rhodes, Alexander Sachs, Leroy Frazer, Patrick Dugan, Michael Daley, Rikers Island Frank, John H., Terry Dunne, Hodges Lewis, Lenora Gidlund, Michael Lorenzini, Robbi Siegel, Coralie Hunter, Kris Puopolo.

My teenagers kept me in touch with the Westchester police, so that in a way helped the book. My wife had long faith and "long green," and perhaps her long bet will pay off.

This book would not exist without the ruthless editing of Bill Thomas and the gentle agenting of Esther Newberg (or perhaps it's the other way around) . . . and, of course, not without the dueling agendas of Devery and Roosevelt.

You can reach me at rzacks@forbiddenknowledge.com.

NOTES

KEY TO FREQUENTLY USED SOURCES

HCL	Henry Cabot Lodge
HCL Papers	Henry Cabot Lodge Papers
Lexow	*Report and Proceedings of the Senate Committee to Investigate the Police Department of the City of New York*
MOR I	*The Letters of Theodore Roosevelt*, Vol. I
MOR II	*The Letters of Theodore Roosevelt*, Vol. II
NYCMA	New York City Municipal Archives
NYES	*New York Evening Sun*
NYH	*New York Herald*
NYPD	NewYork Police Department Museum
NYS	*New York Sun*
NYT	*New York Times*
NY Trib	*New York Tribune*
NYW	*New York World*
People vs. Gardner	*The People of the State of New York vs. Charles W. Gardner*
TRB	Theodore Roosevelt Birthplace
TRC	Theodore Roosevelt Collection at Harvard University
TRP	Theodore Roosevelt Papers at the Library of Congress

PROLOGUE

2   **"If the bloody bitch had turned up the leather"**: *People of the State of New York vs. William McGlory*, Court of General Sessions, Dec. 28, 1891, Trial no. 19, "Trial Transcripts of the County of New York, 1883–1927," Lloyd Sealy Library, John Jay College of Criminal Justice.

3   **"The traffic in female virtue"**: Timothy Gilfoyle, *City of Eros*, p. 248.

3   **"Fornication. Three windows at a time"**: "In the Matter of the Charges Preferred Against Captain Jos. B. Eakins," testimony of illustrator Charles Higby, p. 273 (microfilm), New York Public Library.

4   **"She's a ballet dancer; first she dances on one leg"**: *Actionable Offenses: Indecent Phonograph Recordings from the 1890s*, Archephone Records #1007, 2007, CD and liner notes.

4   **"Plenty of girls to help you drink the best of cheer"**: Richard O'Connor, *Hell's Kitchen: The Roaring Days of New York's Wild West Side*, p. 82.

5   **"He was tremendously excitable"**: William Muldoon interview with J. F. French, transcript, TRB.

5   **"Here lies all the civic virtue"**: Richard Rovere, *Howe and Hummel: Their True and Scandalous History*, p. 104.

5   **"Never quiet, always in motion"**: "Roosevelt in New York," *Washington Post*, June 14, 1895, p. 6.

6   **"little ease where Theodore Roosevelt leads"**: Jacob Riis, *The Making of an American*, p. 212.

CHAPTER 1: PARKHURST AND THE SIN TOUR

7   **"a lying, perjured, rum-soaked and libidinous lot"**: The sermon text is in *Our Fight with Tammany* by Charles Parkhurst (NY, 1895), pp. 8–25.

9   **"If a family is burned out"**: George Washington Plunkitt, *Plunkitt of Tammany Hall*, p. 37.

9   **"Hell, did you weigh them dry?"**: Alfred Hodder, *A Fight for the City: The Story of a Campaign of Amateurs*, p. 145.

9   **"a vile exchange of favors"**: Thomas Beer, *The Mauve Decade*, p. 144.

10   **"a damnable pack of administrative bloodhounds"**: Parkhurst, *Our Fight with Tammany*, pp. 8–25.

10   **"nothing but rumor, nothing but hearsay"**: Ibid., pp. 42–45.

10   **"district attorney had lived an immoral life"**: Ibid., p. 40.

10   **"never again be caught in the presence of the enemy"**: Ibid.

11   **"I still flatter myself that I whirled him"**: Charles W. Gardner, *Doctor and the Devil*, p. 32.

11   **"so coarse, so bestial, so consummately filthy"**: Parkhurst, *Our Fight with Tammany*, p. 74.

11   **"a fashion plate of a dead year"**: Gardner, *Doctor and the Devil*, p. 32.

12   **"South Carolina uncle"**: Ibid., p. 13.

12   **"a breach of Cherry Street etiquette"**: Ibid.

13   **"old enough to have been the mother of Columbus"**: Ibid., p. 16.

14   **"Hey, whiskers, going to ball me off?"**: Ibid., p. 18.

14   a **"200-pound"** drunken woman: Ibid., p. 20.

14   **"Show me something worse"**: Ibid., p. 64.

14   **"stained yellow" by "innumerable quarts of tobacco"**: Ibid., p. 25.

15   **"kerosene oil, soft soap, alcohol and the chemicals"**: Ibid., p. 27.

15   **"the absolute silence"**: Ibid., p. 36.

15   liked to play the **"finger game"**: William McAdoo, *Guarding a Great City*, p. 149.

16   **"the floating scum of thousands of saloons"**: Gardner, *Doctor and the Devil*, p. 44.

16   **"a blue satin skirt that reached to her knees only"**: Ibid., p. 47.

16   **"I suppose none of the police officers"**: Ibid., p. 52.

17   **"unquestionably the biggest single advertisement"**: William F. Mulhall, "The Golden Age of Booze," *Valentine's Manual*, no. 7 (1923): 126–37.

17   **"a scraggly little thin woman"**: Gardner, *Doctor and the Devil*, p. 66.

18   **"This is *rather* a bright company"**: Ibid.

18   **"the girls refused to dance"**: Ibid., p. 67.

18   **"Hold up your hat!"**: Ibid.

19   described as their **"summer outfits"**: "Parkhurst's Can-Can," *NYES*, Apr. 6, 1892, p. 1. The New York newspapers of April 6–8 and May 6–7, 1892, provide many details (some trial testimony disagrees with the chronology in Gardner's book): "What Dr. Parkhurst Saw," *NYS*, p. 1; "Hattie Adams's Defense," *NYES*; "Dr. Parkhurst a Witness,"

NYT, Apr. 7, 1892; "Two to One for Mrs. Adams," *NYS*, p. 1; "The Jury Did Not Agree," *NYT*, Apr. 8, 1892, p. 8; "Hot for Parkhurst," *NYES*; "Parkhurst's Sightseeing," *NYS*; "Parkhurst and Erving Tell Their Stories," *NYH*, May 6, 1892; "Hattie Adams Found Guilty," *NYH*; "Hattie Adams Convicted," *NYS*, May 7, 1892.

19 **"whose airs were those of a young girl"**: Gardner, *Doctor and the Devil*, p. 58.

19 **"pretty, painted, powdered" "plumpest and best looking"**: Ibid., p. 59.

20 **"decidedly pretty French women" "consumptive looking girl"**: Ibid., p. 60.

20 **"most of the testimony . . . unprintable"**: "Young Erving Broke Down," *NYS*, May 10, 1892, p. 1.

20 **"A person who carnally knows"**: Silvernail, *The Penal Code and Code of Criminal Procedure of the State of New York*, p. 139.

20 **French circus.** Anthony Comstock gave a deposition regarding a circus he witnessed nearby at 224 Greene Street on June 14, 1878. The performance by five women perhaps gives an idea of what else Parkhurst might have seen that so upset him. Comstock stated that he saw women: "licking or pretending to lick one another's sexual organs . . . drinking beer upon the vagina of one girl by the other, placing a cigar in the rectum of one of the girls, who [had] thrown her limbs and feet above her head, one girl getting on top of another, and pretending to go through the act of carnal intercourse, each girl being nude . . . sucking one another's breast." *People v. DeForest*, Court of General Sessions, July 2, 1878, District Attorney Papers, New York City Municipal Archives (hereafter NYCMA).

21 **"like a successful lot of ballet dancers"**: Gardner, *Doctor and the Devil*, p. 62.

21 **"the most brutal, most horrible exhibition"**: Ibid.

21 **"Don't tell me I don't know"**: Parkhurst, *Our Fight with Tammany*, pp. 59–78.

22 PARKHURST'S CAN CAN **and** PARKHURST'S SIGHT-SEEING: "Parkhurst's Can Can," *NYES*, Apr. 6, 1892, p. 1; "Parkhurst's Sight-seeing," *NYS*, May 6, 1892, p. 1.

22 **Hattie Adams hired the leading team**: Trial coverage from the *NYS*, *NYES*, *NYW*, *New York Evening World*, *NYT*, and *NYH*, May 5–7, 1892

22 **" 'I cannot elevate him to the level of my contempt' "**: "Hot For Parkhurst," *New York Evening World*, May 6, 1892, p. 1.

22 **"Are your guests single women?"**: "Hattie Adams's Defense," *NYES*, Apr. 7, 1892, p. 1.

22 **"hatchet-faced" curly-haired brunette**: "Triumph for Parkhurst," *NYW*, May 7, 1892.

22 **"put her arm around your neck?"**: "Young Erving Collapses," *NYW*; "Young Erving Broke Down," *NYS*, May 10, 1892.

22 **"Where am I? What day is it?"**: Ibid.

22 **"extreme nervous prostration"**: "Erving's Testifying Ended," *NYS*, May 11, 1892.

23 **"from orgy to orgy"**: "Parkhurst Scored," *New York Evening World*, May 10, 1892, p. 1.

23 **"sharper eyes than the 3,000 policemen"**: Gardner, *Doctor and the Devil*, p. 71.

24 **"I seen my opportunities and I took 'em"**: Plunkitt, *Plunkitt of Tammany Hall*, p. 8.

CHAPTER 2: THE STING

25 **Theodore Roosevelt Jr.:** Future president Theodore Roosevelt (1858–1919) was originally called "Theodore Roosevelt Jr."; when his father died in 1878, he dropped the "Jr." from his name. When he had a son in 1887, he called the boy Theodore Roosevelt Jr.

27 **"swine styes, bone-boiling establishments"**: New York Association for Improving the Condition of the Poor, Annual Report, 1858, p. 38.

27   **"you could do almost what you liked"**: "Richard Croker Young at 67," *NYS*, Nov. 29, 1908, Sec. 3, p. 10.

28   **"Standin' up to a bar"**: "William S. Devery in the Role of Judge," *NYT*, Mar. 29, 1901, p. 3.

28   **"I couldn't risk a load"**: "Devery: A Study," *NYT*, August 3, 1902.

28   **"Have you noticed any stray graft"**: Lincoln Steffens, *The Autobiography of Lincoln Steffens*, Vol. 1, p. 333.

29   **"people who monkey with the police"**: *The People of the State of New York vs. Charles W. Gardner: Stenographer's Minutes—General Sessions Before Recorder Smyth* (New York, 1893) (hereafter *People vs. Gardner*), Feb. 3, 1893, p. 23.

29   **"playing cards with a lot of prostitutes"**: Ibid.

29   **"I will get square with you"**: Ibid.

29   **"tall, well-developed woman"**: *NYW*, Feb. 2, 1893. Newspaper coverage provides key details omitted from bare-bones trial transcripts. Key dates: Feb. 1, 2, 3, 4, 7, 8, 9, 1893.

30   **"three or four ladies"**: *People vs. Gardner*, Feb. 1, 1893.

31   **"lot of disgusting pictures"**: "Paid Money to Gardner," *NYT*, Feb. 2, 1893; "How She Trapped Gardner," *NYW*, Feb. 2, 1893; *People vs. Gardner*, testimony.

31   **"everything on the calendar except keep a w-h-o-r-e"**: Ibid.

32   **"An inmate of a house of prostitution"**: "The Eight French Women," *NYW*, Jan. 15, 1893.

33   **"Joseph Lewis, alias 'Hungry Joe'"**: Thomas Byrnes, *Professional Criminals of America*, pp. 167–70, 205–206.

33   **"peach on his confederates"**: Richard Wheatley, "The New York Police Department," *Harper's New Monthly Magazine*, Mar. 1887, p. 513.

33   **"I'll have it for you on Monday morning"**: Steffens, *Autobiography*, Vol. 1, p. 222.

34   **"chased the thieves all the way to Europe"**: Riis, *Making of an American*, p. 219.

34   **"You're a nice girl"**: *People vs. Gardner*, Feb. 1, 1893.

34   **"terrible rumpus in this town"**: Ibid.

35   **"you stop short of co-habitating"**: Ibid., Feb. 6, 1893.

35   **"these psalm-singing sons-of-bitches"**: Ibid., Feb. 1, 1893.

35   **"Where is our little wife?"**: Ibid.

36   **"Search his left hand pocket"**: Ibid., Feb. 2, 1893.

36   **"If it was good enough for you to take"**: Ibid.

36   **"Don't give us any chin music"**: Ibid., Feb. 6, 1893.

37   **"100 school-teachers like you on my list"**: "Parkhurst's Man Trapped," *NYS*, Dec. 6, 1892, p. 1.

37   **"If the police would only show as much interest"**: Ibid.

37   **"You are a BAD woman, are you not?"**: *People vs. Gardner*, Feb. 1, 1893.

37   **"she was too under the influence"**: Ibid., Feb. 3, 1893.

38   **dubbing Gardner the "vilest" of men**: "Gardner and Parkhurst," *NYT*, Feb. 10, 1893.

39   **"objected to Gardner's blackmailing anyone"**: Parkhurst, *Our Fight with Tammany*, p. 148.

CHAPTER 3: THE REWARD

40   **"Jewtown"**: Jacob Riis, *How the Other Half Lives*, chap. 10.

40   **"New Israel"**: Frank Moss, *American Metropolis: From Knickerbocker Days to the Present Times, New York City Life in All Its Phases*, Vol. III, p. 160.

40   hosted the "Pig Market": Riis, *How the Other Half Lives*, chap. 10.

40   "disorderly house connected with licensed saloons": Gardner, *Doctor and the Devil*, p. 46.

41   "disorderly women and drunken men sang low songs": The [New York] Press. *Vices of a Big City: An Expose*, p. 51. An extraordinary block-by-block guide to the brothels and gambling joints of Manhattan.

41   "I'm prettier than your wife": Citizens Union, *Campaign Book of 1901*, Citizens Union Papers, Rare Book Room, Butler Library, Columbia University.

41   "I would be protected to run along quiet": New York State, *Report and Proceedings of the Senate Committee to Investigate the Police Department of the City of New York* (Albany, 1895; New York: Arno Press/NYT, 1971) (hereafter Lexow), Vol. I, p. 1124.

42   "We had very little conversation": Ibid., pp. 958, 964.

42   "if you hadn't a dollar in your pocket": "She Paid Them All," *NYH*, Aug. 17, 1894, p. 4 (testimony before Police Board). See also coverage in the *NYT, NY Trib*, and *NYS*.

42   "$1.50 for Man Shark": Ibid.

43   "if one of them women cows": Lexow, Vol. II, p. 1538.

43   find a "condom" or to use a "syringe": "In the Matter of Charges Preferred Against Jos. B. Eakins," p. 1004.

44   "*You* did some high kicking?": "Parkhurst's Little War," *NYS*, Oct. 28, 1893.

45   "smash him in the face?": Ibid.

45   he told reporters he was "disgusted": "Superintendent Byrnes Vexed," *NYT*, Oct. 29, 1893, p. 10.

46   "criminal charge of neglect of duty": *NYW*, Apr. 2, 1894, p. 7.

46   "drinks," "merry-making," and "high-kicking": "Devery Failed to Act," *NYW*, Apr. 5, 1894, p. 1; trial coverage from *NYS, NYH, NYW, NYT, NY Trib*, Apr. 5–10, 1894. (Often each reporter heard the testimony slightly differently.)

47   "fight somewhere on Fourth Street": "Byrnes Called as a Witness," *NYH*, Apr. 6, 1894, p. 4.

47   reputation on the force was "good": "Supt. Byrnes's Testimony," *NYT*, Apr. 7, 1894, p. 9.

47   His "leonine" mane of now graying hair: "Capt. Devery on Trial," *NYT*, Apr. 5, 1894.

47   "Parkhurst movement directed against": "Dr. Parkhurst Testifies," *NY Trib*, Apr. 6, 1894, p. 3.

48   he called reformers "little tin soldiers": "Mr. Devery's Opportunity," *NYT*, Aug. 26, 1901. "wings": "Devery Raps Croker and the Triumvirs," *NYT*, June 4, 1902.

48   dismissed Parkhurst as an "enthusiastic ecclesiastic": "Captain Devery Is Acquitted," *NYH*, Apr. 10, 1894, p. 5.

48   he felt the "building tremble": "Capt. Devery Acquitted," *NYS*, Apr. 10, 1894, p. 1.

49   "to discriminate among disorderly houses": "Capt. Devery's Acquittal," *New York Evening Post*, Apr. 10, 1894, p. 2.

49   "No event has transpired": Parkhurst, *Our Fight with Tammany*, p. 231.

49   "it all ran on depraved lines": Charles Parkhurst, *My Forty Years in New York*, p. 140.

CHAPTER 4: POLICE ON THE GRILL

51   "division of political patronage": E. L. Godkin, ed., *The Triumph of Reform*, p. 118.

51   "Me and the Republicans are enemies": Plunkitt, *Plunkitt of Tammany Hall*, p. 51.

51   **Prince of Plasterers**: M. R. Werner, *Tammany Hall*, p. 162.

52   **"a miserable contemptible liar"**: Lexow, Vol. I, p. 592ff. for McClave testimony; "Evidence of Bribery," *NY Trib*, May 22, 1894, p. 1.

52   **"smiling as if he were going to the circus"**: "McClave and Bribery," *NYW*, May 22, 1894.

52   **"in the form of a check on the Fifth Avenue Bank"**: *NYW, NY Trib,* and *NYS*, May 22, 1894.

52   **a "scoundrel" and a "forger"**: Ibid.

53   **"railroaded to Sing Sing"**: Godkin, *Triumph of Reform*, p. 125.

54   **"a ship sighted the Statue of Liberty"**: "The Lines are Broken," *NYW*, June 22, 1894, p. 1.

54   **"I have given up more scissors"**: Ibid., p. 2.

55   **"lots of men swearing to anything"**: Lexow, Vol. V, p. 4896.

55   **"What the hell do I care"**: Ibid., Vol. II, p. 2086.

56   **thirteen serious "symptoms"**: "Barred Out the Doctors," *NYT*, Aug. 12, 1894, p. 8; "Tried Though Away," *NYH*, Aug. 16, 1894.

56   **"My husband's life"**: Ibid.

56   **"in the best of health"**: "M'Laughlin The Next!" *NYS*, Aug. 16, 1894, p. 1

56   **"hearty" appetite**: "Four Sergeants Dismissed," *NYT*, Aug. 16, 1894, p. 8; *NYH*, Aug. 16, 1894, p. 5. (Her name appears as Laura Schilling, Louise Schilling, and Louisa Scheuler.)

56   **"I got tired of earning money"**: Ibid.

57   **"I would literally have given my right arm"**: TR to Henry Cabot Lodge (hereafter HCL), Oct. 24, 1894, Roosevelt, *The Letters of Theodore Roosevelt*, Vol. VIII, ed. Elting Morison and John Blum, p. 1433.

58   **"some of the clubbers 'looked the part' "**: "Clubbing a Minor Offense," *NYT*, Oct. 3, 1894; "Brutal Police Before Lexow," *NYW*, Oct. 3, 1894; Lexow, Vol. III, p. 2825ff.

58   **"The city is redeemed"**: "Strong and Reform!" *NYW*, Nov. 7, 1894, p. 1.

58   **"The wildest hopes of Republicans"**: "W. L. Strong Elected," *NY Trib*, Nov. 7, 1894, p. 1.

58   **"cohesion of public plunder"**: Godkin, *Triumph of Reform*, p. 126.

59   **"I am sorry, almost"**: Lexow, Vol. V, p. 4923ff., Dec. 14, 1894; "$15,000 for Creeden!" *NYS*, Dec. 14, 1895, p. 1.

59   **"take great risks even to your own danger"**: Lexow, Vol. V, p. 4966ff.; "Creeden Confesses," *NYS*, Dec. 15, 1894, p. 1.

60   **"the Crowning Exposures"**: *NY Trib*, Dec. 22, 1894, p. 1.

60   **"a battering ram could not have lodged another unshattered human"**: "Police Secrets Out," *NYS*, Dec. 22, 1894, p. 1.

60   **a tall, "handsome," imposing**: Ibid.

60   **"These dives were resorts for the criminals"**: Lexow hearings, Vol. V, p. 5325 (Schmittberger's testimony on pp. 5311–5384).

61   **"And who was the captain"**: Ibid.

62   **"He did ask me one time"**: Ibid., p. 5370.

62   **"I was given the tip"**: Ibid., p. 5373.

62   **"Unless an absolute emergency arises"**: Ibid., p. 5374.

62   **"told me to take care of her"**: Ibid., p. 5376.

63   **"Send that man back there"**: Ibid., p. 5363.

63   **"only $200 a month in the Tenderloin?"**: Ibid., p. 5375.

63   "I feel that the pillars of the church": Ibid., p. 5382.

63   "Few well-posted citizens": "The Crowning Exposures," NY Trib, Dec. 22, 1894, p. 1.

63   "Byrnes Alone in Favorable Light": Ibid.

64   "I own my residence at 58th Street": Lexow, Byrnes testimony, Dec. 29, 1894, Vol. V, pp. 5709–5758; see also "Byrnes Large Fortune," NY Trib, Dec. 30, 1894, p. 1; "Byrnes May Quit," NYS, Dec. 30, 1894, p. 1; "Byrnes and His Money," NYT, Dec. 30, 1894.

65   "to detect Limburger cheese": Quoted in M. R. Werner, It Happened in New York, p. 112.

65   shut down the city's "pool rooms": Ibid., p. 5745.

66   "I desire not to be an obstacle": Lexow, p. 5755.

66   "Scotland Yard, Paris or New Jersey": Ibid., p. 5756.

66   "the sensation of the country": "What the Committee Has Done," NYT, Dec. 30, 1894.

66   "all-controlling and overshadowing dread": Lexow, Vol. I, p. 24.

66   "established caste . . . with powers": Godkin, Triumph of Reform, p. 126.

CHAPTER 5: ENTER CRUSADER ROOSEVELT

68   "by killing the man who objected": New York Advertiser, Apr. 10, 1896, TR Scrapbook, in Theodore Roosevelt Papers, TRP.

69   "The tenements stank": Steffens, Autobiography, p. 239.

69   "Hello, Jake": Ibid., p. 257.

70   "Every police attendant": "New Police Board," NYH, May 7, 1895, TR Scrapbook, TRP.

71   "It was all breathless and sudden": Steffens, Autobiography, p. 258.

71   "my main prop and comfort": TR to Riis, Apr. 18, 1897, TRP.

71   "closest to me" during those years: Theodore Roosevelt, An Autobiography, p. 168.

71   "knew nothing of police management": "Commissioner Roosevelt," NYH, July 14, 1895.

71   found the department completely "demoralized": "Administering the New York Police Force," Atlantic Monthly, Sept. 1897.

71   "with a minimum of clients": Avery Andrews, Citizen in Action: The Story of Theodore Roosevelt as Police Commissioner (unpublished manuscript, 1945), p. 23. Available at the New York Police Department Museum (hereafter NYPD); this version appears more candid than the one in the Theodore Roosevelt Collection (hereafter TRC), Houghton Library, Harvard.

71   bringing a "can of coffee": "New Board Tries Cops," NYS, May 9, 1895, p. 9.

72   "Are there not hundreds": "Trials Are Trials Now," NYW, May 9, 1895, p. 3.

72   "How are you goin' to interest": Plunkitt, Plunkitt of Tammany Hall, p. 15.

73   "What is the distance between Tokyo and Canarsie": "Points About Policemen," Brooklyn Eagle, May 27, 1895, p. 2.

73   "open competitive examinations for all positions": "Civil Service Reform," NYT, May 9, 1895, p. 8.

73   "Of Corset Will Be Necessary": NYW, Apr. 10, 1887.

73   "took the breath out of the old stagers": "Roosevelt's Girl Secretary," NYW, May 10, 1895, p. 1.

73   "young, small and comely, with raven black hair": Ibid.

74   "obliged to restrain the virtuous ardor": Corinne Roosevelt Robinson, My Brother Theodore Roosevelt, p. 159.

74 **"I should be content with a copper cent"**: "A Slap at Byrnes," *NYES*, May 10, 1895, TR Scrapbook, TRP.

75 **"This bill is thoroughly bad and vicious"**: "Rejected by the City," *NYW*, May 11, 1895.

75 **"He slays a hippopotamus**": "Roosevelt in New York," *Washington Post*, June 14, 1895, p. 6.

75 **"No matter how grave the charge" "If I were an eloquent man"**: "Vetoed by the Mayor," *NYT*, May 11, 1895, p. 9.

75 **"intermittent delusion that he was a shrewd politician"**: Riis, *Making of an American*, p. 211.

75 **"a lovable gentleman of the Old School"**: Avery Andrews, *Citizen in Action*, p. 14, NYPD.

75 **"The old man is a brick, isn't he?"**: "Rejected By the City," *NYW*, May 11, 1895.

76 **"Parker is my mainstay; he is able and forceful but a little inclined to be tricky. Andrews is good but timid and 'sticks in the bark.' Grant is a good fellow but dull and easily imposed on; he is our element of weakness"**: TR to HCL, May 18, 1895, Henry Cabot Lodge Papers, Massachusetts Historical Society (hereafter HCL Papers). (These lines were deleted from published letters edited by Morison.)

76 **"need not be ashamed to show ourselves"**: Jacob Riis, *Theodore Roosevelt the Citizen*, p. 131.

77 **"The ordinary politician is as keen"**: "Police Appointments," *New York Evening Post*, May 14, 1895.

77 **"It is time that an example was made"**: "Police Reform Begins," *New York Journal*, May 16, 1895.

77 **"I want every decent man on the force"**: "They Do Mean Business," *NY Trib*, May 14, 1895.

79 **"beds in constant vibration"**: "Charges Preferred Against Captain Jos. B. Eakins," testimony by Arthur Dennett, p. 389.

79 **"man content to live on his salary"**: "No Need Now of Kelly," *NYT*, Dec. 17, 1894.

79 **"I have never worked harder"**: TR to (Anna) "Bamie" Roosevelt, May 13, 1895, Roosevelt, *The Letters of Theodore Roosevelt*, Vol. I, ed. Elting Morison and John Blum (hereafter MOR I), p. 456.

79 **known for his "flippant audacity"**: Walt McDougall, *This Is the Life*, p. 107. Pulitzer biographer James McGrath Morris discovered a cache of letters that reveal that thirty-year-old star reporter Brisbane was then having an affair with Pulitzer's forty-year-old wife, Kate. When apart, they wrote of "telegraphing" themselves to each other. The couple would break up the following year and Brisbane would quit the *World* and go on to have a long profitable career working for archrival William Randolph Hearst.

79 **"Sing, heavenly muse, the sad dejection"**: Arthur Brisbane, *NYW*, May 17, 1895, p. 1. Publisher Pulitzer, often out of town, forbade reporters from taking bylines but Brisbane sometimes ignored the edict.

80 **TR brought a "moral purpose"**: Riis, *Making of an American*, p. 212.

80 **"good natured, half indulgent, half amused deference"**: *NYES,* May 11, 1895, TR Scrapbook, TRP.

81 **"they are cynics of the worst sort"**: Lincoln Steffens, "The Real Roosevelt," *Ainslee's Magazine*, Dec. 1898.

81 **"I shall move against Byrnes at once"**: TR to HCL, May 18, 1895, MOR I, p. 458.

CHAPTER 6: SLAYING THE DRAGONS

82   **"There is not, except among law breakers"**: James and Daniel Shepp, *Shepp's New York City Illustrated*, p. 415.

82   **"To force Byrnes out publicly"**: *NYW*, May 25, 1895, p. 1.

83   **"the men will belong to very few clubs"**: *NYS*, "Police Board Reforms," May 18, 1895, TR Scrapbook, TRP.

83   **"would have just the opposite effect upon me"**: Ibid.

83   **"more of a mugwump than a Republican"**: *Boston Daily Globe*, May 19, 1895, p. 29.

83   **"There is nothing of the purple in it"**: TR to Bamie, June 28, 1896, MOR I, p. 545.

84   *all* **the rules must be strictly enforced**: *NYS*, "Police Board Reforms," May 18, 1895.

84   **put on the calendar "at once"**: Ibid.

84   **"practically been a dead letter"**: *NYW*, "Byrnes Talks Reform," May 19, 1895, p. 16; *NYS*, "Stirring Up the Police," May 19, 1895, p. 3; *New York Advertiser*, May 21, 1895, TR Scrapbook, TRP.

84   **"harsh, violent, coarse, profane or insolent language"**: New York City Police Department, *Manual Containing the Rules and Regulations of the Police Department of the City of New York*, p. 104.

85   **"Well, the instructions was"**: "Charges Preferred Against Jos. B. Eakins," testimony of Peter McCarty, p. 1424.

86   **"certain evils which I fear cannot possibly be suppressed"**: TR to Lucius Burrie Swift, Apr. 27, 1895, MOR I, p. 447.

86   **"a wild man, ridiculous, sensational, unscrupulous"**: Steffens, *Autobiography*, p. 215.

86   **dubbing him a "good fellow"**: TR to HCL, Sept. [no date], 1895, MOR I, p. 478.

86   **"If a man has President Cleveland"**: *NYW*, "Business, Not Politics," May 22, 1895, p. 1.

87   **"simple, practical and common sense"**: Ibid.

87   **"politeness as a sign of dignity not subservience"**: Ibid.

87   **"a policeman in full uniform open a door for a man"**: Ibid.

87   **"I'm a young man yet and never felt better"**: *NYS*, "Wanted, More Policemen," May 22, 1895, p. 3.

87   **"full enough of brute strength and courage"**: *NYW*, May 25, 1895, p. 1.

87   **"the most venomously hated"**: Wheatley, "New York Police Department," p. 500.

88   **"walking matches at Madison Square Garden"**: "Will Byrnes Follow?" *NYW*, May 25, 1895, p. 2.

88   **"I've been living on rump steak"**: Lexow, Vol. V, p. 5569 (often misquoted as "chuck steak").

88   **"I take a liberal view of the matter"**: "The Ways of the Police," *NYT*, May 4, 1884, p. 3.

88   **"they were fashionable"**: Lexow, Vol. V, p. 5467.

89   **"Corner lots in Japan"**: Ibid., Vol. V, pp. 5431, 5456; "Kellam's Trial for Forgery," *NYT*, Mar. 13, 1895 (John Goff reminiscing).

89   **looking "annoyed and angry"**: "Will Byrnes Follow?" *NYW*, May 25, 1895, p. 2.

89   WILLIAMS GONE, BYRNES TO GO: *NYES*, May 24, 1895.

90   **"muttonhead"**: TR to HCL, Dec. 26, 1896, HCL Papers (this word deleted from MOR I).

90   **"Inspector Williams has asked for retirement"**: "Williams Off the Force," *NYS*, May 25, 1895, p. 1.

90 **"Goodbye"**: Ibid.

90 **"last rescue boat"**: Ibid.

90 **"I ain't ashamed"**: "Williams Is Out of It," *New York Press*, May 25, 1895, TR Scrapbook, TRP.

90 **"Murderers and thugs"**: "Williams Off the Force" *NYS*, May 25, 1895, p. 1.

91 **"how he could give"**: "To Force Byrnes Out," *Chicago Tribune*, May 25, 1895, p. 3.

91 **"worth $1.5 million and every dollar"**: *NYS, NYW, NYH*, and other dailies, May 25, 1895.

91 **board later issued a statement**: "Byrnes May Soon Retire," *NYT*, May 26, 1895.

92 **"Admiral of the United States Navy"**: "Chief Byrnes No Longer," *NYS*, May 28, 1895.

92 **"Never have I felt sadder"**: "Byrnes Is Ex-Chief," *NYW*, May 28, 1895.

92 **"fortunes of war"**: Ibid.

92 **"Why Frank this is nonsense"**: Ibid.

92 **"Even the newspaper reporters"**: Ibid.

93 **"Not one of us"**: Riis, *Making of an American*, pp. 219, 222.

93 **"the very opposite of Roosevelt"**: Ibid.

93 **"a keen, handsome little man"**: "Capt. Peter Conlin in 1864," *NYT*, July 12, 1896.

93 **"getting the police department under control"**: TR to Bamie, June 2, 1895, MOR I, p. 459.

93 **"more full of life energy"**: Edith to Bamie, June 1, 1895, Anna Roosevelt Cowles Collection (MS Am 1834.1), in TRC, Houghton Library, Harvard University.

CHAPTER 7: MIDNIGHT RAMBLES

94 **"one of the longest and busiest streets"**: Shepp, *Shepp's New York*, p. 74.

95 **"Where in thunder does that copper sleep?"**: Riis, *Making of an American*, p. 214.

96 **"I have read your book"**: Riis, *Theodore Roosevelt the Citizen*, p. 131.

96 **"the happiest by far"**: Ibid.

96 **"one of my truest and closest friends"**: Riis, *Making of an American* (introduction by TR), p. xiii.

96 **"snoring so that you could hear"**: "Roosevelt's Stroll," *New York Press*, June 8, 1895.

96 **"Is that the way you patrol your post?"**: "Roosevelt as Roundsman," *NY Trib*, June 8, 1895.

96 **"Come now, get a hustle on"**: *New York Press*, June 8, 1895.

96 **"Officer, is this the way"**: Bits of dialogue from this avalanche of coverage: "A Modern Haroun Al Raschid," *Brooklyn Eagle*, June 7, 1895; "Police Caught Napping," *NYT*, June 8, 1895; "Roosevelt on Patrol," *NYS*, June 8, 1895; "Roosevelt's Stroll," *New York Press*, June 8, 1895; "Out on Patrol," *New York Advertiser*, June 8, 1895; "Roosevelt Out Incognito," *NYW*, June 8, 1895.

97 **"if the whole police force had dropped dead"**: "Roosevelt as a Roundsman," *New York Evening World*, June 7, 1895.

97 **"What the %$#%$# is that your business?"**: *Brooklyn Eagle*, June 7, 1895; "Sly Police," *New York Journal*, June 8, 1895; coverage by *New York Press* and *NYW*, June 8, 1895.

97 **"May I ask who you are"**: *Brooklyn Eagle*, June 7, 1895.

98 **"huge frightened guardians of the peace"**: TR to Bamie, June 8, 1895, MOR I, p. 461.

98 **HUNTS IN VAIN FOR POLICEMEN AFTER MIDNIGHT**: *New York Evening World*, June 7, 1895.

98 **"The passing policeman is afraid"**: *Brooklyn Times* as quoted in *NY Trib*, June 11, 1895, p. 7.

98 **"These midnight rambles are great fun"**: TR to Bamie, June 16, 1895, MOR I, p. 463.

99 **"finest avenue on the American continent"**: Shepp, *Shepp's New York*, p. 76.

99 **"the first class theaters"**: E. Idell Zeisloft, *The New Metropolis*, p. 636.

99 **"I drank it just to see"**: "After the Saloon Men," *NYT*, June 11, 1895, p. 9.

99 **"bad women openly walk Broadway"**: *Town Topics*, June 13, 1895, p. 12. The arch, gossipy "Saunterings" column of *Town Topics* helped inspire the *New Yorker*'s "Talk of the Town."

100 **"I did not see a patrolman putting forth"**: "Andrews On Post," *New York Evening World*, June 10, 1895.

100 **"I want you all to understand"**: "After the Saloon Men," *NYT*, June 11, 1895.

101 **an "earthquake" shake-up**: "Police Earthquake," *New York Advertiser,* June 14, 1895.

101 **"this is Execution Day"**: "Shots Don't Disturb Roosevelt," *NYW*, June 14, 1895, p. 7.

102 **"narrow unlighted apologies for streets"**: "Caught Seven Asleep," *New York Press*, June 15, 1895, p. 82, TR Scrapbook, TRP.

102 **"No bluecoat was lounging"**: Ibid.

103 **"suggested a veritable departmental millennium"**: "Brass Buttons Loose," *New York Recorder*, June 15, 1895.

103 **"Your precinct is in very good order"**: "Caught Seven Policemen," *NYS*, June 15, 1895.

103 **"shouting or singing of drunks"**: Cornelius Willemse, *Behind the Green Lights*, p. 58.

103 **"It was a dog's life"**: Max Fischel, interview typescript, TR Subject File "Police Commissioner," in Pringle Folder at TRC/Harvard.

104 **"green, their favorite color"**: Cornelius Willemse, *A Cop Remembers*, pp. 73, 89.

105 **"more or less mad dogs"**: Jacob Riis, "The Police Department of New York," *The Outlook*, Nov. 5, 1898, p. 583.

105 **"cops who have never taken a dollar"**: Willemse, *A Cop Remembers*, p. 105.

106 **"Mayor of the Bowery"**: "Lights Out at Twelve at Mike Lyons's Now," *NYT*, June 23, 1905.

106 **"Three young men walked into 'Mike' Lyons"**: "And Lo, It Was Roosevelt," *NYW*, June 15, 1895.

107 **"Mr. Roosevelt expects his dream of discipline"**: "Police Earthquake," *New York Advertiser*, June 14, 1895.

107 **"long time since a New York policeman"**: *The Outlook*, June 22, 1895, pp. 1085, 1089.

107 **"to the handle"**: "Sandwiches Not a Meal," *NYT*, July 2, 1895.

CHAPTER 8: THIRSTY CITY

109 **"jugglers, acrobats . . . and rope-dancers"**: C. D. Rust, *Penal Code of the State of New York*, Section 277.

109 **selective enforcement of the law**: "Vain Plea to the Mayor," *NYT*, June 30, 1895; *NYW*, July 5, 1895. He started out with the phrase "lax enforcement." He used "partial enforcement" in "Roosevelt Tells Why," *NYW*, July 6, 1895.

109 **"The saloons form"**: Roosevelt, *Historic Towns: New York*, p. 219.

109 **"I do not deal with public sentiment"**: *NYES*, June 20, 1895 (mistakenly identified as *NYS* in TR Scrapbook, TRP, and in *The Works of Theodore Roosevelt*, compiled by Hermann Hagedorn).

110 **"New York has never been so shocked and surprised"**: "Enforcement of Liquor Laws," *Review of Reviews*, August 1895.

110 **"The Excise Law didn't bother us"**: "Coney Island Went Wet," *NYT*, June 24, 1895.

110 **"This city is ruled entirely by the hayseed"**: Plunkitt, *Plunkitt of Tammany Hall*, p. 28.

111 **"impractical"—being opposed by 19/20ths of the population**: "Talking About Liquor," *NYT*, Jan. 25, 1884, p. 1.

111 **"Archie loves me better than anything"**: TR to Bamie, June 23, 1895, MOR I, p. 463; see also "Memories of Corinne Robinson Alsop," interview transcript, 1965, Theodore Roosevelt Birthplace, New York (hereafter TRB).

112 **"we'll bust your head open with an ax!"**: "Captain Bourke's First Meeting with Theodore Roosevelt," typescript, Oct. 1, 1923, box #79, TRB. (Bourke worked at the Theodore Roosevelt Birthplace after retiring from the NYPD.) Fight story supplemented by newspaper accounts (all June 24, 1895): "Mike Callahan Beaten," *NYW*; "Callahan Up in Court," *NYES*; "Saloon Shades Useless," *NYT*.

113 **"The first man who interferes, I'll shoot down like a dog"**: "Mike Callahan Beaten," *NYW*, June 24, 1895, p. 1.

114 **"All this talk about the impossibility"**: "Excise Law Must Be Respected," *NYT*, June 25, 1895, p. 9.

114 **"I do not thank you"**: *NYS*, June 25, 1895.

114 **"You have done very well indeed!"**: "Pulls Really Gone," *NYW*, June 26, 1895, p. 2.

115 **"How do you want it, French or American?"**: "Charges Preferred Against Captain Jos. B. Eakins," testimony of William Sawyer, pp. 568, 599.

115 **"notorious liars"**: "Advised Against Appeal," *NYT*, June 25, 1895, p. 9. See also "Captain Devery Is Reinstated," *NYH*, June 4, 1895; "Decided in Devery's Favor," *NY Trib*, June 4, 1895; "Devery Is Reinstated," *NYT*, June 4, 1895; and "To Fight Devery," *New York Evening World*, June 10, 1895.

116 **"to moderate" his "zeal" . . . "listen to a lecture"**: McDougall, *This Is the Life*, pp. 116, 140.

116 **"wide toothsome grin"**: "A Joke On Our Nervous Policemen," *NYW*, June 30, 1895, p. 25.

117 **"none of the false dignity of most great men"**: McDougall, *This Is the Life*, p. 131.

117 **"Not only all my class"**: TR to Bamie, June 30, 1895, MOR I, p. 463.

118 **"pretzels, frankfurters and sauerkraut, Limburger"**: Zeisloft, *New Metropolis*, p. 272.

118 **"On every side are family groups, father, mother"**: Helen Campbell, Thomas W. Knox, and Thomas Byrnes, *Darkness and Daylight; or Lights and Shades of New York Life*, p. 470.

118 **"harsh" and "tyrannical" enforcement**: Coverage by the *NYES*, June 29, 1895; "Germans Up in Arms," *NYT*, June 29, 1895; "Strong Defies Beer Men," *NYW*, June 29, 1895; "No Sunday Liquor," *NYH*, June 30, 1895, TR Scrapbook, TRP, May 7, 1895, to May 9, 1896, microfilm reel No. 454 at Library of Congress; see also Ferdinand Iglehart, *King Alcohol Dethroned*, p. 199.

118 **"dry sense of humor"**: Avery Andrews, *Citizen in Action,* p. 10, NYPD.

120 **"the risk of falling off the plank"**: "Climax of Dry Sundays," *NYT*, July 1, 1895.

120 **"sat around a table with a bottle of whiskey"**: "Was Hard to Get a Drink," *NYS*, July 1, 1895.

121 **" 'growlers' concealed in hat boxes"**: Ibid.

121 **"The law is no good anyhow"**: "New Police Allies," *NYW*, July 1, 1895, p. 2.

121 **"WE VOTED FOR REFORM AND THIS IS WHAT WE GET"**: Ibid., p. 1.

121 **"So dry a Sunday and so dull a Sunday"**: "Was Hard to Get a Drink," *NYS*, July 1, 1895.

121   **"If the Sunday laws were properly adjusted"**: *NYW*, June 24, 1895.

122   **"After making a tour of the beer saloons"**: *Town Topics*, June 20, 1895, p. 11.

122   **"I have now run up against an ugly snag"**: TR to Bamie, June 30, 1895, MOR I, p. 464.

123   **"Elliott has sunk to the lowest depths"**: Edith to her mother, Aug. 10, 1894. Quoted in Sylvia Jukes Morris, "Edith Kermit Roosevelt," p. 142.

124   **"There once was an old fellow named Teedie"**: Elliott to Archibald Gracie, Sept. 5, 1873, quoted in David McCullough, *Mornings on Horseback*, p. 125.

124   **"He was distinctly the polished man of the world"**: TR to Corinne Roosevelt Robinson, Aug. 29, 1894, MS Am 1540, TRC.

125   **"partly to drown the smell of my bedfellow"**: Elliott to Theodore Roosevelt Sr., Jan. 9 and 12, 1876, quoted in McCullough, *Mornings on Horseback*, p. 148.

125   **"I enjoy being with the old boy so much"**: Ibid., p. 228.

125   **"he took some ale to get the dust out of his throat"**: TR to Corinne, Sept. 12, 1880, quoted in McCullough, *Mornings on Horseback*, p. 228.

125   **"She is so pure and holy"**: Carleton Putnam, *Theodore Roosevelt, the Formative Years*, p. 209, quoted in Edmund Morris, *The Rise of Theodore Roosevelt*, p. 132.

126   **"It is the life, old man. *Our* kind. The glorious freedom, the greatest excitement"**: Elliott to TR, Apr. 24, 1881, quoted in McCullough, *Mornings on Horseback*, p. 240.

126   **"one of the most brilliant weddings of the season"**: "The Roosevelt-Hall Wedding," *NYT*, Dec. 2, 1883, p. 3.

126   **"drank like a fish and ran after the ladies"**: McCullough, *Mornings on Horseback*, p. 247.

126   **"amateur circus exhibition"**: "The Funeral Next Friday," *NYH*, Aug. 16, 1894, p. 3.

127   **"horns played a little"**: Joseph P. Lash, *Eleanor and Franklin*, p. 37. Elliott was the father of Eleanor Roosevelt, who married her distant cousin Franklin Delano Roosevelt. Edith once commented about her: "Eleanor has been here too. Poor little soul; she is very plain. Her mouth & teeth seem to have no future but as I wrote Theodore the ugly duckling may turn out to be a swan" (Edith to Bamie, May 18, 1895).

127   **"chaffed"**: TR to Bamie, undated letter #294 among letters from TR to Bamie, MS Am 1834, TRC. A birth certificate announced the arrival of Elliott R. Mann, Mar. 11, 1891; he worked at Chase Bank in New York City, and died in California on Dec. 20, 1976, without meeting his half sister Eleanor Roosevelt.

127   **"It is like a brooding nightmare"**: TR to Bamie, Feb. 15, 1891, MS Am 1834, TRC.

127   **"I regard it as little short of criminal"**: TR to Bamie, Mar. 1891, MS Am 1834, TRC.

127   **"His curious callousness and selfishness"**: TR to Bamie, May 23 and June 7, 1891, MS Am 1834, TRC.

128   **"It is his business to be an expert in likenesses"**: TR to Bamie, July 12, 1891, MS Am 1834, TRC.

128   **"DEMENTED BY EXCESS"**: "Elliott Roosevelt," *NYH*, Aug. 18, 1891, p. 11.

128   **"Dear Elliott has been such a loving tender brother"**: Corinne to Douglas Robinson, Mar. 19, 1881, quoted in "Mornings" pp. 243–244.

129   **financial decisions**: McCullough, *Mornings on Horseback*, p. 278; Morris, *Rise of Theodore Roosevelt*, p. 301; Morris, *Edith*, p. 138; Rixey, *Bamie*, pp. 45, 52.

129   **"I wish emphatically to state"**: "A Personal Assertion," *NYH*, Aug. 21, 1891.

129   **"I live in constant dread of some scandal"**: Edith to her mother, Aug. 10, 1894, Morris, *Edith Kermit Roosevelt*, p. 142.

129   **"utterly broken, submissive and repentant"**: TR (in Paris) to Bamie, Jan. 21, 1892, MS Am 1834, TRC (TR, upset, misdated it 1891).

130   **"This morning, with his silk hat, his overcoat"**: Lash, *Eleanor and Franklin*, p. 38.

130   **"DO NOT COME"**: Ibid., p. 44.

130   **"He is now laid up from a serious fall"**: TR to Bamie, July 29, 1894, MS Am 1834, TRC.

130   **"The terrible bloated swelled look was gone"**: Corinne to Bamie, Aug. 15, 1894, MS Am 1834.1, TRC.

131   **"would have been in a strait jacket"**: TR to Bamie, Aug. 14–18, 1894, MS Am 1834, TRC; also quoted in Morris, *Edith Kermit Roosevelt*, pp. 143–144.

CHAPTER 10: LONG HOT THIRSTY SUMMER

133   **"determined attitude"**: "Police Board's Crusade," *NYT*, July 18, 1895.

133   **"Blue laws and blue skies"**: *NYH*, July 29, 1895.

133   **"ALBANY'S MAYOR BLIND"**: "New York Alone Dry," *NYW*, July 15, 1895, p. 2.

133   **for whiskey, "cold tea"**: *New York Advertiser*, July 8, 1895, Avery Andrews scrapbook, TRC.

134   **"Go into a drug store and tell the member of the Lucrezia Borgia"**: *Washington Post*, "Dyspepsia is Epidemic," July 18, 1895, p. 3.

134   **"a colored youth turned a crank"**: "Wide Open," *NYW*, July 22, 1895.

135   **"even sapped the moisture and coolness from the overnight watermelon"**: Ibid.

135   **"I am not going to take any blank from any blankety-blank blank man"**: "Callahan Arrested Again," *NYW*, July 22, 1895; "Callahan on the Rack," *NYS*, July 23, 1895; "Callahan Pays a Fine of $5," *New York Evening World*, July 23, 1895; "Callahan Escapes," *New York Evening World*, July 30, 1895; "Callahan's Immunity," *NYW*, Aug. 1, 1895.

135   **"police to arrest lemonade peddlers or druggists"**: "Excise and Sunday Laws," *NYT*, July 13, 1895, p. 1; "Only Water to Drink Now," *NYH*, July 13, 1895, p. 3; "No Sunday Soda Water," *NYW*, July 13, 1895, p. 2.

136   **"The average citizen . . . has been leading a life of crime"**: "Warning! Read These Sunday Blue Laws," *NYW*, July 28, 1895, p. 30.

136   **"It is an awkward and ugly fight"**: TR to HCL, July 14, 1895, MOR I, p. 466.

136   **"I have plunged the [New York City] Administration"**: TR to Bamie, July 4, 1895, MOR I, p. 465.

137   **"narrow, harsh and unreasonable"**: "Hill on the Blue Laws," *NYW*, p. 1; "Mr. Hill Says 'Agitate,' " *NYT*, p. 8, July 12, 1895.

137   **"waste of time for the criminal classes and their allies"**: "Roosevelt Unyielding," *NYW*, July 16, 1895, p. 3.

137   **"a little tin Czar"**: *NYW*, July 16, 1895, p. 6.

138   **"as full as an L"**: "Mr. Roosevelt's Defiance," *NYW*, July 17, 1895, p. 1.

138   **"What is right in the Union Club is not wrong"**: Ibid.

138   **"I come here to speak caring nothing for . . ."**: Text of speech carried in most New York City dailies, including the *NYW*; see also "Roosevelt's Retort to Hill," *NYH*, p. 3; "Mr. Roosevelt Answers," *NYT*, p. 1, July 17, 1895.

139   **"Your speech is the best"**: For description of July 18 telegram, see TR to HCL, July 20, 1895, MOR I, p. 469.

140   **"I'll sit in the electric chair"**: *NYW*, July 22, 1895.

140   "orderly": *NY Trib*, July 23, 1895, p. 12.

140   "raise its voice against this wholly un-American doctrine": "Roosevelt Tells Why," *NYW*, July 29, 1895, p. 2.

140   "syrups," "confectionary": "Soda Water Is Left Us," *NYW*, July 21, 1895, p. 5.

140   "Roosevelt don't know how to lift the canvas": *Washington Post*, July 18, 1895.

140   "New York is rapidly becoming a jay and hayseed": *Town Topics*, July 11, 1895, p. 12.

141   "he has had such a worn and tired look": Edith to Bamie, July 29, 1895, Anna Roosevelt Cowles Collection, MS Am 1834.1, TRC.

141   Edith, of course, persists in regarding me as a frail": TR to HCL, Aug. 8, 1895, MOR I, p. 474.

141   "strongest and most hopeless": "The Case of Capt. Eakins," *New York Evening Post*, Aug. 3, 1895.

142   "You have got one of those daisies": "Charges Preferred Against Captain Jos. B. Eakins," testimony of Eakins, p. 3942.

142   "colored wenches": Ibid., p. 3927.

143   "talk about except whorehouses": Ibid., p. 4016.

143   "You think this is a crime?": Ibid., p. 4049.

144   "you thought this trial was a crime": Ibid., p. 4128.

144   "sifting" through the charges: "War Declared Against Grant," *NYH*, Aug. 4, 1895.

144   "I would not do it if I were a policeman": "Grant Not in Favor," *Chicago Tribune*, Aug. 4, 1895.

145   "We deeply regret": "Police Board Is Split," *NYS*; "Col. Grant May Resign" *NYT*, p. 1; Aug. 4, 1895, *NYH*.

146   "If my means permitted it": *NYH*, Aug. 4, 1895, p. 4.

146   "I admit it was wrong": "Made Up in Secret," *NYW*, Aug. 6, 1895.

146   "Grant is a good-natured, brave . . . give him a thorough dressing down . . . Indeed I think he rather likes me and wishes to work with me": TR to HCL, Aug. 27, 1895, HCL Papers (deleted from MOR I).

147   " 'Saw dust!' ": "A Bomb for Roosevelt," Aug. 6, 1895; *NYS*, "A Bomb for Roosevelt," Aug. 6, 1895; *NYW*, "Sawdust Game for Roosevelt," Aug. 6, 1895; *NYH*, Aug. 6, 1895.

148   "stout, gaudily dressed woman": "Eakins Trial Ended," *NYH*, Aug. 6, 1895.

148   "throw her down with the niggers": Ibid., p. 4301.

149   "To let you alone on the street": "Charges Preferred Against Captain Jos. B. Eakins," testimony of Gertie Long, p. 4294.

149   "have got their fling on these women": Ibid., p. 4297.

149   "copper women": Ibid., p. 4369ff.

150   "first dirty thing I have ever done": Ibid., p. 4344.

151   "the home becomes the scene of a debauchery": "Attacks Police Methods," *NYT*, p. 1; "Roosevelt's Defiance," *NYW*, p. 1, Aug. 8, 1895.

151   "Never in the memory of any man": "Roosevelt's Defiance," *NYW*, p. 1, Aug. 8, 1895.

152   "Never in my life did I receive such an ovation": TR to HCL, Aug. 8, 1895, MOR I, p. 475.

152   "Individual members of the police force": "Wide Open," *NYW*, Aug. 12, 1895, p. 1.

152   "Copper Jim": *Washington Post*, "Copper Jim and Brodie," Aug. 17, 1895, p. 2.

153   his *Evening Sun* article: Riis, "Roosevelt's Tour," *NYES*, Aug. 19, 1895. Amusingly different rival accounts (both Aug. 19, 1895): "Roosevelt on a Peseas," *NYW*; "Roosevelt on the Bowery," *NY Trib*.

154   "comically untrue": "Roosevelt On The Watch," *New York Evening World*, Aug. 19, 1895.

154 **"we ought not to have the saloons open on Sunday"**: TR to HCL, Aug. 22, 1895. Roosevelt and Lodge, *Selections from the Correspondence of Theodore Roosevelt and Henry Cabot Lodge, 1884–1918*, p. 165; see also HCL Papers.

155 **"Cleopatra's needle"**: "Roosevelt Labor Lost," *NYW*, Aug. 14, 1895, p. 14.

155 **"As soon as we begin to send"**: "To Try All Excise Cases," *NYT*, Aug. 15, 1895.

156 **"dignity of the court"**: "Big Saloon Men Give In," *NYS*, Aug. 24, 1895.

156 **"I am deeee-lighted"**: Ibid.

156 **"distinct greenish hue"**: "Money Came in a Flood," *NYW*, Aug. 31, 1895.

157 **"For the child was dead"**: "The Law Is Supreme," *New York Evening World*, Aug. 26, 1895, p. 4.

157 **"with the Decalogue [Ten Commandments] and the Golden Rule"**: "Honesty At The Polls," *NYT*, Sept. 4, 1895.

157 **" 'biggest man' in New York today"**: *Chicago Times-Herald*, July 22, 1895.

157 **"You are rushing so rapidly to the front"**: HCL to TR, Aug. 31, 1895, Roosevelt and Lodge, *Selections from the Correspondence*, p. 169.

CHAPTER 11: THE ELECTION

158 **"one of the half dozen best-known men in the United States"**: *Boston Daily Globe*, May 19, 1895, p. 29.

158 **"When Platt takes snuff, every Republican sneezes"**: Mayor Robert Van Wyck before the Mazet committee, quoted in the *NYT*, May 17, 1899, echoing a *New York Daily News* cartoon, Oct. 16, 1895.

159 **"such a mixture of good and bad"**: *NYH*, Apr. 16, 1903.

159 **"singularly lacking in political sense of the large kind"**: HCL to TR, Sept. 12, 1895, Roosevelt and Lodge, *Selections from the Correspondence*, p. 177.

160 **"Whoever pushes you up the apple tree"**: "Why Roosevelt Loved the Dear Old Bowery," Box #76, J. F. French folder, TRB.

160 **"tame, thin, indifferent"**: "Platt Yields to Rural Statesmen," *NYT*, Sept. 18, 1895, p. 1.

160 **"no gag law in this Republican meeting"**: "Favors Blue Laws," *NYW*, Sept. 18, 1895.

160 **"sentiment to which I am sure every Republican"**: Ibid.

161 **"liberty to levy blackmail"**: Ibid.

161 WARNER MILLER STAMPEDES: *NYW*, Sept. 18, 1895.

161 **"ill drawn and ill considered"**: TR to HCL, Sept. 1895 (no date), MOR I, p. 478.

161 **"courageous and enthusiastic support"**: Ibid., p. 480.

161 **"You do not realize how you have impressed"**: HCL to TR, Sept. 22, 1895, Roosevelt and Lodge, *Selections from the Correspondence*, p. 179.

162 **"Multiply 252 by 504 and divide the product by 378"**: New York City Police Department, *Annual Report*, 1896, p. 100.

162 **"antecedents"**: Ibid., p. 82.

163 **"He must not be a drinking man"**: *NYH*, Aug. 11, 1895; Avery Andrews scrapbook, TRC.

163 **"this officer" and "that officer"**: Coleman fight: "Night Sticks for the Police," *NYT*, Sept. 24, 1895; "Delehanty Dead," *NYES*, Sept. 25, 1895; trial coverage: "Was It Self-Defense?" *NYW*, Oct. 6, 1895.

164 **"The skull-crushing, bone-breaking night club"**: *NYW*, Sept. 25, 1895.

164 **"more religion in the end of a nightstick"**: Cornelius W. Willemse, *Behind the Green Lights*, p. 35.

164 **"the officer merely crippled the criminal"**: Roosevelt, *An Autobiography*, p. 180.

164 **"easily overpowered"**: "Night-Sticks in Use Again," *NYW*, Sept. 24, 1895.

165 **"hide in the toilet room or the cellar"**: *Town Topics*, Sept. 19, 1895, p. 10.

165 **"honest enforcement of the law"**: Various newspapers, Sept. 26, 1895, including *NYW*, "Tammany's Foes Marched Out."

166 **"brooms, etc." $41,190.95**: M. R. Werner, *Tammany Hall*, p. 166.

166 **"a bill legalizing counterfeit money"**: Ibid., p. 177.

166 **"some old-fashioned people considered"**: "Our Kings," *Harper's Weekly*, Sept. 30, 1893.

166 **"mild-mannered, soft-voiced, sad-faced"**: William Allen White, "Croker," *McClure's*, Feb. 1901, p. 325.

167 **"I do not think we have impaired our chances"**: TR to HCL, Aug. 27, 1895, MOR I, p. 476.

167 **"What a jolly saucy procession"**: " 'Teddy' Beamed on 'Em,' " *New York Recorder*, Sept. 26, 1895.

167 ***"Prosit!"***: "Home Rule Parade," *New York Advertiser*, Sept. 26, 1895.

167 ***"Wo ist der Roosevelt? Ich wurde ihn sehen"***: "Won the Paraders," *NYH*, Sept. 26, 1895.

168 **"and other signs of swelldom"**: *New York Advertiser*, Sept. 26, 1895.

168 **"best of all floats . . . an excellent conceit"**: "Reviewed By Roosevelt," *NYT*, Sept. 26, 1895.

168 **"Tie those up"**: Ibid.

168 **"Good bye, it's been great fun"**: "Parade for Sunday Beer," *NYS*, Sept. 26, 1895.

169 **"not in any way responsible for Rooseveltism"**: TR to HCL, Oct. 3, 1895, MOR I, p. 483.

169 **"Mr. Lauterbach looks important in N.Y. City"**: HCL to TR, Oct. 30, 1895, Roosevelt and Lodge, *Selections from the Correspondence*, p. 197.

170 **"The cowardice and rascality of the machine Republicans"**: TR to HCL, Oct. 3, 1895, MOR I, p. 483.

170 **"A bomb exploding in Tammany Hall"**: "For Another Seventy," *NYW*, Oct. 2, 1895, p. 1.

170 **"Down with Tammany. Down with Platt"**: "Dr. Parkhurst on Platt," *New York Evening Post*, Oct. 7, 1895; "A Fusion Ticket," *NYW*, Oct. 8, 1895, p. 2.

170 **"We insist that every citizen is entitled"**: "Fusion Comes Hard," *NYW*, Oct. 7, 1895.

171 **"I'm no Tammany man"**: "Fusion with Croker," *NYW*, Oct. 9, 1895.

171 **"The attitude of the Germans"**: TR to HCL, Oct. 11, 1895, MOR I, p. 484.

171 **"I can't help writing you"**: Ibid.

172 **"to meet it or run away like cowards"**: "Miller Unmuzzled," *NYW*, Oct. 16, 1895, pp. 1–2; "Opposes Home Rule," *NYT*, Oct. 16, 1895, pp. 1–2.

173 **" 'I don't care a rap for the consequences' "**: "Giving Tammany a Boost," *NYW*, Oct. 18, 1895, p. 1.

173 **"Why, of course, it would not be due to that"**: "Roosevelt up to Date," *NYW*, Oct. 20, 1895, p. 4.

173 **"was terribly angry"**: TR to HCL, Oct. 18, 1895, MOR I, p. 486.

173 **"crank vote"**: *NYH, NYT*, Oct. 21–22, 1895.

174 **"It has been an awful struggle"**: TR to HCL, Oct. 20–23, 1893, MOR I, p. 490.

174 **"The Germans behave very badly"**: HCL to TR, Oct. 23, 1895, Roosevelt and Lodge, *Selections from the Correspondence*, pp. 192–193.

174 **"Thank Heaven there is only one week more"**: TR to Bamie, Oct. 27, 1895, MS Am 1834, TRC.

174 **"I have made the police force work like beavers"**: TR to Henry White, Oct. 28, 1895, MOR I, p. 492; see also Theodore Roosevelt, "Taking the Police Out of Politics," *The Cosmopolitan*, Nov. 1895.

175 **"mattress vote"**: TR to HCL, Oct. 29, 1895, MOR I, p. 493.

176 **"for the good of the service"**: "Blues Shifted," *New York Advertiser*, Oct. 30, 1895, p. 1; "Many Police Votes Lost," *NYW*, Nov. 6, 1895, p. 5.

177 **"danced the war dance of the great eastside" "spank"**: "Urchin Terrors Raided," *NYW*, Nov. 6, 1895, p. 5.

177 **"Weather Prediction"**: *NYS*, Nov. 5, 1895, p. 1.

178 **"It looks as if the godly are on top"**: *NYW*, Nov. 6, 1895, p. 4. (On p. 1, the paper contradicts itself, stating "6 p.m.")

178 **colossal tower of Pulitzer's *World***: Architectural historians cite 309 feet as the height of the *World*'s office building; the newspaper staff cited 375 feet. (Ornaments and flagpoles graced the top.) The statue of Diana stood 341 feet off the ground, atop Madison Square Garden tower, which also featured ornamental details.

179 **"characters were made to perform absurd feats"**: "News Promptly Given," *NYT*, Nov. 6, 1895, p. 8.

179 **"a kaleidoscopic jumble of stale cartoons"**: "The World Had the News," *NYW*, Nov. 6, 1895, p. 4.

179 **"returns as yet are not unfavorable"**: "How Returns Were Received," *NYT*, Nov. 6, 1895.

180 **"the folly of the Good Government Clubs"**: Ibid.

180 **"I did it!" . . . "substantial for Roosevelt"**: "News Promptly Given," *NYT*, Nov. 6, 1895, p. 8.

180 **"riotous hilarity"**: "And the Tiger Howled On," *NYW*, Nov. 6, 1895, p. 4.

180 **"Teddy Roosevelt . . . became bewildered at the figures for Tammany"**: *Tammany Times*, Nov. 11, 1895.

180 **"thugs" over the "quarreling psalm-singers"**: *Town Topics*, Nov. 14, 1895, p. 11.

181 **"But for the exasperating effect of Mr. Roosevelt's"**: *NYW* (quoted in the *Los Angeles Times*, Nov. 6, 1895).

181 **"gigantic foghorn"**: "A Word With Mr. Roosevelt," *NY Trib*, Nov. 7, 1895, p. 6.

181 **"another year of his Puritanical administration"**: "Roosevelt and M'Cook," *NYW*, Nov. 7, 1895, p. 3.

181 **"most orderly and honest election"**: "Law Must Be Enforced," *NYT*, Nov. 7, 1895, p. 13.

182 **"every single [newspaper] has attacked me"**: TR to Bamie, Nov. 10, 1895, Roosevelt, *Letters from Theodore Roosevelt to Anna Roosevelt Cowles, 1870–1918*, p. 162.

182 **"The political outlook is rather discouraging"**: Ibid., Nov. 16, 1895.

CHAPTER 12: CRACK UP . . . CRACK DOWN

183 **"I have got the screws on pretty tight now"**: "Putting on the Screws," *NYT*, Dec. 3, 1895.

183 **"a humorous race prone to look upon the Italian as a 'dago'"**: "Bootblacks Alarmed Again," *NYS*, Dec. 2, 1895.

184 **"He has grown several years older in the last month"**: Bigelow to HCL, Akiko Murakata, *Selected Letters of Dr. William Sturgis Bigelow.* p. 84.

185 **"I am anxious about him"**: HCL to Bamie, Dec. [no date], 1895, Lillian Rixley, *Bamie: Theodore Roosevelt's Remarkable Sister*, p. 89.

185 **"Call the roll"**: "Capt. Eakins Has to Go," *NYW*, Nov. 27, 1895, p. 3.

186 **"as gross an act of injustice as . . . a Massachusetts witch burning"**: *New York Mercury*, Nov. 30, 1895.

186 **"The board is striving to attract"**: "Charges Preferred Against Captain Jos. B. Eakins," p. 36.

187 **"they should never be fined; they should be imprisoned"**: Roosevelt, *Autobiography*, pp. 196–198.

187 **"would remove three-quarters of the present force"**: *New York Recorder*, Nov. 28, 1895.

188 **"Don't, don't"**: "Her Night of Horror," *NYW*, Dec. 6, 1895; "Sent Her to the Workhouse," *NYH*, Dec. 6, 1895.

188 **"I'm a good girl, judge"**: Ibid.

189 **"Me no see her home"**: "Mott Sticks to His Decision," *NYH*, Dec. 7, 1895, p. 3.

189 **"walking out in the night and a street walker"**: Ibid.

190 INNOCENT LIZZIE SCHAUER: *NYW*, Dec. 6, 1895, p. 3.

190 **"wayward and incorrigible"**: "Lizzie Schauer on the Island," *NYH*; "Lizzie on the Island," *NYW*, Dec. 8, 1895; "Her Sad Life Story," *NYW*, Dec. 9, 1895, pp. 1–2.

191 **death of Gen. William Wells**: "39 Grove Street Raided," *NYS*, Dec. 8, 1895.

191 **"and fill it with negroes at $5 a month"**: Grove St. brothel information, New York Press, *Vices of a Big City*, pp. 37–39.

191 **"hat manufacture"**: "39 Grove Street Raided," *NYS*, Dec. 8, 1895, p. 1. See also (all Dec. 8, 1895): "Raided After 35 Years," *NYW*; "Raided It After Thirty-Five Years," *NYH*; "Triumph for the Police," *NYT*.

193 **"decided blond"**: "Pretty Women Faint in Court," *NYH*, Dec. 9, 1895, p. 7.

193 **"the house was pulled"**: "Mrs. Street in Court," *NYT*, Dec. 9, 1895.

194 **"I can stake my life on Lizzie Schauer's character"**: "Lizzie on the Island," *NYW*, Dec. 8, 1895, p. 2.

194 **"a loathsome disease"**: Ibid.

194 **"nothing more difficult to determine than virginity"**: Dr. Nicolas Venette, *Tableau de l'amour conjugale*, p. 95.

196 **"I order that she be discharged"**: "Miss Schauer Free," *NYH*, Dec. 10, 1895.

196 **"If the officers arrested her without cause"**: "Lizzie Schauer's Arrest," *NYS*, Dec. 12, 1895, p. 9; see also "Conlin Backs Up His Men," *NYW*, Dec. 15, 1895.

196 **"Oh mama, you don't believe the charge"**: " 'May Daly' Discharged," *NYS*, Dec. 10, 1895, p. 5.

CHAPTER 13: CHRISTMAS: ARMED AND DANGEROUS

198 **"I would rather welcome a foreign war!"**: TR to Bamie, Jan. 19, 1896, MOR I, p. 510.

199 **"Jewseph Pulitzer"**: *The Journalist*, July 12, 1884, p. 1, as quoted in *Pulitzer* by J. M. Morris.

199 **"gold-ridden, capitalist-bestridden, usurer-mastered future"**: TR to Bamie, Nov. 13, 1896, MOR I, p. 566.

199 **"He has a perfect right to speak"**: "Gathered About Town," *NYT*, Feb. 15, 1897.

199 **"purely American"**: Ibid.

199 **"Pick out about forty"**: James Bronson Reynolds, "Meeting an Emergency with the Mailed Fist," Ethel Armes anecdotes, TRB.

200 **"longest beaked noses on the force!"**: Ibid.

200   **"I am going to assign you men"**: Ibid.

200   **"great bulk of the Jewish population"**: Roosevelt, "The Ethnology of the New York Police," *Munsey's*, June 1897, p. 398.

200   **"Down the main aisle passed the agitator"**: Reynolds, "Meeting an Emergency."

201   **"Rector Hermann Ahlwardt, the noted anti-semite"**: "Eggs for Herr Ahlwardt," *NYW*, Dec. 14, 1895.

201   **"round, fat, good-natured, shiny-faced"**: "Jew Baiter in a Tumult," *NYS*, Dec. 13, 1895, p. 1.

201   **"can you find a single Jew?" "Go down to the eastside"**: Ibid.

201   **"roar of rage"**: "Eggs for Herr Ahlwardt," *NYW*, Dec. 14, 1895.

202   **"Any one else would have thrown straight"**: "Eggs for Herr Ahlwardt," *NYT*, Dec. 14, 1895.

202   **"I am neither afraid of Jews"**: Ibid.

202   **"Some of my most intimate friends"**: "No Welcome for Ahlwardt," *NYT*, Dec. 7, 1895.

202   MECCA OF OUTLAWS: *NYW*, Dec. 16, 1895, pp. 1–2.

204   **"tried to make a Puritan"**: "Mayors Talk of Reform," *NY Trib*, Dec. 18, 1895; "Strong's Confession," *NYW*, Dec. 18, 1895; "Mayor Strong's Experiences," *NYS*, Dec. 18, 1895; "Three Mayors Dine," *New York Advertiser*, Dec. 18, 1895.

204   **"laughed louder and longer"**: "Reformers in a Verbal Clash," *New York Recorder*, Dec. 18, 1895.

205   **"The *World* printed a list of criminals"**: "Mayor Strong's Experiences," *NYS*, Dec. 18, 1895.

205   *Professional Criminals of America*: The borrowings abound between "Mecca of Outlaws" and the book.

205   **"The mayor is just sick of Teddy"**: "The Mayor Only Jested," *New York Mercury*, Dec. 19, 1895.

206   **"rather gloomily"**: TR to HCL, Dec. 23, 1895, MOR I, p. 502.

206   **"Don't imagine that I really get very blue"**: TR to HCL, Dec. 27, 1895, MOR I, p. 503.

207   **a center diamond the "size of a hazelnut"**: "Theft of Burden Jewels," *NYT*, Dec. 29, 1895, p. 1; "One Thief or More?" *NYW*, Dec. 30, 1895; "No Clue to the Gems," *NYW*, Dec. 31, 1895.

207   **"the police system has permitted the existence"**: "Theft of Burden Jewels," *NYT*, Dec. 29, 1895.

207   **"Ted Roosevelt is going about the country"**: *Washington Post*, Dec. 31, 1895.

208   **"We are having a great deal of anxiety with our detective bureau"**: TR to Bamie, Dec. 29, 1895, Roosevelt, *Letters from Theodore Roosevelt*, p. 167.

208   **"worked through the squeal of some thief, or ex-thief"**: William Howe and Abraham Hummel, *Danger! A True History of a Great City's Wiles and Temptations*, p. 111.

208   **"They are just as much in the dark"**: "How to Stop Our Epidemic of Crime," *NYW*, Dec. 1, 1895, p. 21.

209   **"The sweet-tongued orchestra in the belfry"**: "Welcome the New Year," *NYT*, Jan. 1, 1896; "By By '96 Howdy '97," *NYW*, Jan. 1, 1897, p. 2 (for similar celebration).

209   **"I don't see what else I could have done"**: TR to Bamie, Dec. 22, 1895, Roosevelt, *Letters from Theodore Roosevelt*, p. 167.

CHAPTER 14: I AM RIGHT

211   **"I asked him if we'd be legislated out of office"**: "Roosevelt on the Rack," *NYW*, July 8, 1896; "Mr. Roosevelt a Witness," *NYT*, July 8, 1896; "Parker Again Testifies,"

NY Trib, July 8, 1896; "Parker Hearing Closed," *NY Trib*, July 8, 1896; "End of Parker Hearing," *NYT*, July 9, 1896.

211 **"entirely pleasant and cold-blooded"**: TR to HCL, Jan. 19, 1896, MOR I, p. 509.

212 **"perhaps the best spent of my life"**: TR to Bamie, Jan. 19, 1896, MOR I, p. 510.

212 **"I alone am Right!"**: "Police Commissioner Roosevelt from His Latest Photograph Taken by Himself," *NYW*, July 21, 1896, p. 1.

213 **"thrived and fattened through dishonesty and favoritism"**: (Roosevelt's speech to Methodists): "Roosevelt's Defiance," *NYS*, Jan. 21, 1896, p. 8; "Defends Police Board," *NYT*, Jan. 21, 1896, p. 9; "Roosevelt Is Excited," *NYW*, Jan. 21, 1896, p. 1.

214 **passed two resolutions . . . "just warfare against crime"**: "Roosevelt's Defiance," *NYS*, Jan. 21, 1896, p. 8.

214 **Riis knew the place all too well**: Riis, *Making of an American*, p. 166. For Riis's story of tramping and the bitter memory of his dog being killed, see pp. 41–45.

215 **"The system encourages pauperism"**: "Station Lodgings to Go," *NYS*, Jan. 22, 1896.

215 **"On a cold night in a comfortable home"**: Lyman Abbott, *Darkness and Daylight*, p. 46.

216 **"skulkers, loafers, outcasts and criminals"**: Helen Campbell, "Underground Life in New York," in Ibid, p. 431. See also, in this volume, Thomas Byrnes, "Low Lodging Houses," pp. 645–656.

216 **"The metropolis . . . attracts them in swarms"**: Riis, *How the Other Half Lives*, pp. 66–72.

216 **"Society for the Suppression of Benevolence"**: Edwin G. Burrows and Mike Wallace, *Gotham: A History of New York City to 1898*, p. 1160.

216 **"We are satisfied from numerous investigations"**: Robert De Forest to Mayor Strong, Dec. 30, 1895, Mayor's Papers, William L. Strong, microfilm roll #37, NYCMA.

216 **"An Experiment in Misery" "came to his nostrils"**: Stephen Crane, *The New York City Sketches of Stephen Crane*, pp. 33–42. Excellent and amusing resource for fin de siècle New York.

217 **"Yet hundreds of men and women"**: Helen Campbell, *Darkness and Daylight*, p. 420.

217 **"without employment" "not giving a good account of himself"**: C. D. Rust, *Penal Code of the State of New York*. The vagrancy law then also included habitual drunkards, persons unable to pay for disease cures, especially venereal disease, prostitutes, beggars, and persons in disguise.

218 **"unwise philanthropy"**: Roosevelt summed it up in his letter. TR to Mayor Strong, Feb 27, 1897, in Board of City Magistrates, *Annual Report*, p. 12.

218 **"lazy, dissipated, filthy, vermin-covered, disease-breeding"**: "Wandering Willies Must Work," *NYW*, Jan. 29, 1896, p. 8; "Police Lodgings Must Go," *NY Trib*, Jan. 29, 1896, p. 4.

219 **"Skeptical" Roosevelt**: Avery Andrews, *Citizen in Action*, p. 146, NYPD. Andrews argues that his bicycle policing led to founding the New York Police Department's first traffic squad.

219 **"jounced" up and down**: Roosevelt, *Autobiography*, p. 184.

219 **"shot a passerby in the leg"**: Avery Andrews, *Citizen in Action*, p. 152, NYPD.

220 **"Chances are you could tackle ten policemen"**: "Police to Have Pistol Practice," *NYT*, Nov. 1, 1895.

220 **"Policeman O'Donnell raised his pistol and fired. Bang!"**: "Told to Shoot to Kill," *NYW*, Dec. 31, 1895, p. 5.

220 **"A trained marksman can disable a man"**: "Coppers on Bicycles and at Pistol Practice," *New York Journal*, Dec. 11, 1895.

220 **"incalculable value to the force"**: Peter Conlin to TR, Jan. 19, 1897, in New York City Police Department, *Annual Report*, 1896, p. 20.

221 **"sarcasm and criticism"**: "Ward Detectives Again," *NYW*, Jan. 2, 1896, p. 5.

221 **"He is dead game and very efficient"**: TR to HCL, Aug, 27, 1895, HCL Papers (text deleted from MOR I).

221 **"He has exactly the peculiar knowledge"**: TR to Corinne, Aug. 1, 1895, Theodore Roosevelt, Correspondence and Compositions (MS Am 1540), TRC.

222 **"could be replaced with advantage by two high class clerks"**: Ibid.

222 **"queer as Dick's hat"**: Ibid.

222 **"He detested a misplaced comma"**: Louis S. Posner, "I Remember 300 Mulberry Street When!" *Spring 3100*, March 1962, p. 11. The eighty-four-year-old former secretary reminisced about the Police Board.

222 **"his mind was so independent and logical"**: Samuel Parsons, in a letter to the *NYT*, July 10, 1920.

222 **"the secret and evasive Parker and the open, direct emphatic Roosevelt"**: Avery Andrews, *Citizen in Action*, p. 31, NYPD.

222 **"very much impressed with Parker"**: William Travers Jerome, interview by Henry F. Pringle, 1929, Pringle folder, TRC.

222 **"men who have done special service"**: "New Form of Promotion," *NYT*, Aug. 1, 1895.

223 **"seniority, merit and [include a] *competitive* exam"**: "Conlin Sole Applicant," *NYT*, Dec. 4, 1895, p. 16; *NYS*, Dec. 4, 1895.

224 **"exceptionably able and trustworthy"**: "Minutes of the Trial of Andrew Parker," testimony, July 7, 1896, Vol. II, NYCMA.

225 **"Since I wrote it, I'll stand by it"**: "The Luck of Roosevelt's Tierney," *NYW*, Dec. 23, 1896; "Mr. Roosevelt a Witness," *NYT*, July 8, 1896; Parker trial minutes, NYCMA.

226 **"Theodore Roosevelt Tierney"**: Born Oct. 23, 1896, birth certificate #45132, New York City birth records, 1891–1902.

226 **"By the mobilization of the thieves, thugs and murderers in New York"**: *Washington Post*, Jan. 25, 1896.

226 **"War on the Banana Skin"**: *NYT*, Feb. 9, 1896, p. 11.

227 **"Who is 'Ted-dy' Roos-e-velt?"**: "Roosevelt Talks to Students," *Chicago Daily Tribune*, Feb. 23, 1896.

228 **"to redeem themselves and earn their self-respect"**: "Its Clean Beds Popular," *NYT*, Mar. 12, 1896.

228 **"able-bodied and strong" by a "physician who watched them as they bathed"**: Josephine Shaw Lowell to Mayor Strong, Apr. 29, 1896, Mayor's Papers, William L. Strong, microfilm roll #37, NYCMA.

229 **"drunken roughs ripe for mischief"**: Riis, *Making of an American*, pp. 154–155.

229 **"I wish you would stop him from talking so much"**: Joseph Bucklin Bishop, *Theodore Roosevelt and His Time*, Vol. 1, pp. 62–63.

230 **"I am getting this force into good shape"**: TR to Bamie, Feb. 25, 1896, MOR I, p. 516.

CHAPTER 15: DEVERY ON TRIAL

231 **"so right with Devery"**: Citizens Union, *Touchin' On and Appertainin' To Mr. Deputy Commissioner Devery*.

232 **"hypothesis of guilt by circumstantial evidence"**: "One Juryman Obtained," *NYT*, May 18, 1896, p. 3; "Language in Court," *NYT*, May 18, 1896, p. 4.

233 **"Principal Highway Robberies and Burglaries of Fifty Days"**: *NYW*, Jan. 21, 1896, p. 2.

233 **"It would be quite impossible to catalogue and refute"**: "Reports Not Verified," *NYT*, Mar. 19, 1896, p. 8; "The Police Board Angry," *NY Trib*, Mar. 19, 1896, p. 13; "Roosevelt Attacks the World," *NYW*, Mar. 19, 1896, p. 4; "World Infamy Laid Bare," *NYS*, Mar. 19, 1896, p. 1; "Scored by Police," *NYH*, Mar. 19, 1896, p. 5.

235 **"The only thing I am afraid of is"**: TR to Bamie, Mar. 9, 1896, MOR I, p. 521.

236 **"We present a simple statement of facts to-day"**: "Roosevelt's Raid," *NYW*, Mar. 19, 1896, p. 6.

236 **"The ego of the board is in danger of eclipse"**: "Conlin Shows His Hand," *NYW*, Mar. 23, 1896, p. 16.

236 **Commissioner Parker, "at first the least prominent of the quartet"**: "Police in Politics," *NYH*, Mar. 28, 1896, p. 4.

236 **"like a highwayman who says 'Pay me money or I will arrest you'"**: "Capt. Devery's Trial," *NYT*, Mar. 25, 1896, p. 14; additional coverage, first day of trial: "Devery Under Fire," *NYH*, Mar. 25, 1896, p. 8; "Bribe in Handshake," *NYW*, Mar. 25, 1896, p. 4.

239 **"glibly denied everything important" "How long did you do this 'Special Duty'?" "So it drifted along"**: Second day of testimony: "Sleepy Devery Trial," *NYW*, Mar. 26, 1896, p. 16; "Alibi for Devery," *NYH*, Mar. 26, 1896, p. 4; "Devery Tries an Alibi," *NYS*, Mar. 26, 1896, p. 3.

240 **third and final day of testimony in Devery trial**: "Devery Jury Locked Up," *NYT*, p. 3; "Devery's Jury Is Locked Up," *NYH*, p. 5; "Devery's Jury Is Out," *NYW*, March 27, 1896.

242 **verdict in Devery trial**: "Devery Is Acquitted," *NYH*, Mar. 28, 1896, p. 4; "Capt. Devery Acquitted," *NYW*, Mar. 28, 1896, p. 1; "Captain Devery Goes Free," *NY Trib*, Mar. 28, 1896, p. 1; "Capt. Devery Acquitted," *NYT*, Mar. 28, 1896, p. 1.

242 **"not the kind of man"**: "Devery Is Acquitted," *NYH*, Mar. 28, 1896, p. 4.

242 ROOSEVELT KING IN NAME ONLY: *New York Journal*, Mar. 27, 1896.

243 **"It was a political shenanigan of a high"**: Avery Andrews, *Citizen in Action*, p. 193, NYPD.

CHAPTER 16: SURPRISES

244 **"will effectively and promptly solve"**: "To Enforce Raines Law," *NYT*, Mar. 31, 1896, p. 1.

244 **It raised the drinking age from sixteen to eighteen years old**: *Bonfort's Wine and Spirit Circular*, Mar. 25, 1896, pp. 425–438 (entire text of Raines Law); "Raines Bill Provisions," *NYW*, Mar. 14, 1896.

245 **The Raines law required**: "Raines Law Problems," *NYT*, Apr. 1, 1896; "Surety Companies' Profits," *NYT*, Apr. 19, 1896; "A Good Thing for Platt's Son," *NYW*, Apr. 6, 1896, p. 1; "Platt Son Opens Shop," *NYW*, Apr. 17, 1896, p. 5.

245 **"the same idea of public life"**: Roosevelt, *The Letters of Theodore Roosevelt*, Vol. II (hereafter MOR II), p. 1473, quoted in *Mornings on Horseback*, p. 255.

245 **"hundreds of gallons of beef stew"**: "Mourn the Free Lunch," *NYW*, Apr. 2, 1896, p. 2.

245 **"like a horde of locusts"**: "To Enforce Raines Law," *NYT*, Mar. 31, 1896, p. 1.

246 RAINES MAKES A THIRST: *NYW*, Apr. 5, 1896.

246 **"unobstructed view of the bar"**: "Raines Law in Force," *NYT*, Apr. 6, 1896, p. 1.

246 **"I am going to Canarsie"**: "Must Give up the Business," *New York Evening World*, Mar. 26, 1896.

247 "**desirous of promoting only Republicans**": "Police in Politics," *NYH*, Mar. 28, 1896.

247 **"spike Conlin's guns"**: "To Head Off Parker," *NYW*, Apr. 2, 1896, p. 12.

247 LOOK FOR LIVELY FUN: *New York Press*, Apr. 9, 1896, LC Scrapbook, TRP, p. 293.

248 **"simple matter to end such deadlocks"**: "Austin Police Bill," *NYH*, Apr. 10, 1896.

248 **"I would not like to kill Mr. Parker"**: "Words Not Minced by Mr. Roosevelt," *New York Press*, Apr. 10, 1896.

248 **"I want the chief to be subject to the control of the Board"**: "In Favor of Roosevelt," *NYW*; "They Explain," *New York Advertiser*, Apr. 10, 1896.

248 **"consistency is the hobgoblin"**: "In Favor of Roosevelt," *NYW*, Apr. 10, 1896.

249 **Your board transferred policemen**: "Contest Taken to Albany," *NY Trib*, Apr. 10, 1896.

249 **"Never in the history of the force"**: "Give Mr. Parker the Lie," *NYT*, Apr. 16, 1896, p. 2; see also TR to Edward Lauterbach, Apr. 10, 1896, MOR I, p. 525.

250 **"Those statements are false"**: "Minutes of the Trial of Andrew Parker," Vol. II, p. 980, NYCMA.

250 **"so heated a wrangle"**: TR to Frances "Fanny" Parsons, Apr. 12, 1896, Letters to F.T.S.D. Parsons, MS Am 1454.41, TRC.

250 **"Walsh, *Dem.* strongly espoused by Roosevelt"**: TR to Edward Lauterbach, Apr. 10, 1896, MOR I, p.528.

251 **"I shall insist on being furnished with an ax"**: Apr. 11, 1896, *New York Advertiser*, Avery Andrews scrapbook, TRC.

251 **"That statement of Mr. Parker that he is responsible"**: TR to Edward Lauterbach, Apr. 10, 1896, MOR I, pp. 525–533.

252 **"If I had nothing worse than bombs"**: "Roosevelt's Fame Rises on a Bomb," *New York Journal*, Apr. 14, 1896.

253 POLICE REFORM LOST: *NYW*, Apr. 17, 1896, p. 1.

253 **"Roosevelt generally knew how to handle men"**: Avery Andrews, *Citizen in Action*, p. 188, NYPD.

253 **"I regret that Commissioner Roosevelt"**: "Give Mr. Parker the Lie," *NYT*, Apr. 16, 1896, p. 2.

253 **"Lauterbach queered us before the Senate Committee"**: TR to HCL, Apr. 11, 1896, MOR I, p. 533.

254 **"It was to be done through Commissioner Parker"**: TR to Mayor Strong, Apr. 28, 1896, with copy of McMorrow's April 20th confession attached, "Mayor's Letters," William L Strong, microfilm (Roll #36; Subject files: Police Dept.), NYCMA. Other details emerge: "Both Say Mr. Parker Lied," *NYS*, Dec. 30, 1896; "Roosevelt's Queer Stab at Parker," *NYW*, Dec. 30, 1896; "Parker's Name Connected with Charges of Bribery," *NYH*, Dec. 30, 1896; "Parker Baits Roosevelt," *NYS*, Dec. 31, 1896.

255 **"We did not suppose you would care"**: TR to Mayor Strong, Apr. 21, 1896, MOR I, p. 534.

255 **"I had quite a time with the mayor last night"**: TR to Avery Andrews, Apr. 22, 1896, MOR I, p. 535.

255 **"I cannot be sure of Parker's financial honesty"**: TR to Bamie, Apr. 26, 1896, MS Am 1834, TRC.

257 **"There's no fake hotel about this place"**: "Drinks All You Want," *NYW*, Apr. 13, 1896, p. 4.

257 **"one of the busiest places in New York"**: " 'Hotels' Not Molested," *NYT*, Apr. 20, 1896, p. 8.

257　**"eggs boiled to an indigestible degree of hardness"**: "Rum Ruled the City," *NYW*, Apr. 20, 1896, p. 2.

257　**"traffick in liquor"**: "Heavy Blow to Raines Bill," *NYH*, Apr. 8, 1896, p. 4; see also "Clubs Resolve to Fight," *NYW*, Apr. 3, 1896, p. 3.

258　DRINKS? ALL YOU WANT: *NYW*, Apr. 13, 1896, p. 4.

258　**"meal"**: Ibid.

258　**"guest"**: "Dry Sundays Are Over," *NYW*, Apr. 15, 1896, p. 16.

258　RUM RULED THE CITY: *NYW*, Apr. 20, 1896, p. 1.

258　**"We'll have to stop the drinks for a few minutes"**: *New York Evening World*, quoted in the *Los Angeles Times*, May 12, 1896, p. 6.

258　**"Ten beers and one hard boiled egg"**: "Question About a Meal," *NYT*, Apr. 22, 1896, p. 3.

258　**"The police have special instructions just now"**: Ibid.; see also "Mr. Conlin to Go Abroad," *NYS*, Apr. 22, 1896.

259　**"Who says Max Hochstim aint running a genuine hotel?"**: "Cold, But Beer Flowed," *NYW*, Apr. 27, 1896, p. 2.

259　**"I nominate Theodore Roosevelt"**: "Roosevelt Rules," *New York Press*, May 2, 1896; "He Named Mr. Roosevelt," *NYT*, May 2, 1896.

259　**"practical joke"**: May 2, 1896, *New York Evening Post*, Avery Andrews scrapbook, TRC.

260　**"looked like it had seen better days"**: Inspection account: "Roosevelt Sees Sunday Bars," *New York Journal*, May 4, 1896, in both TR scrapbook (TRP) and Andrews scrapbook (TRC).

260　**"an old dessicated ruin of dust-laden bread"**: Eugene O'Neill, *The Iceman Cometh* (1940), opening scene.

261　**"The practical effect is merely to charge double"**: "Differ in Opinions," *New York Advertiser*, May 5, 1896.

CHAPTER 17: DUEL

263　**"derives more joy from teasing reformers"**: "Talk of Pistols by City Rulers," *New York Press*, May 6, 1896.

264　**"expected to be better than the old one"**: "Pure Cussedness, Says the Mayor," *NYH*, Feb. 21, 1896, p. 7.

264　**"in the interests of the criminal classes"**: "Fitch's Refusal Arouses Wrath," *NYH*, Apr. 15, 1896, p. 8.

264　**"everybody in journalism, in office or in politics"**: Reply to Mr. Roosevelt," *NYH*, Apr. 16, 1896, p. 7.

265　**"Remember you are keeping this money away"**: Duel threat scene: "Call for Pistols in Mayor's Office," *NYH*, May 6, 1896, p. 6; "Fitch Said Pistols," *NYW*, May 6, 1896, p. 16; "Roosevelt and Fitch at It," *NY Trib*, May 6, 1896, p. 9; "Mayor Stopped the Row," *NYT*, May 6, 1896, p. 8.

266　**"he has often punctured grizzly bears"**: *NYES*, May 6, 1896, Avery Andrews scrapbook, TRC.

266　**"a matter easily arranged with any sane person"**: "Transfer of Funds," *NYT*, May 8, 1896, p. 9.

266　**The *Evening News* ran a cartoon**: May 6, 1896.

267　**"Yesterday I lost my temper with Fitch"**: TR to HCL, May 6, 1895, MOR I, p. 537. (The published edition leaves out "lying little blackguard.")

267   **"What is a private member?":** "Wordy Police Row," *NYT*, May 16, 1896, p. 8.

268   **"endless petty rows with Parker & Fitch":** TR to Bamie, May 17, 1896, MOR I, p. 542.

268   **"Officer, give me that beer":** "Roosevelt Chases a Cop," *NYS*, May 20, 1896; "Chased by Roosevelt," *NYW*, May 20, 1896, p. 9; "Chased by Mr. Roosevelt," *NY Trib*, May 20, 1896, p. 1.

269   **"goes away often to lecture":** *New York Recorder*, May 20, 1896, Avery Andrews scrapbook, TRC.

270   **"paid May Williams and Gussie Rous":** Brothel expenses: "Shocked by Reform," *NYW*, May 20, 1896; "Bills of Police Spies," *NYS*, May 20, 1896; "Light Shed on Police Reform," *NYH*, May 20, 1896.

271   **"I first take off my wedding dress":** "Pilar-Morin Testifies," *NYS*, May 19, 1896.

272   **Mrs. Grannis . . . "sacredness of marriage":** "Mlle. Pilar-Morin, the Pantomimist," *NYW*, May 19, 1896, p. 5.

272   **Belasco . . . "highly moral":** "Pilar-Morin Testifies," *NYS*, May 19, 1896.

272   **"invasion of the sanctity of the nuptial chamber":** "Faded Orange Blossoms," *NYW*, May 26, 1895.

272   **"Paid for Woman: $10; Wine: $20; Cigars: $2":** Brothel expenses: "Shocked by Reform," *NYW*, May 20, 1896; "Bills of Police Spies," *NYS*, May 20, 1896; "Light Shed on Police Reform," *NYH*, May 20, 1896.

272   **"Cab hire, dress suits, patent-leather shoes":** *New York Recorder*, May 21, 1896, MS Am 1834, Avery Andrews scrapbook, TRC.

273   **"illicit sexual intercourse":** Mayor's Papers, William L. Strong, microfilm roll #36, NYCMA; see also "Reply to Justice Pryor," *NYT*, May 21, 1896, p. 2.

273   **"at heart the best interests of the city":** Mayor Strong to Andrew Parker, May 20, 1896, Mayor's Papers, William L. Strong, microfilm roll #36, NYCMA; see also "Mr. Parker on the Stand," *NYT*, July 3, 1896.

274   **"I am on pretty good terms with the old boy now":** TR to Bamie, May 26, 1896, MS Am 1834, TRC.

274   **"It was the most courteous and proper method":** Andrew Parker to Mayor Strong, May 27, 1896, Mayor's Papers, William L. Strong, microfilm roll #36, NYCMA; see also "Mr. Parker on Stand," *NYT*, July 3, 1896.

274   **"You can judge my astonishment":** Mayor Strong to Andrew Parker, *NYT*, May 28, 1896; "Mr. Parker on Stand," *NYT*, July 3, 1896.

274   **"the resigning kind":** "Parker Asked to Resign?" *NYW*, May 28, 1896, p. 9.

CHAPTER 18: BACK IN BLUE

275   **"any forenoon":** Frank Moss, note, May 19, 1896, Society for Prevention of Crime papers, Rare Book Room, Butler Library, Columbia University.

275   **D.A. dropping indictments:** "Indicted Police Go Free," *NYW*, May 22, 1896, p. 3. Good summary of cases stemming from Lexow.

276   **they made the papers:** "Devery's Friends Indignant," *NYH*, May 31, 1896, p. 7; "Capt. Devery Left Out," *NYT*, May 31, 1896, p. 16.

276   **calèche drawn by two "prancing bays":** "Good Riders and Marchers," *NYT*, June 2, 1896, p. 1.

277   **Chief Conlin, "buoyant and beaming":** "Bluecoats on Parade," *NYW*, June 2, 1896.

277   **"storm of hisses":** Ibid.

277   **" 'What if I did blackmail people?' ":** "The Parade of the Police," *NY Trib*, June 2, 1896, p. 2.

CHAPTER 19: PARKER TRIAL

279 **"his most easily proven sin"**: TR to Bamie, June 12, 1896, MS Am 1834, TRC.

279 **"trivial, mere rot" "schoolboy complaint"**: "Parker to Be Tried," *NYW*, June 9, 1896, p. 16.

280 **"as much a trial of me as of Parker"**: TR to Bamie, July 12, 1896, MOR I, p. 546.

280 **"happy as a big sunflower"**: "Parker Case Fizzles," *NYW*, June 12, 1896, p. 9.

280 **"Rather to my surprise, General Tracy"**: TR to Bamie, June 14, 1896, MOR I, p. 543.

281 **"the respectable age of 46"**: Phillip Jessup, *Elihu Root*, p. 191.

282 **"That kind of evidence is laughable"**: "Mr. Parker's Absence," *NYT*, June 13, 1896, p. 8; "Parker Trial Drags," *NYH*, June 13, 1896, p. 5; "Parker's Turn to Laugh," *NYW*, June 13, 1896, p. 9; *NY Trib*, June 13, 1896, p. 13.

283 **"Today we are having a terrific storm"**: Edith to Bamie, June 13, 1896, MS Am 1834.1, TRC.

283 **"While I greatly regret the defeat of Reed"**: TR to Bamie, June 20, 1896, MOR I, p. 543.

283 **"stage manager" "two rival stars of comedy"**: "Tracy Treads on Teddy's Toes," *NYH*, p. 6; "Mr. Roosevelt's Button," *NYT*, p. 8; "Colonel Kipp Still a Witness," *NY Trib*, June 20, 1896.

284 **"To pee or not to pee"**: Patrick Feaster and David Giovannoni, liner notes, *Actionable Offenses: Indecent Phonograph Recordings from the 1890s*, Archeophone Records #1007, 2007, CD.

285 **"You have got enough evidence out of me"**: "Parker Case a Bubble," *NYW*, June 30, 1896, p. 9.

286 **speculated whether a "fool"**: TR to HCL, Mar. 1, 1897, HCL Papers.

286 **"I see my friend shakes his head"**: "Mr. Tracy Scores Mr. Roosevelt," *NYH*, June 30, 1896, p. 5.

286 **"He jumped around like a tin monkey"**: "Parker Case a Bubble," *NYW*, June 30, 1896, p. 9.

287 **"He found out things I never knew"**: "Field Day for Mr. Parker," *NYT*, July 2, 1896, p. 6.

287 **"I was most frequently in consultation with Mr. Parker"**: Ibid.; see also "Mr. Parker a Worker," *NYW*, p. 14; "In Behalf of Parker," *NY Trib*, p. 4, July 2, 1896.

288 **"as stuffy as a lower east side hall bedroom"**: "Mr. Parker on the Stand," *NYT*, p. 8.

288 **"I want to say right here"**: "Asked Parker to Resign," *NYW*, July 3, 1896, p. 14; "Their Tart Notes," *NYH*, July 3, 1896; "Mr. Parker Testifies," *NY Trib*, July 3, 1896, p. 5; "Mr. Parker on the Stand," *NYT*, July 3, 1896, p. 8.

289 **"I have always been nervous before a contest"**: TR to Fanny Parsons, July 10, 1896, MS Am 1454.41, TRC.

290 **"Was the business of the board postponed"**: Roosevelt's testimony: "War Now on Words," *NYH*, July 8, 1896, p. 9; "Roosevelt on the Rack," *NYW*, July 8, 1896, p. 9; "Roosevelt a Witness," *NYT*, July 8, 1896; "Parker Again Testifies," *NY Trib*, July 8, 1896, p. 9.

293 **"You rescheduled to suit your own convenience"**: "End of Parker Hearing," *NYT*, July 9, 1896, p. 8. For more testimony: "Parker Has a Word," *NYH*, July 9, 1896, p. 10; "Parker Trial Closed," *NYW*, July 9, 1896, p. 9; "Parker Hearing Closed," *NY Trib*, July 9, 1896, p. 9.

294 **"It has by no means been made clear"**: "The Case Against Commissioner Parker," *NYT*, July 10, 1896.

294 **"I scored a complete victory over General Tracy"**: TR to Fanny Parson, July 10, 1896, MS Am 1454.41, TRC.

294 **"with Parker not six feet distant"**: TR to Bamie, July 12, 1896, MOR I, p. 546.

294 **"Thank goodness the Parker trial is over"**: Edith to Bamie, July 9, 1896, MS Am 1834.1, TRC.

294 **"six or eight months"**: TR to HCL, July 31, 1896, Roosevelt and Lodge, *Selections from the Correspondence*, p. 229.

CHAPTER 20: RESTLESS SUMMER

296 **"unending warfare against crime"**: "Roosevelt to the Captains," *NY Trib*, July 17, 1896, p. 2.

297 **"Good Evening" to the man's "Hello"**: "Broadway to Her Rescue," *NYW*, July 17, 1896.

298 **"Of course, I can only tell you"**: TR to HCL, July 29, 1896, MOR I, p. 551.

298 **"He is a good natured, well meaning, rough man"**: TR to HCL, July 30, 1896, MOR I, p. 552.

298 **"No spoils politician ever dared to do"**: "Grant and Parker at It," *NYH*, Aug. 1, 1896.

298 **"Ten Minutes in the Latin Quarter" "exceptionally thin covering of flesh-colored stockingnet"**: "Police Stopped the Show," *NYS*, July 23, 1896.

299 **a pair of "double thick" shoulder-to-toe tights**: "Tights as Exhibit 'D,' " *NYW*, July 24, 1896.

299 **"Where she ought to be slender, she is too thick"**: *Town Topics*, July 30, 1896, p. 13.

300 **"conscienceless adventurer with no morals of any kind"**: TR to Bamie, Aug. 9, 1896, MS Am 1834, TRC.

300 **"nobody could be more amusing than the host"**: Maria Storer, "How Theodore Roosevelt Became Assistant Secretary of the Navy: A Hitherto Unrelated Chapter of History," *Harper's*, June 1, 1912, p. 8.

301 **"it would be well for me to accept Assistant Secretary"**: TR to Bellamy Storer, Aug. 10, 1896, MOR I, p. 556; see also Maria Storer, *Theodore Roosevelt the Child*, p. 16.

301 **"He listened attentively, spoke very warmly"**: TR to Maria Storer, Aug. 10, 1896, MOR I, p. 556; see also Storer, *Roosevelt the Child*, p. 17.

301 **"heated term"**: TR to Bamie, Aug. 15, 1896, MOR I, p. 557.

301 **"The heat did not reach 100 degrees"**: Daniel van Pelt, *Leslie's History of Greater New York*, p. 544.

301 **"a genuine flavor of pestilence"**: TR to Bamie, Aug. 15, 1896, MOR I, p. 557.

301 **"remove either the horses or his shop"**: Roosevelt, *Autobiography*, p. 200.

302 ONE QUART PER FAMILY: "205 Victims of the Heat in One Day," *NYW*, Aug. 11, 1896, pp. 1–2.

303 **"wish to repudiate their debts"**: TR to Bamie, July 26, 1896, MOR I, p. 550.

303 **"some numerical incantation known as the silver standard"**: Thomas Beer, *Stephen Crane*, p. 137.

303 **"a personally honest and rather attractive man"**: TR to Bamie, July 19, 1896, Roosevelt, *Letters from Theodore Roosevelt*, pp. 187–188.

304 INEFFICIENCY OF TEDDY'S RECRUITS: *New York News*, Aug. 13, 1896, Avery Andrews scrapbook, TRC.

304 **"the most remarkable exhibition of mismanagement"**: "Well, Bryan Spoke" and editorial, *NYS*, Aug. 13, 1896.

305   **"The filling of the Garden"**: "The Danger of Crowds," editorial, *NYT*, Aug. 14, 1896.

305   **"Bryan fell perfectly flat here"**: TR to HCL, Aug. 13, 1896, Roosevelt and Lodge, *Selections from the Correspondence*, p. 230.

306   **"What does your father do?"**: "A Scramble for Free Ice," *NYT*, Aug. 15, 1896, p. 8.

306   **"Prize fights have been conducted"**: "Parker Bursts a Bomb," *NYW*, Aug. 21, 1896, p. 11.

306   WAR IN THE BOARD: *NYH*, Aug. 21, 1896, p. 5.

CHAPTER 21: CAMPAIGNING FOR McKINLEY AND HIMSELF

308   **"riding over the great plains"**: TR to Bamie, Sept. 13, 1896, Roosevelt, *Letters from Theodore Roosevelt*, p. 192.

308   **"Roosevelt cannot see a dozen yards away"**: "Roosevelt on a Ranch," *Omaha World Herald*, reprinted in *Washington Post*, Sept. 6, 1896; "Roosevelt on His Ranches," *NYT*, Sept. 20, 1896, p. 12.

308   **"affairs are very much demoralized in Michigan"**: TR to HCL, Sept. 14, 1896, MOR I, pp. 559–561.

308   **"done nearly all I could do"**: TR to Bamie, Nov. 8, 1896, MOR I, p. 566; see also "The bulk of my work here is over," TR to Cecil Spring Rice, Aug. 5, 1896, p. 554.

309   **"overjoyed"**: TR to HCL, Sept. 18, 1896, Roosevelt and Lodge, *Selections from the Correspondence*, p. 235.

309   **"amused with that graceless sheeny"**: Ibid.; see also HCL Papers.

309   **"the basest set in the land"**: "Roosevelt on Honesty," *NYW*, Sept. 12, 1896, p. 3.

310   **Cabot made "remarkably good speeches"**: TR to Bamie, Oct. 4, 1896, Roosevelt, *Letters from Theodore Roosevelt*, p. 195.

310   **"silly and wicked enough to fit well"**: "A Rally in Oneida County," *NYS*, Sept. 30, 1896; "Enthusiasm in Gloversville," *NY Trib*, Oct. 1, 1896.

310   **"a garret room"**: Roosevelt and Lodge, *Selections from the Correspondence*, p. 236, footnote by HCL accompanying Sept. 18, 1896 letter; see also "Clouds Cleared Away at Canton," *San Francisco Call*, Oct. 3, 1896.

310   **"McKinley is bearing himself well"**: TR to Bamie, Oct. 4, 1896, Roosevelt, *Letters from Theodore Roosevelt*, p. 195.

310   **"it was simply delightful to be with you"**: TR to HCL, Oct. 6, 1896, Roosevelt and Lodge, *Selections from the Correspondence*, p. 237.

311   **"Did you get my note about the Canton incident?"**: TR to Bellamy Storer, Oct. 24, 1896, Storer, *Roosevelt the Child*, p. 18.

311   **"I have been nineteen years in the service"**: "Old Charges to Be Tried," *NYH*, Oct. 9, 1896, p. 7.

312   **"It is remarkable that lawyer Moss"**: "Would Ruin the Force," *NYW*, Oct. 9, 1896.

312   **"No one Commissioner would be able"**: "Is Devery Being Persecuted?" *NYH*, Oct. 11, 1896, sect. 3, p. 4.

313   **"I let myself go"**: TR to Bamie, Oct. 22, 1896, Roosevelt, *Letters from Theodore Roosevelt*, p. 196.

313   **"Instead of a government of the people"**: "Text of Mr. Roosevelt's Speech," *Chicago Tribune*, Oct. 16, 1896, p. 1; "Teddy Hits the Pops," *Chicago Daily*, Oct. 16, 1896, p. 1.

313   **"I made a success of it"**: TR to HCL, Oct. 21, 1896, MOR I, p. 237.

314   **"triumph of patriotism"**: *NYT*, Nov. 5, 1896, p. 8.

315   **"I should rather have you speak in my behalf"**: TR to Bellamy Storer, Nov. 19, 1896, Storer, *Roosevelt the Child*, p. 20.

315 **"if he thinks I am hot-headed and harum-scarum"**: Ibid. p. 23.

315 **"spoke of you with great regard"**: HCL to TR, Dec. 2, 1896, Roosevelt and Lodge, *Selections from the Correspondence*, pp. 240–242.

316 **"my influence is nothing compared to yours"**: HCL to Bellamy Storer, Dec. 2, 1896, HCL Papers.

316 **"The main reason why I would care to go"**: TR to HCL, Dec. 4, 1896, Roosevelt and Lodge, *Selections from the Correspondence*, p. 243.

316 **"only people for whom I really care"**: TR to HCL, Dec. 9, 1896, MOR I, p. 570.

CHAPTER 22: BELLY DANCERS AND SNOW BALLS

318 **"to drive out crime and iniquity"**: "Chapman and Egypt Tell," *NYS*, Jan. 13, 1897, pp. 1–2; see also "Captain Chapman Testifies," *Brooklyn Eagle*, Jan. 13, 1897, pp. 1–2; "Chapman's Version of It," *NY Trib*, Jan. 13, 1897, p. 9; "Capt. Chapman on the Stand," *NYW*, Jan. 13, 1897, p. 1; "Chapman on the Stand," *NYT*, Jan. 13, 1897, p. 11. The Chapman case drew enormous coverage in the New York City newspapers from Dec. 22, 1896, to Jan. 14, 1897.

319 **"It seems we are to have no privacy"**: Cora Routt testimony: "Dinner Chapman Raided," *NYS*, Jan. 9, 1897, pp. 1–2; dialogue during raid taken from later trial testimony, including: "That Pompeian Feast," *NYW*, Jan. 9, 1897, pp. 1–2; "It Was No Sunday-School," *NY Trib*, Jan. 9, 1897, p. 14.

320 **"played bear"**: Edith to Corinne, Dec. 23, 1896, MS Am 1785, TRC.

321 **indignation and outrage**: "The Invasion of Sherry's," *NY Trib*, Dec. 22, 1896; "Raided for Revenge," *NYH*, Dec. 22, 1896; "Police Outrage, Say the Diners," *NYW*, Dec. 22, 1896, p. 1.

321 **"A perfect whirlwind of denunciation"**: "Police Outrage, Say the Diners," *NYW*, Dec. 22, 1896, p. 1.

321 **"as the devil hates holy water"**: "Parkhurstian Insolence," *NYS*, Dec. 22, 1896.

322 **"unfitted him"**: "Police Secret Leaked," *NYW*, Dec. 22, 1896, p. 2.

322 **"That muttonhead Grant has suddenly gone in with Parker"**: TR to HCL, Dec. 26, 1896, HCL Papers.

324 **"My thighs were to be covered"**: "True Story of Seeley Dinner," *NYW*, Dec. 31, 1896, pp. 1–2. (Little Egypt's affidavit.)

324 THE INVASION OF SHERRY'S: "The Invasion of Sherry's," *NY Trib*, Dec. 22, 1896.

324 **"to be watched, and guarded"**: "Roosevelt's Moral Crusade," *Washington Post*, Dec. 23, 1896, p. 6 (quotes item in Hearst's *New York Journal* and expands on it).

324 **"The bad taste shown by young men"**: "A Case for Investigation," *NYT*, Dec. 22, 1896.

324 **"a house of entertainment of the highest character"**: "Vindication or Dismissal," *NYT*, Dec. 23, 1896.

325 **"She proved so uninteresting and so unentertaining"**: "True Story of Seeley Dinner," *NYW*, Dec. 31, 1896, pp. 1–2. (Herbert B. Seeley's affidavit.)

325 **"brokers on the Consolidated Exchange"**: "Annoyed Clinton B. Seeley," *NYH*, Dec. 24, 1896, p. 4.

326 **"an absolute untruth" "highest rating of any of the commissioners"**: "A Question of Veracity," *NYT*, Dec. 25, 1896, p. 3.

326 **"ideal Xmas"**: TR to Bamie, Dec. 26, 1896, Roosevelt, *Letters from Theodore Roosevelt*, p. 200.

326 **"rude, boisterous, insolent and arbitrary manner"**: "Squabble Over Chapman," *NYS*, Dec. 29, 1896.

327 **"The higher the standing of the people"**: "Chapman Trial Held Up," *NYW*, Dec. 29, 1896, p. 4.

327 **"I move that the charges be referred"**: Ibid.

327 **"The papers have fiercely denounced the Captain"**: "Chapman May Be Tried," *NYT*, Dec. 29, 1896.

327 ALDERMAN HALL PULLS WIRES FOR HIS FRIEND: "Chapman Trial Held Up," *NYW*, Dec. 29, 1896, p. 4.

328 **"I cut the pages out"**: "Roosevelt's Queer Stab at Parker," *NYW*, Dec. 30, 1896; "Parker's Name Connected with Charges of Bribery," *NYH*, Dec. 30, 1896, p. 4; "Both Say Mr. Parker Lied," *NYS*, Dec. 30, 1896, p. 8.

329 **"We joked about it"**: *New York Advertiser*, Dec. 31, 1896, Avery Andrews scrapbook, TRC; "Parker Baits Roosevelt," *NYS*, Dec. 31, 1896.

329 **"I should consider it a great favor"**: "Put Roosevelt in a Corner," *NYW*, Dec. 31, 1896.

329 **"Fuzzy Wuzzy"**: *New York Advertiser*, Dec. 31, 1896, Avery Andrews scrapbook, TRC. An interesting side note: the mayor had an intact copy of the *four*-page confession, which remains among his official papers, attached to TR's letter of Apr. 20, 1896.

330 **"Here matters are worse than ever"**: TR to HCL, Jan. 2, [1897] (misdated 1896), MOR I, p. 504. This inadvertent error—clearly revealed by a McKinley cabinet appointment reference in the same letter—has led numerous historians to place the TR–Parker feud in full fury far too early.

330 **"When I was at Harvard"**: "Roosevelt and the Fighters," *Washington Post*, Nov. 19, 1896, p. 6, quoting *NYS*.

330 **"Little Egypt's Own Story"**: "True Story of Seeley Dinner," *NYW*, Dec. 31, 1896, pp. 1–2 (Little Egypt and Herbery B. Seeley's affidavits; interview with Little Egypt).

331 **"We find all the diners guilty"**: *Town Topics*, Jan. 7, 1897, p. 12.

332 **"Gee! I wish I was a witness"**: "Sherry and Bitters," *NYW*, Jan. 8, 1897, pp. 1–2 (first day of trial).

332 **"bestial in the extreme" "obscene"**: "Dinner Chapman Raided," *NYS*, Jan. 9, 1897, pp. 1–2; "That Pompeian Feast," *NYW*, Jan. 9, 1897, pp. 1–2; "It was No Sunday-School," *NY Trib*, Jan. 9, 1897, p. 14 (2nd day of trial).

333 MILK BELOW: "Chapman's Trial Winds Up," *NYS*, Jan. 14, 1897, p. 2.

333 **"coon monologues" "pure filth"**: Lottie Mortimer testimony on third day of trial: "Shame: Doings at Seeley's Orgy," *NYW*, Dec. 10, 1897, pp. 1–2; "Police Raid at Sherry's," *NYS*, Dec. 10, 1897, pp. 1–2.

334 **"She is a strange sort of creature"**: Little Egypt's testimony on fourth day: "Egyptian's Story," *New York Evening Journal*, Jan. 12, 1897; "Chapman and Egypt Tell," *NYS*, Jan. 13, 1897, pp. 1–2; see also "Captain Chapman Testifies," *Brooklyn Eagle*, Jan. 13, 1897, pp. 1–2; "Chapman's Version of It," *NY Trib*, Jan. 13, 1897, p. 9; "Capt. Chapman on the Stand," *NYW*, Jan. 13, 1897, p. 1; "Chapman on the Stand," *NYT*, Jan. 13, 1897, p. 11.

334 **"principal topic of conversation in the city"**: "Chapman's Trial Winds Up," *NYS*, Jan. 14, 1897, p. 2.

335 **"Is it true that the Seeleyites"**: Ibid.; see also "Seeley Guests Mute," *NYW*, Jan. 14, 1897, p. 3.

335 **"asked me where I was going"**: *NYH*, Jan. 23, 1897.

335 **"Will it be necessary for a woman"**: Ibid.

336 precinct map without an "escort": "Captain Chapman Justifies His Raids," *NYH*, Jan. 25, 1897, p. 4.

336 **"We do not quite understand why the men"**: "Will Wrangle No More," *NY Trib*, Jan. 9, 1897, p. 14.

336 **"The streets of New York City are infested"**: "Dennett's Last Report," *NYW*, Jan. 10, 1897, p. 33.

337 **"A man's home is his castle"**: "Chapman's Raid Upheld," *NYS*, Feb. 4, 1897.

337 **"If he erred at all, he erred on the right side"**: "Chapman Is Exonerated," *NYT*, Feb. 4, 1897, p. 3.

CHAPTER 23: WHERE'S THE EXIT?

338 **"New York is now convulsed"**: TR to Bamie, Jan. 31, 1897, MOR I, p. 577.

338 **"New York is credited by outsiders"**: "Dr. Rainsford's Advice," *NYT*, Jan. 23, 1897.

339 **"too historically correct for these modern and more Puritanical days"**: *Town Topics*, Feb. 18, 1897, p. 4.

339 **"The working people do not read the accounts"**: "A Modern Masquerade," *Munsey's*, May 1897, p. 192.

340 **"You have bitten off bear's heads"**: "The Ball of the 600," *NYW*, Feb. 12, 1897, p. 2.

340 **"The complaint is such nonsense"**: "Why Police Close Streets," *NYT*, Feb. 14, 1897, p. 20.

340 **"We were immensely amused"**: TR to Bamie, Mar. 14, 1897, MOR I, p. 585.

341 **"The chief has not felt inclined"**: "Conlin Ignores Andrews," *NY Trib*, Feb. 17, 1897, p. 12.

341 **"Parker's fine Italian hand"**: Avery Andrews, *Citizen in Action*, p. 202, NYPD.

341 **"I dislike to be made use of as a missile"**: "Conlin Ignores Andrews," *NY Trib*, Feb. 17, 1897, p. 12.

342 **"I will not get into a discussion"**: "The Bertillon System," *NYT*, Feb. 18, 1897, p. 4.

342 **"I have no explanation whatever to make"**: "Bearded Roosevelt," *Boston Globe*, Feb. 20, 1897, p. 5.

343 **"Take off your hat"**: "Hats Part of His Uniform," *NYT*, Feb. 19, 1897, p. 3.

343 **"A fight between Teddy and the United States"**: *Washington Post*, Feb. 20, 1897, p. 6.

343 **"substitute carrier"**: "'Hats Off!' They Cried," *NYW*, Feb. 19, 1897, p. 12.

344 **"highly insubordinate" "subversive of discipline"**: Mayor's Papers, William L. Strong, microfilm roll #36, NYCMA; "Charges Against Conlin," *NYT*, Feb. 25, 1897, p. 12.

344 **"No, I want to kill it"**: "Charges Against Conlin," *NYT*, Feb. 25, 1897, p. 12.

345 **"areola, radiating, orange, tone dark, periphery"**: "On Bertillon's Lines," *NYW*, Feb. 26, 1897, p. 5.

345 **"custody of criminal records"**: "Answers Conlin's Friend," *NYT*, Mar. 2, 1897, p. 3.

346 **"galloping waltz" "pedigree"**: "Got 350 in This Raid," *NYW*, Mar. 6, 1897, p. 1.

347 **"Discharged." "Discharged." "Discharged."**: "Calls Arrests Unlawful," *NYW*, Mar. 7, 1897, p. 9.

347 **"Oh, go away"**: Ibid.; "Newmarket Prisoners Let Go," *NYT*, Mar. 7, 1897; see also "Police Captain Sued," *NYT*, Mar. 28, 1900.

349 **"You have been in my thoughts day and night"**: HCL to TR, Mar. 8, 1897, Roosevelt and Lodge, *Selections from the Correspondence*, pp. 252–254.

350 **"a little like bawling"**: TR to HCL, Mar. 10, 1897, Ibid., p. 254.

350 **"I have no idea what I should do next"**: TR to Bamie, Mar. 14, 1897, MOR I, p. 585.

350 **"writ of prohibition"**: "Captain Devery's Trial Stopped," *NY Trib*, Mar. 12, 1897, p. 2.

350 **"No more than two members of the board can belong"**: "Captain Devery's Injunction," *NYT*, Mar. 13, 1897, p. 5.

350   **"no more vicious system"**: Ibid.

351   **"fake" clubs**: "Raines Held Up Platt," *NYW*, Mar. 11, 1897, p. 5.

351   **"if the Democrats went to Sing Sing"**: "Tangle Over Excise," *NYW*, Mar. 13, 1897, p. 2.

351   A DISORDERLY HOUSE: *Washington Post*, Mar. 15, 1897, p. 4, quoting the *Brooklyn Eagle*.

352   **"many socialists and anarchists"**: TR to HCL, Mar. 19, 1897, MOR I, p. 586.

352   **"I was poked in the ribs"**: "Roosevelt Was Hissed," *NYS*, Mar. 17, 1897.

352   **"I saw 20,000 gentlemen"**: "Bitter Attack on Roosevelt," *NYW*, Mar. 17, 1897, p. 3; "Police Methods Attacked," *NY Trib*, Mar. 17, 1897.

352   **"were in the habit of visiting churches"**: Ibid.; see also "Roosevelt Was Hissed," *NYS*, Mar. 17, 1897; "Hot Attack on Roosevelt," *NYT*, Mar. 17, 1897, p. 3.

354   **"Edith got hold of the first"**: TR to HCL, Mar. 19, 1897, MOR I, pp. 585–587.

355   **"gentlemanly and lamblike Roosevelt"**: E. W. Ordway to Charles B. Spahr, undated handwritten note added to TR's letter to E. W. Ordway, Mar. 23, 1897, TRC MP-2.

355   **"he then *thinks himself* out of office"**: "Admissions by the Police Board," *NY Trib*, Mar. 23, 1897, p. 4.

355   **"For a big man, Devery has crawled through"**: "How Devery Stood Up," *NY Trib*, Aug. 25, 1901.

356   **"If you are at liberty to say a good word"**: TR to HCL, Mar. 25, 1897, HCL Papers.

356   **"You know the Mayor makes up his mind"**: TR to HCL, Mar. 28, 1897, HCL Papers.

356   **"weak and treacherous"**: TR to HCL, Mar. 29, 1897, MOR I, p. 591.

356   SINBAD HAS EVIDENTLY LANDED: TR to HCL, Apr. 6, 1897, Roosevelt and Lodge, *Selections from the Correspondence*, p. 266.

356   **"astonished"**: TR to Bamie, Apr. 11, 1897, MOR I, p. 593.

356   **"I do not object to any amount of work"**: TR to Henry White, Apr. 16, 1897, MOR I, p. 593.

357   **"a municipal affliction" "personal bereavement"**: Charles Parkhurst to TR, Apr. 16, 1897, TRP.

357   **"Theodore Roosevelt will have to be obliged"**: *NYW*, Apr. 7, 1897, p. 6.

357   **"What a glorious retreat!"**: "Senate Confirms Roosevelt," *NYW*, Apr. 9, 1897, p. 1.

EPILOGUE

358   **"the sporting man was in such good spirits"**: "Preparing for 'Wide Open' City," *NYH*, May 23, 1898.

358   **"utter unscrupulousness" "wide open"**: *NYT*, May 22, 1898, p. 18.

358   **"a fair and impartial enforcement"**: "Devery Against a Wide Open City," *NYH*, May 25, 1898.

358   **"no more fit to be chief of police"**: Steffens, *Autobiography*, p. 330.

359   **"Teddy's Terrors"**: Morris, *Rise of Theodore Roosevelt*, p. 614.

359   **"Are you afraid to stand up"**: Theodore Roosevelt, *The Rough Riders*, p. 126.

359   **"Three days I have been at the extreme front"**: TR to HCL, July 3, 1898, MOR I, p. 846.

359   **"We've been having the devil"**: Robert Ferguson to Edith, July 1898, Arizona Historical Society.

360   **"Alone in Cuba"**: "Mr. Dooley on Ivrything and Ivrybody," p. 106.

360   description of gambling payoffs: "The City's Crying Shame," *NYT*, Mar. 9, 1900, p. 1.

361   **"I have found out one reason"**: TR to HCL, Feb. 3, 1900, MOR I, p. 1166.

361   **"Don't you realize there's only one life"**: MOR I, footnote, p. 1337.

361 **"tactics and methods of intimidation upon respectable citizens"**: "Grand Jury Indicts Chief of Police," *NYT*, Nov. 6, 1900, p. 1; "Devery Indicted; Roosevelt Forces Orders Withdrawal," *NYW*, Nov. 6, 1900, p. 1; "Devery's Order Rescinded," *NY Trib*, Nov. 6, 1900, p. 1.

361 **"obnoxious order"**: Roosevelt, *Autobiography*, p. 312.

361 **"They're crazy!"**: "Devery's Order Rescinded," *NY Trib*, Nov. 6, 1900, p. 1.

361 **"I hope you noticed how I called down [Tammany Boss] Croker"**: TR to HCL, Nov. 9, 1900, MOR I, p. 1413.

362 VIVE LE ROI: Bigelow and Lodge to TR, Sept. 14, 1901, Murakata, *Selected Letters*, p. 183.

362 **"drop them all into the river"**: "Fat a Virtue in Devery's Eye," *NYH*, Oct. 31, 1903.

363 **"What animal comes from the bushes"**: Aaron Hoffman, *My Policies*, Library of Congress typescript (1915).

363 **"efforts were crowned with entire success"**: Roosevelt, *Autobiography*, p. 175.

364 **"fanatical gusto"**: TR mentioned in "Devery on Vice," *NYT*, Aug. 17, 1901.

364 **"The New York police force . . . did not reform"**: Lincoln Steffens, "The Real Roosevelt," *Ainslee's*, Dec. 1898.

364 **"Devery was always on trial for something"**: "William S. Devery," *NYT*, June 23, 1919, p. 12.

364 **"Devery's generosity was well known"**: " 'Big Bill' Insolvent at Death," *NYT*, May 4, 1929.

364 **"I wish about forty police captains would die"**: "Bingham Wishes 40 Captains Would Die," *NYT*, Apr. 14, 1908.

365 **"by furnishing drinks or a good supper"**: Report on 245 W. 39th Street, Lillian Wald Papers, Box #91, Rare Book Room, Butler Library, Columbia University.

365 **"Amateur Competition"**: Lothrop Stoddard, *Master of Manhattan: The Life of Richard Croker*, p. 166.

365 **"There are no better men anywhere"**: Roosevelt, *Autobiography*, p. 194.

365 **"all that I had warred against while Commissioner"**: Ibid., p. 310.

SELECTED BIBLIOGRAPHY

I. MANUSCRIPT COLLECTIONS

Arizona Historical Society, Tucson, AZ. Letters of Robert "Fergie" Ferguson.

Butler Library, Columbia University. Lillian Wald Papers, Society for the Prevention of Crime papers.

Houghton Library, Harvard University, Cambridge, MA. Theodore Roosevelt Collection, including extensive memorabilia, letters, photos, articles; Henry F. Pringle's research notes for his biography of TR; Avery D. Andrews's scrapbook and memoir.

Library of Congress. Theodore Roosevelt Papers (microfilm), Society for the Suppression of Vice blotters.

Lloyd Sealy Library, John Jay College of Criminal Justice, City University of New York. Papers of the Shibles family (1890s New York City police officers); "Trial Transcripts of the County of New York, 1883–1927" (extraordinary collection including more than 3,000 New York City trial transcripts).

Massachusetts Historical Society, Boston. Papers of Henry Cabot Lodge, including TR letters.

Morris Library, Southern Illinois University, Carbondale, IL. Frederick D. Grant letters.

New York City Municipal Archives. Mayor's Papers, especially microfilm roll no. 36, William L. Strong's Police Department letters; court records; minutes of Andrew Parker trial.

New York Police Department Museum Library. Draft of Avery Andrews memoir (*Citizen in Action*); police artifacts, including early Bertillon cards.

New York Public Library. "Committee of Fifteen" papers.

Theodore Roosevelt Birthplace, New York. Transcripts of interviews with Roosevelt family members including his sister Anna and daughter Alice; journalist Ethel Armes's TR anecdotes; J. F. French interviews with politicians; Edward Bourke's reminiscences.

Census and genealogical data obtained from www.ancestry.com.

II. MAGAZINE ARTICLES

Andrews, Avery D. "The Police Control of a Great Election." *Scribner's*, February 1898.

Comstock, Anthony. "Pool Rooms and Pool Selling." *North American Review*, November 1893.

Leary, John J., Jr. "Roosevelt on Prohibition." *McClure's*, November 1919.

"The Madison Square Garden Weather Vane: The Huntress Diana." *Scientific American*, December 26, 1891.

Matthews, Franklin. "The Cost of Tammany Hall in Flesh and Blood." *Harper's Weekly*, October 13, 1900.

———. *World's Work.* "Character of American Police," October 1901.

Posner, Louis. "I Remember 300 Mulberry Back When!" *Spring 3100,* March 1962.

"Progress of the World." *Review of Reviews,* June 1895.

Ralph, Julian. "Theodore Roosevelt, a Character Sketch." *Review of Reviews,* August 1895.

Ruhl, Arthur. "The Caliph and His Court." *McClure's,* October 1901.

Steffens, Lincoln. "The Real Roosevelt." *Ainslee's,* December 1898.

Stein, Harry H. "Theodore Roosevelt and the Press: Lincoln Steffens." *Mid-America,* April 1972.

"Theodore Roosevelt and the Problem before Him." *Leslie's Weekly,* October 10, 1895.

Wheatley, Richard. "The New York Police Department." *Harper's New Monthly,* March 1887.

White, William A. "Platt." *McClure's,* December 1901.

III. SELECTED MAGAZINE ARTICLES BY THEODORE ROOSEVELT (ARRANGED CHRONOLOGICALLY)

"Machine Politics in New York City," *Century,* November 1886.

"Six Years of Civil Service," *Scribner's,* August 1895.

"The Enforcement of Law," *Forum,* September 1895.

"Closing the Saloons on Sundays," *McClure's,* October 1895.

"The Issues of 1896," *Century,* November 1895.

"Taking the New York Police Out of Politics," *Cosmopolitan,* November 1895.

"The Ethnology of the New York Police," *Munsey's,* June 1897.

"Municipal Administration: The New York Police Force," *Atlantic Monthly,* September 1897.

"Roll of Honor of the New York Police," *Century,* October 1897.

"Reform Through Social Work," *Fortnightly Review,* December 1901.

"The American Woman," *Ladies' Home Journal,* June 1905.

IV. BOOKS

Allen, Frederick L. *The Lords of Creation.* Chicago: 1935.

Anbinder, Tyler. *Five Points: The 19th-Century New York City Neighborhood That Invented Tap Dance, Stole Elections and Became the World's Most Notorious Slum.* New York: 2002.

Anon. *Life in Sing Sing by Number 1500.* Indianapolis, IN: 1904.

Asbury, Herbert. *Sucker's Progress: An Informal History of Gambling in America.* New York: 1938.

Baker, Paul R. *The Gilded Life of Stanford White.* New York: 1989.

Bartlett, D. W. *Cases of Contested Elections in the House of Representatives, from 1865 to 1871, Inclusive. Digest of Election Cases.* Washington, DC: 1870.

Bayor, Ronald, ed. *The New York Irish.* Baltimore: 1996.

Beer, Thomas. *Stephen Crane: A Study in American Letters.* Garden City, NY: 1923.

———. *The Mauve Decade.* Garden City, NY: 1926.

Berman, Jay S. *Police Administration and Progressive Reform: Theodore Roosevelt as Police Commissioner of New York.* New York: 1987.

Biographical Directory of the State of New York. New York: 1900.

Birdseye, Charles. *Revised Statutes, Codes and Laws of the State of New York.* New York: 1889.

Bishop, Joseph B. *Theodore Roosevelt and His Time Shown in His Own Letters*. 2 vols. New York: 1920.

Blum, John M. *The Republican Roosevelt*. Cambridge, MA: 1954.

Board of City Magistrates. *Annual Report*. New York: 1897.

Breen, Matthew. *Thirty Years of New York Politics Up-to-Date*. New York: 1899.

Brooklyn Daily Eagle. A Visitor's Guide to the City of New York on the Occasion of the Return of Admiral Dewey. Brooklyn, NY: 1899.

Brooklyn Daily Eagle Almanac. Brooklyn, NY: 1897.

Brooks, Van Wyck. *The Confident Years: 1885–1915*. New York: 1952.

Brown, George W., Jr., ed. *General Ordinances of the City of New York under the Greater New York Charter*. New York: 1901.

Brown, Henry C. *In the Golden Nineties*. Hastings-on-Hudson, NY: 1928.

Brown, T. Allston. *A History of the New York Stage, from the First Performance in 1732 to 1901*. 3 vols. New York: 1903.

Bryce, James. *The American Commonwealth*. London: 1889.

Buk-Swienty, Tom. *The Other Half: The Life of Jacob Riis and the World of Immigrant America*. New York: 2008.

Burne-Jones, Phillip. *Dollars and Democracy*. New York: 1904.

Burns, Ric, and James Sanders. *New York: An Illustrated History*. With Lisa Ades. New York: 2005.

Burrows, Edwin G., and Mike Wallace. *Gotham: A History of New York City to 1898*. New York: 1999.

Butler, Richard J. *Dock Walloper: The Story of "Big Dick" Butler*. New York: 1933.

Byrnes, Thomas. *Professional Criminals of America*. New York: 1886. Reprint New York: Lyons, 2000.

Byron, Joseph. *New York Life at the Turn of the Century*. New York: 1985.

———. *Photographs of New York Interiors at the Turn of the Century*. New York: 1976.

Cahan, Abraham. *The Rise of David Levinsky*. New York: 1917. Reprint 1993.

———. *Yekl and the Imported Bridegroom and Other Stories of Yiddish New York*. New York: 1896/1898, reprint 1970.

Campbell, Helen, Thomas Byrnes, and Thomas W. Knox. *Darkness and Daylight: Lights and Shadows of New York Life*. New York: 1891, reprint 1896.

Carlisle, Robert J., ed. *An Account of Bellevue Hospital*. New York: 1893.

Carlson, Oliver. *Brisbane: A Candid Biography*. New York: 1937.

Caroli, Betty B. *The Roosevelt Women*. New York: 1998.

Cashman, Sean D. *America in the Gilded Age: From the Death of Lincoln to the Rise of Theodore Roosevelt*. New York: 1984.

Citizens Union. *Touchin' On and Appertainin' To Mr. Deputy Commissioner Devery*. New York: 1901.

Clarke, Joseph I. C. *My Life and Memories*. New York: 1925.

Collier, Peter. *The Roosevelts: An American Saga*. With David Horowitz. New York: 1994.

Collins, Percy [Price Collier, pseud.]. *America and the Americans from a French Point of View*. London: 1897.

Committee of Fifteen. *The Social Evil: With Special Reference to Conditions Existing in the City of New York*. New York: 1902.

Conboy, Kenneth. *The Reforming Impulse: Theodore Roosevelt and the New York Police*. Master's thesis, Columbia University, 1980.

Corry, John A. *A Rough Ride to Albany: Teddy Runs for Governor*. New York: 2000.

Costello, Augustine E. *Our Police Protectors: History of the New York Police*. New York: 1885.

Crane, Stephen. *Maggie: A Girl of the Streets and Other Tales of New York*. New York: reprint 2000.

———. *The New York City Sketches of Stephen Crane*. Edited by R. W. Stallman and E. R. Hagemann. New York: 1966. [Articles on opium dens, Tenderloin, bicycles, etc.]

———. *Stephen Crane: Letters*. Edited by R. W. Stallman and Lillian Gilkes. New York: 1960.

Czitrom, Daniel, and Bonnie Yochelson. *Re-Discovering Jacob Riis: Exposure Journalism and Photography in Turn-of-the-Century New York*. New York: 2007.

Dalton, Kathleen. *Theodore Roosevelt: A Strenuous Life*. New York: 2002.

Dash, Mike. *Satan's Circus: Murder, Vice, Police Corruption and New York's Trial of the Century*. New York: 2007.

Davis, Richard Harding. *The Adventures and Letters of Richard Harding Davis*. Edited by Charles B. Davis. New York: 1974.

Dilworth, Charles, ed. *The Blue and the Brass: American Policing 1890–1910*. Gaithersburg, MD: 1976.

Dolan, Jay P. *The Immigrant Church: New York's Irish and German Catholics, 1815–1865*. Baltimore: 1975.

DuMaurier, George. *Trilby*. New York: 1894.

Dunlop, M. H. *Gilded City: Scandal and Sensation in Turn-of-the-Century New York*. New York: 2000.

Dunne, Finley P. *Mr. Dooley in Peace and War*. Boston: 1914.

Einstein, Lewis. *Roosevelt, His Mind in Action*. Boston: 1930.

Emmet, Thomas. *Incidents of My Life*. New York: 1911.

English, T. J. *Paddy Whacked: The Untold Story of the Irish American Gangster*. New York: 2005.

Feaster, Patrick, and David Giovannoni. CD liner notes. *Actionable Offenses: Indecent Phonograph Recordings from the 1890s*. Archeophone Records, 2007. [Excellent notes accompanying fascinating CD]

Flexner, Abraham. *Prostitution in Europe*. New York: 1920.

Gallagher, Thomas. *Paddy's Lament: Ireland, 1846–1847, Prelude to Hatred*. New York: 1982.

Gardiner, Alexander. *Canfield*. Garden City, NY: 1930.

Gardner, Charles W. *The Doctor and the Devil, or Midnight Adventures of Dr. Parkhurst*. New York: 1894.

Gilbert, Frank. *Criminal Law and Practice of the State of New York*. Albany, NY: 1922.

Gilfoyle, Timothy J. *A Pickpocket's Tale: The Underworld of Nineteenth-Century New York*. New York: 2006.

———. *City of Eros: New York City, Prostitution, and the Commercialization of Sex, 1790–1920*. New York: 1992.

Godkin, E. L., ed. *Triumph of Reform, a History of the Great Political Revolution, November 6, 1894*. New York: 1895.

Goldman, Emma. *Living My Life*. 2 vols. New York: 1931, reprint 1970.

Gosnell, Harold F. *Boss Platt and His New York Machine: A Study of Political Leadership of Thomas C. Platt, Theodore Roosevelt and Others*. New York: 1924, reprint 1969.

Greater New York Illustrated and over 100 Selected Views of Greater New York. New York: 1899.

Greeley, Andrew M. *The Irish Americans: The Rise to Money and Power*. New York: 1981.

Gunn, Thomas B. *Physiology of New York Boarding Houses*. New York: 1857.

Hagedorn, Hermann. *The Boys' Life of Theodore Roosevelt*. New York: 1918.

———. *The Roosevelt Family of Sagamore Hill*. New York: 1954.

Hickey, John J. *Our Police Guardians*. New York: 1925.

Hodder, Alfred. *A Fight for the City: The Story of a Campaign of Amateurs*. New York: 1903.

Hofstadter, Richard. *The Age of Reform*. New York: 1955.

Hole, Reynolds S. *A Little Tour in America*. London: 1895.

Homberger, Eric. *The Historical Atlas of New York City: A Visual Celebration of Nearly 400 Years of New York City's History*. New York: 1994.

———. *Mrs. Astor's New York: Money and Social Power in a Gilded Age*. New York: 2002.

Howe, William, and Abraham Hummel. *Danger! A True History of a Great City's Wiles and Temptations*. Buffalo, NY: 1886.

Howells, William Dean. *A Hazard of New Fortunes*. New York: 1890, reprint 2002.

Hoyt, Charles H. *The Dramatic Works of Charles H. Hoyt*. Vol. 3, *A Trip to Chinatown*. New York: 1901.

Iglehart, Ferdinand. *King Alcohol Dethroned*. New York: 1917.

Irvine, Alexander. *From the Bottom Up: The Life Story of Alexander Irvine*. New York: 1910.

Jackson, Kenneth T., ed. *The Encyclopedia of New York City*. New Haven, CT: 1995.

Jeffers, H. Paul. *Commissioner Roosevelt: The Story of Theodore Roosevelt and the New York City Police, 1895–1897*. New York: 1994.

Jessup, Phillip. *Elihu Root*. New York: 1938/1964.

King, Moses. *King's Handbook of New York City*. New York: 1892.

———, ed. *Notable New Yorkers of 1896–1899*. New York: 1899.

Kluger, Richard. *The Paper: The Life and Death of the New York Herald Tribune*. New York: 1986.

Kneeland, George. *Commercialized Prostitution in New York City*. New York: 1917.

Knerr, George Francis. *The Mayoral Administration of William L. Strong, 1895–1897*. Master's thesis, New York University, 1957.

Kohn, Edward P. *Hot Time in the Old Town: The Great Heat Wave of 1896 and the Making of Theodore Roosevelt*. New York: 2010.

Kroeger, Brooke. *Nellie Bly: Daredevil, Reporter, Feminist*. New York: 1994.

Kurlansky, Mark. *The Big Oyster: History on the Half Shell*. New York: 2006.

Lardner, James, and Thomas Reppetto. *NYPD: A City and Its Police*. New York: 2000.

Lash, Joseph P. *Eleanor and Franklin: The Story of their Relationship, Based on Eleanor Roosevelt's Private Papers*. New York: 1971.

League of American Wheelmen. *Fifty Miles around New York: A Book of Maps and Descriptions of the Best Roads, Streets and Routes for Cyclists and Horsemen*. New York: 1896.

Lender, Mark E., and James K. Martin. *Drinking in America: A History*. New York: 1987.

Lessard, Suzannah. *The Architect of Desire: Beauty and Danger in the Stanford White Family*. New York: 1997.

Lockwood, Charles. *Manhattan Moves Uptown: An Illustrated History*. Boston: 1976.

Lodge, Henry Cabot, and Theodore Roosevelt. *Hero Tales from American History*. New York: 1895.

Logan, Andy. *The Man Who Robbed the Robber Barons*. New York: 1965.

London, Jack. *John Barleycorn: Alcoholic Memoirs*. New York: 1913.

Longworth, Alice Roosevelt. *Crowded Hours*. New York: 1935.

Lowe, David G. *Stanford White's New York*. New York: 1999.

Lydston, G. Frank. *The Diseases of Society: The Vice and Crime Problem*. Philadelphia: 1906.

Maas, Peter. *Serpico*. New York: 1973.

MacLeod, Xavier D. *Biography of the Hon. Fernando Wood, Mayor of the City of New York*. New York: 1856.

Mahoney, Charles S. *Hoffman House Bartender's Guide*. New York: 1912.

Marshall, Jim. *Swinging Doors*. Seattle, WA: 1949.

Matthews, Brander. *Vignettes of Manhattan*. New York: 1894.

Mayer, Grace M. *Once Upon a City: New York from 1890 to 1910*. New York: 1958.

McAdoo, William. *Guarding a Great City*. New York: 1906.

McCabe, James D. *New York by Gaslight*. New York: 1882, reprint 1984.

McCullough, David. *Mornings on Horseback: The Story of an Extraordinary Family, a Vanished Way of Life, and the Unique Child Who Became Theodore Roosevelt*. New York: 1981.

McDougall, Walt. *This Is the Life!*. New York: 1926.

Millard, Candice. *The River of Doubt: Theodore Roosevelt's Darkest Journey*. New York: 2005.

Miller, Kerby, and Paul Wagner. *Out of Ireland: The Story of Irish Emigration to America*. Washington, DC: 1994.

Mooney, Michael M. *Evelyn Nesbit and Stanford White: Love and Death in the Gilded Age*. New York: 1976.

Morris, Edmund. *The Rise of Theodore Roosevelt*. New York: 1979.

———. *Theodore Rex*. New York: 2001.

Morris, James McGrath. *Pulitzer: A Life in Politics, Print, and Power*. New York: 2010.

Morris, Sylvia J. *Edith Kermit Roosevelt*. New York: 1990.

Moss, Frank. *American Metropolis: From Knickerbocker Days to the Present Times, New York City Life in All Its Phases*. New York: 1897.

Murakata, Akiko. *Selected Letters of Dr. William Sturgis Bigelow*. Ph.D. dissertation, George Washington University, 1971.

New York City Chamber of Commerce. *Papers and Proceedings of Committee on the Police Problem, City of New York*. New York: 1905.

New York City Police Department. *Annual Report*. New York: 1895, 1896, 1897. [Best source for dept. statistics during TR's police tenure]

New York Police Department. *Manual Containing the Rules and Regulations of the Police Department of the City of New York*. New York: 1891 and 1901 editions.

The [New York] Press. *Vices of a Big City: An Expose*. New York: 1890.

New York State. *Report and Proceedings of the Senate Committee to Investigate the Police Department of the City of New York* [Lexow Committee]. 5 vols. Albany: 1895; New York: 1971.

New York State Assembly. *Report of the Special Committee Appointed to Investigate the Local Government of the City and County of New York*. 2 vols. Albany, NY: 1884.

———. *Report of the Special Committee of the Assembly Appointed to Investigate the Public Offices and Departments of the City of New York* [Mazet Committee]. 5 vols. Albany, NY: 1900.

O'Connor, Richard. *Hell's Kitchen: The Roaring Days of New York's Wild West Side*. Philadelphia: 1958.

O'Toole, Patricia. *When Trumpets Call: Theodore Roosevelt After the White House*. New York: 2005.

Okrent, Daniel. *Last Call: The Rise and Fall of Prohibition*. New York: 2010.

Orth, Samuel P. *The Boss and the Machine: A Chronicle of the Politicians and Party Organizations*. New Haven, CT: 1919.

Parkhurst, Charles H. *My Forty Years in New York*. New York: 1923.

———. *Our Fight with Tammany*. New York: 1895.

Patterson, Jerry E. *The First Four Hundred: Mrs. Astor's New York in the Gilded Age*. New York: 2000.

Plunkitt, George Washington. *Plunkitt of Tammany Hall: A Series of Very Plain Talks on Very Practical Politics Delivered by ex-Senator George Washington Plunkitt. . . .* Edited by William Riordon. New York: 1948.

Powers, Ron. *Mark Twain: A Life.* New York: 2005.

Pringle, Henry F. *Theodore Roosevelt: A Biography.* New York: 1931.

Reid, Mayne. *Boy Hunters or Adventures in Search of a White Buffalo.* New York: 1869.

Richardson, James F. *The New York Police: Colonial Times to 1901.* New York: 1970.

Riis, Jacob A. *How the Other Half Lives.* New York: 1890.

———. *The Making of an American.* New York: 1923.

———. *Theodore Roosevelt, the Citizen.* New York: 1903.

Rixley, Lillian. *Bamie: Theodore Roosevelt's Remarkable Sister.* New York: 1963.

Robinson, Corinne Roosevelt. *My Brother Theodore Roosevelt.* New York: 1921.

Roosevelt, Theodore. *An Autobiography.* New York: 1913.

———. *Historic Towns: New York.* New York: 1891/new postscript 1896.

———. *Letters from Theodore Roosevelt to Anna Roosevelt Cowles, 1870–1918.* New York: 1924.

———. *The Letters of Theodore Roosevelt.* 8 vols. Edited by Elting Morison and John Morton Blum. Cambridge, MA: 1951. [Main printed source for TR letters, though occasionally sanitized]

———. *The Naval War of 1812.* New York: 1882.

———. *The Rough Riders.* New York: 1899.

———. *The Winning of the West.* 4 vols. New York: 1889–1896.

———. *The Works of Theodore Roosevelt.* 24 vols. Edited by Hermann Hagedorn. New York: 1923–1926.

———, and Henry Cabot Lodge. *Selections from the Correspondence of Theodore Roosevelt and Henry Cabot Lodge, 1884–1918.* New York: 1925.

Rovere, Richard. *Howe and Hummel: Their True and Scandalous History.* New York: 1947.

Rust, C. D. *Penal Code of the State of New York.* New York: 1895.

Samuels, Charles, and Louise Samuels. *Once Upon a Stage: The Merry World of Vaudeville.* New York: 1974.

Sante, Luc. *Lowlife: Lures and Snares of Old New York.* New York: 1991.

Schachne, Carolyn. "Some Aspects in the History of the Police Department of the City of New York." Master's thesis, Columbia University, 1940.

Schlereth, Thomas J. *Victorian America: Transformations in Everyday Life, 1876–1915.* New York: 1991.

Shepp, James, and Daniel Shepp. *Shepp's New York City Illustrated: Scene and Story of the Metropolis in the Western World.* Chicago: 1894.

Silvernail, William. *The Penal Code and Code of Criminal Procedure of the State of New York.* Albany, NY: 1902.

Sloat, Warren. *A Battle for the Soul of New York: Tammany Hall, Police Corruption, Vice and Reverend Charles Parkhurst's Crusade Against Them, 1892–1895.* New York: 2002.

Stallman, R. W. *Stephen Crane: A Biography.* New York: 1968.

Social Register, New York. New York: 1895.

Steffens, Lincoln. *Autobiography of Lincoln Steffens.* New York: 1931, reprint 1958.

Stoddard, Henry L. *As I Knew Them: Presidents and Politics from Grant to Coolidge.* New York: 1927.

Stoddard, Lothrop. *Master of Manhattan: The Life of Richard Croker.* New York: 1931.

Storer, Maria L. *Theodore Roosevelt the Child.* London: 1921.

Stout, Glenn. *Yankees Century: 100 Years of New York Yankees Baseball.* Boston: 2002.

Strong, George Templeton. *The Diary of George Templeton Strong*. Edited by Alan Nevins and Milton Thomas. Vols. 3 and 4. New York: 1952.

Sweetser, M. F. *How to Know New York City*. New York: 1895.

Tolman, William H. *Municipal Reform Movements in the United States*. New York: 1895.

Townsend, Edward W. *Chimmie Fadden, Major Max & Other Stories*. New York: 1895.

Townsend, John D. *New York in Bondage*. New York: 1901.

Walling, George. *Recollections of a New York Chief of Police*. New York: 1887.

Washburn, Josie. *The Underworld Sewer: A Prostitute Reflects on Life in the Trade, 1871–1909*. Lincoln, NB: 1997.

Welch, Richard. *King of the Bowery: Big Tim Sullivan, Tammany Hall and New York City from the Gilded Age to the Progressive Era*. Cranbury, NJ: 2008.

Werner, M. R. *It Happened in New York*. New York: 1957.

———. *Tammany Hall*. Garden City, NY: 1928.

Willemse, Cornelius W. *Behind the Green Lights*. New York: 1931.

———. *A Cop Remembers*. New York: 1933.

Wister, Owen. *Roosevelt: The Story of a Friendship, 1880–1919*. New York: 1930.

Wondrich, David. *Imbibe! From Absinthe Cocktail to Whiskey Smash. . . .* New York: 2007.

Zeisloft, E. Idell. *The New Metropolis: 1600—Memorable Events of Three Centuries—1900 from the Island of Mana-Hat-Ta to Greater New York at the Close of the Nineteenth Century*. New York: 1899.

V. TRIAL TRANSCRIPTS

In the Matter of Charges Preferred Against Jos. B. Eakins. New York: 1896. (Microfilm typescript of Police Board hearing, 4,397 pages, available at New York Public Library.)

The People of the State of New York vs. Charles W. Gardner: Stenographer's Minutes—General Sessions Before Recorder Smyth. New York: 1893. (Available at New York Public Library.)

Roosevelt vs. Newett: A Transcript of the Testimony Taken and Depositions Read at Marquette, Mich. Privately printed, 1914, by W. Emlen Roosevelt.

ILLUSTRATION CREDITS

Page 1
TOP RIGHT: Photo courtesy Saint-Gaudens National Historic Site, Cornish, NH

Page 2
TOP: Brown Brothers
BOTTOM: *The New Metropolis* by E. Idell Zeisloft (1899), p. 518

Page 3
TOP: Municipal Archives, City of New York, Court of General Sessions, box 118, folder 1249
BOTTOM: Municipal Archives, City of New York. Court of General Sessions, box 119, folder 1257

Page 4
TOP: (Jacob Riis, Richard Hoe Lawrence, Henry G. Piffard) Museum of City of New York [90.13.2.95]
MIDDLE: (Jacob Riis, Richard Hoe Lawrence, Henry G. Piffard) Museum of City of New York [90.13.2.198]
BOTTOM: Jacob Riis, Museum of City of New York [90.13.4.165]

Page 5
TOP: C. M. Gilbert. Library of Congress [3c17936u]
BOTTOM, LEFT: Library of Congress, 1913 [13589-u]
BOTTOM, RIGHT: *Tammany Hall* by M. R. Werner (Doubleday, 1928), p. 494; photo c. 1900

Page 6
TOP: William-Adolphe Bouguereau, 1873
BOTTOM: *The New Metropolis* by E. Idell Zeisloft (1899), p. 325

Page 7
TOP: Museum of City of New York, Byron Co., 1897 [93.1.1.18453]
BOTTOM: Museum of City of New York, Byron Co., 1898 [93.1.1.18122]

Page 8
TOP: Theodore Roosevelt Collection, Harvard College Library (560.22-001)
MIDDLE: Theodore Roosevelt Collection, Harvard College Library (560.22-001)
BOTTOM: T. C. Platt album. TRC/Harvard (Roosevelt R500.P69a)

Page 9

TOP: *Review of Reviews,* June 1895, p. 625. TRC/Harvard (Roosevelt 335.R32, p. 625)
MIDDLE: "Professional Criminals of America" by Thomas Byrnes (1886)
BOTTOM: Public domain. New York Public Library Digital Gallery image of *Harper's New Monthly Magazine,* March 1887, p. 500

Page 10

TOP: Museum of City of New York, Byron Co. [93.1.1.18373]
MIDDLE: *New York Recorder,* June 15, 1895
BOTTOM: *New York Commercial Advertiser,* July 13, 1895

Page 11

TOP: *The New Metropolis* by E. Idell Zeisloft (1899), p. 140
MIDDLE: "American Metropolis" by Frank Moss, Vol. II (1897), p. 378
BOTTOM: H. Rocher. TRC/Harvard (520.12-018)

Page 12

TOP: (Jacob Riis) Museum of City of New York [90.13.1.246]
MIDDLE: Library of Congress, 1898
BOTTOM: Library of Congress, 1901

Page 13

TOP: Museum of City of New York, Byron Co. [93.1.1.7745]
MIDDLE: (Jacob Riis, Richard Hoe Lawrence) Museum of City of New York [90.13.1.92]
BOTTOM: Museum of City of New York [90.13.1.2]

Page 14

TOP: Museum of City of New York, Byron Co., Kid McCoy fight, 1900 [93.1.1.2713]
MIDDLE: *New York Evening Telegram,* Nov. 19, 1896
BOTTOM: *New York News,* May 6, 1896

Page 15

TOP: L. Reutlinger, Duvernoy Casino, Paris, c. 1890
MIDDLE: Library of Congress, c. 1900
BOTTOM: E. Agelou, c. 1900

Page 16

TOP, LEFT: Bain News Service. Library of Congress
TOP, RIGHT: Courtesy of Bill Cleary, great-grandnephew of Big Bill Devery
BOTTOM: TRC/Harvard (560.52 1905-129)

INDEX

ALSO BY RICHARD ZACKS

AN UNDERGROUND EDUCATION

*The Unauthorized and Outrageous Supplement
to Everything You Thought You Knew About Art, Sex,
Business, Crime, Science, Medicine, and Other Fields
of Human Knowledge*

Astonishing facts! Bizarre photographs! Endlessly enthrall-
ing (and occasionally perverse) anecdotes! Just a small taste
of the intellectual smorgasbord contained in this volume.
Did you know: That the 1949 Nobel Prize for Medicine
went to a man who performed lobotomies . . . with a house-
hold ice pick? That Pocahontas was a spokesperson for
the tobacco industry? That Pope Leo XIII appeared in an
advertisement for cocaine-laced wine in the 1880s? That
the first pediatric guide written in the United States recommended that expectant mothers breastfeed puppies? That
Thomas Edison secretly helped develop the electric chair in
a scheme to have the lethal machine named after his archrival, George Westinghouse?

Reference